Intellectual Property Strategies for the 21st Century Corporation

A Shift in Strategic and Financial Management

LANNING G. BRYER, SCOTT J. LEBSON, AND MATTHEW D. ASBELL

WILEY

John Wiley & Sons, Inc.

Published by John Wiley & Sons, Inc., Hoboken, New Jersey.
Published simultaneously in Canada.

For general information on our other products and services or for technical support, please contact our Customer Care Department within the United States at (800) 762-2974, outside the United States at (317) 572-3993 or fax (317) 572-4002.

Wiley also publishes its books in a variety of electronic formats. Some content that appears in print may not be available in electronic books. For more information about Wiley products, visit our web site at www.wiley.com.

Library of Congress Cataloging-in-Publication Data:
Bryer, Lanning G.
    Intellectual property strategies for the 21st century corporation / Lanning G. Bryer, Scott J. Lebson, Matthew D. Asbell.
        p. cm.
    Includes index.
        ISBN 978-0-470-60175-4 (hardback)
    1.   Intellectual property—United States—Management.   2.   Business enterprises—Law and legislation—United States.   I. Lebson, Scott J.   II. Asbell, Matthew D.   III. Title.
    KF2979.B729 2011
    346.7304'8—dc22   2010048919

Printed in the United States of America

10 9 8 7 6 5 4 3 2 1

To my parents, Mort and Rella, and my wife's parents, Josephine and Eugene, who I miss dearly but honor and treasure their memory, love, and wisdom.

Lanning G. Bryer

For Susan and the boys, Matthew and Luke.

Scott J. Lebson

To my loving wife, Aline, and our parents, Sucha, Michael, and Luiza, for setting the examples to which I aspire and supporting my efforts with their love, encouragement, and patience.

Matthew D. Asbell

Contents

Preface

I nstead of "May you live in interesting times," if Confucius were alive today, he might say "We live in interesting times!" Much of the world has been deeply affected by recession. Political tensions in many regions of the world are acute including places where there is no ongoing conflict. Currencies and markets are fluctuating in exceedingly unpredictable fashions. Technology is developing more swiftly than ever could have been imagined in previous centuries. The climate change debate is resulting in initiatives being proffered that may change, for better or worse, how companies traditionally operate. Through all this activity, businesses must protect their revenue streams and contain their expenses while continuing to seek new markets and customers for their products and services to remain competitive.

Change in the economic world is occurring faster and more radically than few could predict. As globalization advances, traditional rules of the economic game are being challenged. Businesses must be in a position to adapt quickly to change, as making decisions based upon traditional considerations can be a dangerous premise. Variables that impacted prior quarters and prior years may be different than those that will influence future financial performance. In the past, external conditions were considered a constant, and internal factors were used to predict organizational performance. That is no longer necessarily the case. It is dangerous, if not fatal, to create an economic or worldview rooted in the recent past. How can business executives and managers compensate for past understandings and ways of management and future change? One way is to explore and investigate changes in the economic environment to better understand which variables impact critical business processes.

The property rights that these businesses own, use, license, and sell cannot be separated from the same rigorous review. It is an indisputable fact that these rights are often the lifeblood of a company. These rights can include many components, including tangible property, such as real estate and inventory, as well as intangible rights, such as intellectual property, which includes patents, trademarks, service marks, copyrights, design rights, and trade secrets. The ownership and management of these intellectual property rights for many corporations fittingly occupy a significant investment of time and money. How intellectual property owners have historically chosen to acquire, develop, protect, maintain, leverage, and enforce their limited monopoly rights in intellectual property is a study and a book unto itself. However, the purpose of this particular series is to examine the decision making processes, activities, and changes thereto of significant corporate intellectual property owners in the new century and millennium. In this case, size matters.

Why not explore the decision-making processes and activities of all IP owners? Although similarities obviously exist between all IP owners, IP owners with significant portfolios have unique issues and challenges of scale, investment, oversight, law, and development. Moreover, the lessons to be learned from the processes and activities of large corporations can sometimes be applied with some modification to growing companies. As a result, we propose to explore the corporate ownership and management of IP rights in these books. The first book, *IP Strategies for the 21st Century Corporation,* focuses on the strategic decision making that occurs in this process. It is meant to be the view from 20,000 feet by senior decision makers, executives, general counsel, and IP counsel. What strategic corporate or tax issues involving corporate IP ownership need to be considered? How does a corporation expand markets or grow its IP portfolio? How does a corporation keep its IP pipeline full without incurring unnecessary expenses? How has the Internet changed business models and activities and what are the related IP issues? These and other topics that we explore in this first book are detailed in the following chart.

Chapter Title	Authors	Affiliations*
Corporate Strategies, Structures, and Ownership of Intellectual Property Rights	Lanning G. Bryer and Deepica Capoor Warikoo	Ladas & Parry LLP
Properly Evaluating a Target with Intellectual Property Rights	David Drews	IP Metrics LLC
Growth through Acquisition or Merger	Diane Meyers	PPG Industries, Inc.
Penetrating New Markets through Extension of Goods or Product Lines or Expansion into Other Territories	Toshiya Oka	Canon, Inc.
Intellectual Property: From Asset to Asset Class	James E. Malackowski	Ocean Tomo, LLC
Strategic Patent Management after the Boom: Managing the R&D and Patent Pipeline	Marc S. Adler	Marc Adler LLC
Global Piracy and Financial Valuation of Intellectual Property Revisited: Threats, Challenges, and Responses	Robert Lamb and Randie Beth Rosen	Stern School of Business, New York University; Formerly an associate at Orrick, Herrington & Sutcliffe
When to Litigate: The Rise of the Trolls	Raymond DiPerna and Jack Hobaugh	Ladas & Parry LLP; Blank Rome, LLP
Using Insurance to Manage Intellectual Property Risk	Kimberly Klein Cauthorn and Leib Dodell	Duff & Phelps; ThinkRisk Underwriting Agency, LLC
Exploring Alternative Dispute Resolution	Alicia Lloreda	Jose Lloreda Camacho & Co.
Outsourcing and Offshoring of IP Legal Work	Olga Nedeltscheff	Limited Brands, Inc.
Intellectual Property Legal Process Outsourcing	Marilyn O. Primiano	Pangea3, a division of Thomson Reuters, Legal

Satisfying Ethical Obligations When Outsourcing Legal Work Overseas	Michael Downey	Hinshaw & Culbertson LLP
The Brave New World of Web 2.0 and the 3-D Internet: How to Prepare Your Company to Participate	Steve Mortinger	IBM, Inc.
Managing Green Intellectual Property	Larry Greenemeier	Scientific American (A Division of Nature, Inc.)
Accounting and Tax Policies as They Relate to Intellectual Property	Howard Fine and Andrew Ross	Gettry Marcus Stern & Lehrer, CPA, P.C.
Intellectual Property Valuation Techniques and Issues for the 21st Century	David Blackburn and Bryan Ray	NERA Economic Consulting

*The views of the authors are not necessarily those of their employers or affiliates.

We find the second book is equally important to the management of corporate IP rights. We have titled our forthcoming second book *IP Operations and Implementation for the 21st Century Corporation*. Having explored and understood better the strategic issues and decisions that companies make, this second book will examine how companies are effectively implementing them. How does a corporation cost-effectively obtain or enforce its IP rights? How do corporations control expanded counterfeiting throughout the world? What technological developments are available today that did not exist in years past to help manage this process? How are IP searches and investigations more cost-effectively conducted? How are corporations using IP rights to drive increased revenues and profits? These and other subjects will be explored as follows.

Chapter Title	Authors	Affiliations*
Controlling Counterfeiting	Joseph Gioconda and Joseph Forgione	Gioconda Law Group PLLC
Retention and Preservation in Intellectual Property Cases	Jennifer Martin	Symantec Corporation
Controlling Patenting Costs	John Richards	Ladas & Parry LLP
Trademark Costs: Trimming the Sails in Rough Economic Waters	Robert Doerfler and Matthew Asbell	SVP Worldwide; Ladas & Parry LLP
Domain Names	Dennis Prahl and Elliot Lipins	Ladas & Parry LLP
Creating, Perfecting, and Enforcing Security Interests in Intellectual Property	Scott J. Lebson	Ladas & Parry LLP
Strategic and Legal View of Licensing Patents	James Markarian	Siemens Corporation
Monetizing IP Rights: Licensing In and Out	Kelly Slavitt	Consultant, The Francis Company
Working with Government	David J. Rikkers	Raytheon Corporation

(*continued*)

Chapter Title	Authors	Affiliations[*]
Valuation, Monetization, and Disposition in Bankruptcy	Fernando Torres	IP Metrics LLC
Outsourcing of Branding and Marketing	Terry Heckler	Heckler & Associates
Trademark Searches	Joshua Braunstein	CT Corsearch (a Wolters Kluwer Company)
Pretext Investigation	Jeremiah Pastrick	Continental Enterprises
Model Intellectual Property Internship Programs	Barbara Kolsun	Stuart Weitzman Holding, LLC
The Future's So Green, I Gotta Wear Shades: Maximizing Green Brand Exposure and Minimizing Perceptions of Greenwashing	Maureen Gorman	Davis McGrath LLC
Financial Reporting of Intangible Assets	James Donohue and Mark Spelker	Charles River Associates Inc.; J.H. Cohn

[*]The views of the authors are not necessarily those of their employers or affiliates.

Both books will enjoy the perspective of different players in the process. We are fortunate to have the contributions of a number of respected in-house professionals as well as outside practitioners, service providers, consultants, and academics. The intended purpose is to examine many of these issues from different vantage points. For example, on the topic of outsourcing, we have views from corporate counsel, outside IP counsel, and IP service providers. We are confident that looking at this issue with such a wide lens and from different angles provides greater understanding of the topic. Where possible, we have encouraged authors to consider their subjects from other perspectives and to speculate about changes in practice and attitudes that might yet occur in the future. We hope this approach will provide greater clarity and a deeper understanding of the issues that face everyone who has a role to play in the management and ownership of corporate IP rights in the twenty-first century and beyond.

Lanning G. Bryer
Scott J. Lebson
Matthew D. Asbell
New York, New York
2011

Acknowledgments

The editors owe significant debts of gratitude to many people, without whose time and effort this work would not have been possible.

We are deeply appreciative of the many contributors who submitted chapters, and sections of chapters, to make this work what it is. Our gratitude also extends to Dr. Joseph Cook of Pfizer, Inc. for his early participation in the chapter on valuation techniques. In addition to those who contributed to this book, we are also grateful for the significant contributions of the authors who must endure even longer while waiting for their chapters to be published in the forthcoming companion volume. We further recognize the sacrifices of the various employers with which our contributors are affiliated, although the contents of the books do not necessarily reflect their views.

The editors wish to express their sincerest appreciation to the following law students and recent graduates for their tireless efforts in organizing, researching, drafting, critiquing, and handling necessary correspondence regarding this project: Ms. Ilaria Ferrarini, Mr. Ari Abramowitz, Ms. Marie Flandin, Ms. Caroline Camp, Mr. Alex Silverman, Mr. Jason Kreps, Ms. Shefali Sewak, Ms. Rachelle Fernandes, Ms. Olivia Ruiz-Joffre, Ms. Angela Lam, and Mr. John Glowatz. Without their skill, energy, and dedication, this project would not have been possible.

We thank the splendid professional and trade editors of John Wiley & Sons, Susan McDermott and Judy Howarth and their colleagues, for their encouragement and assistance in making this project a reality.

We are indebted to our law partners and colleagues for their understanding and forbearance, and for believing in the value of this project.

Finally, we are grateful to our spouses and children, who patiently endured the lost evenings and weekends during the birth, development, and publication of this work.

CHAPTER 1

Corporate Strategies, Structures, and Ownership of Intellectual Property Rights

Lanning G. Bryer
Ladas & Parry LLP
Deepica Capoor Warikoo

We are moving toward a global economy where the true strategic asset is IP.
Horatio Gutierrez[1]

Globally, as well as in the United States, intellectual property (IP) rights such as copyrights,[2] patents,[3] trademarks,[4] and trade secrets[5] are considered invaluable intangible assets that hold great economic promise and are, for many companies, a significant source of revenue.[6] Companies develop, acquire, and leverage these intangible assets to enhance the potential of their businesses. Further, the value of these intangible assets is not limited to any particular industry.[7] However, in order to successfully monetize such assets, effective management and utilization of the intellectual property rights is required. In order to properly manage intellectual property rights, company executives have to engage in certain decision making regarding many issues that impact these rights. These issues can include which corporate entity is to own the intellectual property rights, or whether there should be one or multiple owners. When and how should the intellectual property rights be licensed to other groups or entities within the corporate structure? How should the intellectual property rights be managed? Should worldwide rights be managed centrally or locally? How is the company going to best generate income utilizing the intellectual property it owns or acquires? The process of making the decisions regarding these and other issues are handled differently by different executives and different companies. The focus of this chapter is to explore the different options and decisions

that companies have made and are making as they value and strategically leverage these intangible assets.

The Importance of Intellectual Property—A Changing Paradigm

> *What was once relegated to a bean counter is now being taken much more
> seriously in companies.*[8]

Historically, most companies employed a defensive strategy when dealing with
their intellectual property. Litigation was the one significant avenue through
which the value of an intellectual property asset was leveraged, usually as a result
of a third party infringement. More recently, however, statistical data on intellectual property prosecution and litigation indicates that intellectual property rights
are no longer considered a mere bundle of legal rights that need to be asserted in
court to leverage their economic potential[9] (see Figure 1.1); instead, the prevail-
ing view is that these rights are considered a core asset, and its management a
significant business strategy.[10]

In more recent times, companies have recognized the need to utilize their intellectual property as a means for promoting innovation, growth, and development of
the business and revenue generation. Leading companies "use those intangible

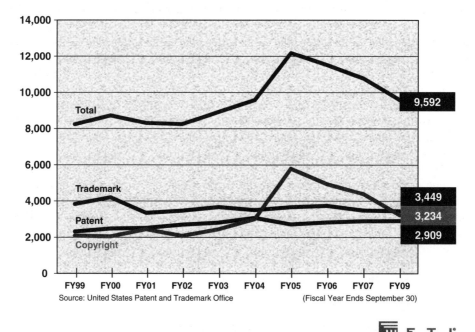

FIGURE 1.1 Intellectual Property Cases Commenced in U.S. District Courts, FY 1999–FY 2008

Source: 2008 Intellectual Property Statistics FTI Consulting, Inc. (March 2009), available at
www.fticonsulting.com/en_us/resources/Documents/2008%20Intellectual%20Property%
20Statistics.pdf (last visited on February 18, 2010).

assets to create new businesses and market their technologies."[11] Gone are the days when software code was protected merely by copyright laws as a defensive strategy.[12] Today, software code is protected through both copyrights[13] and patents,[14] and then leveraged through licensing. Companies elect to patent innovative processes now to garner greater negotiation power as the umbrella of protection has significantly expanded.

In 2006, the last year that the U.S. economy grew in all four quarters, companies with intellectual property assets represented 40 percent of the growth for that year.[15] Undeterred by the subsequent economic downturn, companies continue to increase their ownership of valuable intellectual property, particularly patents,[16] because such assets can translate into significant value for their owners.[17]

Statistics over the last decade strongly suggest that a shift is well underway in corporate attitudes toward acquiring, valuing, and leveraging their intellectual property rights.[18] Intellectual property rights have gone beyond being mere objects of defense strategies, to revenue-earning-core-business-assets requiring special organization and exploitation techniques.

Operational Strategies, Structural Aspects, and Ownership Issues

Traditional intellectual property strategies were aimed at "understanding what inventions to file and in what countries to file them," and assumed that "all key stakeholders have the same point of view . . . on the strategy."[19] The shifting paradigm over the last decade has helped develop numerous strategies for the management of intellectual property assets in the corporate world. Each one is complex and dependent on a number of factors such as the industry, size, global presence, and so forth. The results of a study of 34 companies from eight different industries concluded that "it appears difficult to find a one-size-fits-all strategy for intellectual property at the business-unit level."[20] From a structural aspect, strategy sessions should "involve the corporate, business-unit and functional levels of the organization" in order to properly execute on "IP generation to enforcement."[21]

The two main concerns that dominate the management of intellectual property are legal and business issues. The legal issues related to corporate management most frequently pertain to intellectual property, antitrust and taxation matters. The business concerns pertain to strategically developing management structures and plans, as well as appointing appropriate personnel to play their respective roles to maximize the potential in the intellectual property assets.

Roles: Legal versus Business

> *IP management has dramatically shifted from a purely legal concern to a pervasive business interest that is vital to corporate survival and prosperity.*[22]

Legal professionals are responsible for identifying/selecting, obtaining, protecting, and maintaining the rights in a company's intellectual property. A lawyer's expertise is useful in determining which intellectual property right to obtain[23]—or, if the type of intellectual property right is clear, then the extent of protection that might be necessary.[24] Creating and establishing intellectual property rights is obviously an important foundational role, but maximizing profits from an intellectual property portfolio is not really a lawyer's expertise.[25] As stated by Stephen Fox, "Licensing works well when placed in a business activity that is accountable for profit and loss, rather than in the legal department, which is an expense center."[26]

Intellectual property management is, therefore, a complex task involving the identification of business potential, determination of appropriate business relations that will best leverage the asset's potential, and developing and maintaining relations crucial to such management. Therefore, even though such management is carried out in consultation with the legal department, this is best assigned as a core business role.

Strategies and Structures for the Management of Intellectual Property Rights

While it might be true that companies require managers who "understand (and believe in) IP,"[27] the mere ability to create strategies to manage intellectual property rights is not sufficient. In order to have effective intellectual property rights management, strategies must be accompanied by effective management structures and implementation tools.[28]

Organizational structures governing the management of intellectual property rights are generally either "centralized or decentralized."[29]

In a centralized structure, "decisions are made centrally by a few individuals with others providing support."[30] In such a structure, decisions regarding the management of intellectual property rights are determined at the top level of an organization. Once determined, designated persons/departments are delegated the task of implementing those decisions.

In a decentralized structure, there are "multiple, potentially competing decision makers" where "any firm or individual may decide to undertake a new project."[31] In such a structure, the decision-making process is localized at particular levels of the organization.

Economic literature purportedly favors "decentralized decision structures in economic systems, based on the observation that free-market economies perform better than planned, centralized economies."[32] However, centralized structures can be shaped through policy implementations and offer the lure of lower risk.[33] That being said, a company's decision to adopt either model is dependent on a number of factors, as illustrated here.

Centralized IP Management Structure

> *Intellectual Property Management at IBM is centralized at corporate. The mission: protect and maximize value, a responsibility that goes beyond licensing.*[34]

A centralized intellectual property management structure is "appropriate when the IP is relatively complex, involving multiple licensing issues and/or potential future litigation issues" or where the intellectual property "can be easily accessed from

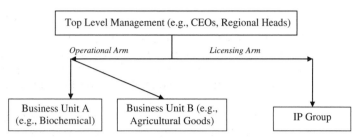

FIGURE 1.2   Centralized IP Model

outside the business unit."[35] As illustrated by Figure 1.2, a "central IP group reports directly to corporate headquarters and manages IP."[36] The IP group receives its orders from the top level executives regarding the management of the corporation's intellectual property rights and coordinates with separate business units and third parties to facilitate various strategic IP-related alliances or arrangements such as licensing and joint ventures.

A centralized management structure is advantageous as it avoids duplication and waste because a single department is delegated the task of managing the company's intellectual property rights and maintaining a network of potential licensees. On the other hand, it has been argued that a centralized system would be inefficient because "no central planner can possibly have all of the necessary local and national information to make the right decisions."[37] Despite such arguments, companies have devised and implemented successful centralized IP management structures.

For instance, IBM pioneered a patent licensing strategy[38] and management model that is centralized at corporate.[39] Its strategy was to increase its patent portfolio by maximizing trade of IP with others. In order to achieve this, IBM entered into cross-licensing agreements[40] with third parties for the exchange of their respective intellectual property rights. This permitted either party to develop products covering the other's intellectual property right without the fear of an intellectual property rights infringement lawsuit. It was through cross-licensing that IBM gave its "engineering community greater freedom of action" and shortened its time to market.[41] Structurally, IBM's IP group is split into technology, legal, and business, and is comprised of a combination of lawyers, inventors, salespersons, licensing executives, and other businesspeople.[42] In addition to this structural setup, IBM uses a tracking system to supplement its efforts in having a successful patent licensing strategy. IBM's tracking system enables it to determine which patents have "periodically become subject to government-levied maintenance fees,"[43] and which are valuable and worth pursuing, providing the ability to "drop the rest."[44] IBM's successful patent licensing methodology can therefore be attributed to its strategy to expand, its comprehensive structural support that is centralized, and its supplementary measures to achieve its strategy.

Decentralized IP Management Structure

A decentralized intellectual property management structure is useful for entities where "there is no strong need to leverage know-how across the business units and

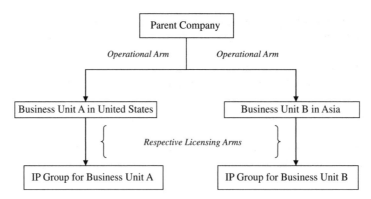

FIGURE 1.3 Decentralized IP Model

the IP issues encountered by the business units are not complex."[45] As illustrated in Figure 1.3, in a decentralized system "each business unit is responsible for its own IP and devotes resources as needed."[46] Additionally, in a decentralized setup, decisions are made at the local level of the organization, resulting in greater employee involvement and input.

For instance, Nestlé S.A. (Nestlé), the parent company located in Switzerland, has 52 operating entities in various countries, including the United States.[47] As regards managing its vast empire of intellectual property, Nestlé follows a complex decentralized structure.[48] Nestlé's intellectual property rights are managed by subsidiaries called Société des Produits Nestlé S.A. (Société) and Nestec, S.A. (Nestec). Société and Nestec own many of Nestlé's trademarks (such as Kit-Kat®) and patents, as well as much of its technical know-how, which they license to various operating entities.[49] In return, the operating entities remit periodic royalty payments to Société or Nestec, as the case may be.[50] This intellectual property management structure is further subdivided by two other entities–Strategic Business Units (SBU) and Strategic Generating Demand Unit (SGDU).[51] SBU concentrates on product development and trademark fidelity for Nestlé's strategic marks[52] and is productcentric.[53] SGDU develops the marketing strategies and determines appeals in geographic markets.[54]

As regards Nestlé's regional presence, operating entities often structure their intellectual property rights management strategies based on regional needs and responses. For instance, Nestlé U.S.A. has a separate identity, and an independent SBU and SGDU that is responsible for managing Nestlé U.S.A.'s day-to-day operations,[55] and for developing and managing its marketing responsibilities.[56] Within this decentralized setup, Nestlé subsidiaries keep apprised of Nestlé U.S.A.'s intellectual property issues and development strategies through personnel called regional intellectual property advisors (RIPAs). However, these RIPAs are employed by Nestlé U.S.A.,[57] and Nestlé does not control the terms of RIPAs' employment agreements or conditions of the licensing agreements that RIPAs enforce. This is one of the indicators that Nestlé's intellectual property management structure is decentralized, and that Nestlé U.S.A. has significant independence when it comes to its intellectual property rights management.

Additionally, in a recent lawsuit it was determined that although Nestlé had the right to control its licensee's activities with respect to the use of its mark through its subsidiaries, its subsidiaries failed to exercise adequate control, and Nestlé[58] merely received the license fees.[59] Such a passive flow of funds from the operating entities to Nestlé did not provide Nestlé with the requisite level of control over the operating entities.[60] The court also found that corporate guidelines developed by Nestlé's SGDU were general guidelines, not corporate mandates that the operating entities were required to follow.[61] The operating entities had their own SGDUs that provided advice based on the relevant regional needs. As a result, Nestlé was found to be a mere beneficial owner with no direct control over the operating entities and their respective SGDUs or SBUs, making Nestlé's intellectual property management structure affirmably decentralized, with its operating entities enjoying a certain amount of corporate independence and flexibility.

Other Management Options

As stated earlier, intellectual property licensing used to be managed solely by attorneys and/or legal departments. An interesting change in this trend is where a company's intellectual property rights are handled by Intellectual Property Holding Companies (IPHCs).

An IPHC is created when "a parent company, the original owner of the intellectual property, establishes a wholly owned subsidiary as a holding company and transfers ownership of its intellectual property company to this newly-created holding company."[62] An IPHC is different from a centralized IP management group set up within a corporation, as in the case of the latter there is no transfer of ownership rights of the company's intellectual property rights.

In essence, an IPHC facilitates the delineation of the management of intellectual property rights to a centralized location for more efficient operation. The primary responsibility of an IPHC is the maintenance and management of the intellectual property rights, and collecting and allocating the income accrued from its licensee (i.e., the parent company and third party licensees) in the form of royalties. For example, Ford Global Technologies, LLC (FGTL) is the wholly owned subsidiary of the Ford Motor Company. FGTL manages the intellectual property rights for the Ford Motor Company, including all aspects of patent, copyright, and trademark licensing.[63] Further, a special team called The Technology Commercialization (TC) Team of FGTL is responsible for marketing and licensing Ford's technology and other proprietary rights for use within and outside the automotive industry.[64] Therefore, to be effective in its operational goals, an IPHC should be an entity that is separate from the parent company, and its operations should be controlled by officers who are independent of the control of the operating company.[65]

A classic example of a hugely successful centralized system for the control and management of intellectual property rights is demonstrated by Hewlett Packard's (HP) Intellectual Property Licensing Group.[66] This group was set up as a wholly owned company to enhance the "visibility, coordination and control of the company's IP assets."[67] In 2003, prior to the launch of its Intellectual Property Licensing Group, the HP board determined that its strategy needed to include "protection" and generation of "value beyond traditional product revenue."[68] To effectuate this strategy, it moved "HP IP into a wholly owned affiliate, required central approval for any out-licensing of HP intellectual property or non-asset agreement and created the HP licensing function."[69] The HP intellectual property licensing function included goals for better protection and strategic utilization of the intangible assets.[70]

At present, the HP Licensing group coordinates across various departments to facilitate licensing needs, including facilitating an appropriate licensing mix of patents, trademarks, copyrights, and know-how, as well as transferring technology to help the licensee's business needs. Intellectual property licensing within HP is broken into separate business groups such as Technology Transfer and Licensing, Patent Licensing, and Brand Licensing.[71] Brand licensing arrangements with HP "typically require an upfront payment, minimum royalty commitment, approved business plan, agreed-upon business metrics, and customary indemnification and insurance provisions.[72] Both parties monitor the licensee's performance on an ongoing basis to ensure that the licensee's business execution is consistent with the standards of the HP brand."[73] Besides the benefits of dedicated and centralized intellectual property rights management, IPHCs have been useful in saving corporations significant state income taxes.[74] For this, a holding company should be incorporated in a location where the income from the exploitation of intangible assets is not taxable.[75] The royalty income will then be considered tax-free for the holding company, and the parent company may claim the royalties paid to the holding company as a tax-deductible business expense.[76] However, an IPHC must not be incorporated merely to avail of taxation benefits; it must be able to justify a substantial business purpose.[77]

In sum, for corporations with large intellectual property portfolios, an IPHC structure may provide significant operational efficiencies and tax benefits.[78]

Strategies for Restructuring

In order to best exploit their intellectual property rights, companies also frequently consider restructuring their ownership and management of intellectual property rights. For instance, prior to reorganizing its structure and setting up the Licensing Group, HP undertook the task of analyzing its portfolio to determine and develop various avenues of revenue generation through licensing.[79] A portfolio review is required to identify and segregate the intellectual property rights that have business potential versus the ones that do not.[80] In HP's case, Joseph Beyers, Vice President, Intellectual Property Licensing, HP, noted that the appropriate determinants are, "the reasons we might want to patent our innovations, . . . what we might want to use in our own products, what we share with others, what we might license to generate revenue, and what we decide we must keep for ourselves."[81] In particular, Mr. Beyers states that HP has "special purpose units" that licensed patents externally and thereafter shared the revenue with the corporation's business units.[82] Most successful organizations consider various strategies for licensing their intangible assets, and in such situations disputes between different business units are bound to arise regarding how best to leverage the assets' potential. At HP headquarters, there is a "specific escalation process" for dispute resolution[83] and it is addressed within a hierarchical system and rarely reaches the chairman and CEO.[84]

Restructuring can be a cost-effective method for streamlining the process by which a company's intellectual property rights can be utilized. An effective intellectual property strategy must consider the intended use of the intellectual property right(s) and the key players who will help develop and leverage it. These include, among others, legal counsel to ensure worldwide legal protection, inventors to create novel products based on the intellectual property rights, business developers to create and maintain commercial liaisons, and marketing professionals to help position the product in the marketplace.

Ownership Issues

Intellectual property rights can be owned by the author/inventor/creator, an assignee,[85] the company employing the author/inventor/creator,[86] under a strategic alliance, or even by an IPHC. However, ownership may not be acquired through licensing arrangements as a license merely transfers a "bundle of rights which is less than the entire ownership interest, e.g., rights that may be limited as to time, geographical area, or field of use."[87] Thus, a licensee merely has the right to exercise certain rights as defined by the license agreement. For example, in a trademark licensing arrangement, the licensee's use of the mark is controlled by the owner of the trademark, but there are no ownership implications.[88] In such a situation, the licensee's use inures to the benefit of the licensor-owner of the mark and the licensee acquires no ownership rights in the mark itself.[89] Therefore, a trademark licensee will merely have the right to use the trademark, subject to the standards set by the trademark licensor-owner as regards the use of such mark.[90]

Ownership of the intellectual property right(s) entails significant advantages. An owner of intellectual property is able to exercise associated rights exclusively as well as prevent others from the unauthorized use of its intellectual property. An owner can enforce its intellectual property rights against a third party, prosecute, and file a patent[91] or trademark application at the United States Patent and Trademark Office (USPTO), as well as foreign patent and trademark offices, where appropriate, and have the right to attract and negotiate with potential investors by virtue of being the record title owner of the particular intellectual property right.[92] Without ownership or being an assignee of the intellectual property rights, broad protection and the means of exploitation will likely be unavailable. However, in certain circumstances, the exercise of the intellectual property right owned may still result in the infringement on another's intellectual property right.[93] For instance, particular caution must be exercised in collaborative alliances that use preexisting intellectual property for developing an extension or improvement to an original product. Here, the lack of properly licensed preexisting rights can limit the value of the ownership of the new rights.[94]

Ownership of intellectual property rights is, therefore, crucial for companies in order to optimally utilize their intangible asset(s). Business strategies for exploiting intellectual property assets must include the consideration of whether owning the intellectual property right is advantageous, or even necessary. For example, where the goal is merely to use and exploit the intellectual property right, ownership of intellectual property rights may not be desirable. Instead, being a licensee of requisite rights, including the right to sub-license, may be sufficient.[95] On the other hand, a company may retain ownership of its intellectual property rights to assess, develop, and implement a business strategy that will best utilize those rights. For instance, a company's business strategy might contemplate ownership for purposes such as developing a portfolio, diversifying its product, or even acquiring newer intellectual property rights to gain a competitive edge.[96]

Developing a company's portfolio is an "aggressive IP strategy" essential for the protection of the company's core products and "commercial interests" and also for protecting intellectual property rights that "may be of interest to non-competing companies."[97] Companies strategically develop their intellectual property portfolio in order to generate income from "the licensing, sale, or commercialization of the IP-protected products or services that may significantly improve the company's market share or profit margins."[98] Companies also leverage their intellectual property portfolio to "maximize the return for investors in the event of a sale, merger or acquisition, or even dissolution."[99]

Product diversification, another important consideration, is crucial to the sustainability of a corporation's business. Product diversification entails strategies for expanding the applicability of the product for direct sale to consumers, as well as for developing and capturing a varied industry appeal. For instance, Canon started with the dream of developing a high quality camera in 1933.[100] Today, through its continued diversification of its products, Canon is a world leader in "professional business, consumer and industrial imaging equipment and information systems."[101]

Strategic alliances is an additional means of leveraging intellectual property rights.[102] Corporations utilize legal tools such as joint venture agreements, mergers and acquisitions, and product development agreements to realize the business potential of their intellectual property rights.

However, a corporation should not assume that ownership of intellectual property rights will automatically lead to significant monetary returns. To ensure a viable return on investment, the benefits of ownership must be weighed against factors such as associated costs, relevant markets, the strength of the intellectual property rights, competitive advantage, jurisdictions, and enforcement strategies.[103]

Costs associated with owning intellectual property include the application, filing, prosecuting, registration and maintenance fees, and enforcement and transaction costs, to name a few. In the United States, a patent is issued by the United States Patent and Trademark Office (USPTO) and the process up to registration itself entails significant costs.[104] Trademark rights may be protectable through common law,[105] but a federal registration, though incurring filing, prosecution, and maintenance costs, bears many advantages.[106] Copyright protection is automatic upon the creation of the work in a fixed and tangible medium, but a registration is required prior to initiating litigation.[107] In addition to these initial costs, transaction costs (such as fees incurred during the negotiation of a licensing agreement) are incurred for developing and licensing of intellectual property rights. Currently, there is a growing trend for multiple entities to align their resources to develop new technology.[108] Though aligning resources, such as sharing costs or pooling investments, might be an important strategic decision, the process of identifying and developing intellectual property rights as a result may become "slower, with greater set-up costs."[109] Transaction costs associated with identifying the existence or ownership of the intellectual property right, determining which intellectual property right can best be leveraged, "bargaining, contracting, maintaining relationships" and negotiating agreements with the partners[110] can be significant and unavoidable.[111] In case of copyrights, though not the most efficient method to leverage an asset, government implemented compulsory licensing schemes may be adopted where the intent is to eliminate negotiation and associated costs[112].

In any event, to avail of the benefits of owning intellectual property rights, companies should first conduct an intellectual property audit in order to take stock of their inventory of trademarks, copyrights, and patents owned, and determine the potential for each through proper valuation.[113]

When considering relevant markets for intellectual property rights, companies should consider both present and potential markets for their products. For existing products, corporations must strategically determine whether the relevant market will ensure a continued or new stream of revenue, with the least amount of capital. An analysis would have to be made of the consumer base, market size, competitors, trends, and any gaps in the market that may be leveraged beneficially.

The issue of ownership involves challenges posed by different structural arrangements. Unlike ownership issues faced by single entities, intellectual property rights owned by multiple entities create additional challenges. Where a company transfers its intellectual property rights to an IPHC, a relatively simple ownership structure results, akin to ownership by the parent company. Here, the IPHC becomes the owner of the intellectual property rights, licensing them back to the parent(s) for a royalty.[114] By virtue of such ownership, the IPHC is entitled to enforce the rights against any unauthorized third party usage.[115] With IPHCs, it is important to note that ownership must be clearly delineated and the transferred rights must not be in "gross."[116]

Ownership issues can become more complicated when multiple entities are involved. This typically occurs when the intellectual property is acquired through purchase, merger or acquisition, joint venture, or other strategic alliance.[117] The ownership of intellectual property rights is particularly complex in cases of joint ownership. Such situations provide a fertile ground for potential problems. Inconsistencies in joint ownership may develop from royalty sharing issues (i.e., a product is covered by copyright and patents) or jurisdictional issues (i.e., a product is marketed in a country where the laws are inconsistent with U.S. law). For example, under U.S. patent law, "any joint owner can use the patent without permission of other joint owners, the exploiting joint owner has no duty to share royalties with any other joint owner, and to enforce a patent, all joint owners must join the suit," but the law in the United Kingdom is directly opposite.[118] In the United Kingdom, in the absence of an agreement to the contrary, each joint owner has the right to exploit the intellectual property right created jointly, provided the other joint owner's consent is obtained.[119] Therefore, although joint ownership is a common feature in joint ventures, and agreements with freelancers and subcontractors, it is important to ensure that the relevant contractual provisions (i.e., ownership, geographic scope, etc.) are carefully drafted to identify the respective rights and anticipate potential pitfalls.

Maximizing the Potential

Through strategic deployment of intellectual property assets, companies can benefit shareholders by protecting market shares, creating cash flow and new markets for existing products through strategic alliances, and taking advantage of available tax benefits.

However, in the course of identifying methods of leveraging a company's intellectual property assets, it can be very beneficial to conduct an intellectual property audit in order to ascertain the current value of the intellectual property.[120] Once such value has been determined, the next step is to determine the most appropriate method for leveraging the assets.

Registration and Prosecution

Some intellectual property rights may exist without registration. For instance, a copyright may exist in the subject matter so long as the material is original and fixed in a tangible medium.[121] In the United States, trademark rights are conferred by the use of an adopted mark in commerce. A common law trademark right extends only as far as the geographic scope of the market where the mark is being used. Therefore, unregistered marks in certain jurisdictions can be protectable under common law, but enforceability of such mark will always be limited by the geographic scope of its use. Similarly, in the United Kingdom, owners of trademarks who are able to prove substantial use of a mark, may succeed in a passing-off action, but such rights are limited in scope.[122] On the other hand, although trade secrets may be protected without registration, rights in a useful invention or an ornamental design only arise from obtaining a patent from the USPTO.

Successful companies are, therefore, quick to recognize that registration of their intellectual property rights may bring many monetary and business advantages. With a patent right, a company can exclude others from developing, using, selling or offering to sell, or importing their patented invention into the United States for a limited duration. Companies use this monopoly to charge higher prices and increase their profit margin, and also reduce competition. As regards trademarks and copyrights, companies require valid registrations to leverage the economic value of the intellectual property rights in an administrative proceeding or in a court of law.[123] However, the mere filing of a copyright application does not satisfy the jurisdictional prerequisite that a copyright be registered prior to initiating a lawsuit.[124]

The registration of intellectual property rights may take multiple forms. A copyright registration protects cartoon characters as an artistic work, for example, but the same work can be protected under trademark law if the characters serve as source identifiers. Warner Bros. Entertainment registers its cartoon characters such as Roadrunner, Tweety, and Daffy Duck under both copyright and trademark laws.[125] This approach not only expands the licensing opportunities, but also helps increase the longevity of protection. In the United States, copyright law provides for a long, albeit definite period of protection,[126] but trademark law provides for an indefinite period of protection, provided periodic renewals are effected and the mark remains in use.[127] Therefore, the artistic expression of the work can be protected for a specified number of years under copyright law, and the elements that function as source identifiers may theoretically be protected in perpetuity under trademark laws.

Strategic Alliances

Companies often seek strategic alliances in order to maximize the value of their intellectual property portfolio. These alliances can be developed through licensing, joint ventures, merger and acquisitions (M&A), and cooperative research and development (R&D) agreements.

LICENSING[128]

A license is a way of extending the value of a brand to a variety of disparate goods and services.[129]

Licensing enables companies to transfer limited usage rights of their intellectual property to a third party without transferring any ownership right to such third party.[130]

Historically, licensing was conducted primarily on an ad hoc basis and was not considered as a significant source of income.[131] However, this perspective changed significantly as corporations realized that intellectual property licensing was a multifaceted tool for generating income and for garnering higher consideration in mergers and acquisitions, or divestures.[132] In 2003, the aggregate corporate sales for companies based on their operating norms for trademark and brand licensing operations were over $225 billion.[133] However, due to the economic climate in 2008, licensing as a means for income generation admittedly suffered. For instance, in 2008, the total royalties collected by brand owners declined due to the decrease in consumer spending.[134] Nonetheless, despite this economic downturn, intellectual property licensing continues to generate significant revenues for many major international companies.[135]

Licensing also helps create new income streams and market opportunities. When companies license one form of intellectual property to develop new products, the new products may in turn be licensed as other forms of intellectual property. For instance, Twentieth Century Fox Licensing & Merchandising (Fox Licensing) launched its most recent and massive licensing and merchandising campaign to introduce "125 products across four key categories: video games, toys, apparel and publishing," in collaboration with "Ubisoft, Mattel, JEM, HarperCollins and Abrams."[136] These licensing deals are expected to result in the creation of new products such as video games, collectible items (e.g., statuettes, life-size busts), clothing, and books. Further, each licensing deal will envision multiple forms of intellectual property that are separate from the intellectual property right in the original product. The new products will have copyright protection for the new artwork, textual work, and software, and trademark rights for the merchandisable articles, branding on videogames, and so forth.

Despite the many benefits of licensing arrangements, a licensee should consider certain risks associated with licensing that a licensor might not be obligated to consider. These risks include return on capital, manufacture and distribution, market shifts in taste, emergence of competition, and rival technologies.[137] Therefore, a licensee would need to ascertain whether licensing the intellectual property right would produce at least "an expected *incremental* economic benefit" from exploiting the work and "after accounting for these risks."[138]

All forms of intellectual property are licensable, including copyrights, patents, and trademarks, provided that such rights are owned and eligible for protection under the law. Common types of license agreements include publishing (e.g., for novels), entertainment (e.g., for live performances), technology (e.g., for product development), and patent and trademark licensing (e.g., for co-branding).

Copyright licensing is often encountered in the entertainment and technology industries. In the entertainment industry, copyrights are relevant to all forms of artwork such as visual/graphical, textual, or other works. Copyright licensing in the entertainment industry is particularly lucrative in this electronically driven day and age, as characters popularized by electronic as well as print media offer ample merchandizing opportunities to companies. Licensing of the copyright is effected by transferring a limited number of rights in a work or transferring all the rights for a limited duration.[139] For instance, an author of a novel could license reproduction and distribution rights to the publisher, but not license the right to make derivative works. The publisher would then have the right to make copies and distribute the same, but not make adaptations, translations, movies, or screenplays. An exclusive copyright license must be in writing to be enforceable.[140] In the technology industry, copyrights are often acquired to protect software. However, like other copyright licenses, a copyright software license would also need to be defined by the intended scope of exploitation. For instance, if the intended purpose is merely to permit a specific technological use, an end user license agreement (EULA) would suffice.[141] However, the same would be insufficient if the purpose is to allow for further development of the work.[142] Licensing in the technology industry is undertaken by various methods, including in-licensing, out-licensing, cross licensing, and securitization. In-licensing is adopted to "quickly fill new product pipelines" and out-licensing to minimize the risks associated with "manufacturing and distribution."[143] The latest trends in technology licensing indicate that companies are actively engaging in cross licensing and out-licensing agreements to not only avail of the resultant monetary benefits, but also to strategically improve a firm's competitive position.[144] Through schemes of cross licensing and out-licensing, firms may be able to prevent potential patent infringement and also develop their portfolio by acquiring existent technology owned by others.[145]

Patent licensing, like other forms of intellectual property, affords opportunities to create revenue as well as inventions through collaborations. As of 2008, patent licensing alone accounted for half a trillion dollars in annual revenue in the United States.[146] Some of the industries in which patent licensing is most common are biotech, engineering, technology, semiconductor, and pharmaceutical.

Patent licensing is relevant at multiple stages of product development. Patent claims are licensed routinely between companies, and for a multitude of purposes. Patents can be licensed for use by the business, to a third party for non-competitive use, to competitors abroad limiting the use geographically, for research and development efforts, and to aftermarket service providers.[147] The common forms of patent licenses include exclusive, non-exclusive, and cross licenses.

Broadly speaking, an exclusive patent license would bar a licensor from entering into an agreement with a third party that is similar to the agreement entered into with the exclusive licensee, or use the patent on its own behalf, unless it retains the rights to do so contractually.[148] However, in practical terms, the exclusivity in patent licenses should depend on the subject matter of what is licensed. This would enable multiple exclusive licenses of the same patent, if the terms are restricted to a particular product or field of use. For instance, a patent for LEDs could be the basis for exclusive license agreements with a car manufacturer or a a stage light manufacturer. Furthermore, as regards royalties in exclusive patent licensing agreements, a licensor may not be able to negotiate higher royalty, since the licensee is the only source of revenue.

A non-exclusive patent license permits the licensee to exercise the rights granted and provides an assurance that the licensor cannot sue him or her on grounds of infringement for uses based on the rights granted.

A cross license, as the name suggests, involves two or more parties who enter into an agreement where there is a mutual exchange of patent rights.[149] Such licenses are usually entered into so that the parties may utilize the other's patents to beneficially develop their products without the threat of litigation from the other.[150] For instance, Toyoda Gosei Co. Ltd. of Japan and Sharp Corp. entered into a cross licensing agreement where each company was permitted to "use inventions related to nitride-based LEDs and laser diodes covered by the patents owned by the respective companies in Japan and in other countries."[151] This deal is expected to ramp up the research and development efforts and also enable the companies to compete in the competitive market for LEDs.[152]

A more recent form of leveraging patents is through patent pools. Initially popular in the consumer electronics industry, patent pools are also gaining momentum with universities and in the biotechnology sector.[153] A patent pool is a "consortium of at least two companies agreeing to cross-license patents relating to a particular technology."[154] Some patent pools were initially found to violate antitrust provisions. In more recent times, patent pools are considered to "have significant pro-competitive effects and may improve a business' ability to survive this era of rapid technological innovation in a global economy"[155] as they "may be viewed as clearing blocking positions, mitigating royalty stacking, promoting the dissemination of technology, and fostering innovation by reducing the potential for, or efficacy of, hold-ups."[156] License revenues may be distributed to "contributory patent owners on a per patent basis (i.e., all patents are treated equally" in determining the basis for sharing of revenue).[157]

TRADEMARK LICENSING—SPECIAL CONCERNS   Companies use trademark licensing as a tool to develop and maintain a global presence, create a secondary stream of revenue,[158] and avoid instances of consumer confusion. Companies effectuate trademark licensing through various relationships, including through a jointly owned subsidiary of multiple parent companies in a mutual trademark holding company (MTHC),[159] through licensing arrangements between the sister companies and between separately owned entities.[160] In fact, one commentator has observed that "in the absence of spinning off brands or mergers between the two parties, the only substantial way to make a dual brand ownership[161] beneficial is to set up a trademark holding company."[162]

Unlike copyright and patent licensing, trademark licensing is governed by a different set of principles. First, trademark licensing assesses (1) whether *goodwill* associated was transferred[163] and (2) whether the licensor maintains adequate *quality control.*[164]

Trademark licensing focuses on the use of the goodwill associated with the mark(s) in order to generate revenue. Goodwill is the advantage of reputation in connection with a business.[165] When licensing a trademark, it should be borne in mind that in the United States a "trademark is simply a symbol of goodwill and cannot be sold or assigned apart from the goodwill it symbolizes"[166] and, therefore, cannot be assigned "in gross."[167] A trademark can, therefore, be transferred only if accompanied with the associated goodwill. However, companies should identify whether goodwill needs to be transferred in other jurisdictions, as not all jurisdictions abide by this principle.[168]

A licensor must exercise quality control over the licensee's use of the licensed mark to avoid loss of its rights in the trademark.[169] The notion of quality control stems from the need to obviate deception on the public.[170] Quality control is maintained by ensuring that the nature and quality of goods and services under the licensed mark is sufficiently controlled by the licensor so that the consuming public can expect consistency and predictability of the quality of the goods/services associated with a mark.[171] The presence of a mere right to control the quality is insufficient; there must be actual control.[172] As a means to better practice, licensing contracts should include provisions regarding the licensor's express right to control the quality of the licensee's products since it is the responsibility of the licensor to maintain the quality associated with its mark.[173] However, the lack of such a contractual provision regarding the licensor's right to inspect and supervise the licensee's operations is not fatal to the question of control.[174] If there is a special relationship between the licensor and licensee, a licensor may justifiably rely on its licensee for quality control.[175] Where there is a failure to exercise adequate quality control, significant risks to trademark rights may result, including cancellation of the registration under which the mark is licensed or the inability to enforce a trademark right against a third party.[176] However, it is to be noted that the standards for quality control are not universally applicable and differ from product to product, and industry to industry.[177] In determining the adequacy of quality control, the facts of each case must be considered.[178] Generally, a mark may be deemed abandoned if the license is not properly policed,[179] or through "naked licensing."[180] Naked licensing results when the licensor does not exercise sufficient control over the licensee's use of the mark, and the mark no longer is a source identifier or a means of quality assurance.[181]

OTHER RISKS AND ISSUES   In addition to ensuring the exercise of quality control, to engage in sound licensing practices in the United States, companies must police the marketplace to prevent competing uses by the licensees, related entities, or third parties where such uses create a likelihood of confusion, dilution, separation from the associated goodwill, or the loss of distinctive character of the mark that is being used or licensed.[182]

There is a likelihood of consumer confusion in a business relationship where the companies combine their existing marks into a new composite mark. Joint owners must take steps to minimize the risk of such consumer confusion by: (1) setting forth the relationship of the parties to establish their actions in tandem; (2) establishing control and supervisory guidelines over the use of the composite mark; (3) discontinuing use of the composite mark, including its possible use as a corporate or trade name, upon termination of the business relationship; (4) prohibiting the use of any of the elements of the composite marks in a stand-alone fashion for the duration of the license; (5) requiring licensing and demarcation of ownership rights and registration status of individually owned elements whenever the composite mark is used. [183]

A trademark can also suffer due to dilution of the mark through blurring or tarnishment.[184] Dilution by blurring is defined as the "association arising from the similarity between the mark or trade name and a famous mark that impairs the distinctiveness of the famous mark."[185] Dilution by tarnishment is defined as an "association arising from the similarity between the mark or trade name and a famous mark that harms the reputation of the famous mark."[186] When a famous mark is the basis of the business relationship, dilution by multiple licensees can occur if the manner in which the mark is used is inconsistent with the equity.[187] For instance, a licensor uses its trademark on a single good such as cereal, but it's licensees use the trademark on different goods such as clothing items or sporting goods. This would result in dilution due to the inconsistent usage by the multiple licensees.

In course of licensing a trademark, companies must include provisions to ensure that the distinctiveness of the mark is maintained.[188] A licensor should not permit the licensee to use multiple licensed marks on a single product or service because such activity results in a loss of distinctiveness of each element.[189] Consumers will be unable to identify the separate and distinct impression, function, or purpose associated with the mark.

Joint Ventures, Mergers and Acquisition

Besides licensing, companies utilize other methodologies to create monetarily efficient alliances that help best leverage their intellectual property assets.

JOINT VENTURES   Companies have long used partnership strategies that offer benefits to the participating organizations. A joint venture (JV) is one such vehicle that "represents a collaborative effort between companies—who may or may not be competitors—to achieve a particular end (e.g., joint research and development, production of an individual product, or efficient joint purchasing)."[190] It may encompass a myriad of business processes, such as the joint cooperation over "research and development, manufacturing, distribution, and sales and marketing."[191] Even though such ventures are often more complex than mergers and acquisitions and "tend to end earlier than expected,"[192] there are a number of advantages. Companies are able to "combine . . . the strengths, expertise, technologies, and know-how of separate [firms] along with [the] sharing of investment costs and risks."[193] A joint venture may be structured to jointly develop a product from scratch, through research and development, or even develop upon a product that might have been acquired by a license agreement. Another typical scenario is where "if the smaller organization doesn't have cash, it could give the larger organization a share in future patent revenues, as well as the right to use the patented technologies."[194] Needless to say, a multitude of intellectual property such as patentable inventions, software codes, reports, trade secrets, or trademarks are developed through such collaboration. Ownership of intellectual property is central to the structural aspects of a joint venture agreement. Companies may retain ownership of preexisting intellectual property, allocate ownership to the respective companies, or own it jointly. However, during such alliances newer intellectual property rights are created based on modified business needs, and the terms of the contract between the parties may not address ownership issues of such newly created intellectual property rights.[195] Joint ventures also suffer from the inherent risk of accessible technology codes. A collaborating company will have access to the other company's technology and consequently, the ability to engineer the product independently. Therefore, joint venture agreements must be structured carefully and include contractual provisions that address ownership, confidentiality, the rights and terms of transfer, term, territory, and scope.

MERGERS AND ACQUISITIONS[196] Companies normally seek to acquire intellectual property rights that would arm them with the ability to create competitively superior products and services that have the potential of maximizing revenue. With such intellectual property rights, companies may successfully stifle competition and gain a significant competitive advantage. Companies often "divest certain intangible assets for a premium at an opportune time" to "yield significant financial benefit" through consolidation.[197] The company that acquires another's intellectual property can benefit through its use for expansion of the business, with an industry specific outlook, or to "simply improve their performance and competitiveness."[198]

In the course of the sale of assets, trademarks and associated goodwill may be acquired even though the transfer agreement does not mention the trademark or other intellectual property rights.[199] However, such automatic inclusion will not occur where the agreement is between a parent company and a wholly owned subsidiary, unless specifically transferred by way of such agreement.[200]

Securitization as Funding for Operations or Purchases[201]

In recent years, intellectual property backed securitization has emerged as an alternate method of financing. The value of securitization backed transactions increased from $380 million in 1997 to $1.13 billion in 2000.[202] Intellectual property backed securitization can generate working capital in a short period of time, and result in "other than cash benefits" such as brand management and protection.[203]

Such securitization takes place when the intellectual property "owner transfers the intellectual property to the investors who, in turn, provide lump sum capital to the" intellectual property owner "and rely on the expected royalty stream from the IP to serve as their return."[204] Intellectual property securitization is, therefore, "speculative" and contemplates a "future flow of revenue" from the intangible assets because "they are based on 'rights' to something that might occur in the future (i.e., future sales from the brand)."[205]

Intellectual property such as trademarks, copyrights, and patents may be securitized if these assets demonstrate a "predictable cash flow or even future receivables that are exclusive."[206] The most famous case of copyright securitization is the Bowie Bond. David Bowie raised $55 million in 1997 through the issue of bonds backed by future royalties from 25 albums that he had recorded prior to 1990.[207] More recently, in 2006, the Dunkin' Brands Inc. were securitized to monetize the company's cash flow.[208] The securitization deal considered "multiple cash flow streams from three distinct brands across multiple jurisdictions. The sources of revenue included franchise royalty fees, licensing fees, lease payments, and other valuable cash flows."[209] Following the financial crisis in 2008, Morgan Stanley launched an intellectual property securitization deal for Vertex Pharmaceuticals worth $250 million.[210] This deal is expected to help "investors get repaid while the drug is still in development."[211] The companies retain their "assets—any upside from other sales and license agreements, without the need to dilute their equity."[212] Additionally, because the securitization was set up with the help of a special purpose vehicle, companies do not bear the risk in case the drug fails.[213]

A relatively new form of IP-backed securitization is brand securitization. A brand securitization transaction requires either the actual sale of the brand to a third party or transference of the risks associated with the brand to the third party, while retaining the ownership of the brand title.[214] The purpose of brand securitization may be either to generate working capital or to ensure other than cash benefits such as effective brand management.[215] For instance, Sears Holding Corp. (Sears) set a "precedent for companies worldwide" by successfully engaging in one of the biggest brand securitization deals.[216] It securitized its core organic brands such as Kenmore, Craftsman, and Die Hard, to one of its wholly owned subsidiaries in Bermuda for "other than cash benefits" such as brand protection, brand management flexibility, and tax and cash benefits. Through such a strategic move, Sears ensured that its securitized core brands were safeguarded in the event Sears itself was subject to any bankruptcy proceedings.[217]

Intellectual property securitization is not a highly utilized tool for generating revenue, as "securitization of assets takes a lot of time and energy, and can be an expensive process. Therefore, intellectual property securitization is not very efficient as an acquisition financing tool, however, it can be as a long-term financing tool [if it achieves a lower cost of capital]."[218]

Tax Considerations[219]

Intellectual property is a taxable asset simply because it is the "primary fuel of the U.S. economic regime."[220]

In developing intercompany structures for the ownership, development, and management of intellectual property, companies must consider taxation issues that will affect intercompany transfers[221] or cost-sharing arrangements.[222] Through cost sharing arrangements, companies elect to bear the costs and risks in exchange for a specified interest in the intangible property, and are able to defer indefinitely their related U.S. taxes.[223] For instance, in 2009 Maxim Integrated Products, one of the most profitable companies in the semiconductor industry, reported revenue of $1.646 billion.[224] To facilitate utilization of its intellectual property by foreign subsidiaries, Maxim Integrated adopted a buy-in and cost sharing arrangement with the foreign subsidiary that pays the U.S. entity for certain operating expenses. Initially, "the cost sharing to the U.S. entity is greater than the benefit achieved by the foreign subsidiary,"[225] but it is expected that the taxes that will be levied as an expense for the U.S. entity will eventually be offset by tax savings on the revenue and profit earned internationally.

Assigning the title in their intangible assets to a wholly owned IPHC, which then licenses back to its parent the right to use the intellectual property,[226] may be another efficient tax strategy. IPHCs have significant tax benefits. First, corporations have the option of setting up IPHCs in the United States without incurring federal taxes under Section 351(a) of the Internal Revenue Code.[227] The assignment of the title in intellectual property in exchange for controlling stock is not recognized as a transfer of property for income tax purposes.[228] However, the Internal Revenue Code does require that the operating company acquire at least 80 percent of the stock.[229] Second, IPHCs are usually set up in states that offer favorable taxation options. The operating company receives deductions for royalties paid under a license as a business expense, thereby reducing the company's income tax liability in its state of operation. However, taxation of IPHCs is becoming increasingly complex as states have begun to employ measures that will block this loophole.[230] A state is permitted to tax the operating company if the operating company has a "physical presence" in that state or receives incomes in exchange for the use of the license.[231]

As an alternative, companies may elect to set up organizational arms offshore to take advantage of the favorable taxation policies. This strategic move helps to develop new funding mechanisms. For instance, because royalties, a form of intellectual property revenue, "flows to the location where the IP is owned . . . significant long-term tax savings can be made from moving IP to a low-tax jurisdiction."[232] Such international venues may be *pure tax havens* where there are "no income taxes levied on local and foreign persons and corporations alike" or offer *tax-free status* to qualifying persons or corporations by distinguishing "between the taxation of locals and that of special categories of offshore persons."[233] Pure tax havens are preferable to optimally exploit intellectual property due to the flexibility they offer.[234]

By transferring ownership and management of the intellectual property to an offshore entity, a company is able to advance its intellectual property exploitation strategy and raise capital. However, various issues must be considered prior to setting up such a corporation. Besides the setup costs, a company must obtain "shareholder approval" if it is a public company, assess the "requirement and availability of professional offshore management," consult with U.S. tax counsel on how to "mitigate ultimate U.S. taxation and isolate U.S. income from the worldwide income," and also determine the appropriate timing of initiating such a setup.[235] Companies must ensure that their IPHCs overseas are safeguarded from any bankruptcy proceedings that may be instituted against the operating company and the insolvency of the operating company will not affect the IPHC's revenue.[236]

Legal Concerns—Antitrust

Intellectual property laws enable right holders to own and use their intellectual property to the exclusion of others. However, the grant of such a right is not absolute. A system of checks and balances helps keep the exclusionary nature of intellectual property rights in check. First, the historical basis for creating laws that protect intellectual property rights (i.e., the promotion of knowledge and art[237]) helps justify the grant of such rights. Second, such exclusive rights are also kept in check by antitrust laws. Although antitrust laws are designed primarily to curb anti-competitiveness and remedy unfair business practices, these laws also limit the exclusivity associated with intellectual property rights by scrutinizing the operations of companies to determine whether the ownership or use of such rights violates the spirit of productive competition. A recent effort to curb anti-competitiveness by the Federal Trade Commission (FTC) is evinced by its complaint against Intel Corp. (Intel) which alleges that Intel adopted anti-competitive measures in order to capture, maintain, and manipulate the market for Central Processing Units (CPUs) and Graphic Processing Units.[238] This action in the United States follows closely in the footsteps of the large fines levied in Europe and Korea against Intel for bullying "computer makers into buying all, or nearly all, of their [Intel's] CPUs . . . or risk losing potentially billions of dollars in rebates."[239]

It is evident that today's market has expanded through globalization, and as a consequence, many countries are harmonizing their legal norms to promote international business relations. Parallels may be drawn between the antitrust laws of the United States and the European Union. In the United States, the relevant antitrust laws are found in Section 7 of the Clayton Act, Sections 1 and 2 of the Sherman Act, and Section 5 of the Federal Trade Commission Act.[240] The Clayton Act proscribes anti-competitive mergers.[241] Sections 1 and 2 of the Sherman Act are supplementary provisions wherein Section 1[242] sets the prohibitory tone by identifying the specific anti-competitive conduct, and Section 2[243] pertains to specific results that are anti-competitive in nature. The Federal Trade Commission Act proscribes "unfair methods of competition."[244] Additionally, the Hart-Scott-Rodino Anti-Trust Improvements Act of 1976[245] subjects larger transactions to pre-merger notification and reporting requirements. In the European Union, Article 81 of the European Community Treaty (ECT) prohibits "cartels and other concerted practices that distort competition" and "is roughly comparable to Section 1 of the Sherman Act."[246] Article 82 of the ECT addresses "abuse of dominant position" similar to Section 2 of the Sherman Act.

However, despite this seeming uniformity in the spirit of the laws of the United States and the European Union, companies should recognize that significant differences exist between the approaches employed by the two legal systems. Generally speaking, if business is being conducted outside of the United States, any differences in the respective countries' antitrust laws must also be considered. Returning to the example of the antitrust laws in the United States and the European Union, companies in the United States have learned the hard way that the European Union has a different approach to antitrust laws as compared to the United States.[247] The United States focuses on identifying anti-competitiveness that might result from horizontal relationships rather than vertical ones and is, therefore, pro-competitive.[248] The European Union is structured to protect competitors. As a consequence, a merger between two large entities might pass the muster in the United States, but fail in the European Union.[249]

Conclusion

The management of intellectual property has become more complex and sophisticated with the spread of the global economy and the shifting sands of business markets and company strategies. Intellectual property rights have evolved from being almost exclusively tools of defensive corporate strategies to being avenues of significant revenue generation and market penetration. However, with this recognition, corporations often have had to reevaluate and restructure their approach in developing and leveraging intellectual property rights. Structural and management decisions, as discussed in this chapter, are most successful when based on the particular needs, philosophy, and concerns of the company, which often evolve as the company or industry grows or changes. Management and ownership of intellectual property rights are critical to ensuring that companies are properly positioned to be able to successfully execute their business strategies.

Notes

1. PricewaterhouseCoopers, "Exploiting Intellectual Property in a Complex World, Technology Executive Connections," Vol. 4, June 2007 (statement of Horratio Gutierrez).

2. 17 U.S.C. §§101 et seq.

3. 35 U.S.C. §§1-376 et seq.

4. 15 U.S.C. §§ 1051 et seq.

5. Uniform Trade Secret Act (adopted in 46 states) and the Economic Espionage Act, 1996, 18 U.S.C. §1831–1839.

6. Licensing Industry Merchandisers' Association (LIMA), "Licensing Revenues Decline 5.6% in 2008, Brand Owners Look to Position Themselves for the Future," June 2, 2009, www.email repository.com/GL/060209li/index.html (last visited on February 25, 2010) (providing estimated licensing revenues by property).

7. Even though distinctive marks/brand names may be specific to goods/services, such marks/names appeal to all industries because entities want to distinguish themselves from their competitors and capture consumer recognition. Protection from disclosures of confidential information is achieved through trade secret law and again is not limited to any one industry.

8. Eric W. Pfeiffer, "Mine Games," June, 2002, statement of Bruce Berman, www.forbes.com/asap/2002/0624/060.html (last visited January 9, 2010).

9. 2008 Intellectual Property Statistics, FTI Consulting, Inc., March 2009, www.fticonsulting.com/en_us/resources/Documents/2008%20Intellectual%20Property%20Statistics.pdf (last visited February 18, 2010).

10. Ron Carson, "Get Your Assets in Gear: Aligning IP Strategy and Business Strategy," Innovation Asset Group, www.wipo.int/sme/en/documents/pdf/ip_business_strategy.pdf (last visited March 4, 2010).

11. Business Wire, February, 2005, statement of Doyal Bryant. "Many people, lawyers in particular, are still looking at IP assets as a bundle of legal rights that you need to assert in court in order to get some money out of them," however, "some leading companies, like ours, are starting to use those intangible assets to create new businesses and market their technologies."

12. Copyright protected against literal copying of the code. However, not all aspects of a software code are copyrightable. See *Computer Assocs. Int'l v. Altai*, 982 F.2d 693 (2d Cir. 1992); *Lotus Dev. Corp. v. Borland Int'l. Inc.*, 49 F.3d 807 (1st Cir. 1995).

13. 17 U.S.C. §§ 101 et seq.

14. 35 U.S.C §§ 101 et seq.

15. "Patent Reform in the 111th Congress: Hearing of the Senate Committee on the Judiciary," Federal News Service, Inc., March 2009 (statement of Sen. Patrick J. Leahy (D-Vt)).

16. IFI Patent Intelligence's list of 2008's top patent owners based on 2008 USPTO data, in order of rank, is: International Business Machines Corp., 4,186 patents; Samsung Electronics Co. Ltd. KR, 3,515 patents; Canon K K Jp, 2,114 patents; Microsoft Corp., 2,030 patents; and Intel Corp., 1,776 patents.

17. Intel's Financial Report (2008): Intel's intellectual property assets had a net value of $624 million for December, 2008 and the estimated value of intellectual property assets acquired was worth $68 million in 2008. Available at http://files.shareholder.com/downloads/INTC/817654389x0x284346/74829b05-7cd8-4ae2-a3b6-3ccfd5c2fcec/Intel_2008_Annual_Report_and_Form_10-K.pdf (last visited January 11, 2010). IBM's Financial Report (2008): Intellectual Property and Custom Development income increased from $958 million in 2007 to $1,153 million in 2008: Available at ftp://ftp.software.ibm.com/annualreport/2008/2008_ibm_annual.pdf (last visited January 11, 2010).

18. Carson, "Get Your Assets in Gear," 33–35.

19. John Cronin and Paul DiGimmarino, "Understanding and Unifying Diverse IP Strategy Perspectives," *Intellectual Asset Management* (January/February 2009).

20. Markus Reitzig, "How Executives Can Enhance IP Strategy and Performance," *MIT Sloan Management Review* (2007), 41.

21. Ibid., 40, providing a graphical representation for an integrated IP strategy.

22. Robert Shearer, *Business Power: Creating New Wealth from IP Assets* (Hoboken, NJ: John Wiley & Sons, 2007), 99.

23. A lawyer's skills are useful in determining the appropriate intellectual property right protection, such as a copyright for protecting literary works, trademark for brands, trade dress, patent design, and so forth.

24. A lawyer's skills are useful in determining the extent of protection even where the type of intellectual property right has been identified. For instance, whether a certain mark is better protected as a word mark, a stylized mark, a composite, or a color composite mark.

25. Alan Cohen, "Licensing's In and Lawyer's Out," *American Lawyer Media L.P.,* 2004. (statement of David Klein).

26. Ibid. (Statement of Stephen Fox, former vice president and deputy general counsel for intellectual property at Hewlett Packard Company.)

27. Joseph B. Root, "Re-Fighting the Last War: Dot-Com Ideas in the 21st Century," *Intellectual Property Today* (February 2008) quoting Kevin Rivette and David Kline, *Rembrandts in the Attic,* 1999.

28. Ibid.

29. Bo Carlsson, Monica Dumitriu, Jeffrey T. Glass, Craig Allen Nard, and Richard Barrett, "Intellectual Property (IP) Management: organizational processes and structures, and the role of IP donations," *Journal of Technology* (February 2008). This paper examines IP management in U.S. companies based on in-depth interviews and online survey data.

30. Tim Wu, "Intellectual Property, Innovation, and Decentralized Decisions," *Virginia Law Review* 92, no. 1 (2005): 104.

31. Ibid.

32. Ibid., 104.

33. Ibid., 104–105.

34. "IBM's Patent/Licensing Connection." *Industry Week* March 2003, statement of Jerry Rosenthal, IBM's former VP of intellectual property and licensing business.

35. Carlsson et al., note 29 above, at 554.

36. Ibid. at 555.

37. Wu, note 30 above, at 106, quoting F.A. Hayek, "The Use of Knowledge in Society," 35 *Am. Econ. Rev.* 519 (1945). ("If we possess all the relevant information, if we can start out from a given system of preferences and if we command complete knowledge of available means, the problem which remains is purely one of logic . . . . This, however, is emphatically not the economic problem which society faces . . . . [T]he "data" from which the economic calculus starts are never for the whole society "given" to a single mind which could work out the implications, and can never be so given.")

38. "IBM's Patent/Licensing Connection," *Industry Week*, March 2003, statement of Louis Galambos. ("They [IBM] have learned how to use licensing as a strong positioning factor in global markets.")

39. Ibid.

40. Wikipedia, "Cross Licensing," http://en.wikipedia.org/wiki/Cross-licensing (last visited March 12, 2010).

41. Ibid.

42. www.law.com/jsp/article.jsp?id=1202430463695 (last visited October 22, 2009).

43. John Teresko, "IBM's Patent/Licensing Connection," March, 2003, www.industryweek .com/articles/ibms_patent/licensing_connection_1228.aspx (last visited March 12, 2010).

44. Ibid.

45. Carlsson et al., note 29 above, at 555.

46. Ibid.

47. In re: Chocolate Confectionary Antitrust Litigation, MDL No. 1935 (M.D. Pa.) (Aug. 11, 2009).

48. Ibid.

49. Ibid. at 8.

50. Ibid.

51. Nestlé does not have direct control of the SBU or the SGDUs.

52. In re: Chocolate Confectionary Antitrust Litigation, MDL No. 1935 (M.D. Pa.) (Aug. 11, 2009) at 9, fn 10 indicating that "strategic marks are those assigned to large families of products, such as Nescafe.®"

53. Ibid.

54. Ibid.

55. Ibid. at 48, noting that Nestle's executives do not serve concurrently on the operating entity's board and the operating entity's board's CEO and executive officers manage the day-to-day affairs of the operating entity.

56. Ibid. at 44.

57. Ibid. at 50.

58. Ibid., indicating that "Société personnel have the right to inspect Hershey Global's facilities and monitor product quality, and nothing in the record establishes that Nestlé S.A. employees participate in these activities."

59. Ibid.

60. Ibid.

61. Ibid. at 44, indicating that Nestle's SGDUs offer pricing strategies were merely advisory and the operating entities are free to create their own.

62. See Lanning Bryer and Matthew Asbell, "Combining Trademarks in a Jointly Owned IP Holding Company," *The Trademark Reporter,* May–June 2008. Also see Pamela Chestek, "Control of Trademarks by the Intellectual Property Holding Company," *41 IDEA* 1 (2001): 5–7.

63. www.fordbetterideas.com/tc/mainframe.html (last visited January 7, 2009).

64. Ibid.

65. See Pamela Chestek, "Control of Trademarks."

66. "HP Announces Intellectual Property Licensing Group to Leverage Growing Patent Portfolio," January, 2004, www.hp.com/hpinfo/newsroom/press/2004/040112c.html (last visited March 4, 2010).

67. Ibid.

68. Joe Beyers, "IP Licensing at Hewlett Packard, Patent Engineering lecture," March, 2008 at p.7.

69. Ibid.

70. Ibid. at 8.

71. www.hp.com/hpinfo/abouthp/iplicensing/ (last visited March 4, 2010).

72. "Intellectual Property: Brand Licensing," www.hp.com/hpinfo/abouthp/iplicensing/brand.html (last visited September 23, 2009).

73. Ibid. Also see note 114 below.

74. See also Howard Fine and Andrew Ross, "Accounting and Tax Policies as They Relate to Intellectual Property," in *IP Strategies for the 21st Century Corporation.*

75. Bryer, note 63 above, at 860–861.

76. Ibid. at 861.

77. See *Sherwin-Williams Company v. Commissioner of Revenue,* 438 Mass. 71 (2002)

78. It is recommended that a tax lawyer be consulted before considering restructuring and incorporating an IPHC.

79. PricewaterhouseCoopers, note 1 above at 17 (statement of Joseph Beyers, Head of IP, HP).

80. See also Toshiya Oka, "Penetrating New Markets through Extension of Goods or Product Lines Expansion into Other Territories," in *IP Strategies for the 21st Century Corporation.*

81. PricewaterhouseCoopers, note 1 above at 17 (statement of Joseph Breyers Head of IP, HP)

82. Ibid.

83. Ibid.

84. Ibid.

85. In case of patents, an assignee is generally not permitted to file a patent application for registering the right. See Appendix R Patent Rules, §1.46 Assigned inventions and patents.

In case the whole or a part interest in the invention or in the patent to be issued is assigned, the application must still be made or authorized to be made, and an oath or declaration signed, by the inventor or one of the persons mentioned in §§ 1.42, 1.43, or 1.47. However, the patent may be issued to the assignee or jointly to the inventor and the assignee as provided in § 3.81.

86. See "Works Made for Hire Under the Copyright Act of 1976," United States Copyright Office, www.copyright.gov/circs/circ09.pdf (last visited December 15, 2009).

87. See "Manual of Patent Examining Procedure," Chapter 300 Ownership and Assignment, www.uspto.gov/web/offices/pac/mpep/mpep_e8r3_0300.pdf (last visited March 12, 2010).

88. Lanham Act § 5, 45 U.S.C.A §1127 providing that: A "related company means any person whose use of the mark is controlled by the owner of the mark w.r.t. the nature and quality of the goods or services on or in connection with which it is used."

89. See McCarthy on Trademarks, Assignment and Licensing, §18:52 quoting *Watec Co., Ltd. v. Liu*, 403 F.3d 645, 74 U.S.P.Q2d 1128 (9th Cir. 2005). The court affirmed the jury verdict that the foreign manufacturer was the owner of the trademark and that the U.S. importer and distributor's licensed use inured to the benefit of the foreign manufacturer.

90. See Lanham Act, note 91 above.

91. See Appendix R Patent Rules, note 88 above.

92. Ibid.

93. Gary H. Moore, "Joint Ventures and Strategic Alliances: Ownership of Developed Intellectual Property —Issues and Approaches," *The Computer and Internet Lawyer* September, 2007.

94. Ibid.

95. Ibid. at 2, explaining that patent rights developed under a broad patent cross license arrangement might become equally available to the cross licensees due to the collaborative nature of the agreement. See also James Markarian, "Strategic and Legal View of Licensing Patents," and Kelly Slavitt, "Monetizing IP Rights: Licensing In and Out," in *IP Operations and Implementation for the 21st Century Corporation*, (forthcoming).

96. See also James Markarian, "Strategic and Legal View of Licensing Patents," and Kelly Slavitt, "Monetizing IP Rights: Licensing In and Out," in *IP Operations and Implementation for the 21st Century Corporation*, (forthcoming).

97. Hung H. Bui, "Practical Strategies to Develop an IP Portfolio and Avoid Mistakes Pertaining to IP for High-Tech Startup and Small Technology Companies," *Intellectual Property and Technology Magazine,* June, 2005, www.ipfrontline.com/downloads/IP_Start_Up_Strategies.pdf (last visited March 15, 2010).

98. Ibid.

99. Ibid.

100. See History of Canon available at www.canon.com/about/history/; Canon: Sustainability Report (2008) available at www.canon.com/environment/report/pdf/report2008e.pdf; Canon Technology Highlights (2009) available at www.canon.com/technology/pdf/tech2009e.pdf (last visited January 11, 2010).

101. Ibid.

102. See discussion *supra* Strategic Alliances and accompanying text.

103. Christopher M. Kalanje, "WIPO-WASME Special Program on Practical Intellectual Property Issues—Ownership of IP Assets," October 2003, www.wipo.int/edocs/mdocs/sme/en/wipo_wasme_ipr_ge_03/wipo_wasme_ipr_ge_03_12.pdf.

104. USPTO, General Information Concerning Patents (January 2005) available at www.uspto.gov/patents/basics.jsp#functions (last visited February 23, 2010). Also see American Intellectual Property Law Association (AIPLA) Report of the Economic Survey to determine the average patent costs.

105. USPTO, Trademark FAQs, www.uspto.gov/faq/trademarks.jsp#Basic002 (last visited February 23, 2010).

106. USPTO, Trademark Process, www.uspto.gov/trademarks/process/index.jsp (last visited February 23, 2010). ("Federal registration has several advantages, including a notice to the public of the registrant's claim of ownership of the mark, a legal presumption of ownership

nationwide, and the exclusive right to use the mark on or in connection with the goods or services set forth in the registration.")

107. In case of a copyright litigation, registration is a legal prerequisite. See 17 USCS § 412 (registration is a prerequisite to avail of statutory damages and/or attorney's fees).

108. Nitin Aggarwal and Eric A. Walden, "Intellectual Property Bundle (IPB): Managing Transaction Costs in Technology Development Through Network Governance," http://ssrn.com/abstract=1372286 (last visited December 10, 2009) at fn 13 and 33.

109. Ibid. at 1.

110. Ibid. at 9.

111. Companies may adopt non-negotiable license terms as in shrink-wrap/click-wrap agreements.

112. Richard A. Posner, "Transaction Costs and Antitrust Concerns in the Licensing of Intellectual Property," 4 *J. MARSHALL R. INTELL. PROP. L.* 325 (2005).

113. Mohan Rao, "Valuing Intellectual Property in Licensing Transactions," *The Licensing Journal,* June/July 2008, stating that valuation of intellectual property is undertaken for "four purposes: (1) in the context of licensing transactions or acquisition, including as part of a business acquisition; (2) for regulatory compliance, such as in transfer pricing; (3) as collateral in financing or for intellectual property-backed securitization; or (4) in the context of litigation.". However, IP is one of the most difficult assets to value and its valuation may be undertaken by various means. See PricewaterhouseCoopers, note 1 at 18:

- Conducting a comparative analysis with other companies of profits earned due to IP assets owned, or the lack thereo
- Conducting a comparative analysis between the total revenues earned between branded and unbranded products
- Calculating potential savings due to the IP assets owned
- Conducting a comparative analysis of sales of similar assets.

For other strategies for valuation of IP, see Ted Hagelin, "Competitive Advantage Valuation of Intellectual Property Assets: A New Tool for IP Managers," *The Journal of Law and Technology,* 2003, 79. Also see "The New Role of MBA in Licensing," *Intellectual Property Today"* (February 1999) stating that "Intellectual property valuation [for technology] includes valuing the technology, determining manufacturing costs, determining royalties and methods of payment, evaluating the exclusive licensing against non-exclusive licensing and assessing financial damages for litigation purposes. Understanding the value of technology is a fundamental component in determining the above financial objectives and in devising business and technology marketing strategies. The technology's value underlies the terms of licensing negotiations and provides a guideline in selecting proper marketing strategies."

114. See also James Markarian, "Strategic and Legal View of Licensing Patents," and Kelly Slavitt, "Monetizing IP Rights: Licensing In and Out," in *IP Operations and Implementation for the 21st Century Corporation,* (forthcoming).

115. See discussion *supra* Other Management Options and accompanying text in this chapter.

116. The assignment of trademark rights must not be in "gross," that is, the assets of the holding company should not be equitably owned by the operating company. The owner is the entity that controls the use and that is the proper party to apply for and obtain registration. See *In re Wella* A.G. 787 F.2d 1549, 229 U.S.P.Q. 274 (Fed Cir, 1986) (emphasizing that either the licensor or the operating corporation must be the registrant of the licensed mark).

117. See note 106 above.

118. Joseph Yang, "IP Ownership And Usage Rights in Joint Developments: Alternatives to Joint Ownership," *The Licensing Journal*, January 2004.

119. See Joint Ownership, www.ipo.gov.uk/types/copy/c-ownership/c-jointauthors.htm (last visited January 10, 2010). Also see Section 36 of the Patent Act of 1977.

120. See Rao, note 116 above.

121. *Martha Graham School and Dance Foundation, Inc. v. Martha Graham Center of Contemporary Dance, Inc.,* 2004 U.S. App. LEXIS 20904 (2d Cir., October, 2004). Under the 1976 Act, works that were created on or after January 1, 1978, acquired statutory copyright upon creation. The act extended this protection to works created before January 1, 1978, provided the work was not in the public domain or copyrighted. Also see 17 U.S.C § 302(a) and 303(a).

122. "Registering a Mark in the U.K," www.out-law.com/page-375 (last visited January 11, 2010).

123. USPTO FAQs stating that a federal trademark registration affords the owner "constructive notice" of a valid claim of ownership, the ability to file infringement actions in federal courts and the ability to prevent importation of infringing foreign goods bearing the owner's mark, available at www.uspto.gov/faq/trademarks.jsp#Basic002 (last visited November 18, 2009).

Similarly, a copyright registration affords the owner a prima facie presumption about the ownership and validity of the copyright. Further, upon registration, a copyright owner has the ability to file an infringement action in federal courts and may be entitled to statutory damages and attorney's fees. See note 110 above.

124. See *Do Denim v. Fried Denim,* No. 08 Civ. 10947, 2009 U.S. Dist. LEXIS 51512, at *7 (S.D. N.Y. June 17, 2009). Also see 17 U.S.C. §411(a) ("no civil action for infringement of copyright in the U.S. work shall be instituted until pre-registration or registration of the copyright claim has been made in accordance with this title").

125. Jean-François Bretonnière, Melanie Howlett, and Grégoire Corman, "Licensing Strategies: defensive protection and active exploitation," www.iam-magazine.com/issues/Article.ashx?g=5789fb19-ece0-4b4c-a33b-2288ad4a971e (last visited December 10, 2009).

126. See 17 U.S.C. § 302 –305.

127. USPTO, Trademark FAQs, www.uspto.gov/faq/t120052.jsp (last visited January 12, 2010), stating that:

"For a trademark registration to remain valid, an Affidavit of Use ("Section 8 Affidavit") must be filed: (1) between the fifth and sixth year following registration, and (2) within the year before the end of every ten-year period after the date of registration. The registrant may file the affidavit within a grace period of six months after the end of the sixth or tenth year, with payment of an additional fee." The registrant must also file a §9 renewal application within the year before the expiration date of a registration, or within a grace period of six months after the expiration date, with payment of an additional fee. "Assuming that an affidavit of use is timely filed, registrations granted PRIOR to November 16, 1989 have a 20-year term, and registrations granted on or after November 16, 1989 have a 10-year term."

128. See also James Markarian, "Strategic and Legal View of Licensing Patents," and Kelly Slavitt, "Monetizing IP Rights: Licensing In and Out," in *IP Operations and Implementation for the 21st Century Corporation,* (forthcoming).

129. Developing and licensing technology: another source of revenue; FW FOCUS: TECHNOLOGY Franchising World (April 1, 2008) (statement of Gary R. Duvall).

130. Note that licenses are distinguishable from assignments in that licenses can be exclusive or non-exclusive and the owner invariably retains certain rights allowing the third party to

exercise specified, but not all rights. An assignment, on the other hand, is more like a sale that effectively transfers ownership and all associated rights.

131. George A. Frank, "Licensing IP Rights: Why, How, What, and When—A Corporate Perspective," *The Licensing Journal* (June/July 2004).

132. Ibid. at 2.

133. EPM Communications, Inc., "Minor on Revenue Line, Healthy for Bottom Line," Exclusive Survey of Trademark/Brand Licensors, *Licensing Letter* (May 2003).

134. Louis P. Berneman, Iain Cockburn, Ajay Agrawal and Shankar Iyer, U.S./Canadian Licensing In 2007-08: Survey Results, March, 2009, www.lesfoundation.org/survey/pdfs/2008 SurveyResults.pdf (last visited March 15, 2010). Also see note 6 above.

135. Cameron Gray, "A New Era in IP Licensing: The Unit License Right Program," *The Licensing Journal* (Nov./Dec. 2008) (stating that due to few mandatory disclosure requirements, "the quantitative figures do not adequately convey the importance and reach of IP licenses in the United States. . . . However, an indication of the magnitude of the transactions can be gleaned from the following:

> IBM's annual licensing revenue is consistently more than $1 billion
> Qualcomm Incorporated has posted more than $400 million in licensing revenue per quarter in recent years
> Deloitte Touche Tohmatsu estimated that technology patent licensing revenues in North America surpassed $500 billion in 2007
> In 2008, Northwestern University sold royalty rights to the drug Lyrica for a reported $700 million
> In 2005, Emory University sold royalty rights to its HIV drug for a reported $540 million
> In 2006, NYU reported more than $150 million in licensing income").

136. Press release, "Twentieth Century Fox Licensing & Merchandising Launches Ground breaking Merchandising Program for the Year's Most Anticipated Film—Avatar," *Market Watch*, December, 2009, www.marketwatch.com/story/twentieth-century-fox-licensing-merchandising-launches-groundbreaking-merchandising-program-for-the-years-most-anticipated-film-avatar-2009-12-10 (last visited January 11, 2010)

137. See Rao, note 116 above, at 21.

138. Ibid.

139. Licensing is distinguishable from an assignment in which all the copyrights in a work will be transferred without any limitation in duration.

140. See 17 U.S.C § 204. See also Kelly Slavitt, "Monetizing IP Rights: Licensing In and Out," in *IP Operations and Implementation for the 21st Century Corporation,* (forthcoming).

141. Typically, EULAs contain restrictions imposed by the manufacturer/author on the use of the product. See www.webopedia.com/TERM/E/EULA.html (last visited March 13, 2010).

142. Agreements such as "Development and License Agreements" provide collaborating parties the right to develop a product further and the ability to make necessary modifications, instead of merely using it based on the terms provided by a manufacturer/author in an EULA.

143. See PricewaterhouseCoopers, note 1, at 28.

144. Ulrich Lichtenthaler, "Product Business, Foreign Direct Investment, and Licensing: Examining Their Relationship in International Technology Exploitation," *Journal of World Business,* (October 2009).

145. Ibid at 3.

146. Mohan Rao, note 116 above, at 1.

147. Andrew J. Sherman, Esq., "Strategies for Leveraging Intellectual Property Through Licensing, Joint Ventures, Alliances and Franchising," June, 2001, www.netpreneur.org/advisors/ip/images/Strategies_for_IP.pdf (last visited November 18, 2009).

148. See USPTO, 35 U.S.C. 261 Ownership; assignment (explaining that "an exclusive license may be granted by the patent owner to a licensee. The exclusive license prevents the patent owner (or any other party to whom the patent owner might wish to sell a license) from competing with the exclusive licensee, as to the geographic region, the length of time, and/or the field of use, set forth in the license agreement," www.uspto.gov/web/offices/pac/mpep/documents/0300_301.htm (last visited January 12, 2010).

149. See http://en.wikipedia.org/wiki/Cross-licensing (last visited March 13, 2010).

150. See www.entrepreneur.com/tradejournals/article/178615552.html (last visited March 13, 2010).

151. Tracy Wang, "Japan's Toyoda Gosei and Sharp enters into a LED cross-licensing agreement," LED inside, December 28, 2009, www.ledinside.com/toyoda_LED_20091228 (last visited February 20, 2010).

152. Ibid.

153. See note 139 above.

154. Wikipedia, Patent Pool, available at http://en.wikipedia.org/wiki/Patent_pool (last visited December 15, 2009).

155. Ibid., 6.

156. Gray, note 139 above, at 27.

157. Ibid. at 28.

158. See Jean-François Bretonnière, Melanie Howlett and Grégoire Corman, "Licensing Strategies: defensive protection and active exploitation," *Licensing in the Boardroom,* 2008, www.iam-magazine.com/issues/Article.ashx?g=5789fb19-ece0-4b4c-a33b-2288ad4a971e (last visted March 15, 2010) (stating that recently, the Louvre licensed the "use of its name to Abu Dhabi for 30 years for a tidy sum of US $520 million.").

159. See Bryer, note 63 above.

160. Lanham Act § 45, 15 U.S.C. § 1127 ("related company" as "any person whose use of a mark is controlled by the owner of the mark with respect to the nature and quality of the goods or services on or in connection with which the mark is used.").

161. See Christian Dorffer and David Aaker, "Brand Papers—Dual Brand Ownership," *Brand Strategy,* April 10, 2006, 30.

162. See Bryer, note 63 above, quoting Christian Dorffer and David Aaker, "Brand Papers—Dual Brand Ownership," *Brand Strategy,* April 10, 2006, 30.

163. See *Topps Co. v. Cadbury Stani S.A.I.C.,* 454 F. Supp. 2d 102 (S.D.N.Y. 2006) (stating that a trademark is simply a symbol of goodwill and cannot be sold or assigned apart from the goodwill it symbolizes), citing *Marshak v. Green,* 746 F.2d 927, 929 (2d Cir. 1984) (citing Lanham Act §10, 15 U.S.C. § 1060).

164. See *Barcamercia Int'l Trust v. Tyfield Imports, Inc.,* 289 F.3d 589, 598 (9th Cir. 2002) ("Licensor is required to exercise control over the license to ensure that the nature and quality of goods are consistent and meet the standards set by the licensor.").

165. Mark A. Greenfield, "Good Will as a Factor in Trademark Assignments—A Comparative Study," *Trademark Reporter* 60, no. 2 (1970): 173.

166. Ibid., quoting *Topps Co. v. Cadbury Stani S.A.I.C.,* 454 F. Supp. 2d 102 (S.D.N.Y. (2006) (stating that a trademark is simply a symbol of goodwill and cannot be sold or assigned apart from the goodwill it symbolizes) citing *Marshak v. Green,* 746 F.2d 927, 929 (2d Cir. 1984) (citing Lanham Act §10, 15 U.S.C. § 1060).

167. See *Topps Co. v. Cadbury Stani S.A.I.C.,* 526 F.3d 63 (2d Cir. May 15, 2008) ("An assignment "in gross" is a purported transfer of a trademark divorced from its goodwill, and it is generally deemed invalid under U.S. law").

168. See Lanning, note 63 above, at 845, fn 56 referencing Mark A. Greenfield, "Good Will as a Factor in Trademark Assignments—A Comparative Study," to indicate that some countries allow for the assignment in gross of trademark rights independent of any transfer of goodwill.

169. See *Barcamercia Int'l Trust v. Tyfield Imports, Inc.,* 289 F.3d 589, 598 (9th Cir. 2002) (Plaintiff was unable to demonstrate "any involvement whatsoever regarding the quality of the wine and maintaining it at any level," and as a consequence engaged in naked licensing of its mark and forfeited its rights).

170. See *Dawn Donut Co. v. Hart's Food Stores, Inc.,* 267 F.2d at 366 ("[T]he Lanham Act places an affirmative duty upon a licensor of a registered trademark to take reasonable measures to detect and prevent misleading uses of his mark by his licensees or suffer cancellation of his federal registration."); see also McCarthy on Trademarks and Unfair Competition, § 18:42 (indicating that the trademark owner not only has the right to control quality, but also an obligation to do so).

171. See Greenfield, note 169 above.

172. See *Alligator Co. v. Robert Bruce Inc.,* 176 F. Supp. 377 (E.D. Pa. 1959) (even though the license agreement contained adequate provisions for quality control by the licensor, the court refused the licensor's summary judgment motion on the grounds that only a trial would clarify the factual issues of "what the parties actually do in carrying out the agreement").

173. See McCarthy, note 174 above.

174. See *Stanfield v. Osborne Indus. Inc.,* 52 F.3d 867, 871, 34 U.S.P.Q.2d (BNA) 1456, 1460 (10th Cir. 1995) ("The absence of an express contractual right of control does not necessarily result in the abandonment of a mark, as long as the licensor in fact exercised sufficient control over its licensee."); Moore Bus. Forms, Inc., 960 F.2d 489 (5th Cir 1992) ("there need not be formal quality control where particular circumstances [indicate] that the public will not be deceived").

175. See *Stanfield v. Osborne Indus., Inc.,* 52 F.3d 867, 872 (10th Cir. 1995) ("In cases in which courts have found that a licensor justifiably relied on a licensee for quality control, some special relationship existed between the parties"); *Transgo, Inc. v. Ajac Transmission Parts Corp.,* 768 F.2d 1001, 1017-18 (9th Cir. 1985) (in light of the fact that licensor supplied at least 90 percent of the components sold by the licensee and there had been years without complaint, and "[d]ue to [licensor's] association with [licensee] for over ten years and his respect for his ability and expertise, [licensor] felt he could rely on [licensee] to maintain high standards by performing his own quality control").

176. See Lanning, note 63 above.

177. See McCarthy, Restatement Third, Unfair Competition §33, comment c (1995), indicating that there can be no general standard for quality control. For instance, quality control applied for licensing a soft drink mark on a T-shirt may be totally inadequate for the purposes of quality control applied for a pharmaceutical trademark for use on prescription drugs.

"Cases both under the Lanham Act and common law apply a flexible standard responsive to the particular facts of each case. The ultimate issue is whether the control exercised by the licensor is sufficient under the circumstances to satisfy the public's expectation of quality assurance arising from the presence of the trademark on the licensee's goods or services."

178. See McCarthy on Trademark §18:58. Also see *Doebler's Pennsylvania's Hybrids, Inc. v. Doebler,* 442 F.3d 812 (3rd Cir. 2006) (a triable issue of fact existed that one family member, in his dual roles in the alleged implied licensor and licensee companies, "ensured that [licensee's] use of the mark was conducted with appropriate quality controls").

179. See *Procter & Gamble Co. v. Quality King Distributors, Inc.,* 123 F. Supp/2d 108 (E.D.N.Y. 2000) (Trademark will be deemed abandoned where the registrant licenses the mark and fails to police the license).

180. Naked licensing is an "[u]ncontrolled licensing of a mark whereby the licensee can place the mark on any quality or type of goods or services," raising "a grave danger that the public will be deceived by such a usage." 2 McCarthy on Trademarks § 18:48; also see Restatement (Third) of Unfair Competition § 33 cmt. b (1995) (Naked Licensing is "[w]hen a trademark owner fails to exercise reasonable control over the use of a mark by a licensee," such that "the presence of the mark on the licensee's goods or services misrepresents their connection with the trademark owner since the mark no longer identifies goods or services that are under the control of the owner of the mark" and the mark can no longer provide "a meaningful assurance of quality."); *Barcamercia Int'l Trust v. Tyfield Imports, Inc.,* 289 F.3d 589, 598 (9th Cir. 2002) (plaintiff engaged in naked licensing and was stopped from asserting rights in the mark because its quality control measures were insufficient, inasmuch as that the plaintiff engaged in minimal tasting of the wine, did not document the times of the tasting, and failed to demonstrate knowledge of reliance on actual quality control or on any ongoing effort to control quality).

181. In determining whether a trademark licensor engaged in naked licensing, the facts of each case must be considered and the burden of proof is stringent. See *Doebler's Pennsylvania's Hybrids, Inc. v. Doebler,* 442 F.3d 812 (3rd Cir. 2006) quoting *Creative Gifts, Inc. v. UFO,* 235 F.3d 540, 548 (10th Cir. 2000); *Tumblebus Inc. v. Cranmer,* 399 F.3d 754 (6th Cir., 2005) quoting *Exxon Corp. v. Oxxford Clothes, Inc.,* 109 F.3d 1070, 1075-76 (5th Cir.), cert. denied, 522 U.S. 915, 118 S.Ct. 299, 139 L.Ed.2d 231 (1997) ("Because naked licensing is generally ultimately relevant only to establish an unintentional trademark abandonment which results in a loss of trademark rights against the world, the burden of proof faced by third parties attempting to show abandonment through naked licensing is stringent").

Minority Views: North America, Inc. v. Magic Touch GmbH, 124 F.3d 876 (7th Cir. 1997) ("Naked licensing law is full of contradictory case law with some authorities requiring strict oversight by licensors and others taking a more lenient approach."). Some indicate that stipulation in the contract is sufficient, even if no actual control is exercised. *Ideal Toy Corp. v. Cameo Exclusive Prods., Inc.,* 170 U.S.O.Q. 596 (TTAB 1971) (proper "control" found where licensor had a right to control, even though there was no evidence of actual control). Other Courts have held that reliance on licensee's own quality control efforts may "be deemed as the taking of reasonable measures to protect quality of the goods bearing the mark."

182. See Lanning, note 63 above, at 840.

183. Ibid. at 841.

184. See Trademark Dilution Revision Act, 109 P.L. 312, 120 Stat. 1730 (2006).

185. Ibid.

186. Ibid.

187. See Lanning, note 63 above, at 843.

188. See Intangible Business Ltd., Ingredient branding case study: Intel, www.intangiblebusiness .com/store/data/files/360-Ingredient_branding_case_study_Intel.pdf.

189. See Lanning, supra note 63, at 844 quoting Saul Lefkowitz, "Double Trademarking—We've Come a Long Way," 63 TMR 11, 15 (1983) ("The use of each mark applied to the product must not confuse the purchasing public as to its function or purpose, or derogate the trademark rights of anyone who contributed to the creation of the product, or those who handle the product during its journey to the market place.")

190. See *Addamax Corp. v. Open Software Found.*, 152 F.3d 48 (1st Cir., 1998) at fn 2.

191. Nigel Parker, "Intellectual property issues in joint ventures and collaborations, *Journal of Intellectual Property Law & Practice.* 2, no. 11 (2007): 729.

192. Ibid., citing *Collaborating to Compete: Using Strategic Alliances and Acquisitions in the Global Marketplace*, McKinsey & Company, Inc., 1993, J. Bleeke and D. Ernst (eds).

193. See Kurt M. Saunders, *Marquette Intellectual Property Law Review* (2003).

194. Fancher, Deloitte & Touche, in "Mine Games," *Forbes ASAP* (June 2002).

195. Broox W. Peterson, "Protecting Your Intellectual Property from Your Strategic Alliance Partner," 2008, www.bwplawyer.com/uploads/Protecting_Your_Intellectual_Property_From_Your_Strategic_Alliance_Partner.pdf (last visited December 7, 2009).

196. See discussion in Chapter 2.

197. Ibid.

198. Oracle recently acquired Sophoi to "monetize digital content and enable better financial control of content assets," according to the VP of products at Oracle Communications, Liam Maxwell, www.crn.com.au/News/158080,oracle-buys-up-ip-management-firm-sophoi.aspx (last visited January 20, 2011). Also see the press release indicating that this collaboration will help Oracle "bring innovative end-to-end solutions to the media and entertainment industry," www.oracle.com/corporate/press/2007_may/sophoi.html (last visited November 18, 2009).

199. Lanning G. Bryer, Scott J. Lebson, Intellectual Property Assets in Mergers and Acquisitions, www.wipo.int/sme/en/documents/pdf/mergers.pdf (last visited on January 20, 2011) at 4.

200. Ibid., citing to Glenn A. Gunderson and Paul Kavanaugh, *Intellectual Property in Mergers & Acquisitions,* Trademarks in Business Transactions Forum, International Trademark Association, Sept. 16–17, 1999. See also Fernando Torres, "Valuation, Monetization, and Disposition in Bankruptcy," in *IP Operations and Implementation for the 21st Century Corporation,* (forthcoming).

201. See also Scott Lebson, "Creating, Perfecting, and Enforcing Security Interests in Intellectual Property," in *IP Operations and Implementation for the 21st Century Corporation,* (forthcoming).

202. See David Edwards, "Patent Backed Securitization: Blueprint For a New Asset Class," Gerling NCM Credit Insurance, www.securitization.net/pdf/gerling_new_0302.pdf (last visited March 15, 2010).

203. See Ruth L. Taylor, Rudy Becerra, Patricia Stuart and Spencer A. Case, "Securitization of brand names: Basic concepts and its use in practice," *Journal of Brand Management* (2009).

204. Mohan Rao, "Valuing Intellectual Property in Licensing Transactions," *The Licensing Journal* (June/July 2008): 1.

205. See Taylor et al., note 207 above, at 63.

206. WIPO, "The Securitization of Intellectual Property Assets—A New Trend," www.kipo.ke.wipo.net/sme/en/ip_business/finance/securitization.htm (last visited Nov. 2, 2009).

207. Matt Morris, "Royalty Securitizations—Were "Bowie Bonds" Just a Fad?," www.cfi-institute.org/VP%20-%20Royalty%20Securitizations%20-%20Morris.html (last visited Nov. 2, 2009).

208. Ambac, Dunkin' Brands Securitization Marks Milestone for Innovative Private Equity Financing, www.ambac.com/pdfs/Deals/Dunkin.pdf (last visited on January 20, 2011).

209. Ibid.

210. "Morgan Stanley unveils $250m Securitization," *Financial Times,* July 2009, www.ft.com/cms/s/0/f0f05d54-6f2c-11de-9109-00144feabdc0.html?nclick_check=1 (last visited Nov. 2, 2009).

211. Ibid.

212. Ibid.

213. Ibid.

214. See Taylor et al., note 207 above, at 65, elaborating on a true sale securitization or a synthetic securitization.

215. Ibid at 63.

216. Ibid at 68. Also see Reuters, "Sears Securitizes its Brand Names," April 5, 2007. www.reuters.com/article/idUSN0523890220070405 (last visited February 20, 2010).

217. Ibid.

218. Kelly Holman, "A Starring Role for IP? As the securitization market comes back to life, private-equity firms are finding deal flow in intellectual property. Will the structured finance market support IP deals?," *Investment Dealers' Digest* (July 31, 2009) quoting John Fargis, Managing Director, U.S. Media Investment Banking, Jefferies & Co., www.allbusiness.com/banking-finance/financial-markets-investing-securities/12609889-1.html (last visited December 10, 2009).

219. See also Howard Fine and Andrew Ross, "Accounting and Tax Policies as They Relate to Intellectual Property," in *IP Strategies for the 21st Century Corporation.*

220. Xuan-Thao N. Nguyen, "Holding Intellectual Property," *State Tax Notes,* November 21, 2005, at fn 19. The author states that "Indeed, intellectual property has become so significant that the Federal Bureau of Investigation has admitted:

These valuable products, collectively known as 'Intellectual Property (IP), are the primary fuel of the U.S. economic engine. . . ."

221. Perry D. Quick and Timothy L. Day, "Management of IP: Intercompany Transfers, Offshore Planning, and Recent Developments Regarding Cost Sharing," *The Licensing Journal* (January 2006).

222. Ibid. at 15, explaining cost sharing arrangements as contemplated by the U.S. transfer pricing regulations.

223. Ibid. at 16.

224. CQ Transcriptions LLC, Third Quarter, Products Earning Conference Call, Maxim Integrated Products (April 2009).

225. Ibid.

226. See Lanning, note 63 above, at fn 15. Also see Christine Bauman and Michael Schadewald, "More States Challenge Trademark Holding Companies," *The CPA* Journal April, 2004, at 38, available at www.nysscpa.org/cpajournal/2004/404/essentials/p38.htm; John Dull and Michael Bredahl, "Great Opportunities in an IP Holding Company Beyond Tax Savings," *Intellectual Property Today,* January 2002, at 8; Susan Barbieri Montgomery and Leonard Schneidman, "*Intellectual Property Transfers—Holding Companies* in *Intellectual Property Assets in Mergers and Acquisitions* 13.4. (L. Bryer ed., 2002); State Income Tax Strategies, 1-7 Taxation of Intellectual Property §7.06 (2006).

227. 26 U.S.C. §351(a) (2007). Transfer to corporation controlled by transferor.

"No gain or loss shall be recognized if property is transferred to a corporation by one or more persons solely in exchange for stock in such corporation and immediately after the exchange such person or persons are in control (as defined in section 368(c)) of the corporation)."

228. Ibid.

229. 26 U.S.C. § 368 (c) (2007). Also see Lanning, note 63 above, at 860–861.

230. Certain states have attempted to counter the tax-free status of IPHCs by employing the argument that an economic nexus exists. See note 185 above.

231. *Quill Corp. v. North Dakota,* 504 U.S. 298 (1992) (the physical presence of a corporation was required to establish substantial nexus and thereby allow the state to tax such corporation); *Geoffrey Inc. v. S.C. Tax Commissioner,* 437 S.E.2d 13 (S.C.), cert. denied, 114 SCt 550 (1993) (by licensing the use of intangibles in South Carolina and receiving income in exchange of such use, Geoffrey had substantial nexus and minimum contacts with the state for the purposes of Due Process Clause and the Commerce Clause); *Lanco, Inc. v Division of Taxation,* N.J. Sup. Ct., Oct. 12, 2006; cert. denied; U.S. Sup. Ct., 06-1236, (June 18 2007) (Although the Delaware trademark holding company had no physical presence in New Jersey, because it derived income through a licensing agreement with a company conducting retail operations in New Jersey, the plaintiff had income tax nexus in New Jersey. Also, the Court noted that the holding in Quill is appropriately confined to sales and use tax); *A&F Trademark, Inc. v. Tolson,* 605 S.E.2d 187 (N.C. Ct. App. 2004), cert. denied, 126 U.S. 353 (2005) (the out-of-state trademark holding company licensed its intangibles for use in North Carolina and, therefore, there was sufficient tax nexus).

232. "What Are the Advantages and Disadvantages of Locating IP Offshore?," *Managing Intellectual Property* 85 (December 2008): 90–91.

233. Lanning Bryer, *Intellectual Property Assets in Mergers and Acquisitions,* 2001, at 14.1.

234. Ibid.

235. Ibid at 14.2–14.4.

236. Jamal Smith, "Offshore Securitization of IP Assets," *Mondaq Business Briefing,* May 28, 2008.

237. Article I, Section 8, Clause 8 of the United States Constitution:

"To promote the Progress of Science and useful Arts, by securing for limited Times to Authors and Inventors the exclusive Right to their respective Writings and Discoveries."

238. www.ftc.gov/os/adjpro/d9341/091216intelcmpt.pdf (last visited January 8, 2009).

239. Jordan Robertson, "Intel Hit With More Antitrust Charges In FTC Suit," Associated Press, December 16, 2009, www.businessinsider.com/intel-hit-with-more-antitrust-charges-in-ftc-suit-2009-12 (last visited March 14, 2010).

240. The Clayton Act, 15 U.S.C. § 18 (2007); The Sherman Act, 15 U.S.C. § 1 and 2 (2007); The Federal Trade Commission Act, 15 U.S.C. § 45 (2007).

241. The Clayton Act, 15 U.S.C. § 18 (2007).

242. The Sherman Act, 15 U.S.C § 1 (2007) § 1. "Trusts, etc., in restraint of trade illegal; penalty.

Every contract, combination in the form of trust or otherwise, or conspiracy, in restraint of trade or commerce among the several States, or with foreign nations, is declared to be illegal. Every person who shall make any contract or engage in any combination or conspiracy hereby declared to be illegal shall be deemed guilty of a felony, and, on conviction thereof, shall be punished by fine not exceeding $100,000,000 if a corporation, or, if any other person, $1,000,000, or by imprisonment not exceeding 10 years, or by both said punishments, in the discretion of the court.

243. The Sherman Act, 15 U.S.C § 1(2007) § 2. "Monopolizing trade a felony; penalty.

Every person who shall monopolize, or attempt to monopolize, or combine or conspire with any other person or persons, to monopolize any part of the trade or commerce among the several States, or with foreign nations, shall be deemed guilty of a felony, and, on conviction thereof, shall be punished by fine not exceeding $100,000,000 if a corporation, or, if any other person, $1,000,000, or by imprisonment not exceeding 10 years, or by both said punishments, in the discretion of the court."

244. The Federal Trade Commission Act, 15 U.S.C. § 45 (2007).

245. The Hart-Scott-Rodino Act of 1976, 15 U.S.C. § 18 (a) (2007).

246. See Larry Bumgardner, "Antitrust Law in the European Union: The law is changing—but to what effect?" http://gbr.pepperdine.edu/053/euantitrust.html#1 (last visited March 14, 2010).

247. Ibid.

248. Department of Justice, "US and EU Approaches to the Antitrust Analysis of Intellectual Property Licensing: Observations from the Enforcement Perspective," April 2004. www .justice.gov/atr/public/speeches/203228.htm (last visited January 8, 2010). Also see Coco, "Antitrust liability for refusal to license intellectual property: a comparative analysis and the international setting," *Marquette Intellectual Property Law Review* (Jan. 1, 2008) (The Department Of Justice–Federal Trade Commission Guidelines for the Licensing of Intellectual Property adopted the "rule of reason." These guidelines clarify that "[a]s with any other tangible or intangible asset that enables its owner to obtain significant supra-competitive profits, market power or (even monopoly) that is solely the 'consequence of a superior product, business acumen, or historic accident,' does not violate [per se] antitrust laws." Case law has thus "shaped the refusal-to-license-the-IP law").

249. See William Drozdiak, "European Union Kills GE Deal," *Washington Post,* July 4, 2001, at A1. Also see Larry Baumgardner, "Antitrust Law in the European Union," commenting on EU's denial of the proposed merger between General Electric and Honeywell even though the United States had approved it.

CHAPTER 2

Properly Evaluating a Target with Intellectual Property Rights

David Drews

IPmetrics Intellectual Property Consulting

O ne of the primary vehicles used by companies interested in growth is the acquisition of or merger with a separate company. The benefits of such a strategy are
obvious. These may include allowing the acquirer to expand its market share, extend
its operations into new markets, or offer a larger selection of products and services.
Although not the case in every situation, the decision to go forward with a certain
acquisition or merger often hinges on the intellectual property (IP) that the target
company owns or controls. Whether it is leading edge technology or a "category
killer" brand name, IP can make or break a deal.

In this chapter, I explore the impact that IP has on mergers and acquisitions
(M&A), the various forms of IP that may be important or attractive to an acquirer,
and the methods necessary for properly evaluating a takeover or merger target.

Intellectual Property in Mergers and Acquisitions[1]

Statistics indicate that M&A activity has declined in the wake of the recent economic
difficulties. While 2007 was a record-setting year with transaction levels at or near all-
time historical highs, overall deal value during 2008 decreased by 38 percent compared to 2007 and transaction volume dropped by 18 percent.[2] These declines were
largely the result of tighter lending restrictions and more expensive credit. Nevertheless, several major M&A deals have taken place recently, all of which featured significant IP assets.

When the Financial Accounting Standards Board issued the Statement of Financial Accounting Standard (SFAS) 141, *Business Combinations,* in 2001, it required the
identification and valuation of intangible assets such as trademarks and patents when
accounting for the purchase price of an acquired company. This accounting rule has
allowed interested parties to see the relative importance of the intangible assets

TABLE 2.1 Examples of Intellectual Property in M&A Transactions

Year	Buyer	Target	IP Value	Purchase Price
2008	InBev	Anheuser-Busch	$40,903,000	$40,280,000
2007	Altria	Middleton	$ 2,800,000	$ 2,900,000
2007	AstraZeneca	Medimmune	$16,832,000	$15,653,000
2006	Johnson & Johnson	Pfizer CH Unit	$15,132,000	$16,000,000
2005	Procter & Gamble	Gillette	$64,679,000	$53,436,000
2005	Bank of America	MBNA	$28,810,000	$34,579,000
2005	Boston Scientific	Guidant	$24,458,000	$28,358,000
2004	JPMorgan Chase	Bank One	$42,825,000	$58,546,000
2004	Bank of America	FleetBoston	$36,396,000	$47,253,000
2002	Pfizer	Pharmacia	$58,469,000	$55,972,000

acquired with the purchase or merger of a target company, as this information is frequently reported in the annual 10-K filings required of all public companies.

For example, when Bank of America acquired Merrill Lynch in 2008, $5.8 billion of the $29.1 billion purchase price was allocated to identified intangible assets, including $1.3 billion for the Merrill Lynch trade name, and an additional $5.4 billion was allocated to goodwill.[3] In addition to expected economies of scale, the goodwill "represents the value expected from the synergies created from combining the Merrill Lynch wealth management and corporate and investment banking businesses with the Corporation's capabilities in consumer and commercial banking."[4] In other words, the goodwill is recognition of additional intangible benefits to be enjoyed as a result of the acquisition.

Similarly, when InBev purchased Anheuser-Busch in 2008, the provisional purchase price allocation of the €40.3 billion cash purchase price included €16.7 billion for the intangibles, the vast majority of which are indefinite-lived brands such as Budweiser and Michelob.[5] Expected synergies were identified as the primary component of the €24.7 billion in goodwill.[6] (The inclusion of significant acquired liabilities is the main reason the sum of these two parts appears to be larger than the total purchase price.) Other examples of recent deals with significant IP are included in Table 2.1.

Identifying Intellectual Property in a Potential Target

The first step in assessing the IP rights in a potential target is to identify the full scope of IP and intangible assets to be included. These may include marketing assets such as trademarks, brand names, slogans, and the like. Technology assets such as patents, software, trade secrets, and know-how may also be important. In the entertainment industry, copyrights may be responsible for the majority of a firm's overall market value. The key is to perform thorough research on these assets so that a comprehensive understanding of the full extent of intangible assets is understood.

Categories of Intellectual Property and Intangible Assets

Many of these assets will be readily apparent, with some likely being the primary driver behind the interest in acquiring the target entity in the first place. Others will only become obvious after some due diligence has been performed. The following list of intangible assets, including some examples, may likely be of importance in a merger or acquisition.

Intangible Asset Possibilities in Potential Merger Targets

> Trademarks (corporate, umbrella, product line, product)
> Brand names and trade names (goodwill, image, cachet)
> Internet assets (domain names, proprietary systems, data capture)
> Trade dress (packaging, color schemes, uniform themes)
> Marketing campaigns (slogans, jingles, mascots, catchphrases)
> Promotional concepts (loyalty clubs, frequent buyer programs)
> Product warranties and service guarantees
> Patents (utility, design, plant, methods)
> Trade secrets (formulas, know-how, lab notes, plant design)
> Software (proprietary code, licenses)
> Training programs, customer service policies, educated workforce
> Noncompete agreements and management contracts
> Customer lists (databases, mailing lists, survey results)
> Copyrights (ad copy, publishing rights, music, films, photographs)
> Licenses (both grants of rights and government approval)
> Favorable lease terms/options

The presence or absence of these assets can be determined by a thorough investigation of the target's past and current activities. A review of historical press releases or news items may provide clues as to the existence of certain intangibles. Past acquisitions or divestitures will likely have affected the portfolio of brands and technologies produced and marketed by the target, and new product introductions or expansions into new geographies may indicate that additional patent applications and trademark registrations were pursued.

Eventually, discussions with members of the target's management team will be imperative. Employees of the target who are likely to have knowledge of these various assets include those with responsibilities in legal, operations, marketing, and product development departments. The legal team should have a comprehensive listing of all patents and patent applications, common law trademarks, trademark registrations, and copyrights. They will also be most familiar with the firm's policies regarding the safekeeping of trade secrets and may have participated in the negotiation of any important contracts, such as noncompete agreements, intangible asset licenses, or favorable lease arrangements.

Operations and product development personnel will likely have the most knowledge of early stage technology, processes, know-how, and formulas. Marketing personnel will have information on past and current brand-building efforts, often including survey and efficacy data.

Asset Bundles, Synergies, and Overlap

When conducting this initial due diligence, a key objective should be to understand how these various assets interact. For example, there are likely to be complementary aspects among the brands, trademarks, trade dress, slogans, advertising campaigns, and other marketing assets. The same is probably true for technical assets such as patents, trade secrets, know-how, and proprietary processes. The relative strength of these asset bundles depends on how well they have been managed and what priorities have been in place under the previous management team.

Once the various assets and asset bundles have been identified, it is necessary to determine how they interact with the other assets and asset bundles in the target firm. For example, which brands and trademarks go with which technology bundles? Which patents will begin to expire, thereby potentially weakening their associated asset bundles?

Of key importance is the identification of any potential overlaps between the acquired assets and assets that already exist in the acquirer. If the acquirer already has a particular asset niche covered, and there is not likely to be a strategic reason for acquiring that particular asset, such as defensive positioning, there will be little or no demand for that asset bundle. The price paid for an asset will be less when the perceived need is lower. An unfortunate but all-too-frequent example is when an acquired firm's brands and technology are prized, but the assembled and trained workforce is considered to be redundant. No premium is paid to acquire the labor force and layoffs usually follow such an acquisition. This may be short-sighted, however, in cases where the trained workforce embedded in the target has knowledge of proprietary processes and formulas that are vital to the success of the brands or technology desired by the acquirer.

One of the primary drivers behind any merger or acquisition is the perceived synergy between the two companies. This is no less true for the intellectual property and intangible assets involved, which may be responsible for most of the hoped-for benefits. While antitrust considerations may sometimes be an issue, there are numerous examples of competitors merging to form a stronger overall company. Many of the recent mergers in the airline industry fall into this category, with strong regional brands coexisting and benefiting from the efficiencies of scale and reduction of redundancies resulting from the merger.

In addition to geographic consolidation, many potential synergies may result from mergers or acquisitions. Following is a brief list of some important synergies.

Potential Synergies Resulting from Mergers and Acquisitions

Market share improvement
Increased/strategic product offerings
Proprietary technology
Geographic distribution
Efficiencies of scale
Complementary expertise

Verification of IP Rights

After the IP has been identified, steps must be taken to ensure that the uncovered assets and asset bundles are indeed valid.

Registrations, and More

For many assets, verifying the validity may be a simple verification of existing contracts and licenses, along with their associated amendments. For those assets with formal registrations, such as trademarks and patents, it is imperative that the maintenance fees have been paid and the registrations have been kept intact. In addition to the requirement of continued use in the marketplace, a trademark has required filings and fee payments at its 6- and 10-year anniversaries, and every 10 years thereafter. The current standing of a particular trademark's United States registration may be confirmed using the Trademark Applications and Registrations Retrieval (TARR) system at the USPTO website.[7] Similarly, the status of state registrations may be confirmed by checking with the appropriate secretary of state in each jurisdiction.

For a patent, the fee payments necessary to keep a patent registration current are due at the 3.5-, 7.5-, and 11.5-year anniversaries. As with the federal trademark information, the current status of a patent or patent application can be researched at the USPTO web site.

Also, patents, trademarks, and copyrights may have many complementary registrations in other jurisdictions around the world. As noted previously, the legal department or outside IP counsel for the target should be able to provide a comprehensive listing of all foreign trademark, patent and copyright registrations. Each of these jurisdictions has a distinct regimen for maintenance of IP registrations. Local counsel will likely be necessary (and valuable) in assessing the current status of these complementary rights.

Commercial Validity

An additional aspect to the validity of these assets will be their commercial validity in the marketplace. In other words, do these assets truly have meaning or importance in the marketplace? For example, even though a trademark registration has been maintained and marginally used in commerce, it may be associated with a product line that has essentially been neglected and may not be as important as it once may have been. Also, a proprietary process for manufacturing widgets may indeed have been a valuable and well-guarded secret 5 or 10 years ago, and may even still be an important process for the target, but if the industry has moved beyond that technical expertise in the interim, thereby making that process relatively obsolete among the players in the industry, it will be less important and less valuable to the acquirer, even though the validity of the trade secret has been conscientiously maintained. A similar analysis should be conducted regarding any patents the target may hold, although these may provide the basis for important developments that have taken place subsequently.

When it comes to patents, the granting of a patent does not necessarily mean that those rights will be vindicated by the courts. It may be prudent for the acquirer to research other patents, products, and processes in that particular field with an emphasis on locating prior art, especially if the ultimate use is expected to be a licensing or enforcement program.

This portion of the due diligence is more of a common sense, big picture approach to the target evaluation process. How does the intellectual property held by the target fit in with the IP that we already hold? How does it fit into the current marketplace? Does the acquisition of this IP truly provide us with the benefits that we think it does? Many of the questions covered by this aspect will have already been answered when the target was selected in the first place, as the acquisition of certain technology and/or trademarks may have been the reason for the initial interest.

Case Study

A simple case study provides an example as to why the identification and verification of IP rights can be so important. As you are undoubtedly aware, the U.S. automobile industry has experienced severe difficulties over the past several years. One of the primary suppliers to the industry, Company XYZ, had filed for bankruptcy and various bidders were vying for the plants, equipment, and existing contracts.

One participant in the liquidation process was pleased with its due diligence and successful bid for several European plants, until it discovered that it had not secured the patents, trade secrets, and proprietary processes used in those plants. Those assets were owned by a separate U.S. subsidiary, Company ABC. Because of this, the new owner of the plants and equipment was not legally able to produce the products covered by the existing contracts (or new ones) without obtaining a grant of rights from Company ABC.

Once this unfortunate situation was discovered, the bidder was forced to undergo a new set of negotiations with Company ABC to obtain those rights. Ultimately, the patents, trade secrets, and related know-how were acquired by the bidder for several million dollars.

The lesson learned by the bidder in this case study is to never assume that IP rights used in an operation are indeed owned by that operation. It may be the case that those rights are available via a license that could be cancelled on change of ownership or, as in the case cited here, the rights may be held by a separate entity that is not part of the business being acquired, but were being used by the target due to the common ownership of the two subsidiaries.

Evaluating IP in the Target

Once the IP has been identified and its validity in the marketplace and via formal registrations, whichever is necessary, has been verified, it is essential for the acquirer to determine the role of the acquired IP in the new entity. This process is necessary whether the ultimate form of the transaction is an acquisition or a merger. The decisions made during this portion of the analysis will reflect the proposed use or fit of the acquired IP and acknowledge the purpose of the acquisition or merger. While the expected endgame for many of the acquired assets was probably settled on prior to the initiation of the due diligence, this is a necessary step for any assets uncovered during the identification portion of the due diligence process, and any new information associated with those assets previously identified may change the initial plan of action.

Strategic versus Financial Acquisitions

There are two broad categories of drivers for the utilization of acquired IP in an M&A target: strategic and financial. Financial acquisitions are those in which the primary driver for acquiring the IP is to increase the cash flow received from the usage of the IP. There may be lucrative licensing agreements in place for a patent, or a well-known brand may be able to command a significant price premium in the market-place. Good examples of financial acquisitions are those undertaken by so-called patent trolls, wherein the cash flows associated with enforcing the acquired patents are the primary reason for the purchase.

Strategic acquisitions do not necessarily have a strong direct financial argument be-hind their acquisition, but may help prevent others from offering a competing product in the marketplace or may complete the family of offerings associated with a particular product line. An example of a strategic acquisition is the recent purchase of Palm by Hewlett-Packard. This acquisition enables HP to compete in the wireless handheld mar-ket, which helps to counter their archrival Dell's recent move into this market.

Determining whether a strategic or financial purpose exists for each asset or as-set bundle will impact how the asset is handled post-acquisition.

Important Aspects to Consider

When deciding whether a strategic or financial purpose lies behind the acquisition of IP in an M&A target, it is important for the acquirer to consider the following aspects:

- Impact on acquirer's operation.

    How does this particular asset or asset bundle fit in with the existing mix of assets, the operation, and the business strategy going forward? Does it require additional complementary assets beyond those being acquired to utilize it to its full potential? Is there significant investment necessary to unlock the potential or is it a turn-key operation? Will it drain away significant management attention and capital from existing investment priorities or cash cows?

- Cash flow, both existing and potential.

    What cash flow does this asset or asset bundle generate right now? Can it be improved by implementing our existing sales/manufacturing/distribution pro-cesses? Are there potential cash flows that are more likely/efficiently achieved in our hands versus those of the target? Is the cash flow from licensing/sale more attractive than the cash flow from ongoing utilization/production?

- Market share/market positioning.

    What is the market share of the acquired asset or asset bundle? What is the positioning of the assets? How do they interact with/affect/complement our existing assets/product offerings?

- Defensive positioning.

    Does the asset or asset bundle provide protection against competitors in cer-tain markets/product categories? Does it provide additional product offerings/ more market share in certain categories? Does it remove or lessen the possibility of being targeted for infringement litigation?

- Relevant litigation history.

    Have the assets been involved in any litigation proceedings, either offen-sively or defensively? What was the outcome? Does it provide the basis for enforcement or licensing operations? Is it more or less likely that the assets can be utilized in an unencumbered way going forward?

- Public relations.

   How are the assets viewed in the marketplace? Do they enhance or harm our existing reputation? Can certain actions (donation/joint venture) improve our standing in the community at large?

What Is the Endgame?

After considering these and many other aspects of the assets and asset bundles, it is necessary to determine the likely utilization or handling of the assets going forward. The various options available to the acquirer include the following:

- Incorporate into existing operation.

   The brands, trademarks, and technologies may be folded into the acquirer's existing operation. This may also be true of various intangibles such as an educated workforce, noncompete agreements, proprietary processes, and copyright portfolios. The vast majority of acquired IP usually falls into this category.
- Stand-alone product line, operating segment, and so on.

   For well-known brands and associated technologies, the existing operation may be implemented in a fashion very reminiscent of the preexisting operation. In this case, some of the background operations and redundancies may be reduced in an attempt to capture efficiencies of scale.
- Sell the IP.

   Those assets and asset bundles that do not fit in with the acquirer's business strategy going forward may be sold, either individually or in coordinated bundles. The redundant operations referred to previously may also be sold off.
- License the IP.

   Other assets may be good candidates for implementing or expanding a licensing program, which allows for a certain amount of control over how the assets are utilized in the marketplace while still providing income. The income from a licensing program is typically generated at a lower level of expense than a manufacturing or distribution operation.
- Joint venture.

   The acquired assets may be the acquirer's contribution to a joint venture designed to exploit the IP. This option allows the acquirer to benefit from the assets while also profiting from the specific industry management, manufacturing, or marketing expertise of the joint venture partner.
- Abandon/donate.

   Finally, the acquired assets or asset bundles can be either abandoned or donated. The abandonment of patents or trademarks removes the burden of maintenance expenses. The donation of certain assets such as patents or trademarks is unlikely to generate any financial benefit, but may provide positive public relations benefits with strategic research and nonprofit institutions.

Looking Ahead

In too many cases, the intellectual property and intangible assets associated with an acquisition or merger are not given the proper attention by either the buyer or seller. This can result in nasty surprises like that presented in this chapter's case study. At a minimum, it can lead to inaccurate pricing or ineffective management of the acquired assets. However, as companies gain a better understanding of the extent of their IP rights portfolios, both in-house and as part of potential targets, these adverse outcomes are likely to be minimized or eliminated. There is evidence that the requirements of SFAS 141 are forcing companies to take a closer look at the IP being acquired and to promote its consideration to a higher priority rather than a last-minute effort that gets addressed as Appendix G in the ultimate deal memorandum. Deal participants who forgo a comprehensive due diligence effort in regard to the IP rights may find themselves in a very disadvantageous position.

In addition to more and higher priority attention being given to the IP rights in a deal, it is likely that more deals will be confined to the acquisition of the IP rights as stand-alone assets rather than as part of a full company merger or acquisition. This kind of focused activity has been increasing in recent years and will likely continue to gain momentum.

I'd like to present a few final thoughts regarding developments that may impact the future of IP rights in mergers and acquisitions. First, because the USPTO is being more diligent in its review of claims in patent applications, patents covering broad-based invention claims will be less likely to be granted. This will constrain the ability of rights holders to exclude competitors from the marketplace, and may make any acquired patents less valuable from a strategic perspective.

Conversely, the Trademark Dilution Revision Act of 2006 essentially creates a situation wherein "famous" trademark rights may cover a range of goods and services beyond their actual class designations.[8] The implication of this is that a famous trademark may be more valuable than would otherwise be the case. Alternatively, a registered trademark that is similar to a famous trademark may not offer protection against a charge of dilution, and may therefore have little or no value in the marketplace.

Conclusion

Whenever an acquisition or merger takes place, there are usually numerous intangible assets and intellectual property involved. The proper identification, validation, and evaluation of the assets, synergies, and options available regarding the IP in an acquisition target will lead to more accurate pricing and more effective management of the assets. Finally, it is likely that IP rights will become more important in mergers and acquisitions as time goes on, and a well-informed participant will be better positioned to act accordingly.

Notes

1. See also Diane R. Meyers, "Growth through Acquisition or Merger," in *Intellectual Property Strategies for the 21st Century Corporation.*

2. Stephen Older, Jeffrey Rothschild and Harold Davidson, "By the Numbers," *The Deal Magazine,* March 31, 2009, www.thedeal.com/magazine/ID/025193/community/by-the-numbers.php.

3. Bank of America 2008 Annual Report, 130.

4. Ibid., 129.

5. InBev NA 2008 Annual Report, 74–75.

6. Ibid., 75.

7. http://tarr.uspto.gov.

8. This act led the U.S. District Court for the Western Division of Kentucky to rule that trademark dilution caused by tarnishment was likely in *V Secret Catalogue, Inc. v. Moseley*, even though Victoria's Secret did not have trademark registrations in Moseley's product classes, which led to a permanent injunction against Moseley.

CHAPTER 3

Growth through Acquisition or Merger

Diane Meyers
PPG Industries, Inc.

There are many advantages and reasons for growth through acquisition or merger. Organic or internal growth might take longer than the business would like, or there might be cost issues, timing issues, or other barriers that prevent internal growth from being a practical option. Joining forces in some way with another company to achieve one or more particular goals might not give the business the desired level of profit or control. In such circumstances, growth through acquisition is the most effective option.

Acquisitions and mergers can follow several different formats. For example, in a stock acquisition, where one company acquires the stock of another company, the acquired company still exists in its pre-acquisition form (until the acquirer chooses to make changes), but will be under the control of the acquirer. An asset acquisition, however, involves the acquisition of only certain assets of a company; in this situation, the company whose assets are acquired will likely continue to exist and will not be under the control of the acquirer. In the case of a merger, all assets of the non-surviving entity are acquired by the surviving entity by operation of state law.

This chapter focuses on issues to be considered after the target company has been identified. Maybe you are a member of the team assigned to perform due diligence on the target, maybe you are a member of the team assigned to "do the deal," or maybe you are a member of the team responsible for integrating the acquiree into your company or affecting the merger of the companies. A good place to start your work is to understand the goal or goals your company wants to achieve through the merger or acquisition. This is, therefore, a very important question to ask as you begin your work.

The Merger or Acquisition Target[1]

Just as there are a number of reasons why a company would choose to grow through merger or acquisition (M&A), there are a number of objectives that the company may wish to achieve through such a transaction. In addition to understanding these goals or objectives, another question you should consider at the outset is why this particular company *is* a target. This understanding will help you to consider the transaction in the proper context and help you to focus on what is most important to your company.

All companies likely have the same M&A objective: growth. The type of growth, however, can take many forms. Some of these are discussed later in this chapter and were, no doubt, some of the objectives of the largest M&A deals, in terms of transaction value, that occurred during the past two decades as shown in Table 3.1.

Geographic Growth

The fastest and perhaps easiest way to expand in or into a geographic area is by acquisition of, or merger with, a company established in that area. Industries that are regional in nature may see growth opportunity by merger of two complementary regional businesses. Both large and small companies desiring to expand into geographic markets in which they currently do not have a presence, or to grow in regions where they are underrepresented, may choose to do so through the acquisition of, or merger with, regional players. An acquiring company may wish to tailor its brands or products for a regional or even local market and may accomplish this most efficiently through acquisition of a regional or local company.

Many companies desire expansion into other countries and onto other continents. In the past 15 to 20 years, U.S. companies have acquired hundreds of billions of dollars in assets from companies outside the United States. During the same period, a number of U.S. companies have been acquired by foreign owned entities. For instance, U.S. companies generated $68.03 billion in mergers and acquisitions from abroad in 1996, up from $61.42 billion in 1995. During this time, foreign investors consummated 16 transactions that have been deemed megadeals in the United States, of which 11 were made by investors from Western European countries.[2]

Globally, the value of cross-border M&A deals has mostly been on the rise for the past decade or so.[3] According to the United Nations Conference on Trade and

TABLE 3.1 Top M&A Deals Worldwide by Value from 1990 to 2009[4]

Rank	Year	Acquirer	Target	Transaction Value (in bil. USD)
1	1999	Vodafone AirTouch PLC	Mannesmann AG	202.8
2	2000	American Online Inc.	Time Warner	164.7
3	2007	Shareholders	Philip Morris Int'l Inc.	107.6
4	2007	RFS Holdings BV	ABN-AMRO Holding NV	98.2
5	1999	Pfizer Inc.	Warner-Lambert Co.	89.2
6	1998	Exxon Corp.	Mobil Corp.	78.9
7	2000	Glaxo Wellcome PLC	SmithKline Beecham PLC	76.0
8	2004	Royal Dutch Petroleum Co.	Shell Transport & Trading Co.	74.6
9	2006	AT&T Inc.	BellSouth Corp.	72.7
10	1998	Travelers Group Inc.	Citicorp	72.6

Development (UNCTAD), the total value of worldwide cross-border merger and acquisition sales rose for consecutive years from 1991 to 2000, and again from 2003 to 2006 as shown in the graph in Figure 3.1.[5]

A major area of growth of all kinds (including organic growth, joint venture formation, and other partnerships, in addition to M&A), has been in markets that were previously inaccessible to outside companies. This has been particularly observed in the former Soviet Union countries. For example, in the past several years, Heineken N.V. has acquired a number of breweries in Russia to expand the market share of Heineken in Russia to 14 percent.[6]

Similarly, significant growth has been observed in emerging regions, such as India and China. The increase in China's deal-making appetite is largely a result of buoyancy in its domestic stock markets, rising demand for energy and resources, and consolidation within the consumer and telecom sectors.[7]

According to the Press Trust of India, by January, 2010, the volume of M&A activity in the country more than doubled over that of the same period during the previous year: There were 29 domestic deals worth $2.3 billion in January, 2010, compared with 14 transactions worth $0.59 billion during the same period in 2009. The majority of the deals were targeted toward telecommunications, logistics, and the banking, finance, and insurance industries—worth a total of $2.1 billion, $164 million and $117 million respectively, according to financial research services provider V.C. Edge.[8]

While the decline of Emerging to Developed (E2D) activity continues, there are indications that such activity could be about to accelerate. Chinese companies are showing greater interest in overseas acquisitions, prospecting for deals and conducting plenty of feasibility studies.[9] This trend is reflected in the rise of cross-border M&A net purchases by mainland China from $12,053 million in 2006 to $36,861 million in 2008.[10] Activity out of the Middle East, too, is increasing and this will only accelerate once the local Sovereign Wealth Funds (SWFs) make their move, inspiring others to follow.[11]

In India, cross-border M&A activity has been on the rise, with net sales increasing from $4.4 trillion in 2006 to $9.5 trillion in 2008, and net purchases rising from $6.7 trillion to $11.6 trillion during the same period.[12] Presently, however, the Indian buyers sit relatively quietly, waiting for bank lending to begin again, as their preference has always been to work with debt rather than equity. When that happens, and the acquisitive Indian corporate base rumbles back into life, the gap between E2D and Developed to Emerging (D2E) deal values could narrow extremely rapidly. While India dominated E2D deals until 2008, China now leads the way, having completed 20 deals in the first half of 2009, and recording 30 more in the second half. India, on the other hand, registered just 25 deals in 2009, accounting for one-seventh of the E2D deals in the year.

The Middle East registered 17 deals between February and August, 2010, which was an increase from the five deals registered in the first half of the year. Central and Eastern Europe remain the most popular D2E destination with 1,081 deals since the second half of 2003 (compared to China's 1,023 and India's 713). The United States is still the most popular E2D destination with 345 inbound deals, compared to 259 for the United Kingdom and 116 for Germany. The most acquisitive nations are the United States (1,549 D2E deals) and India (404 E2D deals).[13]

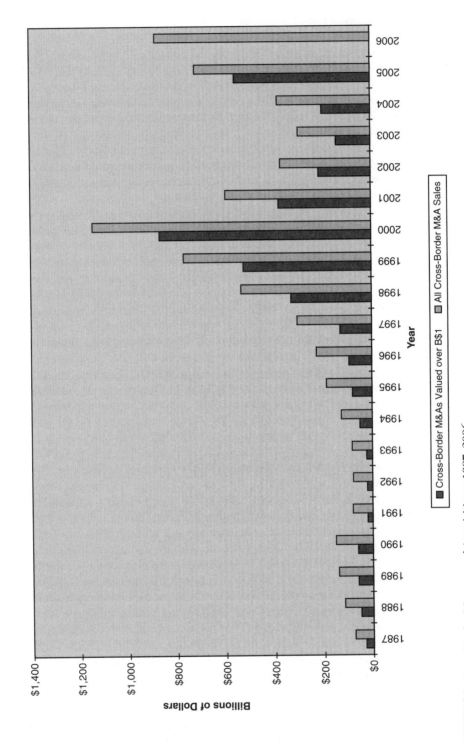

FIGURE 3.1 Cross-Border Mergers and Acquisitions, 1987–2006

Source: UNCTAD.

Sales Growth

While global market share should inherently grow with geographic expansion, there are ways to grow market share without geographic growth. Expansion can occur in your company's currently existing market, in adjacent markets, or in unrelated markets.

EXISTING MARKET Expansion in one's current market could be achieved by acquisition of a company that sells the same type of products. Perhaps their product is superior to yours or vice versa, or maybe the products are of comparable quality. Perhaps the other company wishes to exit this particular market, and is interested in selling a branch of the company or assets of the company that relate to the particular market. Since you are no longer competing with the other company for sales of these products, assuming the customers are still there, your customer base or market share should grow. For example, in 2007 ZipCar and Flexcar merged. Both companies offered flexible "car sharing" options to customers, who can make online car reservations to fit their usually local and/or short-term needs. There is a limit of miles per day for which the car can be driven, and cars can be reserved for as little as one hour. The merger saw ZipCars' 3,500 vehicle fleet in 35 markets combine with Flexcars' fleet of 1,500 vehicles in 15 markets.[14] Both companies were pioneers in the car sharing idea. The merger "accelerates that big idea into the mainstream."[15] Thus, the merger of two companies with the same product allowed the surviving entity to increase its market.

In another example, in 2008, PPG Industries, Inc. reached an agreement with BASF North American business to acquire the latter's coil extrusion coatings business, which serves the construction, appliance, transportation, heating, ventilation and air conditioning, lighting fixture, and extrusion industries.[16] The acquisition allowed PPG to add both products and customers to its existing coil business.

A somewhat different example of this point is the acquisition of Marvel Entertainment by the Walt Disney Company. Disney is in the business of marketing, promoting, and commoditizing characters and stories. Marvel has over 5,000 characters. The acquisition of Marvel allowed Disney to "do what they do best." The acquisition added to Disney's product line of characters, and likely strengthened Disney's position as a leader in this industry.[17]

ADJACENT MARKETS Another way to grow sales is to expand into adjacent markets. The acquisition of Tween Brands by Dress Barn on June 25, 2009, for $157 million illustrates an acquisition that was used to gain access to an adjacent market. Dress Barn targets professional women with its Dress Barn stores, and younger women with its maurices stores, and desired to enter the girls' apparel market. Tween brands operated the Justice stores, which targets 7- to 14-year-olds, and was a perfect target for Dress Barn to achieve its objective of entering this market. The combined stores are expected to generate $2.4 billion in annual sales.[18]

UNRELATED MARKETS An acquisition or merger may also be used to get into a market in which your company has no presence and in which there might not even seem to be a logical adjacency. For the right kind of company, this can make perfect sense.

For instance, when Berkshire Hathaway, which is purely an investment entity and does not produce anything but returns for investors, spent $30 billion on a train company, namely, Burlington Northern Santa Fe, it was not to realize any synergies, per se, but simply because Warren Buffett thought the target was undervalued.[19]

In another example, eBay Inc., a company that manages an online auction and shopping web site, in unrelated diversifications, acquired (1) Skype Ltd., a company that developed and operated Voice Over Internet Protocol software, and (2) StumbleUpon, an online discovery engine that allows its users to discover and rate Web pages, photos, and videos that are personalized to their interests. Similarly, General Electric has diversified into banking, real estate, aircraft leasing, and so on.[20]

The last scenario, acquisition in an attempt to grow into an area in which your company does not currently exist or in which there is no logical adjacency, comes with a red flag. What plan does your company have for managing the acquired company? Will it be integrated somehow into the existing structure and, if so, what modifications to that structure will be needed? Will the acquisition be operated as a stand-alone company and, if so, what support will the company need? A plan of action, preferably prior to acquisition, is really in order. Buying something with the thought "we'll figure out later what to do with it" is not likely to lead to success.

Similarly, defensive acquisitions are also prevalent in the corporate world and are typically used to thwart a hostile takeover by making a potential target less attractive to—that is, too large for—potential acquirers. A small to midsized company may be the target of a larger company. By acquiring one or more other small companies, the target may make itself too large to be acquired. For example, maybe the potential acquirer would not want, or be able, to pay what would be needed to acquire the newly expanded target, or perhaps such an acquisition would not pass antitrust scrutiny. One company may acquire another to prevent its competitor from doing so, or by acquiring a small company rather than allowing its merger with another, might avoid the formation of a midsized competitor. Of course these defensive acquisitions will likely provide other benefits in terms of market share growth, geographic growth, and the like; their defensive value may, however, be their biggest value.

Technology Growth

One key objective in many transactions is to increase the technology offered by the acquiring company. The target may have technology that your company simply does not have. The acquired technology may fill a gap in your company's current product line, or may allow your company to expand into one or more other product lines. Such expansion can be in the same market, an adjacent market, or a totally unrelated market.

Take, for example, the merger between pharmaceutical giants Pfizer and Wyeth in January, 2009. Pfizer was facing the expiration of the patent for its best-selling drug, Lipitor, as well as several others. Indeed, Lipitor is said to have accounted for almost a quarter of Pfizer's bottom line. Unfortunately, the research and development (R&D) pipeline at Pfizer did not look very promising. Acquiring Wyeth bolstered its waning drug portfolio—and leveraged a competitive advantage by tapping into a tight credit market that only a company of Pfizer's stature could access. It was the right deal for Pfizer to make and the right time to make it.[21]

Benefits of Mergers and Acquisitions

Why M&A instead of employing other means for your company to solve its problems or achieve its goals? In many cases, M&A offers advantages that other avenues do not.

Speed to Market

Perhaps most obvious of the reasons to choose M&A is the speed with which a company can have a presence in a particular geography, market, or technology. It could take years, if not decades, to get where you can be virtually overnight through an acquisition or merger, assuming you could even get there on your own. Sometimes the incumbent company or companies are so entrenched in a particular space that the market is not willing to accept a newcomer.

Consider Google's acquisition of YouTube. Google had been trying, unsuccessfully, to enter the online video market since early 2005 through its Google Video service. Although YouTube launched shortly after Google Video, YouTube had far greater success. Anxious to increase advertising revenue and accumulate user data through the video market, yet gaining little traction with its own service, Google opted against trying to organically grow Google Video and, instead, bought YouTube in late 2006 for $1.65 billion in Google stock.[22] It was estimated that as of 2007, 20 percent of all Web traffic consisted of YouTube streams.[23] Thus, Google has a huge presence in the online streaming video market by virtue of the acquisition.

Reduced Cost

Another reason to choose acquisition or merger over other avenues is reduced cost. R&D costs to develop new technologies, legal and administrative costs to meet regulatory requirements, costs to obtain intellectual property protection, capital expenses for manufacturing, building infrastructure for product distribution, marketing, and advertising expenses: All these things represent significant costs in the development of products and getting them to market. While at least some of these costs will likely be packaged and included in an M&A deal through the purchase price or other consideration, this might still represent a smaller investment than if the company had paid for these things itself individually over the course of several years.

Moreover, your company may not have the necessary resources to develop the products itself. The costs of R&D personnel with the technical background in the acquired products, manufacturing capabilities for the products, a sales force with expertise in the market may make entering a market or offering a particular technology unattainable by any means other than some sort of relationship with another company.

Economies of Scale and Synergies

There are often significant economies of scale or other synergies that can be realized through M&A. Consider again the scenario when a company with products in one market acquires a company with essentially the same products or same type of products in the same market. Consolidating the resources required to bring each of these product lines to the same market can result in greater profitability for the newly combined product line than was realized by either of the product lines individually. The acquiring company can, for example, run fewer manufacturing sites and fewer distribution centers, and/or employ fewer salespeople and support staff, while at the same time increasing sales. For example, in the PPG acquisition of BASF previously discussed, plants were shut down and production and sales forces consolidated, all allowing for increased product lines with reduced overhead and other costs.

Being able to capitalize on economies of scale may be particularly relevant when both the acquirer and the acquiree have only mediocre profitability in the pre-acquisition situation. Synergies may allow the acquirer to increase margin and profitability along with sales. The same result may be achieved by merger of the two companies—when two C students study together, they may get a B, or even an A.

Synergies outside of those achieved by reducing the combined footprints of the individual companies can also be realized through M&A. Perhaps one company has products in a line that complement, or are used in combination with, the other company's products. For example, Kraft's acquisition of Cadbury—through which Kraft picked up gum and candy brands to go with cookies and crackers from Nabisco—is likely to generate a joint portfolio of more than 40 confectionary brands, essentially creating the world's biggest confectionary company.[24]

Certainty of Income Stream

While all companies, and their stockholders, would jump at the chance to have guaranteed income or certainty of income stream we all know there is no such thing. Purchasing a business that already exists, however, can take away at least some of the uncertainty that accompanies introducing new products or entering a new market: The costs and risks of introducing a new product were borne by someone else. Although there may still be some uncertainty or risk of moving into waters uncharted by your company, the fact that another company was successful in these waters may give your company and its shareholders a comfort level. Acquisition or merger may therefore provide greater certainty of an income stream than entering an unproven market on your own.

Logistics of the Acquisition/Merger

Remember the question asked above—what goal does your company hope to achieve through the M&A? The answer to that question may help guide you in considering the logistics of the due diligence and/or the acquisition or merger itself by focusing your attention on the particular needs of or areas of interest to your company.

There are other questions you should ask up front as well. For example, if the deal is an acquisition, you should ask what is being acquired. In a stock acquisition, the whole target company is purchased; thus, the target is owned by the acquiring company. Will the target company continue to exist after the acquisition? If the target survives in its pre-acquisition form, there is no need to change anything, or at least no immediate need to change anything. What if the target company will be rolled into the acquiring company? This concept is relevant to the transfer of intellectual property rights. More specifically, if the target company continues to exist in its pre-acquisition form, there is no need to transfer the title of the intellectual property to the acquirer, unless the acquirer desires to do so. If the target company will be merged into the acquiring company post-acquisition, the title to any intellectual property of the target will be owned by the acquirer as a matter of law, but the change in ownership to the surviving company should be recorded with any relevant patent and trademark offices around the world.

In an asset acquisition, however, you need to be clear on what assets you are acquiring. Since your company is not taking ownership of the target, you should understand what form, if any, of the target company will remain post acquisition. What rights, if any, will the target retain and what rights does your company need in order to get the full benefit from the acquired assets? Does your company need to license intellectual property from the target for a transition period? For example, maybe you are acquiring a product currently sold under Brand X. Brand X, however, might be a trademark that will be retained by the target for use with other products. A license for the right to use Brand X for a period of time, such as two years, to transition from Brand X to your brand might be needed. Similarly, maybe the target has patents that cover the products you are acquiring as well as the products they are retaining. A license to the patent should be granted to enable you to make, have made, use, sell, service, and import the acquired products. For all forms of acquisition, you really need to understand what exactly is being acquired. Is your company acquiring intellectual property assets? Employees? Facilities? Existing litigation? Ongoing liabilities?

This section is not intended to provide a due diligence checklist; rather, it is intended to provide some food for thought on due diligence and post-acquisition related matters.

Staffing the Due Diligence Team

The person or people managing the due diligence will need to decide who should be on the team and will do so based largely on the nature of the acquisition. A specific question to answer is whether an intellectual property attorney should be on the due diligence team. The answer, of course, is "It depends." It depends, for example, on what is being acquired. If the acquisition is of a plant, manufacturing equipment, and a product line that has been sold for decades, it is not likely that intellectual property (IP) plays a large role.

Even in situations where no IP appears to be changing hands, having an IP attorney involved (if not formally on the team) is still advisable. An IP attorney, along with a labor attorney, should consider any employment issues raised by the acquisition. Employee contracts should be reviewed whether the target company's employees will join you or not. These employees could have valuable technical or commercial information and their obligation to maintain this information in confidence post-employment should be confirmed. Another area that is sometimes overlooked relates to software licenses. Are computers and computer systems being acquired? If so, it should be confirmed that any necessary software licenses can be assigned to the new owner. Here again is an IP-related matter that might arise in a deal otherwise thought to lack IP issues.

When there is IP, specifically patents, trademarks, or copyrights, that will be acquired, an IP attorney should be part of the due diligence team. How many IP attorneys and what expertise they should have depends on a number of factors, some of which are discussed here, but also depends again on what is being acquired. If only a handful of trademarks are being acquired, that would warrant much different staffing than would the acquisition of hundreds of trademarks, patents, and the like. While there are IP attorneys knowledgeable about IP due diligence issues across the various types of IP, it should be recognized that the practice of IP law, specialized as compared to other areas of law, is also specialized within itself. A lawyer versed in patents may not have much knowledge of trademarks and vice versa. Therefore, it might be necessary to have more than one IP attorney on the team. It might also be necessary and/or advisable to enlist outside counsel having the particular expertise you need.

Focus of the Due Diligence Team

We are all finding ourselves to be more resource constrained than ever, and it may be the case that this constraint will play a role on the level of due diligence that is done. Assuming that you do not have a staff with time on their hands and/or an extensive budget to hire outside counsel, you might need to decide just how many of the 100 things on the due diligence checklist you really need to do. In other words, the due diligence checklist you use should really reflect the deal that is being done. Some of this will involve a judgment call, but again, it all goes back to the questions of what is being acquired and what goal or goals your company wishes to accomplish with the acquisition. The determination of what areas will receive lesser scrutiny should be made thoughtfully.

A related question is what the goal or goals are of the due diligence itself. Typically, a goal of due diligence is to determine whether the deal should proceed at all: Does the target company really own the intellectual property it purports to own? Does it really have the profit margin it purports to have? Is it really free from all meaningful threats of litigation or other liabilities? Are you really getting all the assets you need to enter the business? Do the patents actually cover the products? If the answer to any of these questions is "no," that may be enough to call the deal off. Alternatively, significant renegotiation of contract terms might be in order, such as valuation, various pre- and post-closing obligations, indemnification provisions, and the like. In some circumstances, however, your company may have already decided to make the acquisition or do the merger regardless of what your due diligence investigation uncovers. If that is the case, it is still better to know up front what you are buying and take what preventive action you can to minimize any potential risks involved with the merger/acquisition. Finally, one of your goals of the due diligence might be to prioritize the issues to be addressed post acquisition/merger.

Other related questions are: How significant is the target IP to your company? Are you buying major brand names from a soon-to-be former competitor, or are you buying brands that are not well-known, with the plan to phase them out post-acquisition? The answer to this question may indicate how much review of the marks is appropriate. Similar questions can be asked about technology being acquired. Are you acquiring tried and true workhorses of the industry, or are you acquiring new products? The likelihood of a patent infringement issue arising for the former products is not likely, but can the same be said of the latter products?

Related to the importance of the target IP to your company is the question as to how significant the target IP is to your industry. Are you in an industry where the players peacefully coexist or an industry where patents are vigorously asserted and defended? The answer may make a difference in your review of the target patents and products.

Timing is another issue. Has the seller indicated that the deal is off if you cannot close in three days? In some scenarios, the seller might have a "take it or leave it" attitude toward the deal, and be unwilling to allow any significant level of due diligence to occur. Hopefully, you have enough time to complete the due diligence you need and get the answers to the questions you have so you can advise your company accordingly. As with the resource situation, however, timing matters may require you to focus your energy on those issues that are most important to consider and/or resolve in the time frame you have. You should understand, however, that any shortcuts you are forced to take due to timing issues, resource issues, and the like will need to be carefully considered, agreed to, and understood by the due diligence team, and taken with the knowledge that there is risk to doing so.

Whether the acquisition is an asset purchase or a stock purchase may help you in the prioritization. In a stock acquisition, for example, the entire company is acquired and that company continues to exist post-acquisition (until such time that the buyer dissolves it, merges it, etc.). Certain issues, such as intercompany chain of title issues, might not be as urgent in a stock acquisition as in an asset acquisition; they can be cleaned up later. For an asset acquisition, it is a good idea to address as many issues before closing as you can. Although a good asset purchase agreement will include a requirement that the acquired company will help as needed with follow-up issues, frequently referred to as a further assurance clause, the target, or what remains of it, may not always have much motivation to do so after acquisition. Moreover, the target company may not exist very long after the acquisition, and people with the knowledge you need might have moved on. It is better to get as much done before closing as you can, when you still have some leverage to get the assistance you require.

Domestic versus International M&A

Acquisition of, or merger with, another company is complex enough when the acquiring company is in the same country. Acquisition or merger across country borders is even more complex. The most important word of caution that can be offered here is not to assume that the law of one jurisdiction is the same as that of another. Get help from local counsel! You may even need help determining what laws are relevant, and the answer may be that the laws of many countries are relevant. For example, a Swiss company might be acquiring a French company that has a license agreement governed by British law. With international acquisitions, you will not be able to rely solely on your knowledge of the law in your own country to support these deals. Moreover, cross border deals give rise to considerations that may not be relevant in a domestic transaction, such as export control issues and the Foreign

Corrupt Practices Act (FCPA). In addition to the complexity related to the determination of which country's or countries' laws are relevant, laws in a number of different areas are likely to be relevant. Intellectual property, employment, antitrust, and tax are just some of the areas that will need to be considered. These laws vary from country to country. In some circumstances, the law in which the intellectual property right is registered will control, even if that law has no other apparent relationship to the deal. It is possible that different legal specialists in each area and country will need to be consulted. Even if your company is acquiring another company based in the same country, these issues will all need to be considered if the target has affiliates, subsidiaries, or facilities in other countries.

Post-M&A Issues

So the merger or acquisition has been completed. What now? Often, the team that does the deal hands the work off at this point to an integration team. Decisions will need to be made, if they were not made before closing, as to how to integrate the new business. Will it become part of the existing structure, or will it be operated as an independent business unit? Are there challenges to integration, particularly if companies from two different countries or having facilities in a number of countries are involved? For example, there may be significant cultural differences or even barriers between the two pre-merger companies that will need to be considered and addressed post-merger. Will employees of the acquired company become employees of your company and, if so, what training, as to your company's policies, will be given?

Staffing at your company should also be considered. Will your human resources department and IT department have sufficient resources to support the merger/acquisition, or will employees from the acquired company in these areas be joining the new company?

What about the law department? Will lawyers from the target join your company? Did the company rely on outside counsel for support in certain areas? If the target company used outside counsel, the attorneys for your company should carefully consider whether they would like to continue using that counsel. Chances are, that counsel has historic knowledge that you certainly will not have, and perhaps no one else will have, either. Thus, retaining the legacy outside counsel may prove to be very useful. Perhaps, however, the outside counsel was not very effective, gave less than ideal advice, or had unfavorable staffing or price structures. Although you might eventually replace the target's outside counsel with your own, you should probably resist the urge to do so immediately, first assessing how the legacy outside counsel can be of assistance to you. You may even be in a position to bring the work in-house. For example, maybe the target did not have in-house intellectual property attorneys, but your company does. It might make sense to bring at least the management of the acquired intellectual property in-house.

Another issue that is ideally considered before closing, but quite often is not, is to make sure that the business clearly understands what rights have been purchased. Although there may be some overlap, the team that identified the target and/or the team that did the deal are not likely to be the team that integrates the new business into the existing business. The people on that team will need to be educated as to what they can and cannot do. If your company has acquired all the rights of another company, then not much instruction may be needed. There may be scenarios, however, in which you have purchased only certain assets of the target company. Perhaps those assets provide you with intellectual property and other rights in North America, but not in other parts of the world. You will need to carefully counsel your business as to what can and cannot be done and where, vis-à-vis these rights. This is particularly relevant if the target will continue to do business in areas where you have not acquired rights. The business should also clearly understand any liabilities that have been undertaken by virtue of the merger or acquisition. These liabilities should have been fleshed out during the due diligence process, and should have been addressed and accounted for in the purchase agreements and other closing documents, but again the pre-M&A team and the post-M&A team are not likely to be the same. There should be a handoff of this knowledge.

One particular area to consider is which entity will own the intellectual property post-merger or post-acquisition.[25] This is not always an easy answer, and can be complicated if there are multiple ownerships by subsidiaries or affiliates of the target company in different regions of the world. In addition to the intellectual property laws of the countries in which intellectual property rights are held, consideration must be given to the relevant tax laws. Transfer of intellectual property ownership, even among subsidiaries of the same company, can often have tax consequences. While this issue is noted here as a post-M&A consideration, it is really a decision that more preferably is made preclosing. During closing, various assignment documents and other supporting documents transferring ownership from the target to your company will be executed. These documents will need to be filed with the relevant intellectual property offices in the countries in which intellectual property rights are held to reflect that your company is now the owner of the rights. If these documents assign the IP rights to your company, but it is ultimately decided that these rights should be held by a subsidiary of your company, two sets of documents will need to be recorded: The documents assigning ownership from the target to your company, and the documents assigning ownership from your company to your company's subsidiary. These recordal steps are time-consuming and can often be very costly, particularly if a large amount of intellectual property rights are involved. Having the original assignment from the target to your company's subsidiary eliminates a step and the costs associated therewith.

In addition to the myriad of other things that may change following a merger or acquisition, one of the things that may change for your company is its risk profile. Perhaps you have acquired a relatively small player in the market. Other big players in the market may have largely ignored the target company; they were perhaps too small or too regional to pose any type of threat. Once acquired by your company, however, a different level of threat may exist. While a competitor may have been reluctant for one reason or another to sue the little guy, once your company acquires the little guy that reluctance may disappear. The deep pockets of the acquirer may attract attention that a smaller company just would not attract. Your company's expansion in existing or new markets may also attract unwanted attention. Accordingly, it is appropriate to consider how the merger or acquisition will change the face of the market and how that affects your company's risks of doing business in the market.

Conclusion

The preceding is just a glimpse of some M&A that has occurred in the past two decades, reasons why a company would pursue merger and acquisition, and issues to consider when contemplating, reviewing, and consummating a transaction. Many objectives or goals can be achieved most efficiently through a merger or acquisition; often, merger or acquisition allows more than one goal to be realized. Knowing the goals your company wants to achieve through the transaction will help you to focus your attention in your due diligence investigation to the areas that are of the greatest interest or concern.

Notes

1. See also David Drews, "Property Evaluating a Target with Intellectual Property Rights," in *Intellectual Property Strategies for the 21st Century Corporation.*

2. Annual Survey of Global Takeover Activity, KPMG Corporate Finance, http://actrav.itcilo.org/actrav-english/telearn/global/ilo/multinat/manda.htm (accessed August 31, 2010).

3. "Mergers and Acquisitions—Value of Cross-Border M&A, by Region and Country of Seller/Purchaser, 2006–2009," *Global Finance*, www.gfmag.com/tools/global-database/economic-data/9971-mergers-and-acquisitions-value-of-cross-border-maa-by-region-and-country-of-sellerpurchaser-2006-2009.html (accessed September 14, 2010); also see http://blogs.reuters.com/reuters-dealzone/2010/02/19/keeping-score-cross-border-ma-property-follow-ons/. Also see http://dealbook.blogs.nytimes.com/2010/03/28/geely-of-china-agrees-to-buy-volvo-from-ford/?scp=2&sq=geely%20volvo&st=cse; www.theghanaianjournal.com/2010/07/17/africa-indian-cross-border-mergers-increasing/.

4. "Statistics," Institute of Mergers, Acquisitions and Alliances, www.imaa-institute.org/statistics-mergers-acquisitions.html (accessed January 28, 2011).

5. World Investment Reports 1991—2010, United Nations Conference on Trade and Development (UNCTAD), available at www.unctad.org/Templates/Page.asp?intItemID=1485&lang=1 (accessed November 11, 2010).

6. "Heineken Acquires Ivan Taranov Breweries in Russia," press release, Heineken International, www.heinekeninternational.com/content/live/files/downloads/PressCentre/Heineken%20N.V.%20press%20release%2017082005.pdf (accessed August 30, 2010).

7. "China M&A Activity on the Rise in 2010, Forecasts KPMG Global M&A Predictor," KPMG, January 18, 2010, www.kpmg.com/CN/en/PressRoom/PressReleases/Pages/press-20100118.aspx (accessed September 3, 2010).

8. "Indian Cross-Border M&A Expected to Increase," 2point6billion, www.2point6billion.com/news/2010/02/24/indian-cross-border-ma-expected-to-increase-4168.html (accessed September 15, 2010).

9. "Emerging Economies Already Back on the Cross Border M&A Trail," KPMG Global, www.kpmg.com/Global/en/IssuesAndInsights/ArticlesPublications/Press-releases/Pages/Press-release-Emerging-economies-cross-border-MA-trail-8-March-2010.aspx (accessed September 15, 2010).

10. "Mergers and Acquisitions—Value of Cross-Border M&A, by Region and Country of Seller/Purchaser, 2006–2009," *Global Finance*, www.gfmag.com/tools/global-database/economic-data/9971-mergers-and-acquisitions-value-of-cross-border-maa-by-region-and-country-of-sellerpurchaser-2006-2009.html (accessed September 14, 2010).

11. "Emerging Economies Already Back on the Cross Border M&A Trail," KPMG Global, www .kpmg.com/Global/en/IssuesAndInsights/ArticlesPublications/Press-releases/Pages/Press-release-Emerging-economies-cross-border-MA-trail-8-March-2010.aspx (accessed September 15, 2010).

12. "Mergers and Acquisitions—Value of Cross-Border M&A, by Region and Country of Seller/ Purchaser, 2006–2009," *Global Finance*, www.gfmag.com/tools/global-database/economic - data/9971 - mergers - and - acquisitions-value-of-cross-border-maa-by-region-and-country-of-sellerpurchaser-2006-2009.html (accessed September 14, 2010).

13. "Emerging Economies Already Back on the Cross Border M&A Trail," KPMG Global, www.kpmg.com/Global/en/IssuesAndInsights/ArticlesPublications/Press-releases/Pages/ Press-release-Emerging-economies-cross-border-MA-trail-8-March-2010.aspx (accessed September 15, 2010).

14. "Zipcar," Wikipedia, http://en.wikipedia.org/wiki/Zipcar (accessed September 15, 2010).

15. Dominic Gates, "Seattle's Zipcar Merges with Rival Flexcar," *Seattle Times*, October 31, 2007, http://seattletimes.nwsource.com/html/businesstechnology/2003984391_flexcar31. html (accessed September 15, 2010).

16. "PPG to Acquire BASF North American Coil, Extrusion Coatings Business," PPG Industries, www.ppg.com/corporate/ideascapes/metalcoatings/resources/mcnews/Documents/ 080925BASF_COEX.pdf (accessed August 30, 2010).

17. Brooks Barnes and Michael Cieply, "Disney Swoops into Action, Buying Marvel for $4 Billion," *New York Times*, August 31, 2009, www.nytimes.com/2009/09/01/business/media/01disney.html?_r=1&scp=4&sq=disney%20marvel%20merger&st=cse (accessed September 3, 2010).

18. "Dress Barn (DBRN) and Tween Brands (TWB) Agree to Merger," *StreetInsider,* June 25, 2009, www.streetinsider.com/Hot+List/Dress+Barn+(DBRN)+and+Tween+Brands+(TWB)+Agree+ to+Merger/4754315.html (accessed September 3, 2010).

19. "Berkshire Bets on U.S. with a Railroad Purchase," *New York Times*, November 3, 2009, http://dealbook.blogs.nytimes.com/2009/11/03/berkshire-to-buy-rest-of-burlington-northern-for-44-billion/ (accessed September 2, 2010).

20. "Products and Services," GE, www.ge.com/products_services/index.html (accessed January 28, 2011).

21. Andrew Ross Sorkin and Duff Wilson, "Pfizer Agrees to Pay $68 Billion for Rival Drug Maker Wyeth," *New York Times*, January 25, 2009, www.nytimes.com/2009/01/26/business/ 26drug.html (accessed September 3, 2010).

22. Andrew Ross Sorkin and Jeremy W. Peters, "Google to Acquire YouTube for $1.65 Billion," *New York Times*, October 9, 2006, www.nytimes.com/2006/10/09/business/09cnd-deal.html (accessed September 2, 1010).

23. Nate Anderson, "Deep Packet Inspection Meets 'Net Neutrality, CALEA," *ARSTECHNICA*, July 25, 2007 http://arstechnica.com/hardware/news/2007/07/Deep-packet-inspection-meets-net-neutrality.ars (accessed September 2, 2010).

24. Guy Beaudin, "Kraft-Cadbury: Making Acquisitions Work," Bloomberg BusinessWeek, February 9, 2010, www.businessweek.com/managing/content/feb2010/ca2010028_928488 .htm (accessed August 30, 2010).

25. See also Lanning Bryer and Deepica Capoor Warikoo, "Corporate Strategies, Structures, and Ownership of Intellectual Property Rights," in *Intellectual Property Strategies for the 21st Century Corporation.*

CHAPTER 4

Penetrating New Markets through Extension of Goods or Product Lines or Expansion into Other Territories

Toshiya Oka
Canon Inc.

E very product has its own life cycle. When product sales begin to decline, it may be necessary to introduce a successor product or a new product that adds new functions and features to the existing product to sustain a healthy and profitable business. In order to further expand the business's customer base, it may be necessary to enter into new markets.

This chapter focuses on what intellectual property issues should be considered, especially patents, for penetrating new markets through extension of goods or product lines.

Types of New Business in Connection with Patents

In this section it is shown that new businesses are classified into three categories and those classified businesses have their respective relationship with patents.

Three Types of New Businesses

In relation to product expansion and entry into new markets there is the concept of classifying a new business into three categories: market exploitation model, technology development model, and diversification model.[1] This consists of defining the type of new business using a two-dimensional matrix based on two elements: (1) market and (2) technology. According to this approach, business is divided into four quadrants: whether a market is known or unknown and whether technology is known or unknown. (See Figure 4.1.) Among the four quadrants, the lower left

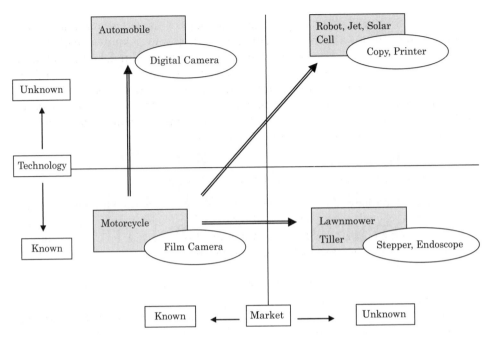

FIGURE 4.1 New Business Matrix

Source: Author created referring to Takeru Ohe, *Why Does Not a New Business Succeed?*, 3rd ed. (Tokyo: Nikkei Publishing Inc., 2008).

(third) quadrant shows a known technology in a known market, which represents the business as it currently exists. The other three quadrants (the first, second, and fourth) illustrate three types of new businesses.

MARKET EXPLOITATION MODEL   This model consists of an existing technology being introduced into a new market or territory. This type of known technology in an unknown market is classified in the lower right (fourth) quadrant and can be referred to as the market exploitation model. For example, Japanese camera manufacturers such as Canon[2] and Nikon[3] entered into the semiconductor exposure field to make steppers[4] using existing optical technology and precision mechanical technology, and Olympus[5] and Pentax (currently Hoya)[6] moved into the medical field to make endoscopes. Honda[7] had motorcycles as its existing business and decided to make tillers and lawnmowers with the use of motorcycle engines. These are examples of the market exploitation model of a new business.

TECHNOLOGY DEVELOPMENT MODEL   In the technology development model, a new product developed with new technology is brought to the market to existing customers. This model is illustrated in the upper left (second) quadrant of the matrix. For example, Nikon, Canon, Ricoh,[8] and other camera makers advanced into the digital camera field. Honda entered the automobile market by targeting its motorcycle customers.

DIVERSIFICATION MODEL   The diversification model is designed to introduce a new product based on new unknown technology into a new unknown market. This model is located at the upper right (first) quadrant of the matrix. In the Japanese camera industry, Canon, Ricoh, Minolta (currently Konica Minolta),[9] and others entered the copy machine market, and eventually evolved to the printer business, including laser printers and inkjet printers. In the case of Honda, it diversified its business into a humanoid robot entitled ASIMO, a business jet named HondaJet, and nonsilicon-type solar cell battery using CIGS compound.

Three Types of New Businesses in Connection with Patents

In the market exploitation model, existing technology is often used for a product and it is likely that patents based on the existing technology have already been obtained. However, when a company enters a new market, it is preferable for the company to file for new patent protection for the new product line.

With respect to the technology development model, new technology is always incorporated into a product and such new technology should be the subject of new patent applications.

With respect to the diversification model, the market to be entered is unknown and the technology and product to be introduced are also unknown. Even though patent protection may have already been obtained, those patents would not be useful for the new product and market in a new field of business. Thus, new technology development is necessary as well as new market exploitation. If a company is delayed in entering into the market, others doing business in the same market may already have obtained patent protection. Therefore, it may be necessary to approach such parties for a license.

Whichever model is considered, it is important to investigate third party patents, that is, conduct a prior art search for the new product and the new market as described in the following section. A prior art search for third party patents should be conducted thoroughly before introducing the product into the market. If prior art is found, it may be necessary to consider designing around, obtaining a license, or discontinuing research and development of the product.

Product Development and Market Exploitation in the 20th Century—Era of Closed Innovation

This section refers to companies' typical product development and marketing style in the twentieth century and describes the importance of a patent prior art search in the product development and marketing.

Proprietary Research and Development—In-House R&D Policy

In the twentieth century, the predominant management style for business was a vertical integration model. According to this model, a company would engage in all research and development, manufacturing, and sale of a product by itself.

To achieve this vertical integration at the development stage, each company made its own central research center. Bell Laboratories and Xerox's Palo Alto Research Center (PARC) are typical examples. Henry Chesbrough, who is an adjunct professor at the University of California, Berkeley and coined the term *Open Innovation*, described this type of management style as "Closed Innovation."[10]

Under the central research center system, the company's main purpose is to obtain a patent right to protect its own product. Moreover, to prevent competitors from entering its market, it may file patent applications for the second and third alternative technologies to expand the scope of protection (i.e., defensive patent applications.) Of course, the company will file patent applications covering technology that is actually used for its product.

When a competitor has patents covering a company's product, the parties could negotiate a cross licensing agreement. Having a large patent portfolio is important in order to secure bargaining power when negotiating a cross licensing agreement.

If a company does not have an effective patent portfolio that could become the subject of a cross license, but wishes to obtain a patent license from a competitor in return for royalties, such licenses are rarely granted, as the competitor often prefers the monopoly of the market to license fees. At the same time, companies generally take a negative view regarding obtaining patent licenses from competitors. This is known as the "Not Invented Here" syndrome.

Prior Art Search—Investigation of Third Party Patents

Whether developing new products based on new technology (i.e., the technology development model), penetrating a new market using existing products or technology (i.e., the market exploitation model), or creating new products to introduce them into the new market (i.e., the diversification model), it is necessary for a company to investigate third party-owned prior patents already in the market.

For this purpose, patent mapping is useful for checking prior art. A patent map is created for each market and each technology sector the company intends to enter. A patent map is useful to find undeveloped areas of the technical sector and to avoid infringing third party patents.

When no prior art is found where a company intends to enter, it files patent applications in the market and technology area. By having many patents in the intended market or technology area, the company is able to protect its new and improved technology and new product by using the technology and preventing others from entering into the market.

Moreover, many patents are useful for cross licensing arrangements. In cross license, for example, it is common for two parties to exchange patents in the same technology sectors. However, in order to enter into an unknown market with an unknown product or technology, it is preferable to negotiate a cross license to be able to use others' patents in a technical area different from the company's, one that covers the unknown technology, product, and market.

When a company tries to break into an existing market, existing participants in the market usually have many patents. Where substantial prior art exists, there are three choices:

1. Design around.

   The company should consider whether it could develop a new product without any third party's patents found as prior art in the market. If there is an alternative technology, the company can use the alternative to change the design of the product.

   However, if existing patents cannot be avoided, the company needs to reconsider its entire strategy. In such instances, designing around is both time-consuming and expensive.

2. Acquisition of a patent license.

   If it is difficult to avoid prior patents, or it takes too much time to design around, the company should consider a license from the patent owner. However, the patent owner would have to be doing its business in the same market and the owner is unlikely to grant a license under the patents to its competitor. When the patent owner's intention is to monopolize the market, the owner has a tendency not to grant licenses to its competitors, even if the patents are royalty-bearing.

   On the other hand, if the existing patent owner would like to enlarge the market for its product to become more profitable, it is likely to grant a license to its competitor. It is more likely for a competitor to obtain a license from the existing patent owner if the competitor's product is limited to a certain market sector that does not compete with the owner's.

3. Discontinuation of the product development.

   When designing around is difficult or impossible, or the company cannot obtain a patent license from a third party, or even if a patent license is obtained but the royalty is too high, it can be argued that this does not constitute a viable business.

   In such instances, the company would be faced with discontinuing product development. This scenario is especially troublesome near the end of product development, prior to introduction to the market, as enormous research and development costs, loss of profits, and the research and development costs of a substitute product are raised.

Recent Product Development and Market Exploitation—Era of Open Innovation

This section states companies current product development and marketing style. In particular, it refers to collaboration with other companies or universities and utilizing government fund, de jure and de fact standards, and patent pool.

Collaboration with Others

Just prior to the end of twentieth century, it was not uncommon for a company to perform all research and development (R&D), production, sales, and finance activities. More recently, there is a tendency for a company to select and concentrate on business in its core field and reduce or withdraw from its tangential businesses. In addition, it is more likely that a company will use not only its internal resources, but also external resources to its advantage. This is referred to as Open Innovation.[11]

As technology becomes more sophisticated, it can be cost prohibitive for one company to perform a series of activities to discover new technologies, invest in R&D, and sell and support the product. Accordingly, utilizing outside resources, including cooperation with other entities from a financial and technical perspective has become advantageous.

COLLABORATION WITH OTHER COMPANIES   Recently, companies are collaborating with other entities on technology development, production, and marketing of products. For instance, assume that a certain company manufactures computer-related hardware; it could:

- Cooperate with a software house to run the hardware.
- Cooperate with a material manufacturer (e.g., copy paper and toner for copying machines).
- Jointly develop a product with a competitor. In this case, the company must be careful because antitrust issues could arise if a product sold as a result of the joint development obtains a dominant position in the market.
- Use a foundry[12] in the case of a semiconductor manufacturer, and use an electronics manufacturing service (EMS),[13] in the case of an electronic equipment manufacturer when the production costs of the company are too high because of low productivity.
- Outsource manufacturing of a product to a company having many patent licenses from third parties due to cross licensing arrangements. In this case, the company entrusted with manufacturing the product can market it without obtaining patent licenses from each of the licensors, if the entrusted company not only has the right to sell its products with its own brand but also has the right to OEM supply.
- Build a relationship with other sales companies, or supply its product to others as an OEM product with their own brand when the sales network of the company is weak.

COLLABORATION WITH UNIVERSITIES   It is not unusual for companies to collaborate with universities and research laboratories having leading edge technology. The university benefits from the financial support while the research results obtained jointly by the university and the company are available to both parties. Treatment and attribution of the joint research results are usually determined in writing between the university and the company.

From the standpoint of the university, the following may be required, however, from the company's view point, the following may not be desired:

- Universities or laboratories seldom execute the research results and the universities or laboratories may request an execution fee or other compensation from a company.
- When a company grants a third party a license under the patents jointly owned by the university and the company, the university sometimes requests a portion of the license fees from the company.

Making research results available to the company via financial support may be more cost-effective than establishing and maintaining its own central research laboratory.

GOVERNMENT FUNDED RESEARCH Universities and private companies can receive research funds from government agencies—such as the National Institute of Health (NIH), Defense Advanced Research Projects Agency (DARPA), and National Institute of Standards and Technology (NIST)—and are thereby able to own any inventions resulting from it. However, government fund recipients are not always free to use the research results. There are some restrictions, such as march-in rights and confirmatory licenses, for such government funded research. According to the confirmatory license rule,[14] when the university or company obtains a patent based on government funded research, it must grant a free, nonexclusive license under the patent to the government agency that granted the funds to the university or the company. If the university or company discontinues prosecution of patent applications relating to the government funded research or maintenance of the patent rights relating thereto, it must assign or transfer ownership of the applications or rights to the government agencies when they require ownership. Furthermore, the march-in rights[15] require the university and company to grant a license under the patents obtained through the government funded research to any third party who wishes to make use of the patents, if the university and company do not practice the patents.

Standardization

Technological standardization is desirable for a company to reduce development and production costs and to expand the market. This subsection explains de jure standard, de facto standard, and patent pool systems.

INTERNATIONAL STANDARD—DE JURE STANDARD AND DE FACTO STANDARD Typical examples of de jure standard are the International Standard (IS) established by International Organization for Standardization (ISO) and the ANSI Standard established by American National Standards Institute (ANSI). Some examples of de facto standard are the TCP/IP that is the Internet communication standard, Ethernet as the LAN connectivity standard, and the VHS format standard for consumer video tapes and VCRs. These formats are widely adopted as de facto standards in the marketplace. In fact, the de facto standard was sometimes confirmed by standardization organizations to become a de jure standard. For example, HTML (Hypertext Markup Language), a language describing Web pages, was originally recognized as a de facto standard and eventually adopted as the de jure standard by ISO in 2000.[16]

If it is possible for a company to widely distribute its own original technology or standard used in its products vis-à-vis the technology development model or diversification model, this can result in a competitive advantage for the company. The company can further leverage its investments in R&D and production facilities, and in some cases the company expects certain amounts of revenue from licensing covering the original technology. If the company's technology development is slower than others or it goes into a new market later than others, it may still effectively use such de jure standard and de facto standard in its products. However, when the company uses these standards, it is usually requested to select either of RF, RAND,[17] or no license as a patent policy. Since the company is required to grant to other members a license on the RF or RAND condition, it is necessary to carefully examine whether the patent policy is beneficial to the company or not.

PATENT POOL   A patent pool system is also effective to meet industry standards. Image compression standard MPEG-2 and wireless LAN standard IEEE 802.11 are typical examples of a patent pool.

In the past, there were more than 20 companies and individual inventors who owned patents concerning optical disk drives. Even if a company tried to make and sell an optical disk drive, it had to pay patent license fees to the tune of no less than 20 percent of the price of a disk drive if it paid at least 1 percent royalty per patent holder. The company would eventually need to abandon commercialization of the disk drive. However, if a patent pool were formed in this field at the time, the company might have been able to make and sell the product by paying a reasonable and acceptable royalty to the pool.

If a patent pool is formed in the market that a company is trying to enter, it should effectively utilize the patent pool for expanding its product, product lines, or territory.

Future Product Development and Market Exploitation

This section describes companies' future product development and marketing style. Especially, it refers to utilization of a company's own patents and technologies, the threat to a non-practicing entity (NPE), and the use of patent commons.

Provide Company's Patents and Technologies to Outside Companies

Companies generally own a sufficient number of patents to protect their own products. The technology covered by the patents is often used in products, although not always. A patent concerning alternative design to block third party entry into the market (i.e., a defensive patent) is not normally used for products. Figure 4.2 shows the total number of Japanese patents owned by patent holders from 2003 through 2008. In the graph, the lower portion illustrates the number of patents that are used for products or have been licensed to others by cross licensing or other licenses. The upper portion signifies the number of patents without use or license (including defensive patents). According to the graph, patents without use or license exceed 50 percent of the total number of patents per year. Many "sleeping" patents are still stored in the attic.

A company may choose to license its patents to third parties in order to supplement its product line with another company's products. One example would be a printer manufacturer who grants a patent license to another company to supply it with consumables such as paper and/or toner and other chemical materials.

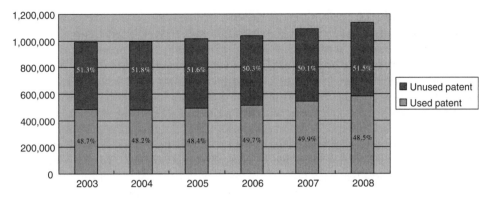

FIGURE 4.2 Total Number of Patents in Japan

Source: Japan Patent Office: "Result of the Survey of Intellectual Property-Related Activities" (2007 and 2009).

In the event that the business of a certain product has been discontinued or doing business is unprofitable for a company because the size of the company is too large to make a profit, the company could license its own patents concerning the business to others. Thereafter, the company will receive from others the supply of the patented products to complement its own product line, and it would be able to get revenue from the license. If the company does not intend to do future business concerning the patents, it may consider selling the patents to others.

Countermeasures for NPE

Cross licensing is an effective means of utilizing third party patents because it enables each of the companies to exchange its respective patents with the others for use in its own products. However, if the third party having the patents does not make or sell any products, cross licensing may not be feasible. The third party may often require unreasonable licensing fees.

This kind of entity is called a non-practicing entity because it does not practice its patents. The term *NPE* might include in a wide sense those companies that were selling their products with use of their patents but subsequently stopped selling them, as well as universities that own their patents but do not have manufacturing facilities and selling ability. In this chapter, the term NPE is defined in a narrow sense as an individual, firm, enterprise, or other entity that does not create its own patents but purchases them from others, and uses or sometimes abuses the patents not for the purpose of manufacturing and selling products but for the purpose of making unreasonable profits from a license fee or litigation settlement. This kind of NPE is a threat to a company that is ordinarily practicing business nowadays. Such an NPE was once called a patent pirate and has also been referred to as a patent troll.

To protect practicing companies from NPEs, a defensive patent aggregation has been organized. Typical examples are Allied Security Trust (AST)[18] and RPX Corporation (RPX).[19] Both organizations purchase patents and license them to their members, who pay an annual membership fee to AST or PRX and agree not to sue their respective members based on the purchased patents. AST members are involved in purchasing patents; however, RPX members are not involved in purchasing and RPX independently decides the patent portfolio to be held. To deal with the threat of NPE, a performing company may use defensive patent aggregators.

Furthermore, nonprofit and private organizations are established to investigate prior art and file requests for reexamination. Public Patent Foundation (PUBPAT),[20] Troll Busters LLC,[21] and Electronic Frontier Foundation (EFF)[22] are typical examples. When an NPE is alleging infringement of its patent rights against a company, the company could engage these organizations to investigate prior art and/or file reexaminations to have the patent deemed invalid. The company can also request an anonymous reexamination. Thus, a company may utilize this type of organization as an effective countermeasure to an NPE.

Use of Patent Commons

Patent Commons is a community in which patents contributing to a certain technology, such as open source software and environment, are offered free of charge to the community to promote the use of the patents among its members. Typical examples are the Patent Commons Project of the Linux Foundations[23] for open source software and Eco-Patent Commons[24] established by IBM, Nokia, Pitney Bowes, and Sony for the environment. Actively using the mechanism of the Patent Commons, a company will be able to expand its product line and develop into new markets.

Conclusion

In the twentieth century, the vertical integration model was the predominant management style for business. Accordingly, a company engaged in all research and development, manufacturing, and sale of a product by itself. The intellectual property such as patents obtained during the company's own research and development had been used for purposes of defending its own business and securing bargaining power for cross licensing agreements.

In the twenty-first century, to promote and expedite research and development activities, it is more important and necessary for a company to collaborate on the research and development with universities or any other entities, in order to procure an idea, technology, and patent license that meets the company's needs from external resources of the world. In addition, it is of strategic importance for a company to grant licenses under its patents to other companies for making and supplying their products or for obtaining royalties from the license of the company's unused patents as well as used patents. It is also of strategic importance for a company to provide or make available its patents to International Standard, a patent pool, or patent commons to create a new market, where the company and any other members can utilize available patents. All these activities are useful tools for penetrating new markets through extension of goods or product lines or expansion into other territories.

Notes

1. Takeru Ohe, *Why Does Not a New Business Succeed?*, 3rd ed. (Nikkei Publishing Inc., Tokyo, 2008).

2. *Canon Inc.*, www.canon.com/corp/ (accessed September 14, 2010).

3. *Nikon Corporation*, www.nikon.com/ (accessed September 14, 2010).

4. Stepper is photolithography equipment using reduced projection exposure that prints a lot of circuit patterns of a photomask or reticle onto a single silicon wafer by moving or stepping the wafer from one exposure location to another.

5. *Olympus Corporation*, www.olympus-global.com/en/ (accessed on September 14, 2010).

6. *Hoya Corporation*, www.hoya.co.jp/english/business/business_05.html (accessed September 14, 2010); PENTAX Corporation merged with HOYA CORPORATION in 2008.

7. *Honda Motor Co., Ltd.*, http://world.honda.com/ (accessed September 14, 2010).

8. *Ricoh Company, Ltd.*, www.ricoh.com/ (accessed January 22, 2011).

9. *Konica Minolta Holdings, Inc.*, www.konicaminolta.com/about/index.html (accessed September 14, 2010); Minolta merged with Konica and became Konica Minolta Holdings, Inc. in August, 2003. Konica Minolta transferred its single-lens reflex camera business to Sony Corporation in March, 2006.

10. Henry W. Chesbrough, *Open Innovation* (Harvard Business School Press, 2003).

11. Ibid.

12. Major foundries are Taiwan Semiconductor Manufacturing Company Limited (TSMC), www.tsmc.com/; United Microelectronics Corporation (UMC), www.umc.com/; and Globalfoundries Inc., www.globalfoundries.com/ (accessed January 22, 2011).

13. Leading electronics manufacturing services are Hon Hai Precision Industry, www.foxconn.com/; Flextronics International, www.flextronics.com/; and Celestica Inc., www.celestica.com/Home/Home.aspx (accessed August 22, 2010).

14. The contractor must provide a nonexclusive, nontransferable, irrevocable, paid-up license for the government to practice or have the invention practiced on its behalf throughout the world. See 37 C.F.R. § 401.14(f)(1).

15. The government's right to require the contractor or an assignee of a subject invention to grant a nonexclusive, partially exclusive, or exclusive license, under reasonable terms, to responsible applicants. See 35 U.S.C. § 203.

16. ISO/IEC 15445:2000.

17. RF stands for "Royalty Free" and RAND means "Reasonable And Non-Discriminatory" terms and conditions. For example, ISO, IEC, and ITU have common patent policy in which a patent holder will select to grant either of (1) a free of charge license, (2) a license on a worldwide, non-discriminatory basis and on reasonable terms and conditions, or (3) no license. See *International Organization for Standardization*, www.isotc.iso.org/livelink/livelink/fetch/2000/2122/3770791/ITU_ISO_IEC_Patent_Statement_and_Licensing_Declaration_Form.pdf (accessed September 15, 2010).

18. AST has 18 members as of January, 2011. *Allied Security Trust*, www.alliedsecurity trust.com/ASTMembers.aspx (accessed January 22, 2011).

19. RPX has 72 members as of January, 2011. www.rpxcorp.com/index.html (accessed January 22, 2011).

20. PUBPAT is a not-for-profit legal services organization whose mission is to protect freedom in the patent system. *Public Patent Foundation,* www.pubpat.org/About.htm (accessed August 22, 2010).

21. Troll Busters LLC states "We file reexaminations to invalidate the patent claims of patent trolls. So like the movie "Mr. and Mrs. Smith" we're hired assassins who shoot to kill the patent claims of patent trolls." *Troll Busters LLC,* www.troll-busters.com/whatDoWeDo.html (accessed August 22, 2010). However, in 2010 PUBPAT filed *qui tam* actions for false patent marking against four companies, and in January 2011, Troll Busters LLC filed a *qui tam* action for false patent marking against 15 companies and both sought half the amount of the penalty of not more than $500 per article based on 35 U.S.C. § 292. This kind of relator of a *qui tam* action is often called a marking troll.

22. EFF investigates and documents the harm that patents are causing to the public interest and files reexaminations of the patents. *Electronic Frontier Foundation,* http://w2.eff.org/patent/wp.php (accessed August 22, 2010).

23. *Patent Commons,* www.patentcommons.org/ (accessed August 22, 2010).

24. "The Eco-Patent Commons: A Leadership Opportunity for Global Business to Protect the Planet," *World Business Council for Sustainable Development,* www.wbcsd.org/DocRoot/4tF7aXkIt0vZODBJobYY/Eco-Patent%20Commons%20Brochure_011008.pdf (accessed August 22, 2010).

CHAPTER 5

Intellectual Property:
From Asset to Asset Class

James E. Malackowski
Chairman and Chief Executive Officer,
Ocean Tomo, LLC

Although you may not be aware of it, intellectual property (IP) is the biggest asset class on the planet, estimated at more than $5.5 trillion in the United States alone.[1] That is bigger than the gross domestic product (GDP) of most countries. Moreover, in the past quarter century there has been a dramatic and permanent shift in corporate value from tangible assets like factories, machines, and land, to intangibles, such as patents, copyrights, trademarks, industrial design rights, and trade secrets. Consider the following research from Ocean Tomo, LLC (OT), a leading merchant bank in the IP space. The data shows that in 1975, only 17 percent of the value of S&P 500 companies was found in intangibles (see Figure 5.1). In 2009, by contrast, 81 percent of the value of these companies is in intangibles. Additional OT research on intangible versus tangible assets, in non-U.S. markets such as Europe and China (using the Euro Stoxx 50 and Shanghai Composite indexes as benchmarks), shows similar results. The message is that value in the companies the world cares about most resides in their protected ideas, rather than in hard assets.

To traders and investors looking for an edge, there is a clear take-away from this data. If you want to find corporate value, you must be able to identify key IP metrics. This is not to say that traditional metrics commonly used to gauge growth and predict stock price targets are obsolete. It is still reasonable, for example, to analyze earnings, read SEC filings, consider macroeconomic factors, monitor insider transactions, and look at technical indicators, just to name a few widespread investment due diligence practices. However, if the majority of a company's value resides in intangibles, it seems self-evident that understanding that value repository gets you closer to knowing what the company is worth. In other words, rather than trying to determine what the company's price/earnings (P/E) ratio ought to be or whether to be a buyer or seller of the stock at the 200-day moving average, go to the real source of value and look to the IP.

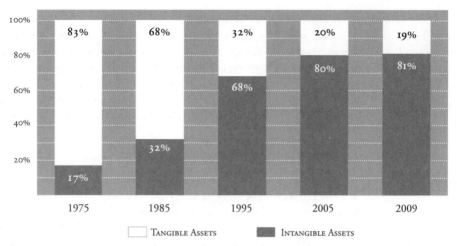

FIGURE 5.1 Components of S&P 500 Market Value
Source: Ocean Tomo LLC.

To put an especially fine point on the subject, it is fair to say that the value of a corporation's IP is a unique, forward-looking indicator of corporate value. The reason for this is intuitive: The most innovative companies, that is, those companies with the strongest IP portfolios, tend to outperform their peers as a result of: (1) the government granted monopoly on the production of the patented, copyrighted, or trademarked product or service; (2) related economies of scale; (3) premium pricing associated with unique features; and (4) lower costs due to protected methods of manufacturing.

So, what sort of data should the prescient trader or investor consider? The following is a good starting list.

- How many patents does a company own?
- Which technologies do those patents cover?
- What is the average age of those patents (patents have a finite life, for example, 20 years in the United States)?
- How many new patents is the company bringing through the pipeline and how many patents is it abandoning? (Companies abandon more than 60 percent of their patents by year 12 because they cost more to maintain than they produce in revenue.)
- What is the value of the company's brand?
- Does the company own valuable trade secrets?
- What is the effect of interest rate fluctuations on the company's research and development budget?
- Is there significant litigation surrounding a company's IP?
- What is the effect of merger and acquisition activity?
- Are there paradigm shifts in a particular technology that will fundamentally alter the way people utilize a product or service (e.g., Blu-ray or hybrid automobile technology)?

Some of this information is readily available. For example, the United States Patent Office produces a voluminous amount of data about issued patents. In reality, however, it is enormously difficult for most traders or investors to incorporate IP metrics into an investment strategy or trading model. Because historically there has not been a central marketplace for IP transactions, as in the cases of foreign exchange, interest rates, equities, or commodities, there is virtually no transparency as to IP transaction prices or volumes and this inhibits even the most motivated market participants.

Introducing IP-Enhanced Indexes

Because markets abhor a vacuum, OT, in partnership with its affiliate the Intellectual Property Exchange International, Inc. (IPXI), has developed a family of IP indexes and related exchange traded funds that IPXI is now introducing to the marketplace. Based on a patented database, the Ocean Tomo PatentRatings® system, that allows for the rating of all U.S. patents (a European patent ratings system developed jointly by OT and the French bank Caisse des Depots will be introduced in 2011), these trading products will enable money managers, investors, and traders to generate *excess returns with less risk* in a transparent, liquid marketplace.

Here's how the IP indexes work. An existing underlying index is chosen, such as the S&P 500, and enhanced by IPXI/OT using a 130/30 weighting; increasing weights in companies with long IP signals and reducing weights in companies with short IP signals. Thus far, IPXI/OT has published four IP-enhanced indexes, based on, respectively, the S&P 500, S&P 1500, Nasdaq 100, and Wilderhill Clean Energy Index. IPXI has the capability to create any IP-based absolute return or benchmarked fund for which size, style, and sector criteria are specified. With respect to the current four indexes, the enhanced index outperformed the underlying index with a better information ratio in each case (see Figures 5.2 through 5.5).

Achieving such performance is like finding a unicorn or getting a clear photo of the Loch Ness monster; it is what every index developer hopes to find: more alpha, less risk. With the IPXI/OT enhanced IP indexes, investors and traders can easily implement two discrete strategies to capture the IP alpha. They can simply buy the enhanced index in place of the underlying, or execute a spread between the underlying and enhanced index and lock in a risk-free profit. While these are the most obvious strategies, it is expected that when the IP-enhanced exchange-traded funds (ETFs) are actively trading, additional strategies will be implemented by traders and investors attracted by the appeal of IP alpha.

IP-enhanced indexes are an exciting innovation but, ultimately, nothing more than a means to an end. IP is a vast and vastly inefficient market. At even a quick glance by any seasoned market participant, the IP market looks a lot like FX or interest rate markets in the 1970s, or energy and stock indexes in the 1980s. In each of these cases, the markets in question were vast and vastly inefficient. However, because the world needed price discovery and liquidity, markets developed. There were fits and starts—nothing as massive as the creation of a global market happens without some amount of chaos—but there was never any doubt that the markets would grow. This is also true with the IP market. Indexes and ETFs are only the

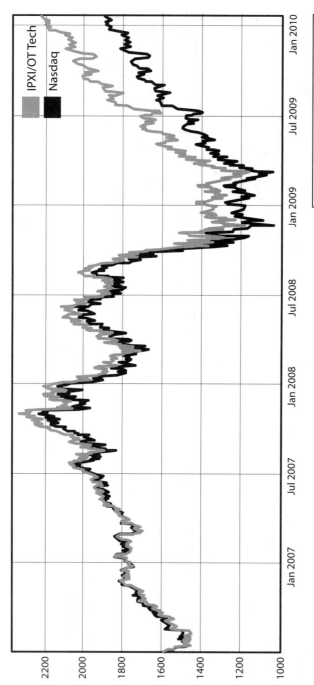

FIGURE 5.2 IPXI/Ocean Tomo Technology
Source: Ocean Tomo LLC.

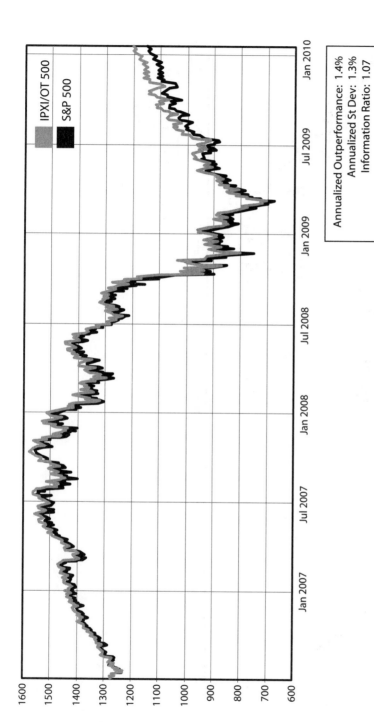

FIGURE 5.3 IPXI/Ocean Tomo 500

Source: Ocean Tomo LLC.

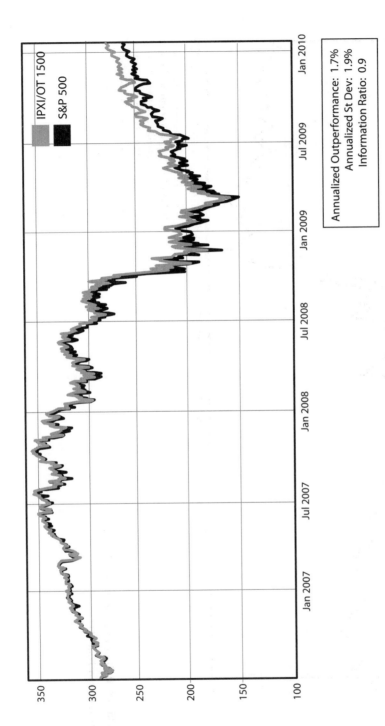

FIGURE 5.4 IPXI/Ocean Tomo 1500

Source: Ocean Tomo LLC.

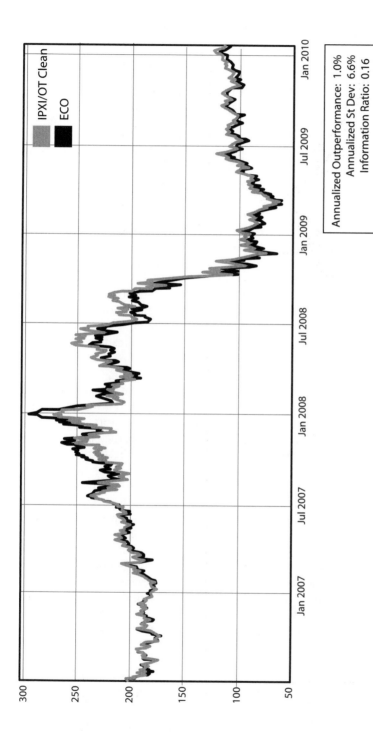

FIGURE 5.5 IPXI Ocean Tomo Clean Energy

Source: Ocean Tomo LLC.

beginning. It won't happen overnight, but as the world's largest and most important asset class, IP is destined to become as transparent and liquid as any market on the planet.

Creating a Market for Intellectual Property

Creating a market for intellectual property is no different than creating a new market for any other type of good, commodity, or asset. When the concept was first revealed, it was guaranteed to be met with skepticism and resistance. Such was the case in 2005 when Ocean Tomo announced that it would be holding the world's first live intellectual property auction. The critics were out full force. In retrospect, many of the comments were credible and intelligent; however, if people had had no willingness to try something new, then there would be no future for innovation.

The idea of a single-lot IP auction is not a new one. For years, intermediaries who market assets for a single company or seller have been conducting small, quasi-public auctions. One of the more noted examples was the bankruptcy sale of the Commerce One Inc. patents in 2004.[2] Many of the market intermediaries or small brokerage shops typically conduct a sealed bid process, which could qualify as a form of auction. This approach certainly has its benefits and limitations.

There are many different theories about why the multi-lot live IP auction approach has been so readily adopted. There are likely several leading reasons that benefit both sellers and buyers:

- *Benefits to sellers:* The auction is a clean, simple process that provides sellers of IP with access to a global network of buyers that they would otherwise be unlikely to reach. This is particularly true for the smaller inventors and venture-backed companies. The auction benefits larger corporate participants by giving them a standard platform where they are able to effectively dictate the terms and price to the market buyers.
- *Benefits to buyers:* Buyers, as well as sellers, have come to enjoy the benefits regarding the transparency of the auction process. Prior to the live IP auction, it was very difficult to know what IP was supposed to sell for. What was its value in a sale versus its value in a license or litigation? These values certainly vary from one another, but with the advent of the multi-lot live IP auction, there are real, tangible, and public IP sales, allowing for comparison to each other, and some framework for what IP, specifically patents, should be selling for based on their qualities and criteria. Large companies have come to appreciate the intelligence that the live auction format for IP brings. The simple knowledge of knowing what is available for purchase, maintaining the ability to participate as a buyer, and ultimately receiving the pricing knowledge of the sale regardless of participation, have all proven quite valuable.

Additionally, the live auction format has changed the game for buyers. It effectively lifted the covers for corporate buyers and forced them to more actively review IP for sale. Historically, a midlevel IP purchasing manager, following the receipt of an announcement of litigation against his or her company on a patent that was recently sold, was able to claim that transactions were private and that he or she had no knowledge that the assets were available for purchase. This excuse is now extinguished for any IP sold through a live auction. The burden has switched to the buyers, as they can no longer hide. They now must pay attention to the IP for sale because it is listed publicly, allowing everyone to examine the offered assets. Buyers can no longer afford not to participate if the assets are interesting or of value to them.

What Exactly Is a Live Multi-Lot IP Auction?

Put simply, a live multi-lot IP auction is virtually identical in style to the age-old auctions put on by well-known auction houses such as Christie's and Sotheby's. It sounds the same. "Going once, going twice, sold." It is a physical forum where parties can participate as sellers, buyers, or onlookers. There are multiple sellers and multiple buyers. There is an auctioneer, an auction service company facilitating the physical event, and the auction company that deals with collecting and managing the consignment and registration processes. Hundreds of people, including members of the local or international press, often attend the event.

Auction Consignments Structure and Rationale

There are many comparisons between a live public auction and a privately represented transaction. Depending on the types of assets, both approaches have great benefits and significant limitations. In facilitating private transactions, one of the difficulties is that the sellers maintain tremendous arbitrary control of the acceptance of terms. Think about the process: A seller contracts with an intermediary or broker, a marketing package is put together and circulated, and offers are received (ideally). Upon receipt of these offers, the seller is free to accept, reject, or counter such offers. However, the seller is typically not bound to accept any of the offers even if they meet or exceed the seller's initial pricing expectations. (The exception here might of course be a provision in the engagement agreement that specified that fees are due from the seller to the intermediary in the event a good faith offer is received at or above a certain amount.)

Depending on its structure, the live auction format addresses this dilemma. All sellers in the auction, whether corporate, individual, or otherwise, are required to, as a condition of participation, execute and notarize all documents necessary for the transfer of the IP at the time of consignment. These agreements include the comprehensive IP Sale Agreements (often called the PPA—patent purchase agreement—in some circles) as well as the simple one-page assignments that are filed at the regional patent offices around the world.

In addition to the transfer agreements, the sellers are all required to set a reserve, or minimum, price at the time of consignment. The reserve is defined as the "lowest fixed price at which an item is offered at an auction sale and (1) at which it will be sold if no higher price is bid, or (2) below which the seller is not obligated to accept the winning bid."[3] Put in simpler terms, the seller agrees to the reserve price, and once the bidding reaches that amount, the seller is obligated to sell the assets. They maintain no unilateral ability to back out of the transaction.

Let's now look at the combination of the execution of the all the documents necessary for the transfer of the IP and the setting of the reserve price, both of which take place at the time of consignment. With both of these actions taken, the seller and the auction company both know, unequivocally, the minimum price and the terms upon which the assets will sell.

Marketing the Event

For a live IP auction, it is critical that all potentially interested parties, no matter how small, are aware of the event and its structure for participation. While it is always necessary to conduct some form of direct contact, marketing becomes critical for an IP auction. In the traditional auction world, a company such as Sotheby's will conduct an international road show of, for example, a collection of paintings to market the assets. Unfortunately, IP is intangible, so showing up with an exhibit of patents is less likely to draw a crowd. The marketing for such an event must be global since IP is utilized worldwide. This universal nature of IP will often necessitate that marketing materials be translated into multiple languages by a diverse group of international native speakers on staff.

The other key issue for a live IP auction is lead time. There is a chain of events for any IP buyers, particularly large corporate buyers, which require sufficient lead time. This includes getting the information to the right person in a company, having them review all the IP available for auction, making a determination that it is of interest, making a further determination after technical and legal due diligence that they would like to acquire such IP, gaining internal approval for the purchase, and authorizing sufficient funds to cover the likely final bid amount and then some. Consequently, any marketing campaign for a live IP auction must begin months in advance of the event.

Buyers and the Auction

When the first multi-lot live IP auction was introduced, it was met with great skepticism, not just from sellers, but especially from buyers; many of these parties were being asked to spend hundreds of thousands, if not millions, of dollars on intellectual property in a forum and under a structure that was foreign to them. After all, how often in the history of arms-length transactions were buyers told, essentially, "These are the terms, there is a set minimum price. Take it or leave it"? The answer is, not often at all. Consequently, it was no great surprise when the widespread buyer adoption for the idea took a few auctions to show real progress.

Over time, many buyers have come to like the live auction format, with a concentrated number becoming quite active. This is particularly due to the transparency and filtering process Ocean Tomo, and now ICAP Ocean Tomo, provide. One of the difficulties in a private transaction is that buyers never know whether they are bidding against another third party or not. They are forced to rely solely on the word of the seller or the intermediary. In a live auction, they can see a paddle go up or a phone bidder place a bid. There are many bidders in the market who prefer this type of format because regardless of what they are ultimately required to pay, they are paying the unquestionable market price of the assets.

The filtering process is an often overlooked component of the auction to many onlookers. For a live IP auction, it is critical that the IP offered for sale be screened with diligence conducted prior to acceptance. Buyers have come to appreciate this value added component. One of the significant problems that plagues buyers of intellectual property is the need to filter through the vast ocean of IP in their respective industries or areas of interest. Sometimes, they will be able to make a quick determination initially that an available IP falls squarely within their industry and interest, only to discover fatal diligence issues later in the process. For example, it would often extinguish any interest if buyers found out that there were exclusive licenses to the IP or that the inventor refuses to execute comprehensive assignments of such IP. Unfortunately for buyers, these types of issues come up often and frequently require buyers to expend legal resources to make these discoveries.

Throughout the entire IP transaction process, buyers are kept completely anonymous. This is one of the oldest tenets of the auction world and an issue of the utmost sensitivity when it comes to intellectual property. When it comes to IP transactions, companies do not want third parties to (1) know that they are even an interested buyer; (2) know what they are willing to pay if they do buy; and (3) have any idea whatsoever regarding the strategic direction of the company and its purchasing plans. In addition, for reasons obvious to the IP professional, the buyers certainly do not want to do anything to trigger additional liability for themselves, particularly a potential willful infringement action years later. No one wants to be the second highest bidder, and the first litigant or licensee. For these reasons an auction company must go to great lengths to protect the identity of its bidders. Extremely sensitive buyers who choose to remain anonymous, even post auction in the public records, often choose to purchase through and assign the assets to a shell company that is set up specifically for the purpose of the purchase. With the birth of Ocean Tomo's auction market now reaching its fifth anniversary, a number of third parties have been able to publish research on successful buyers by compiling public records of assignment and corporate ownership.

Can Buyers Conduct Due Diligence?

Often, there is a public misconception that buyers in a live IP auction conduct no due diligence and purchase the assets on a somewhat blind, uneducated basis. This is certainly not the case, and the thinking itself defies logic. For patents being sold, in any forum whatsoever, conducting appropriate due diligence is the engine behind any transaction. Potential and actual bidders in live multi-lot IP auctions conduct significant amounts of diligence on any of the assets they choose to bid on at the live auction.

The diligence is enabled through a centralized, globally accessible, online due diligence room that houses many of the documents necessary for the diligence of a typical IP transaction. The problem is that IP transactions are often not typical, and buyers must gather other necessary documents on their own or through standard channels. In addition to the transfer agreements, the online due diligence room will typically contain such materials as license agreements, file histories, past assignments, cease and desist letters that were sent out, business plans, corporate authorities, and other materials.

In addition to utilizing an online due diligence room, potential buyers will often need to speak directly with the sellers or inventors of the assets to develop a better understanding of the patent claims, discuss what was conceived or developed by the inventors, or gain some clarity on communications during the prosecution.

Buying at Auction

At auction, the auctioneers will go through one lot at a time in a sequential order. They will then open the bidding at whatever amount they choose, based on their experience as an auctioneer, and look to solicit bids on the lot. There are multiple types of bidders. These include: live bidders with the proverbial bidding paddle, phone bidders, and absentee bidders who elect to leave their bids and authorization amounts with the auction company to place on their behalf. Once the bidding reaches the confidential reserve amount, the auctioneer will make an announcement that the lot is "in the market," meaning it is guaranteed to sell at that point. Often, the urgency that this statement creates will stimulate additional bidding. Ultimately, there will be a winning bidder who will tender funds to the auction company for the purchase. At a date and time following the auction, those funds will be released to the seller of the assets and the assignment and other transfer documents will be released to the buyer.

The Next Chapter

So, does the business of conducting live IP auctions remain stagnant, rapidly grow, or go away? While only time will tell, the likelihood is that it will continue to grow. Companies will continue to have an increasing desire to sell their intellectual assets, and their need for a consistent predictable forum and centralized marketplace will be cornerstone to this need. In addition, as the global understanding develops that IP can be dealt with as an asset separate from the products and other technology, the market for these opportunities can only grow.

Moving to a Traded Exchange

While the auction model will continue to bring price discovery to both the United States and increasingly a growing international market, ultimately transacting patent rights will include a traded exchange.

IPXI has created a marketplace for the exchange of commoditized patent licenses, known as Unit License Right™ contracts (ULRs). IPXI anticipates maturation of this market in three phases: (1) an initial introductory period; (2) one to two years of over-the-counter price discovery focused in the United States; and (3) ultimately, global electronic trading with the introduction of futures and derivative products.

ULRs allow patent owners to license select technology in a non-discriminatory manner via standard form licenses on publicly disclosed terms. ULR contracts address the current inefficiency of technology transfers, including the time, expense, redundancy, and uncertain outcome of traditional bilateral license negotiations. IPXI serves as the intermediary between the patent owner(s) and potential licensees or other buyers. IPXI lists the ULR contracts and facilitates one or more offerings of consumable license rights—the ULR contract. Each ULR contract purchased gives the buyer the right to use a pre-established unit of IP, for example the right to make and sell up to an established quantity of products covered by the patents in question. IPXI is responsible for auditing consumption of ULRs and publicly reporting this information. In the event of infringement, IPXI is generally responsible for coordinating enforcement of the rights under the patent or other IP.

Generally, a ULR offering is presented in multiple tranches with prices for each successive tranche determined based on market adoption and the pricing of the prior tranche. An exemplar offering for 50 million units could be structured as follows: tranche A for 10 million units at $0.50 per unit; tranche B for 10 million units at $0.75 per unit; and, tranche C for 30 million units at $1.00 per unit. There are a number of controls built into the ULR contracts market to assure fair and reasonable pricing, including: market-based standard valuation practices; the experience of market participants; disclosures in the offering documents; IPXI selection committee review and approval; community review of proposed offerings; use of a Dutch Auction, or advance bid allocation market opening; tranche price limits; position limits; declarations of failed offerings; and, ultimately, judicial limitations on pricing through determination of reasonable royalties.

Likewise, the ULR contract market also contains a number of mechanisms to assure fair and reasonable expectations of demand, including mediation; arbitration; accelerated reexamination; and, ultimately, judicial determination of infringement.

Benefits of the Unit License Right™ Contract Model

ULR contracts represent an alternative to traditional debt and equity for purposes of liquidity. ULRs are by definition a far more attractive option, as they are non-dilutive to equity and, unlike debt, the licensing income does not need to be repaid.

As an asset, third party profits associated with the buying and selling of ULRs are generated from an increase in value of the underlying intellectual property as a result of market adoption and use of the technology covered by the patents contained within the ULR. The key tenet of the ULR contract market is that patents create business value from the implementation of associated inventions, for their original owner as well as third party operational users. Further tenets of the ULR contract marketplace include the following.

- Initial offering prices are determined through independent market forces and the experience of buyers.
- Intelligent and structured guidance on pricing is provided through early market adoption in multiple tranches.
- Price adjustment flexibility within disclosed "bands" allows for unexpected changes in market conditions.
- Follow-on offerings are presented based on market conditions reflecting real-time market dynamics of consumption and price.

Although a patent is by its nature only a negative right (i.e., the right to exclude others), vast sums spent annually in research and development seeking new patentable inventions confirms that at its core, patented innovation is seen as a way to create economic value by enhancing the gross margins of its owner or licensee through price premiums, cost reductions, or access to attractive markets.

ULR contracts represent a quantum leap forward in the monetization and recognition of the value created by patented technology. The technology transfer benefits of ULR contracts are numerous and include:

Licensor Benefits

- Efficient monetization of patent portfolios
- Dramatically reduced legal cost
- Avoidance of forced cross licensing
- Outsourced marketing
- Outsourced auditing
- Outsourced enforcement
- Timely reports on licensee usage
- Market-determined fair and reasonable licensing terms
- Flexible rights structures

Licensee Benefits

- Efficiently obtained licenses to patent portfolios
- In-licensing standard contracts
- Ability to resell unused ULR contracts to accommodate reduced future needs
- Fair and level playing field for all prospective licensees
- Formal mechanism by which licensees request that IPXI investigate alleged infringement

Market Players and Economic Motivations

Key market players include IP owners, or sponsors, buyers, and the exchange itself. There are two classes of buyers or demand-side participants: operational users and institutional users. Each participant has its own economic considerations and motivations.

Sponsors are initially expected to be large corporate patent owners who are, in many cases, also operational users. The exchange will not discriminate against sponsors, so it is expected that universities, government funded research organizations, and general non-practicing entities (NPEs) who own quality portfolios will also participate. Indeed, for many operational users, the ULR contract market is expected to bring relief from unrealistic price expectations of NPEs. In any case, sponsors are motivated to maximize licensing income associated with the listing of their patents through ULR contracts on the exchange. Such motivation will necessitate natural compromise between unit pricing and volume elasticity. In general, the exchange will be seeking high volume ULR contracts tending to have relatively modest per unit prices.

Every market will necessarily include operational users. This is practical because as the end consumers of the ULR contract right, they largely create the market demand through their adoption of technology. Participation by operational users is also mandated for any given ULR contract to open, due to exchange rules mandating that they comprise a portion of buyers of the tranche A offering. As the commercializing entity for each technology, most operational users will be long-term market participants. Major interrelated economic considerations of operational users include:

- *Pricing:* Typical practice in evaluating a fair price for technology rights, particularly patent rights, involves a calculation of the incremental revenue or profits a licensee will be able to generate from commercializing the technology and further deciding a fair allocation of the incremental revenue or profit between the inventor or owner of the technology and the user. Operational users will likely employ a similar framework in evaluating the fair value of a ULR contract right. This allocation of value concept itself gives rise to the increasing value of a ULR contract as the technology is widely adopted. The risk of successful technological integration into a product line and commercial demand for the marketable product is a major justification for a heavy allocation of the incremental value to the user and accordingly a lower per unit royalty. As the technology is proven to be successful and valuable, and is therefore more widely adopted in the industry, these risks are diminished and the allocation of the total value of the technology may be allocated further to the underlying technology rights. This is generally reflected in the risk adjusted hurdle rates implicit in the tranche pricing of the initial offering.
- *Risk management preference:* While it is expected that operational user may hold some safety stock of ULR contract rights to support its business, the size of this inventory will be based on the specific company's requirements. Operational users must balance the risk of price volatility with the drawbacks of the capital inefficiencies of excessive inventory. Given that compliance is measured thirty (30) days following the close of a calendar quarter, it is possible for operational users to purchase all required ULR contracts in arrears.
- *Anticipated industry adoption:* An operational user's assessment of the technical capability and strategic intent to adopt a ULR contract-based technology will be a consideration in both pricing and inventory decisions. If the operational user believes a major competitor(s) is unable or unwilling to adopt the technology, it will have a strong position in the market and would have reduced price volatility concerns. Similarly, if an operational user believes that it can more cost-effectively implement the technology and/or extract more value from it than its competitors can, the ULR contract right will have a relatively higher value to it and therefore such a buyer would have decreased concerns about competitors driving up prices for ULR contract rights.

The second class of demand-side participants, institutional users, may or may not participate in a particular ULR contract market. Institutional users do not plan to directly extract value from obtaining ULR contracts by commercializing the underlying technology. They generate profits from ULR contracts by purchasing the rights early in the adoption curve and holding them with the expectation that they will increase in value as a result of independent market forces; ultimately selling into the secondary market at a profit. In effect, institutional users generate returns by taking on the risk that the technology will be proven to be successful and adopted—effectively moving down to lower risk-adjusted hurdle rates.

Institutional users are expected to evaluate each ULR offering solely on the basis of their own financial and IP expertise and judgment as to (1) whether the patents contained within a given ULR contract protect a useful commercial offering and (2) their view as to how quickly the market will adopt the technology, if at all.

In addition, IPXI itself plays a role as an intermediary through its administrative functions. IPXI provides four administrative service components related to ULRs, none of which create incremental value for the ULR contract holder over and above that created by market adoption:

- *Transparency* through publication of the rulebook, posting of each ULR contract offering memorandum, and reporting
- *Opening logistics* assuring initial market pricing without discount by managing the Dutch auction of each ULR
- *Resale* of the ULRs by receiving interest to buy or sell ULR contracts, verifying the required qualifications of participants, and facilitating completion of necessary documentation
- *Policing* of consumption through partnership with an outside audit firm and third party investors in elective litigation enforcement

IPXI and a sponsor may elect to enforce ongoing offerings in cases where operating entities are currently using the technology covered by the patents but have not acquired and consumed the related ULR contracts. In short, an enforcement ULR denotes a decision by the exchange and sponsor to file U.S. District Court litigation or a Section 337 proceeding with the International Trade Commission to enforce compliance for one or more believed infringing users. In such cases, IPXI anticipates partnering with the sponsor or a capital partner who will retain any excess award over and above what is required to purchase the adjudged units from the market. Such excess amounts will not be distributed to ULR contract holders and hence they will receive no value creation from these efforts. It should be noted that the policing efforts of IPXI are similar to those of many similar IP management organizations, including the American Society of Composers, Authors and Publishers (ASCAP) for music or one of several widely recognized patent pools. IPXI will not be involved in any activities that create value for unit holders, such as driving adoption of the technology within ULR contracts. IPXI will not conduct research, publish its views on the benefits of such technology, or promote specific ULR contracts. Neither the audit nor enforcement functions of IPXI create value in ULRs.

IPXI's business model as an exchange can easily be distinguished from patent aggregation firms and patent licensing and enforcement companies (P-LECs) based on the following:

- IPXI will not enforce ULRs without the consent of the original sponsor or patent owner.
- IPXI will not fund enforcement.

- IPXI will not incrementally benefit from the proceeds of any enforcement.
- IPXI's members are not exposed to free-riders who use offered technology without being in compliance.
- IPXI will not accept cash settlement of disputes over compliance; the operational user will be required to purchase required units from the market.

Conclusion

The economic inversion shown through the S&P 500 in Figure 5.1 reflects a quarter century overnight success for IP as an asset class. A review of similar data prior to 1975 shows only the historical bedrock of tangible assets driving company valuations. Similarly, we do not anticipate that a crystal ball view of the next 100 years will show a transition away from value creation through intangible assets, notably IP. We have lived through the intellectual revolution and as a result of the speed of the transition, only now see the emergence of new markets and related reporting functions desperately trying to catch up.

Notes

1. Robert J. Shapiro and Kevin A. Hassett, "The Economic Value of Intellectual Property," *Intellectual Property Report*, October 2005, 2.

2. In 2004, the company Commerce Once Inc. sold its patents in the U.S. Bankruptcy Court for the Northern District of California for $15.5M (EWEEK, www.eweek.com/c/a/Web-Services-Web-20-and-SOA/Commerce-One-Patents-Auctioned-Off/, January 26, 2009). Months later, it was revealed that the buyer was Novell, the Waltham, MA based company delivering software and computer services, Boston Business Journal Online, www.bizjournals.com/boston/stories/2005/05/02/daily1.html (accessed January 26, 2009).

3. BusinessDictionary.com, www.businessdictionary.com/definition/reserve-price.html (accessed January 26, 2009).

CHAPTER 6

Strategic Patent Management after the Boom
Managing the R&D and Patent Pipeline

Marc S. Adler
Marc Adler, LLC

E ffective, business-focused patent strategies can accelerate innovation, improve patent quality, simplify communication, facilitate executive participation, and reduce costs. Lessons learned from existing practices can instruct business executives and patent counsel in reassessing and modifying their patent strategies and procedures to better manage their research and development (R&D) and intellectual property (IP) pipeline during periods of economic uncertainty and changing business models. While this chapter examines existing patent operations in large companies, the lessons and proposals for a new strategic approach are applicable for small companies and individual inventors.

This chapter examines existing patent strategy approaches and their advantages and deficiencies, and offers suggestions for new strategic approaches for existing and emerging technology-based ventures for success in the next decade.

Patent Strategy

Much has been written about patent strategy, but in my opinion, the term *strategy* has been widely misused to refer to tactical aspects such as patent preparation and prosecution practice, litigation and patent management issues, and not planned, proactive patent—business strategies integrated with long- and short-term R&D and financial objectives. In this chapter I examine some of the historical approaches to patent strategy and propose a new approach to offensive and defensive patent strategies and practices for the future.

In order to place the proposed new approach in proper context, it is worthwhile to review the traditional and more recent approaches companies have employed along with their benefits and deficiencies.

The Traditional Corporate Patent Management Model

During the twentieth century companies that had been founded on new technology, and had been able to successfully sustain their innovations and profitability over several decades and product generations, developed internal patent departments and processes to manage their patent operations. These in-house departments created their own attorney, patent agent, search and inventor training programs, and developed and improved their patent process workflows, docketing systems, formal paperwork, and filing systems. In addition to administrative, clerical, and paralegal staff they also added and redirected some, or all, in-house attorneys and patent agents to support research and development activities. Some of these attorneys had prior technical experience with the company. Turnover of in-house patent personnel tended to be low, and management systems, metrics, and processes were developed over time to address their training, performance, and career development. Outside counsel were employed primarily in situations where special legal expertise, litigation, or second, independent opinions were needed.

INWARD FOCUS, BUREAUCRACY, AND REDUCED EXECUTIVE INVOLVEMENT   As companies grew, they generally tended to devote more of their strategies and attorney effort inwardly on their own R&D and invention pipeline, and less frequently, except for infringement issues, externally on the patent activities of their customers and competitors. As this occurred, more attorney time and attention became directed to defensive patent procurement and internal meetings focused on prioritization and compliance with their own procedures and research needs. Unfortunately in order to present this information to research and business management, a considerable amount of energy was devoted by attorneys to the development and presentation of spreadsheets and visual charts in an attempt to summarize and explain complex information at regular internal decision points to various committees and decision makers. While process compliance offered uniformity and some degree of cost control, it also tended to create bureaucracy around implementation, tended to focus more and more on tactical issues, and slowed down those decisions without providing adequate attention and time for broader strategic discussion and planning. The midlevel technical and business managers who were delegated to participate in patent committees often had limited authority, and accordingly the actions that patent committees were directed to take tended to be short range, tactical, and reactive.

Higher level executive participation in broader, proactive defensive and offensive patent strategy discussions became less frequent as the company grew. Most of the proactive patent activities that companies were able to undertake tended to focus primarily on defensive issues around major new product development and internal process improvements, such as improving internal search and databases for product clearance to avoid infringement. Proactive next generation defense and offensive strategies directed toward competitors were often not pursued. Patent strategy discussions on issues such as whether to develop out-licensing programs were considered, but were often rejected by line business managers at the committees as not being of core financial importance to the ongoing manufacturing and operating business (their profit and loss). A few large companies, however, developed broader licensing strategies and internal licensing operations, and some of these became separate business units or profit centers.

Patent "strategy," as the term was most often used by patent attorneys, focused on specific patent claim preparation, their structure (process, product, etc.), and patent application prosecution tactics; while patent "strategy" for executives focused mostly on major infringement issues and operational cost control. The latter activities tended to involve reviews of outside counsel actions having a significant short-term impact on the case, potentially how it could affect operations, and on costs and potential damages. As litigation costs, especially in the United States, rose dramatically, and as these costs often became greater than the combination of the internal department people costs and the patent procurement budget, more attention was paid by patent managers, general counsel, and executives on tactical litigation management issues.

As departments grew, they often separated patent procurement activities from patent enforcement and licensing functions, occasionally using non-patent attorneys for licensing and litigation, thereby further complicating strategic discussions and further distancing in-house patent attorneys from high-level business executives and planned, proactive patent strategy discussions.

This traditional patent organizational model tended to be present in established manufacturing companies, most notably in the chemical, petroleum, and pharmaceutical industries, in some diversified and consumer product companies, and established business machine and telecommunication companies. These companies had frequently been founded with a few key patents and had developed a long-standing and strong respect for internal R&D and patents. The corporate culture and institutional memory of these companies generally supported the patent department's role in generational renewal through innovation and patent procurement.

It's not a simple or quick proposition to create, maintain, and manage a large patent operation inside a company. With growth and acquisitions, and as the number of products, locations, and businesses grew, the more complex it became for patent management to utilize centralized systems. Similarly, as time goes on it becomes more difficult for a company that was successful with a certain business or management model to make rapid changes that impact long-standing culture and established processes. This inflexibility, bureaucracy, internal focus, and inefficiency can be tolerated during growth but can become a serious liability in times of dramatic economic change. In my view, companies employing traditional patent operations and procedures need to reassess their strategic approach and their procedures to become simpler, less bureaucratic, more digitally nimble, and faster. This can be achieved by a combination of higher level offensive as well as defensive patent strategies coupled with internal process modifications. Patent processes can always be made simpler with better accountability, and internal patent process overhauls can be made faster to be less costly while at the same time maintaining or increasing their focus on patent quality. This effort may require some new capital investment for better software. Recent advances in information technology, searching, patent management, and document software can be tremendously valuable in process changes as well as development and implementing a new strategic approach such as by improving analysis, data filtering, decision making, and communicating important information. These process improvement efforts should be undertaken; but, they are the tools for assisting the strategy, they are not the strategy itself.

Established companies need to pay heightened attention to offensive patent strategies, which are externally focused on customers, competitors, universities, and new entrants around the world who have potentially disruptive technologies. They also need to become better at tailoring and coordinating their strategies everywhere they operate.

Business executives do not need to be involved in the design and project management of improved patent processes or systems, but they need to be involved in higher level proactive defensive and offensive strategy development and review. Getting business executives interested in patent strategy requires a new approach. Strategy reviews must be constructed in a way that engages the interest of the highest level executives quickly; and I believe one essential aspect of this is for the strategies to clearly and effectively communicate the financial impact of possible options. Later in this chapter I identify a few specific improvement proposals to address these issues.

Riding the Wave of the New Strategy Model

Newer companies, formed during the last decades of the twentieth century and the first decade of the twenty-first century, especially in the high-tech information technology, semiconductor, and software sectors, started with intellectual property such as proprietary computer code and copyrights, but unlike prior technology founded companies, not always with patents. Over time, however, as they grew and began to face potential competition, they began to utilize the patent system and employed at least one patent attorney on staff. Much of their patent procurement was provided by law firms and outside counsel, some of whom may have assisted in their inception or in early litigation. As time went on, additional in-house attorneys were hired for routine matters to reduce over-dependence on outside counsel, provide help for the solo in-house patent attorney, coordinate outside counsel activities, and provide more services to growing research and development and business needs. But daily demands to keep pace with rapid economic growth and high attorney and management turnover in this tech sector tended to impede or overtake systematic plans for the internal development of proactive patent processes and strategies. There was often no time, or desire among business executives, to engage in long-term strategic planning with patent attorneys. In addition, due to the lack of a long corporate history and culture around patents, and the lures of new start-ups, many companies had difficulty retaining patent attorneys and inventors, making compliance with internal processes difficult.

PATENT STRATEGY DURING THE FIRST DECADE OF THE 21ST CENTURY   During the last decade, as technology-based companies, both established companies and newer entrants, were seeing their businesses ramp up and grow quickly, the strategy moved to one of defensive patent accumulation.

Management often directed chief patent counsels to substantially increase patent filings annually, lower procurement costs, support acquisition activities, and spend minimal effort attempting to avoid infringement if it slowed down new product introduction. Invention harvesting and filing new patent applications as fast as possible was seen strategically as the most important thing, often more important than the quality, specific strategic use, or individual value of each patent.

At about the same time, previously large in-house corporate patent departments generally began to shrink in size, especially in the United States, as more staff was added at new research centers outside the United States, especially in Asia, and companies focused on cost control. Smaller patent departments for the most part did not significantly grow, and previously successful internal training and development programs for in-house patent attorneys were phased out.

Patent strategy under the new model focused more on short-term results, often involving acquisitions. The remaining in-house counsel became more involved with assisting in business transactions involving acquiring or licensing patent portfolios, and as a result the in-house counsel necessarily increased their reliance on outside counsel to prepare and prosecute a greater percentage of the new patent applications as well as to defend the company against infringement allegations. Companies also encouraged early retirement of many of their most seasoned patent specialists, and contracted with a few retirees and convergence firms using a combination of fixed fees and lower priced associates to draft and prosecute patent applications, and highly priced senior litigation partners to defend against infringement charges.

As long as the business continued to grow profitably, ongoing business operations were not enjoined, and potential threats of infringement damages were minimized or at least properly forecasted and factored into the cost of doing business, many companies seemed to be able to accept the increased cost and litigation risks, without adding in-house patent complement. The fastest growing companies were not as concerned about the carrying cost of their own patents or the effectiveness or optimization of their internal processes as were companies that were not growing as rapidly.

The new accumulation and outside counsel-reliant procurement model appeared to be working fairly well, and in some ways it was a psychological relief for top executives and general counsel. They could spend less time with the patent staff. The corporate MBA business elite often skeptically viewed in-house patent attorneys as either conservative or "difficult." They were often criticized for their introspective personalities, poor interpersonal skills, or not seeing the big picture, and for being too concerned with details and process. Business leaders lamented, "Why do they need to constantly remind me of all these detailed patent processes and potential horrors when things seem to be working just fine? We'll react when we need to, but we won't maintain or build costly proactive systems to avoid potential problems." Making matters worse for in-house patent operations was that experienced patent attorneys were few, and hard to recruit, compensate, and retain.

Compared to the traditional model in which the patent attorneys desired to engage the business in proactive, systematic, long-term defensive patent strategies that would require the executives' time and attention, the new model freed executives to travel the world to make deals and expand into emerging markets. To many business executives and general counsels, the new slim and trim model seemed like a win-win.

The new model also led to new ways of viewing patents themselves. Part of the reason was a result of a patent portfolio arms race strategy. The rapid expansion of patent portfolios had the effect of creating dense thickets of patents, which tended to convert patents from individual, strategic assets into defensive tactical weapons carrying the potential litigation deterrent—the threat of mutual self-destruction. Rapid increases in the number of new patent applications distributed among outside counsel, and fewer in-house attorneys, also had the effect of disconnecting individual patents (and claims) from specific commercial products, manufacturing processes, and business plans. More patents were generally viewed as being more important than fewer, higher quality patents. Prosecution efficiency and claim correspondence to specific products and processes became of lesser importance than in the past. Patents and often large groups of patents became viewed as a new type of technocurrency; potentially valuable as intangible options or commodities that could be used as bargaining chips in negotiation or royalty-free cross licenses, as a means for participating in standard setting organizations for new generation products, for generating revenue through package licensing, auctions, and potentially as futures to be traded as a commodity on an exchange.

The traditional patent department and strategy model became frequently denigrated as tired, old thinking and not appropriate for twenty-first century technology. Even traditional assumptions that strong patent rights were important and necessary for growth, that patent clearance could or should be conducted before commercialization, that patents could be enforced, especially in emerging markets, or even that there was a necessary connection between each invention, the patent that protected that invention, and the commercial product and the financial results flowing from the marketing and sale of that product, became ripe for questioning by patent counsel, academics, and economists. Part of the argument against the continued viability of the old model relied on the claimed inherently different nature of high-tech products, due to their short product cycle and the absence of anything close to a one-to-one relationship between a patentable invention and a final product. Many patentable inventions (some contend the ratio is as high as a thousand to one) are required to assemble one high-tech device or application. It is unclear whether this is a truly inherent quality of all high technology products and business models, in a similarly but opposite way that one patent claim to a new active compound is inherently of most value to chemical and pharmaceuticals at the end of the patent life, or whether it was partly a result of group think about the priority of the patent accumulation, difficulty with the self-created patent thickets, and successful manufacturer cross licensing. The problem with increased filing was compounded by the fact that the speed of the innovation and publications in these new technological fields often outpaced the ability of the patent offices and patent laws to keep up or truly understand the technology. Increasing application pendency and the grant of many patents of unclear claim scope and questionable validity further disconnected individual patents from their role under the old strategy model. Expansion of royalty-free cross licensing among manufacturers of entire large patent portfolios tended to maintain the focus on accumulating patents regardless of specific connection to specific products.

Regardless of the exact cause or causes, the new patent strategy model became principally a numbers game for many companies: "Make sure we obtain x percent more patents than we did last year." Companies were tracking competitive patent rankings in the *Wall Street Journal* as if they were synonymous with their degree of innovation. "We are more innovative than the other guy; look at how many more patents we got than they did last quarter: Let's get our ranking higher."

Older patent operations that addressed incremental process improvement, the quality of each application and claim precision and product correspondence, prosecution efficiency, the specific contribution of each patent to business financials, and precommercialization product clearance to minimize the potential risk of infringement, were seen as passé, slow, or not suited to the new technologies; and the boom patent accumulation mentality was in vogue.

During a boom when things have been good, it's easy to assume that they will continue to be good, thus making it easier to take more risks. Naysayers can easily be dismissed as either being too slow, conservative, or pessimistic, and one machismo reaction to such conservatism was for companies to take even bigger risks (e.g., less preacquisition due diligence) for faster, and potentially bigger short-term returns. Blinded by the pressure to deliver quarterly results that met or exceeded analyst predictions, combined with the conventional wisdom that the good times would continue, companies ignored certain warning signs. For example, instead of examining how to conduct patent audits or investigating how to search all new advances in rapidly developing technologies and creating rapid product clearance processes before new product introduction, companies relied on their cross licensing activities, disparaged non-manufacturing patent owners as trolls, and threw up their hands regarding clearance, saying that as a result of the industry's increase in new filings it was impossible to navigate through their patent thickets in a meaningful or precise way in a reasonable period of time.

More simply, when something is too easy and too profitable, complacency and conventional wisdom overwhelm critics who point to the possibility of fundamental problems with underlying assumptions.

Disruption: The Post 2008 Recession

As the real estate and mortgage-backed derivative market collapsed along with financial institutions and easy credit (as well as government bailouts, bankruptcies, stock market declines, and other recent economic debacles), and economic growth slowed, it was inevitable that technology-based companies and their law firms would be adversely affected. In the past, when the economy slowed, new patent filings, patent litigation, and the patent bar as a whole were minimally affected. But this time, as sales took a dramatic nosedive and acquisition synergies began to look more questionable, executive attention turned to the continued increase in patent costs, including the cost of procurement, attorney rates, litigation costs, and substantial infringement damages. Law firm merger mania began to run into unmanageable conflicts and scale problems and some smaller boutiques closed shop or laid off their least productive associates.

Just as in hindsight it is clear that the real estate bubble was a house of cards based on faulty assumptions, the recession or expectations for a slow economic recovery is making companies rethink their underlying patent strategy.

Scrambling to Cut Costs and Adjust to New Realities and Rules

Chief patent counsels are being directed to immediately limit spending and reduce costs by decreasing the number of new filings and pruning portfolios. Since internal patent department head count, convergence programs, and flat fees with law firms had already been implemented to reduce costs, the remaining focus for additional savings became the cost of the portfolio itself. Reducing R&D spending and filing fewer patents is fairly easily and quickly accomplished by fiat, but it is more problematical to properly audit a portfolio to reduce maintenance costs when the portfolio was built without a clearly defined linkage of each patent to ongoing and future products and business strategy. "How do we know which individual patents and applications we need to keep and which to drop if we don't know exactly what we have and what they really cover? We don't even have reliable databases, processes, or the internal staff to manage this." If the new model strategy is based on obtaining as many patents as possible rather than on their linkage with specific products or processes, it is difficult to know where to prune and how deep to cut. Some feel they can simply tighten their belts by examining the portfolio in large groupings of patents, making some educated guesses about what and where to maintain, and hoping for fairly quick economic recovery to resume operating as before, but others are looking for other guidance.

Potential new patent office rules that could increase costs and require additional disclosure of prior art on related applications, or requiring limitations on claims or continuing applications, also created anxiety among patent counsel with poor database and internal processes.

Time to Reassess and Modify

I believe this tough economic period is a perfect time to take a step back and reassess each company's patent strategy and processes, question the fundamentals of the existing business and patent model, and examine whether some of the best practices of the old model and the new model can be combined, while preserving the process discipline of the old model and building on the speed, entrepreneurial energy, and cost benefits of the new model. Improvements to patent strategy can be made while a business is still performing fairly well, but it cannot be done once the bubble bursts.

A Proactive Patent Strategy

An explicit, written patent strategy is not simply a statement of a philosophy such as obtaining patent protection for new products and processes and respecting the valid patent rights of others. A proactive patent strategy is a fiduciary obligation of management to maximize R&D investment and the quality of patent protection while minimizing cost and risk. If the quality, total cost, and explicit business purpose of each patent and the risk of infringement of new products and processes is not clear and measurable from the onset, building or maintaining a patent portfolio, for example as a potential litigation deterrent or for possible licensing, cannot ensure sustainable short- or long-term profitability. In fact, as a company expands its patent portfolio without an explicit strategy, each individual patent tends to become less valuable to the business and less clearly connected to the overall objectives of R&D and patent quality, and operation efficiency declines. Conversely, if significant attention is paid to the development of a clearly defined, business focused, patent strategy, linked with the R&D pipeline, competition, and acquisition prospects, faster and better business decisions, higher patent quality, lower costs, and lower risk can be measurably achieved.

A New Strategic Approach

In any strategic process, there needs to be an explicit plan with clear goals. Whether the company is a multibillion-dollar global enterprise, a start-up, or even an individual inventor, a patent strategy is a useful way to align R&D, patent, and finance. Most new ventures proceed with a business plan having various assumptions, but typically do not have a patent strategy. Patents are typically viewed as a venture capital inducement, an indication that the company has some unique technology that merits investment, but beyond that there is little time taken to plan for future developments or think about how to make the best use of the patented technology and defend against third parties until commercial success of an initial product is achieved. Problems often occur as a result of the lack of a patent strategy when the first entrant is quickly overtaken by another with a similar product or process.

The following new approach can be tailored for any size business or business unit. Because it requires a thorough understanding of the external environment as well as the internal R&D pipeline, it requires more initial time commitment but will return significant dividends. Individuals and small start-ups may feel that they do not have the resources to prepare a patent strategy before establishing market credibility, but I believe that a proactive patent strategy can save small companies significant costs, rework, and risk, and provide for sustainable profitability.

The Strategy Team

The initial organizational issue in the development of a patent strategy is who should be on the team. The patent strategy team should be composed of the individuals whose responsibilities align with and whose performance will depend on the final implementation of the strategy. This is a team effort that needs a team leader or co-leaders. The team should be composed of the business manager, the marketing manager, the researcher or research team (no more than three people), and the patent attorney strategist for that business unit or subunit. The team should also include the business finance manager for that business unit; if not a member of the team, that person should at least be brought in to advise on the financial quantification aspects of the strategy. The patent strategist should have responsibility for leading or co-leading the team with the business manager and should have responsibility for drafting strategy documents and organizing reviews. Patent attorney specialists responsible for filing and prosecuting patent applications for the business unit should attend strategy sessions when needed.

The leaders should set a schedule for completion of strategy tasks and management reviews.

The Review Team

The review team for the patent strategy should include the following individuals: the chief patent counsel, the chief technology officer or highest research manager for that business, the vice president of the business, and other strategic executives in accordance with the business organization. These individuals must be willing to participate in periodic reviews of the patent strategy and be prepared to make decisions on issues brought to them by the strategy team.

Setting the Deliverables

First know what you need to accomplish for the business. For any patent strategy to be successful, it is critical that the business expectations or deliverables from the strategy be clearly documented and quantified. In order to achieve the desired results of a patent strategy, each company should define the desired deliverables (financial as well as qualitative) of the business in the short (this year and the next) and long (2–5 year) term. Since every business, and even subsets of a business, is at a different place in its development, growth, and ultimate product cycle plateau, each has different expectations, and the patent strategy for each business needs be tailored to current reality and future projections. As a result, patent strategies are dynamic and need to be revisited and modified periodically.

The shorter the statement of the strategy and the clearer the metrics, the more likely it will be used. The *strategy statement* is not a document to be placed in a binder and pulled out only when a review is scheduled. The language of the strategy must make sense to the inventors, the patent attorneys, and the financial experts. As a result there may be a statement of an overall objective with more specific dependent strategic initiatives and specific tactics and processes to be employed. The statement needs a time line for each strategic initiative and intermediate review points to measure progress and identify obstacles. Management must be rigorous in conducting reviews and not delegate this to lower level persons with limited authority to make the types of decisions that a strategic business review requires. The patent strategy can be thought of as a subset of a business strategy review that would include many other business processes.

The patent strategy is a planning and implementation process. As a planning exercise it involves addressing a number of basic questions relating to the fundamentals of the business. For example, is this an existing stand-alone business composed of one or numerous products or is it part of a broader business unit that requires it to supply or produce something for the other parts? Is it a new business undergoing market acceptance or one that has achieved significant market share? Is it a geographically limited business or a global one? Does the company expect to expand the business and if so, how: by internal or collaborative research and development, acquisition, geographic expansion, or a combination thereof? Is the business subject to divestment, self-cannibalization, or replacement by disruptive new technology? Who are the key competitors and new entrants and where is disruptive technology likely? What is the existing R&D pipeline? What are the financial parameters for profitability, and so forth?

For each question, it is critical to determine when the business expects the changes or results of the patent strategy to be achieved. As with any strategy, these and other questions and answers need to be addressed and approved by those in charge of the business and then be clearly communicated to R&D as well as the business, finance, and internal patent staff. If the business deliverables expected by the business for each new invention and the external competitive reality is not clearly examined, effective proactive defensive and offensive strategies cannot be achieved.

In some tech areas the business must also grapple with changes in patent law, and operational issues such as how to best collect and protect inventions made at multiple research locations, how to balance trade secret protection, and process patent enforcement, how to respond to non-manufacturing patent owners, and changing laws, such as in the present state of business method and software patents and process claims.

New Business Models and the Internet

Businesses that rely on the Internet as a content distribution vehicle are struggling with strategy issues such as what should be free and how to charge for other things. Since the United States Supreme Court's *State Street Bank* and *In re Bilski* decisions, companies have been seeking to patent new business methods, and the law has been trying to catch up with the technology, especially as it relates to legal issues presented by new technologies and business models often described by process patents as opposed to product patents. Companies are also exploring different collaboration models such as open source development, social networking, and how to properly participate in standard-setting organizations.

What the proper patent strategy for each Internet-enabled new business should be is fundamentally connected with how the company intends to go to market with new products and processes as well as its philosophy regarding exclusivity and openness.

As traditional profit pathways change and the time between conception and commercialization is compressed, patent strategy must be more geared to speed, flexibility, and short-term as well as long-term results. The strategy must fit the existing business model, preferably be flexible, be compatible or adaptable to the next model, and preferably predict the next business model. If profit margins per use of a product or process are driven downward with increased usage and if more technology must be bundled together to achieve the next big thing, collaboration and interchangeability become even more important to achieve maximum penetration and sales volume quickly. A patent strategy that is static and inflexible will not serve the needs of a rapidly changing business.

Because of the speed of new developments some may question whether companies in this technology space need patent protection or how the perceived limits of the patent system itself will limit the usefulness of a patent strategy. Others will approach the speed issue by examining more radical ways to revise their current patent procedures to keep pace with the required speed of the business model. Companies can create new patent procedures leveraging software, artificial intelligence, and self-learning algorithms to continually shrink the time and effort required from conception to patent grant. Competitive, off-line patent analysis combined with open sourcing and accelerated examination need to be factored into the strategy. Patent drafting and prosecution tactics can be used to minimize pendency without sacrificing quality.

For example, how can a company continue to accept weeks from conception to patent application filing and years from filing to grant, if a new application can be accessible to the users and potential competitors in a few months? The time line for the patent process needs to dramatically move much closer to commercial realities for patents in such a fast-paced environment to be relevant to the business. By utilizing clear and explicit patent strategies, much patent prework, due diligence, and analysis can be done off-line from R&D ideation. The correct data and analysis can be timely introduced to the R&D and marketing personnel so that when an idea is discovered that clearly supports the strategy, a patent application can be prepared and filed more quickly, and existing third party patents and applications can be effectively identified and timely engaged. With a clear strategy and optimized procedures it is possible to file patent applications within two weeks of ideation and obtain granted patent coverage within 12 to 18 months of ideation.

Non-Manufacturing Entities and Disruptive Technologies

Can companies afford to continue following their current approach to the challenges of non-manufacturing entity patentees? Can manufacturing companies continue to accumulate patents solely for litigation defense and cross license with other manufacturers? Defending against charges of infringement by an entity that is not concerned about your patent portfolio means the accumulation strategy is not providing an adequate defense. The idea that if you attempt to patent every conceivable idea you will make it harder for others to obtain patents that you may infringe is a costly and imperfect strategy that also has other strategic problems. Is it really impossible or impractical to review all the publications, patent applications, and patents that exist in a new technology area to design around or license others' patents? Are disruptive technologies more frequently likely to occur in information technology areas where physical plant entry barriers are low, and how do disruptive technologies factor into the company's patent strategy? The key to dealing with these questions resides in the ability to conduct and analyze all publications related to the technology and business quickly. I address this more fully in discussing patent clearance procedures.

Whatever patent strategy a company selects to deal with non-manufacturing entities and disruptive technologies, competition in emerging markets (especially those countries which may not recognize certain new technologies as being patentable or where the courts are not predictable), need to be factored into the patent strategy.

One suggested approach to organizational alignment and to deal with R&D expenses and program self-expansion, or creep, is to require that before any significant research and patenting is done the objective of the invention be examined in view of the strategic questions and their strategic statement.

Product managers and marketing managers can help in the development of the patent strategy by clearly defining the overall business strategy, the time lines and financial expectations of the patents, and by providing useful competitive intelligence.

How exactly does the business expect each patent to help reach the business objectives? When referring to deliverables, it is important for management to be clear about the financial metrics, resources, timing, and cost structure to be used to evaluate business and patent operation performance.

For any patent strategy to be successful, it is critical that the expectations or deliverables from the strategy be quantified. Financial metrics should be established for measuring the effectiveness of the patent strategy. I personally favor tracking two financial metrics: product gross profit and product market share. These financial metrics should include all the fixed and variable costs of the patent process, as well as assign a portion of the business financial results to the presence, absence, and effectiveness of the patent strategy by comparing patented products and processes with unpatented products and processes. If licensing is a business function, the costs and returns of licensing (in and out) need to be evaluated based on the resources employed and impact on other business and patent strategies.

Patent strategy must move the dialog with the business away from being solely focused on the cost to acquire, enforce, or defend against third party patents, and soft or qualitative aspects of patent protection, and toward patent protection as a quantifiable portion of the profit equation. While there are many reasons that may account for a new product or process success in addition to patent protection, there needs to be some approximation of the contribution of patent protection to product profitability and market share over time in order to evaluate the proper spend and the return on that spend. The existence of patent protection may not be the only factor that accounts for a new product or process success. This does not mean that the contribution of these intangible rights cannot be converted into financial terms, even if approximate and not exact. For example, if a business sells patented and unpatented products to similar customers, a positive delta profit being achieved by the patented products over unpatented products (for example 10 percent) can be used as a base point for the positive financial return of the patent strategy. This delta can be compared against the entire patent cost for that product and the profit margin can be viewed by product, process, and country to determine the sustainability of the initial profit over time. Without a business financial outlook, patent strategy becomes too qualitative and easily viewed by business management solely in terms of a cost to be reduced, instead of a positive contributor to financial success that should be managed for maximum impact.

The key deliverables of the patent strategy need to align with the business plan and the research plan and pipeline. If research is being conducted in areas that do not fit with the business strategy, whether for the near or long term, should patent resources and costs be expended to protect such inventions? Should such research even be conducted at all? The patent strategy should clearly define what actions, if any, the patent attorneys should expend on technology that the company knows it does not intend to use, or does not wish to license. If licensing out is a strategy to be used to obtain a financial return for noncore technologies, this should be an explicit part of the patent strategy at the onset instead of being an afterthought. If the technology is to be licensed in return for rights under certain third party technology, the strategy needs to identify which patents it must license and how to make the patent protection for the new technology essential for licensees; how it can be leveraged to obtain a license back under a selected third party patent or group of patents quickly and at the right price; and whether a design around is possible.

If these strategies can be established before actual research is started, patent clearance, design around, and possible acquisition or licensing due diligence can be started and completed sooner. Much of this data collection and analysis work can be done offline and outsourced at a reasonable cost without impacting ongoing operations or staff time.

In addition to speeding up acquisition or licensing due diligence, clear strategies can also be used to eliminate patent committee meetings, prioritization, and triage, since the decisions that will be needed can be predetermined simply by reference to the guiding strategy. If an invention is made that clearly fits with the business and patent strategy, everyone will know what needs to be done without waiting months for a committee to endorse the actions that are needed. If an invention does not fit with the line business strategy, the research should either be discontinued or possibly refocused onto strategically important technologies, or alternately be pursued as a potentially disruptive future technology, or be used as part of a defined competitor or offensive patent strategy. The disposition of such nonstrategic new technologies can be contemplated by the strategy so that each does not need to be reviewed by a committee.

Therefore, each new invention can be evaluated against the strategic deliverables as soon as the invention is made, and be prioritized in order of importance for filing based on everyone's understanding of how patent protection for the new invention can best assist the business. As a result, both time and process effectiveness and cost can be dramatically improved.[1]

Auditing the Current Patent Portfolio

It is critically important to precisely know all your patents, pending applications, licensed patents, and new ideas in the pipeline, and where each is in the time line from conception, development, filing, foreign filing, opposition, grant, and expiration.

Taking inventory takes effort, especially if the portfolio is not organized, is decentralized or disconnected from the company's existing and planned new products and processes. In addition to organizing the patents according to products and processes (even if there is no one-to-one correlation, or if a patent is directed to alternative commercial embodiments, or was filed purely for defensive purposes) each should be correlated to each of the closest commercial products and processes to determine overall cost. It is important to know the current profitability and historical financial performance and the business's view of the future timing of the products and processes covered by each patent. If marketing knows that a certain product is coming to the end of its cycle and will soon be replaced, or sold, that fact will help guide patent strategy for that business.

Patent maintenance costs increase exponentially over the life of a granted patent. As a result, knowing when a product will be discontinued or replaced can be very important in auditing maintenance costs. If the first few years of a new product and patent are more important than the last few years of the patent's life, every effort should be made to secure granted patent protection quickly. In this regard, accelerating exam as opposed to deferring examination, such as under the Patent Cooperation Treaty (PCT), may have significant strategic and cost advantages.

No Hidden Costs

In order to define a cost-effective strategy it is necessary to know all the sunk and future costs associated with each patent in the portfolio. In addition to patent attorney costs, governmental patent fees, and maintenance or annuity costs worldwide for each patent, it is also important to examine the administrative and information technology costs associated with the portfolio. It is important to include such costs as those relating to administrative or process delays, such as, fees for extensions of time, and continuation applications. In determining whether in-house or outside counsel should prepare and prosecute patent applications, productivity and cost analysis should be conducted and if, as I believe is often the case, in-house counsel are more cost-effective than outside counsel, changes to the inside/outside resource balance may be in order and more in-house counsel may need to be hired.

I also believe that patent counsel need to examine the quality of each patent application with particular focus on the downstream cost impact of the patent application itself. By this I am referring to the cost and time impact of the number of pages of the specification, drawings, and the number of claims (independent and dependent) presented. Overall costs and time to grant can be reduced by limiting the number of pages of the patent specification and the number of claims, and therefore, the inventory should track the number of pages and claims submitted for each application.

Filing on a worldwide basis typically costs on the order of $250,000 per case over the life of a patent. There are many hidden costs in this process, some resulting from initial foreign country filing decisions and some from charges by outside firms. Examining all these costs can lead to significant process change and cost savings. Since most companies file counterpart applications in multiple foreign countries (independently or using PCT), routine charges from firms such as from redrafting the application to meet country requirements, processing fees for notices, translation costs, and other handling charges, should be broken out and examined because they can be low-hanging fruit for savings. Even the selection of whether to proceed by PCT or not has cost consequences. For example, the advantage of deferring costs under PCT can actually result in higher overall costs than proceeding directly (EPC plus a few important countries) if the specific countries where protection is really required for the business is defined and limited at the time of initial filing. For example, do you really need patent protection in every PCT country for every case or only for certain inventions? Where is the competition filing applications?

The Hidden Cost of Royalties

Another important cost element is the effect and extent of patent license royalties being paid to others as well as the revenue received from out-licensing. In many companies these costs are not carried on the patent department budget and are hidden costs or benefits, but they need to be factored into the overall cost of the operation since they have an impact on strategy. For example, if the company often needs to secure licenses from others to operate, one element of a patent strategy may be how to avoid this in the future or how to minimize its cost. Can a strategy be devised to block the licensor from obtaining important improvement patents by filing on these ideas before the licensor and using those applications as leverage to reduce existing royalty obligations? How profitable are each of the out-licenses compared to the costs involved in negotiating and concluding the license or enforcing the licensed patents against infringers? It is possible that the royalties received from licensing are not reported with the associated costs because of a split in internal organizational structure, such that the licensing group shows a profit but much of the work and cost is maintained in the patent department budget.

Knowing the Customer and Competitors

Just as it is critical to sales and marketing to thoroughly know the customers and the competition, a patent strategy is incomplete if it focuses inwardly only on defending new inventions without thoroughly knowing the patents, pending applications, and publications of the customers and competitors.

Patent landscape information, current awareness watch lists and analysis of customer and competitor patents, publications, and applications can provide significant opportunities for patent strategies. Knowing that a customer is focused on a certain new product or process or how the customer is approaching the solution to an existing problem, can inform and modify your research and marketing to their existing or planned approaches. Knowing that customers or potential customers have filed joint patents with others, or have licensed certain patents from another, is also useful information to your customer and patent strategy.

Knowing each competitor's patent portfolio intimately is critical for a patent strategy. First, it is important to know the technical approach your competitors are employing to solve a customer's problem. It can show the extent to which the competitor has attempted to protect certain approaches, and the cost of that approach, and it can identify gaps in their thinking. Your researchers can utilize this information in deciding on their own approach or it can be useful in an offensive blocking patent strategy. It can also identify key competitor patent applications (watch list) that you may want to license or oppose. Early identification can be useful for design around activities and to avoid infringement or licensing. University, individual, or small entity patents and applications uncovered by an ongoing, competitor patent search may identify disruptive emerging technologies or present other opportunities for acquisition or license at an opportune price point.

An important aspect of externally focused patent strategy is the identification of your key competitors' most important patents; the ones that you wish you had. I call this the envy list. How can we obtain a license under that patent? Offensive patent strategies designed to fence in or block competition advances or force them to license you under their envy patents may be a more targeted and less costly approach to effective licensing than a patent arms race and package cross licensing of low value but equally expensive patents.

Digitally Nimble: Patent Clearance and New Data Management Software

Despite the conventional wisdom that precommercial product clearance is difficult or impossible in certain technology sectors, I am of the opinion that search technologies continue to make substantial advances, and while not perfect they are very valuable tools. I believe that companies that utilize pre-commercialization patent clearance procedures are more cost-effective; they can either avoid or design around potential infringement, or develop an early opposition, reexamination, or licensing strategy earlier and at less cost than settlement during or after extensive litigation. I also believe that despite the number of patents in a given technology area that may be required to commercialize a new product or process, proactive patent clearance analysis is less costly than reacting to third party challenges and potential injunctive relief after product launch. Certainly up-front effort and time is required to do this effectively, since not every one of the third party applications will eventually be granted with blocking claims, and it may be difficult in some instances to be certain about claim construction, but simply waiting until a competitor patent is asserted is not a cost-effective business strategy. Proactivity here is more economical than reactivity.

Illustrative Example: Patent Clearance versus Litigation Cost Comparison[2]

A thorough patent clearance process for a new product or process can involve searches of varying scope and cost. A search process will involve filtering through a series of search iterations to determine the potential relevance of the uncovered references. It is not possible to hypothetically and accurately estimate the exact number of prior art references that will need to be reviewed for every invention, but for the sake of an example, let's theorize that the initial search uncovers 2,000 patents of potential interest that need to be reviewed for relevancy, and that after relevancy review there are 200 patents to review in more detail.

The cost of the search and one or two iterations will be on the order of $2,500 to $5,000. The attorney time to conduct the legal relevancy determination, based on $200 per hour and 10 patents per hour is 2000/10 = 200 hours or $40,000.

Add another 100 attorney hours at $200 per hour for the final legal analysis and opinion, equal to $20,000; the total cost will be $60,000. Obviously, the attorney time and cost will be proportionate to the number of relevant references and the number of inventions to be reviewed.

Let's assume that the company needs to review on the average of *10 new inventions a month*.

The monthly cost for the clearance process would be $600,000 or about *$7 million a year*.

If no clearances are conducted and the company faces an infringement suit in the United States, the cost will be about $100,000 for the initial six months and 2 to 5 million for the first two years of the lawsuit, assuming no settlement. For the purpose of this example let's conservatively assume the litigation cost for the suit is *$3 million* (absent any settlement cost or court assessed damages).

Since I have assumed about 120 new inventions a year, the cost breakeven for the clearance process point occurs if there are less than three infringement suits per year or less than three challenges per 120 new inventions or 2.5 percent.

The overall cost of three suits per year is $9 million versus $7 million for the clearance process, not counting settlement (license fees) or damages.

Skeptics of patent clearance processes point out that despite best efforts, no clearance process will absolutely guarantee catching every possible infringement charge. As a result, they will contend that the cost of the searches should be added to the cost of the suits since lawsuits will be filed despite the clearance process.

If we assume arguendo, that for every 100 inventions, a company that conducts clearances will also be sued at the same rate as a company who does no searches, it means that the company that searches incurs an additional $600,000 per suit for a failed clearance process. That would take the cost from $3 million per case to $3.6 million, or an increase of about 20 percent.

So, while the upside of successful clearance process would result in a savings of $3 million minus $600,000 or $2.4 million (−20 percent) versus $3 million for a lawsuit, the downside of a failed clearance is an additional annual cost of $600,000, or $3.6 million (+20 percent). If the percentage of infringement suits per hundred new inventions is less than the above assumption, then one may argue that a patent clearance process is not economical (+20 percent), but conversely if the percentage of suits is greater than a 3 percent rate, it would seem clearly to be the fiduciary responsibility of a company to attempt to minimize foreseeable legal costs (and damages or injunction) by instituting a clearance process.

Putting it in a different and more positive light:

The entire cost of one litigation avoided pays for five years of a clearance process for 100 inventions per year.

If the preceding economics are reasonable, does it make economic sense not to conduct patent clearances and wait to defend challenges as they arise?

More frequency and experience conducting searches in a technology reduces the cost of subsequent searches and reviews and builds strategic knowledge about the competition.

In summary, although not every relevant third party patent will be asserted against you, ongoing prior art searching is economical if you are frequently being sued. This prior art searching effort may not be 100 percent perfect, and there is a learning curve, but over time the database that will be created by the effort will improve accuracy, reduce subsequent costs, and provide additional information and guidance for the strategy effort.

Does No Prior Knowledge Lead to Broader Inventions?

Some believe the ability of scientists to think creatively is adversely affected by their knowledge of what others have done or are doing, and thus they prefer that their scientists intentionally should be unaware of what others are thinking, so as not to be influenced or contaminated by other approaches to the problem. A contrary view from a patent strategy standpoint is that invention more often is incremental and not totally unrelated to prior approaches, and that patentable inventions are more likely to be identified and enhanced by thorough prior art knowledge. Furthermore it is also likely that by studying how others have attempted to solve a problem, scientists may identify a single flaw in what otherwise would be an excellent solution. "They almost got it, here's where they went wrong, or here's what they missed or didn't understand." It's not always the first inventor that is the most successful, it's often the second person's improvement that makes the idea work either more economically or for a slightly different purpose or just much better. It's also perfectly possible that another has found the best way, and, if so, then it's time to focus on how to compete with it or how to obtain a license instead of spending more money on R&D.

Furthermore, much of this searching and competitive analysis activity can be organized on an outsourced, ongoing continuous basis, managed remotely at a reasonable cost (compared to litigation defense). Information and preliminary analyses from the offline activity can be distributed back into the strategy process. Patent clearances and effective searching and database management is an important but larger topic for another time, and I will simply leave it this way for now: Digital search and semantic analysis and artificial intelligence tools will eventually make continuous searching a standard best practice and not an option, so it is best to start now even if imperfect. Those who learn to manage this process well will see significant cost savings, strategic advantages, and operational business efficiencies.

Improve What You Measure and Measure Only What Is Important

We know the maxim that you improve what you measure, and the corollary that it is important to measure the right things. In designing a patent strategy it is important to select a few key metrics to measure success. As important as it is to measure the right things, it is equally important to limit the number of variables measured, develop specific countermeasures as part of the initial measurement process, and execute changes quickly.

Since speed is an increasingly important variable, I believe the substantive elements to be measured should include tracking time. Patent strategies should not impede innovation or delay new product introduction, and the faster new inventions are identified, filed, and prosecuted to grant, the more effective the strategy. Also, the time needed to clear new products from infringement or identify them for license, the faster new products can be introduced. Measuring time from invention date to filing, and invention date to clearance opinion will focus attention on these two critical initial actions. Measuring time from filing to grant (including all continuing applications) also drives prosecution efficiency, lowers cost, and improves the effectiveness of enforcement. It also drives desirable, best practice quality patent preparation and prosecution activities, such as the use of examiner interviews, early comparative data, and declaration preparation and claim limitation.

It is important to focus on initial actions since errors up front will be more difficult to rectify than issues that come from later stages of a process. Also, rework equals time and money lost that could be avoided. While there are many variables in the complex patent process, if the measurement process becomes burdened by selecting too many measures to track, the process itself can result in excess resource deployment and bureaucracy and loss of speed. There is a balance, and rigorous prioritization is required. Certain metrics will have a bigger impact than others and obviously those that are directly related to the overall objective of the process should be evaluated before minor metrics, that either are dependent on other variables or have a minor impact on the objective.

Metrics: Selection

When I refer to metrics I am typically thinking of five or less metrics maximum. These metrics must focus on quality, speed, and ultimate results. By this I mean that they must be a combination of in-process metrics and result metrics. Each metric must be accurately measured. Ratios of certain metrics may be found to have combinatorial impact.

The development of appropriate metrics may take some trial and error and modification over time. Brainstorming around creative combinations (ratios) can often lead to surprising discoveries and can provide competitive advantage to your strategy. Using baseball as an analogy (apologies to those who don't like sports analogies or baseball itself), for many years players' hitting performance was measured solely by their batting average, the number of hits divided by the number of plate appearances. New metrics have been developed that focus on the frequency a player reaches base regardless of whether he gets a hit (on base percentage); similarly, the absolute number of runs batted in, a traditional measure for power hitters has been supplemented by a slugging percentage focusing on the frequency of extra base hits for the player. These and other statistics have been found useful for a team to best determine where in the lineup each player would have the greatest impact. Similar metrics have been developed for pitchers. In a patent strategy, context patent application filing production divided by pendency may be a useful metric for individual attorney performance, while profitability divided by pendency for each application filed may be a better result metric for strategic impact of a patent. The preceding metric combinations are presented solely for illustrative purpose and each strategy team should tailor the metrics to meet specific strategic objectives.

It is important that your metrics be maintained as confidential in the same manner as your strategy. Metrics must be quantified and be least subject to interpretation as possible.

When selecting the metrics to be used, the team should also define the frequency of data review and the specific actions that will be taken in response to the resulting metrics. Once the results are reviewed, the actions that will be required to be taken should be clear and be executed immediately. Taking the necessary time to decide on a course of action to address the results before the data is collected and analyzed will reduce the response time. There may even be a series of changes to be taken based on the extent of the departure from the desired objective and different responses for different metrics. If the objectives are easily and quickly met, the metrics selection and goal process was not rigorous enough to start with, and the goals need to be reset higher. For example, if a speed goal is to reduce the time from idea conception to granted patent by 50 percent from current state is reached in a year, then you should consider increasing that goal another 25 percent in the next six months. Push the process until new issues or barriers are created and then examine the new issues, make adjustments, and repeat the process.

The metrics should be consistent with and seek to drive certain desired individual performance and behaviors. Positive reinforcement results when those being

measured are being measured by the same metrics that drive their individual performance management goals. In the case of outside counsel, agreed-on metrics can
be used for incentive-based payments.

Management must be careful not to send mixed messages by the metrics selected
and make certain that the actions taken in response are constructive and doable. In
addition, management must pay heightened attention to any quality issues and other
unintended consequences that will require quick corrective action.

Quality: Validity

An effective patent strategy cannot be built on patents of questionable validity. A
strong foundation is required. The quality of each patent application, search, amendment, and response needs to be examined in terms of the ultimate validity of the
patent claims. It makes little sense to spend the time and effort to seek a patent if
the legal presumption of validity of a granted patent can be easily rebutted because
the patent has a fatal flaw. While it is not completely possible to predict which patents will become the most commercially valuable, it is nevertheless better practice to
assume that each patent application will be challenged and therefore each should be
created such that validity and claim scope will survive third-party and court scrutiny.
Doing a high quality job the first time is less expensive in the long run than trying to
remedy major deficiencies after they have occurred. Perfection may not be possible,
but it should be the goal. Patent applications should be reviewed against checklists
and by senior in-house counsel before filing to make certain that each is most likely
to withstand scrutiny. I am suggesting that resources be redirected from quantity to
quality. It is less costly and better strategically to have a smaller portfolio of quality
patents connected with business objectives than to have a larger portfolio of patents
of questionable validity not connected with specific business strategies. More is not
necessarily better, only better is necessarily better. High quality patents that are
granted promptly can have significant competitive deterrent value. Broad claims that
may read on unknown prior art are of significantly less value in the long run than
valid, narrower claims.

Prior art searching is not perfect, but every effort to improve pre-filing prior art
searches will be valuable to ultimate patent quality. Attention to the definition of key
terms, internal specification and claim consistency regarding terminology, ranges,
and supporting data must be focused on to maximize the quality of each patent
application. Overly complicated filing strategies, such as filing without a search or
examples, and using intentionally vague language and very broad claims is not, in
my opinion, the way to obtain a quality patent quickly. The costs of such a, file first
and define the invention later after a PTO search, approach is not cost-effective in the
long run, creates unnecessary file wrapper estoppel, and is not as likely to result in a
high quality patent. Such practices are ultimately self-defeating from strategic, cost,
and time perspectives. Doing it right the first time is always better than trying to
make it right later.

Offensive strategies may require the enforcement of patents. Accordingly,
if enforcement is a key offensive strategy, the team should consider metrics that
relate to successful enforcement at a minimum cost and time. For example, claim

construction may have a significant impact on litigation success. If claim language or claim scope is narrowly construed, validity may be upheld but infringement may be avoided. Similarly, if new prior art is uncovered during litigation that invalidates the asserted claims, or the patent is invalidated for 112 reasons, or if inequitable conduct be found, these findings should be part of the offensive strategy metrics and be fed back into the strategy process and metrics.

In addition to time, some other quality metrics are also useful, such as the number of pages of the patent specification, the number of claims, the frequency of section 112 and 102 rejections in first office actions, and the number of amendments, continuations, and appeals. All these can be tracked and used to drive down costs and increase speed. Whichever metrics you select, it is important that the metric itself represent some aspect of the strategy you are seeking to achieve. Too many metrics will have the opposite effect; resulting in overanalysis and delay, so it is important to minimize the number of metrics selected to those most important to the strategy.

Result Metrics

Finally, the financial contribution of new products and processes, especially gross profit, should be tracked for every product by patent by country. This will clearly show whether the patents are doing their intended job (e.g., excluding lower priced competitive alternatives) or not, over time.

Whether patents withstand challenges to their validity in reexamination, opposition, or litigation is a critical result metric but since not every patent is challenged, it cannot be the only result metric.

While quality and speed may be the most important in-process metric categories, production and cost are very important variables that need to factor into the metric selection.

The point here is not to list all the possible metrics to be selected from, but to encourage patent counsel and their staff to work together with R&D and business to select the metrics appropriate for the business objectives of each business or technology unit for which a strategy is developed. In this manner flexibility is maintained; one size does not fit all businesses.

Review and Communicate the Implementation of the Strategy

If the specific patent strategy is clear, research personnel and the patent attorneys will know what types of inventions are needed, and how they are expected to fit into the business strategy. Patent claims can be drafted by the attorneys to guide inventors toward the patentable inventions the company desires for the strategy. Inventions that do not relate to the strategy or have minor value to the strategy can be discontinued or given lower priority. The priority and expected contribution of each new invention can be assessed at the time it is identified according to the strategy. Setting the strategy up front can identify the countries where each type of new invention will be filed. By having a clearly defined patent strategy before research is undertaken, product clearance can be managed without adversely impacting product commercialization.

Patent Committees Become Obsolete

A clearly defined patent strategy eliminates the need for patent committee meetings to review each invention. No decisions are needed by such committees when a clear strategy exists, since the decision as to what is needed has already been made before the invention has been made.

If clear patent strategies exist, business management does not have to be brought into tactical patent management issues. Instead of serving as a gatekeeper at a patent committee meeting, management can participate in periodic, higher level patent strategy reviews to receive an update on current activities and to spend more time discussing the effectiveness of the strategy according to the metrics and making suggestions for additional actions—licensing, litigation, and collaboration. Since all the costs and financial contributions of each patent can be provided to management, strategic decisions instead of tactical decisions can be made; a better use of management's time.

Simplify Executive Communication

Executives do not need detailed information about the patent process. They want to know the status of the new intellectual property product or process. The strategy regarding each new product and process can be summarized in one slide, with enough detail to provide management with what it needs. The importance of simple, focused communication with management by both researchers and patent staff cannot be minimized. Meetings with management can focus on key issues and problems, and issues can be teed up properly for decisions to be made. If management wants more detail, patent and research can provide management with additional information, but my experience has taught me that executives typically don't want or need much additional detail. They want to know, whatever patent protection is being sought, what the status is of the patent strategy, how the metrics are working, where there are problems, if any, what the solutions and timing are, and whether additional resources are needed. What is "the ask," what decision do you need from them, why, what will it cost, how will they see progress, and when should such progress be seen?

Management can then participate in a review at the correct level, while permitting the patent staff and the researchers to focus more of their time and energy on what they do best.

Meetings can be minimized and made sharper if the preread information is simple and where problems and other issues needing resolution are highlighted beforehand. For example, a patent review meeting can focus on a single issue, even a tactical issue such as, how exactly do we plan to enforce this patent in China or India? The patent attorneys can describe the problem and identify a few possible approaches, and management can use the time at the review to evaluate the options and instruct the patent staff about what they would like them to do and how much time and money they can spend to accomplish this result.

Managing the R&D and Patent Pipeline

R&D is not an exact science; sometimes a solution to a problem can be solved perfectly within a short time and other times years of ongoing R&D will fail to solve the problem. Many companies have instituted what is commonly referred to as stage/gate processes for R&D progress review. As long as the stage/gate R&D process is intimately linked to the strategic deliverable and managed effectively to prevent projects from going on without end, a stage/gate process is a valuable management technique. I believe that with prior art search conducted before substantial effort starts on the R&D effort, false starts can be reduced and potentially blocking patents and patent applications can be identified early. A part of the stage/gate review should include the identification of potentially close patents and patent applications of third parties as well as those owned by the company itself.

By substantial research, I mean a point in time after conception but before resources are directed to evaluate and design a solution. The goal is not to limit creative new ideas but to manage them as part of the strategy in a way that eliminates rework or redesign at a later time. If the legal prior art review can take place simultaneously with the second stage (evaluation post idea conception), if the solution is found, a final legal review can be conducted and the product can move out of the R&D stage/gate process into manufacturing and sales more quickly than if clearance does not start until after a final product for sale has been identified.

Managing the R&D pipeline in this manner will also potentially identify third party patents that cover the new idea early and need to be considered for license or be designed around. Early identification will save time and cost.

Managing the Patent Staff

In-house patent attorneys can be identified as patent specialists and patent strategists. The patent specialists focus on the preparation and prosecution of patent applications, while the patent strategists focus on the business patent strategy and third party matters including licensing, acquisition, and litigation. The skill sets and personality profiles of patent attorneys can be used to match each person with these two functions. Some patent attorneys are highly skilled in the technology and R&D, and are highly productive patent drafters, prosecutors, and opinion writers who desire a structured and predictable work day. They desire and work best as patent specialists. Others are more suited to working more closely with business people and third party matters that may involve more travel and a less predictable work day. Patent specialists can participate in patent review meeting and strategy sessions, but the patent strategist would have the lead role during these meetings and reviews.

While I believe that all inexperienced in-house patent attorneys should start their careers as patent specialists, I am not suggesting that after this initial period there is a hierarchy between patent specialists and strategists. Some patent specialists may desire to spend their entire career as specialists, while others may want to become patent strategists. The career ladders for specialists and strategists having the same length of experience, but which do different types of work should be created equal, and both should be managed to increase their productivity and management expertise over time. During the first five years of their tenure, care should be taken during periodic performance or career reviews to determine which track the attorney aspires to and what additional skills or competencies may be needed to advance their career for that role. If all in-house patent attorneys gain experience initially as patent specialists, an attorney who becomes a strategist can easily opt back into a specialist role if he becomes disenchanted with being a strategist. Managing each in-house patent attorney to maximize individual performance is critical.

A manager wants to obtain the highest quality product and productivity from each person she manages. If a portion of the patent applications that are filed are drafted by outside counsel, quality and other guidelines can be developed and managed by senior in-house specialists. Familiarity with the prior art searches can be of significance in strategy development, and the specialists can be called on to assist the strategy team.

Small Companies and Individual Inventors

A new approach to patent strategy has been described mostly in terms of large companies with in-house attorney staff. Does this approach apply to smaller companies and individual inventors? Certainly smaller companies and individual inventors have less resources than large companies but that does not mean that certain key aspects of the new strategic approach cannot be highly beneficial to them. For example, filing a patent application on a new invention without knowledge of third party patents that could preclude the manufacture, use, or sale of that invention will create a false sense of security for the inventor. At some point after significant additional development or manufacturing resources are expended, the inventor will become aware of such third party patents. Is it not better for the inventor and his or her investors to know about such a potentially fatal situation before such resources are expended? Wouldn't an inventor want to know as much about the potential customers and competitors for the new product or process as early as possible either to identify potential customers for the product, develop useful formulations or modifications to the product for use by customers, or determine the price it should charge for the product based on competitor offerings?

Too often start-ups and individuals may be under the false impression that the filing of a patent application is all that is necessary to protect themselves from competition, but technology and the patent literature are dynamic. The work is not done on the filing of a patent application. A clear patent strategy will provide guidance for additional product or process development and improvements and knowledge of the dynamic prior art will be very useful to provide additional credibility to the business plan projections. Since a small company or individual may have resource or capital limitations, their patent strategy may be less comprehensive, but it should be commensurate with the scope of the business plan and available resources. To do less will likely end up costing more in the long run. It may be that the metrics selected are fewer and more qualitative than those of a company with a track record of commercialized patented and unpatented products, but some metrics will be useful to track progress and ensure that the results achieved match up with the business objectives. Proactive planning is always a more difficult concept for entrepreneurs and small companies, but the additional cost and risks of not conducting a proactive, clear written patent strategy are not warranted or cost justified.

Filing without a Search?

Filing patent applications without first conducting a prior art search is not likely to result in claim coverage as initially presented. Saving a few thousand dollars for the search and spending $10,000 or more on a patent application without a search is not a prudent cost or strategic decision. Those who claim that a search costs too much have not spent significant time evaluating presently available search techniques. The patentability search does not have to be of the same level of detail as a pre-litigation prior art search, but not doing any search and relying on the patent office to conduct the only search, leaves open the real possibility that the entire cost of preparing the application was for naught or that the scope of the claims that may be allowed is much narrower or limited than what was contemplated. This result can lead to significant disparities between the original business plan and the ultimate commercial result.

It does not matter whether the patent strategy utilizes outside counsel or in-house counsel. Outside counsel can perform the same function in developing a patent strategy for small companies and individuals as in-house staff can for larger companies. The key difference is the mindset: namely, that their role needs to focus as much on litigation avoidance as on patent procurement. A patent strategy that does not have defensive and offensive components is not in the best interest of any inventor who wants to be successful over time.

Prognosis for the Future

As all technology-based enterprises realize that their intellectual property protection is the critical component of their sustainable competitive advantage, management will demand, and chief patent counsels will develop, more detailed patent strategies. Chief patent counsel will tailor these patent strategies and review processes in accordance with financial and business objectives as previously discussed. Successful examples of the benefits of these strategies, while confidential to the enterprise, will be appreciated by management, and they will become accepted as a best practice. Patent operations will develop financial balance sheets similar to any operating business, and management will become more engaged in the value added by patent operations. Conventional reactive, internally focused, qualitative responses, and R&D driven patent reviews will be replaced by offensive and defensive patent strategies in all technology sectors, and these strategies will be used by law firms, small companies, and independent inventors as well as large corporations. Case studies of patent strategy, financial metrics and competitively oriented tactical actions may become part of business and law school curricula. As patent counsel become better at communicating these strategies to executive leadership and boards of directors, they may become more sought after as business leaders. Patent staff in large corporations will undergo changes reflecting the strategic and growing realization of the importance of the activity and internal patent staffs will likely expand.

Changes to worldwide patent laws and practices, along with more sophisticated analytical tools, will provide greater opportunities for businesses to evaluate and either challenge or collaborate with emerging competitive third party technologies earlier. Emerging technologies and new business models will continue to disrupt conventional practices and patent strategies will evolve to predict and respond to such disruptions faster.

Search technologies will continue to improve, and patent clearance procedures will become standard means for assessing risk. Litigation will continue to remain a high stakes option when parties are unable to reach business accords, but better information and financial analysis may lower the extent of litigation from its current level.

Conclusion

Patent strategies, R&D, patent operation, and management for the next decade should be reassessed. Companies employing traditional strategy models need to focus more externally and become faster and less bureaucractic. Companies following the new model need to reexamine their part in the patent arms race and begin to examine their underlying processes and their ability to continue doing the same thing in an environment of slower growth. All companies should have explicit and simple patent strategies linked to their business strategies, and the specific patent strategies must be linked to clear process metrics and resulting business financial objectives. Patent quality, speed, and cost control are key drivers for an effective patent strategy. Clear and explicit statements of the strategy and linkage to financial objectives can accelerate innovation and improve business and executive management buy-in to the patent strategy and effort. Patent strategy can utilize some of the traditional strategy best practices such as improved prior art searching and pre-commercialization patent clearances, and focus on application quality and early identification of relevant third party patents and applications, while everyone should thoroughly and regularly review improved information technology and offline techniques to improve speed and lower cost.

Patent strategies should focus on offense as well as defense by developing an external focus on customers and competitors. Internal bureaucracy and processes need to be streamlined to focus on quality, time, and cost. Strategy should focus on proactive actions, and move away from reactive and tactical issues.

Each patent should be thought of as being potentially of critical value; overall, the strategic focus should shift from quantity to quality. In-house patent specialists can lead the effort on patent quality. New business models, disruptive technologies and speed to market are important aspects of a patent strategy and customer and competitor patent analytics are critical to successful navigation. Internal processes should be refined so that litigation can be a strategic offensive weapon.

Notes

1. See also John Richards, "Controlling Patent Costs," in *Intellectual Property Operations and Implementation for the 21st Century Corporation*, (forthcoming).

2. See also Raymond DiPerna and Jack L. Hobaugh Jr., "When to Litigate: The Rise of the Trolls," in *Intellectual Property Strategies for the 21st Century Corporation*.

CHAPTER 7

Global Piracy and Financial Valuation of Intellectual Property Revisited

Threats, Challenges, and Responses

Robert Boyden Lamb
Stern School of Business, New York University
Randie Beth Rosen, Esq.[*]

D ubbed by the FBI to be the crime of the twenty-first century, intellectual property (IP) counterfeiting and piracy has no territorial boundaries, affecting mom and pop enterprises and multinational corporations alike, in industries as varied as pharmaceuticals, computer software, and luxury items.[1] This chapter explores the critical recent legal, financial, and policy developments that have occurred in this area since our first publication exploring it in 1997.[2] We also highlight the alarming new trends of cyber identity theft and cyber terrorism threats, the relationship between IP piracy revenue and international terrorism, and some of the effects that the emergence of new global economic players have produced for intellectual property protections and the freedom of the World Wide Web.

Google versus China: A Case Study for Censorship in the Context of Economic Might

The global economic meltdown of 2007 through 2009, caused in large part by the financial structured derivative securities debacle, has weakened traditional economic

---

[*] The co-authors of this chapter wish to gratefully thank and acknowledge the support and encouragement of Lanning Bryer, Esq. of the New York office of the law firm of Ladas & Parry LLP, as well as the invaluable and dedicated research assistance of Caroline Camp (LL.B., University College of London, England, and LL.M. in Intellectual Property from the Benjamin N. Cardozo School of Law, New York).

stalwarts such as the European Union and the United States. The breadth and growth of new and financially strong players, such as China, has changed the international economic IP climate, as well as the political and policy rules of the game, affecting the business plans and profits of multinational, as well as U.S. companies around the globe. The potential for the resultant intellectual property piracy, as well as the danger of censorship, is alarming and far-reaching.

In the fourth quarter of 2009, China leapt past Japan to officially become the world's second largest economy, after the United States, with a gross domestic product (GDP) of US$4.9 trillion. Assuming an annual growth rate of 4 percent or more than the United States, China's economy could surpass that of the United States within 30 years. On a purchasing power parity basis, it could outpace that of the United States by 2020.[3]

With such a rapidly expanding domestic market, Chinese domestic producers more easily achieve economies of scale. Combined with a rapid push on the part of the Chinese government to attract foreign direct investments and technology in order to modernize its infrastructure, the numerical results are staggering. Indeed, in 2007 alone, China spent nearly $46 billion on information technology (IT)—computers, peripherals, network equipment, packaged software, and IT services. That amount accounted for approximately 1.6 percent of its gross domestic product, supported in excess of 84,000 IT companies with more than 2,400,000 IT industry employees, and generated $3.5 billion in IT-related taxes.[4]

China's rapid financial expansion is not limited to domestic innovation and investment. In 2009, China was the second largest holder of U.S. Treasury debt, at US$755.4 billion, after Japan's $768.8 billion. This amount included substantial holdings in U.S. governmental agencies, such as Fannie Mae and Freddie Mac. This rapidly growing financial dependence on China has substantial potential for disastrous consequences for governmental policy as well as for U.S.-based businesses.[5] In fact, shortly after the U.S. decision to sell more arms to Taiwan, Chinese Major Gen. Luo Yuan stated to China's state-run *Outlook Weekly* magazine that China's "retaliation should not be restricted to merely military matters" but also should be "covering politics, military affairs, diplomacy and economics. . . . We could sanction them using economic means, such as dumping some U.S. government bonds."[6] Nor are U.S. businesses immune from the exercise of China's economic muscle and restrictive policies, as Google recently discovered.

In January, 2010, Google announced that its source code and the Gmail e-mail accounts belonging to human-rights activists and journalists located in China and abroad had been targeted as a way to censor and control access to content from anti-government human rights activists critical of Chinese authoritian policies. Up to 20 other companies, many of them technology providers, had also been affected. Several weeks later, a number of those online attacks had been traced to computers at Shanghai Jiaotong University and the Lanxiang Vocational School, the latter having long time close military connections. Apparently, the unauthorized access to Google's servers was initially gained by exploiting a security flaw in Microsoft's Internet Explorer web browser.[7]

Google has been simultaneously embroiled in a similar battle with Vietnam. On March 31, 2010, Google security engineers reported the presence of malicious spyware software attacking blogs critical of governmental policies. Neel Mehta, a Google engineer, stated that "Infected machines have been used both to spy on their owners" as well as to render inaccessible blogs and web sites containing anti-government content.[8]

In a March 22, 2010 interview for the *New York Times* blog, Google's co-founder, Sergey Brin, stated that due to "subtle and uncertain" negotiations with the Chinese government regarding its censorship and security concerns, Google had decided to reroute queries to its China-based search engine, google.cn, to the Honk Kong site of google.com.hk, where there was no censorship of web searches or political discussions. Mr. Brin declared that "The story's not over yet."[9] Not surprisingly, the Chinese government web filters soon thereafter began automatically to remove "politically sensitive" or "objectionable" material before it could reach Chinese-located user computers, thereby effectively enforcing China's authoritarian control. Google then abruptly canceled the China launch of its new Android[10] cellular smart phones.[11] Before that series of events, Google controlled approximately one-third of the Chinese search engine market, dominated by the Chinese giant Baidu. It is unclear what the effect will be on Google's overall advertising revenues, as the bulk of Google's estimated 2009 $300 million China revenues were from export-oriented companies.[12] Although Google continues to sell advertisements in China via its Hong Kong site, Google.hk, China's Baidu is projected to significantly profit from Google's mainland China departure, in terms of advertising revenue gain and further market penetration. After capturing more than 64 percent of China's Internet search market in the first quarter of 2010, Baidu expects its second quarter revenue to jump 67 percent to 70 percent, far outstripping investors' estimates.[13]

As retribution for Google's actions, the Chinese government appears to have quietly influenced companies to abandon their Google connections. The China-based Tianya.cn portal with an excess of 30 million registered users recently took full control of a social networking service previously jointly operated with Google.[14] China's Unicom also recently announced that it would no longer be using the Google search engine on its Android phones, substituting Microsoft's Bing search engine for it. When asked about the situation, Unicom's president tersely stated that, while his company works with "any company that abides by Chinese law," there was "no co-operation with Google currently."[15] Perhaps taking its cue from this conflict, at approximately the same time, Motorola also switched from Google to Bing as the default search provider on Google-powered Android phones within China, without stating whether the strategic alliance would be expanded to include other countries.[16]

Has there been any financial effect of this conflict for Google? By the end of the first quarter of 2010, Google's stock price had fallen 10 percent, compared to a rise in the Nasdaq Composite (COMPX) of almost 6 percent during the same time period. Google also had a price/earnings-to-growth (PEG) ratio of less than 1.0, suggesting a possibility that its conflict with China has produced at least a tangible short-term financial result for the company.[17] As Google's expansive search and advertising business depends so heavily on providing users with access to increasing amounts of digital content, it must continue to reach and expand into every corner of the globe, including China.[18]

A China without Google also raises the larger concern of rampant criminal industrial espionage, targeting intellectual property from American technology firms and other multinational companies. For example, the fate of Google China's Top100.cn, a free, advertising-revenue supported music portal service, which partners with 14 independent labels as well as four global music companies, is unclear. By offering an alternative to unlicensed copying, Top100.cn was reducing China's wide-spread music piracy. As aptly stated by Duncan Clark, managing director of technology market research firm BDA China Ltd., "Without that, are we back to 'Piracy wins'? Piracy thrives because of censorship."[19]

Nor are China's censorship battles limited to Google. The Yahoo! e-mail accounts of several journalists and activists were recently rendered inaccessible, prompting concerns of compromised accounts and personal safety. Andrew Jacobs of the Beijing Office of the *New York Times*, for example, said in a March 31, 2010 interview that his Yahoo! Plus e-mail account had somehow been set to automatically forward to another unknown account.[20] Stay tuned, the saga continues.

Identity Theft, Cyber Gangs, and Alarming National Security Concerns

Two of the most substantial threats to electronic commerce and national security in the twenty-first century are identity theft and cyber terrorism. Steven Chabinsky, deputy assistant director of the FBI's Cyber Division, recently warned that many "cyber-adversaries" of the United States have the ability to access virtually any computer system they target, and thereby "challenge our country's very existence."[21] Indeed, cybercrime, whether of state secrets, private intellectual property, or personal identifying consumer information, is becoming a very profitable big business, increasingly connected with violent organized crime syndicates.[22]

In 2008, more than 9.3 million individuals were victims of identity theft in the United States. With databases of personally identifiable data increasingly becoming prime targets of computer hackers, identity thieves, and members of organized and sophisticated criminal operations, identity theft is a substantial threat to national economic stability and security.[23] A 2006 survey conducted by the U.S. Federal Trade Commission (FTC) estimated that 8.3 million American consumers, or 3.7 percent of the adult population, became victims of identify theft[24] in the prior year. By 2010, the FTC ranked identity theft as the number one consumer complaint.[25] Previous methods of stealing personal identification or financial information through theft of wallets, purses, banking and credit card statements, or by hacking into online payment systems, are now being supplemented by a wide variety of new techniques, including: dumpster diving,[26] phishing,[27] and pretexting.[28]

No one is immune from becoming a victim of identity theft and cybercrime. In 2009, powerful Federal Reserve Board Chairman Ben Bernanke and his wife became victims of a sophisticated identity fraud ring, after an unknown assailant stole his wife's purse. The perpetrators affected more than 10 major financial institutions, and stole in excess of $2 million, before they were finally identified and apprehended.[29]

The breadth and international scope of the identity theft computer attacks are staggering, and are rapidly becoming increasingly sophisticated. In 2008, for example, Russian hackers hijacked American identities, using the social networking sites of Facebook and Twitter, and refashioned Microsoft software to attack Georgian government web sites during the war between Russia and Georgia.[30] Russian cyber gangs also actively promote web sites selling counterfeit antivirus software, pharmaceuticals, and luxury products.[31] Elsewhere abroad, Chinese hackers recently allegedly stole Indian national security information as well as 1,500 e-mails from the Dalai Lama's office and Tibetan exiles.[32] Finally, French hackers were arrested last fall for an extortion attempt on the management team of the high travel and lifestyle network, ASMALLWORLD.net. The perpetrators claimed they had accessed the member database, and demanded payment of approximately $1 million in exchange for their silence.[33]

The danger of cybercrime is also increasing on a national level, raising alarming economic and security concerns. As intellectual property is now frequently stored in digital form, industrial espionage that exploits weak cyber security simultaneously dilutes investment in innovation while subsidizing the research and development efforts of foreign competitors. National economic strength and technological leadership across industries are thereby significantly compromised.[34]

In May, 2007, Mike McConnell, the former Director of National Intelligence, allegedly told President Bush that "if the 9/11 attackers had chosen computers instead of airplanes as their weapons and had waged a massive assault on a U.S. bank, the economic consequences would have been 'an order of magnitude greater' than those caused by the physical attack on the World Trade Center."[35] Indeed, in May 2009, President Obama labeled cyber attacks "one of the most serious economic and national security challenges" that the United States currently faces.[36] The prior month, the President had created a cabinet level IP cyber security czar position, appointing Melissa Hathaway as its acting director. Officially known as a Cyber Security Coordinator, this position reports to the National Security and National Economic Councils and Department of Homeland Security, manages the U.S. government's interagency cyber security process, and makes recommendations for the nation's cyber policies and standards.[37] By August, however, Hathaway had resigned her post, allegedly for personal reasons.[38] In December 2009, Howard Schmidt, former chief security executive at Microsoft, was finally appointed to fill this critical position.[39]

In a January 26, 2010, interview with reporters from *USA Today*, Secretary of Homeland Security Janet Napolitano stated that "We're seeing increasing attempts to use the Internet not only to connect different people as a facilitator of terrorist groups but also as a possible means of attack. . . . It can be a denial of service attack. . . . It can be fraud or misinformation. It can be the theft of valuable defense information or of intellectual property."[40] The following month, Attorney General Eric Holder announced the formation of a new intellectual property task force within the agency, as part of its effort to combat IP theft and protect national security. The task force plans to work closely with state, federal, and international law enforcement agencies, including the Department of Homeland Security and the Federal Communications Commission, focusing on the links between IP piracy and international organized crime.[41]

There have also been several recent Congressional attempts to stem the threat of identity theft and cyber terrorism, with mixed results. In February, 2007, Senator Bayh introduced S. 522, "The Intellectual Property Enforcement Act of 2007," which attempted to strengthen civil and criminal penalties for copyright and trademark infringement. It would also establish an Intellectual Property Enforcement Network (IPEN), composed of deputy secretaries of the departments of Homeland Security,

Justice, Treasury, Commerce, and State, as well as from the Office of the Attorney General, all charged with spearheading international antipiracy efforts.[42]

No action was taken on the bill after its November, 2007, Senate judiciary hearings.[43] Instead, Senators Leahy and Specter introduced S. 3325, "Prioritizing Resources and Organization for Intellectual Property Act of 2008," which was signed into law the subsequent year.[44] The IPEN is now paired with a designated intellectual property enforcement coordinator, an advisor reporting directly to the President. S. 3325 also amended the Federal Trademark Act[45] to double statutory damages in counterfeiting cases, and eliminated the Copyright Act's[46] registration requirements for civil infringement acts.[47]

Possibly the most ambitious legislative attempt to date to tackle cyber terrorism is the "Cyber Security Act of 2009," S. 773, co-authored and introduced by Senators Rockefeller and Snowe on April 1, 2009.[48] The bill seeks to secure cyber communications and to maintain effective cyber security defenses against disruption by directing the President to establish or designate a cyber security advisory panel and to develop and implement a comprehensive national cyber security strategy, and by requiring the National Institute of Standards and Technology (NIST) to assist with this ambitious endeavor. Should this bill become law, both the Director of National Intelligence and the Secretary of Commerce will be required to submit to Congress an annual report on cyber security threats to, and the vulnerabilities of, critical national information, communication, and data network infrastructure.[49] The bill designates the Department of Commerce to serve as a clearinghouse of cyber security threat and vulnerability information.[50] Although the proposed legislation purports to "bolster market incentives for innovation and excellence in cyber security professional training, products and services,"[51] it also establishes a detailed audit procedure to measure milestones.

Critics of S. 773, such as the Business Software Alliance (BSA) trade organization, however, have expressed concern that the proposed legislation's focus on compliance may hinder the development and use of private sector security innovations.[52] Conscious of the delicate balancing of interests and priorities involved, Senator Rockefeller, as keynote speaker for the BSA's April 29, 2010, cyber security conference, stated that "To secure our country from cyber attacks, we must have shared responsibility between the government and the private sector. . . . As our economy continues to struggle, it has become clearer than ever that economic security is national security. The two are inseparable and we must confront them as one."[53] Time will tell if this is the right approach to achieve such a lofty and critical goal.

Are Proceeds from Counterfeited Goods Funding International Terrorism?

The recessionary times of the last few years have seen a marked increase in counterfeiting and intellectual property piracy on an unprecedented global scale. It is estimated that since 1982, the global trade in illegitimate goods has increased from $5.5 billion to approximately $600 billion annually. Approximately 5 to 7 percent of the world trade is estimated to be in counterfeit goods.[54] Those amounts and numbers of intellectual property piracy and business losses continued to climb during the global economic meltdown of 2008 and 2009, especially in the software market. The worldwide PC software piracy rate rose from 38 percent to 41 percent. The retail value of unlicensed software—representing revenue losses to software companies—broke the $50 billion level for the first time in 2008, with worldwide losses growing by 11 percent to $53 billion, aided substantially by high piracy rate countries such as Brazil, China, and Russia.[55]

At the same time, international trademark filings under the World Intellectual Property Organization's (WIPO) Madrid System for the International Registration of Marks (the Madrid system) dropped by 16 percent in 2009. WIPO's director general, Francis Gurry, recently stated that "Historically, we know that demand for intellectual property rights declines in periods of recession. These downturns are more strongly and rapidly felt in the area of trademarks which are more closely tied to market conditions."[56]

One of the priority watch countries of the International Federation of the Phonographic Industries (IFPI), Brazil sports a piracy industry estimated to be in excess of $1 billion. A recently commissioned report by the U.S.-Brazil Business Council found that 6 out of every 10 music discs or cassettes sold in Brazil are pirate copies. Between 2005 and 2009, Brazilian music sales fell by more than 40 percent, thereby substantially impacting the local music industry.[57] The future does not look good. The report concluded that piracy in Brazil was heavily controlled by organized crime, highlighting Taiwan's role as a leading manufacturer of pirate CDs. In fact, one of the individuals targeted by the specially formed Congressional Investigatory Commission on Piracy (CPI) was Law Kin Chong, charged with allegedly attempting to bribe the chairman of the Congress committee.[58]

Since joining the World Trade Organization (WTO), China has strengthened its legal framework and amended its IPR and related laws and regulations to comply with the WTO Agreement on Trade-Related Aspect of Intellectual Property Rights (TRIPs). Despite stronger statutory protection, however, China continues to be a haven for counterfeiters and pirates. According to one copyright industry association, China's estimated piracy rate of 90 percent remains one of the highest in the world, causing U.S. companies to lose over $1 billion in legitimate business each year. On average, 20 percent of all consumer products in the Chinese market are counterfeit. If a product sells, it is likely to be illegally duplicated, with pirates and counterfeiters targeting both foreign and domestic companies.[59]

Remarkably, Chinese software piracy had reportedly skyrocketed to a staggering 82 percent in 2008![60] Furthermore, gathering information about the Chinese pirated media market remains difficult. The Chinese government prohibits foreign investigators to conduct studies in China, and statistics made available by the government are generally insufficient.[61]

Since the dissolution of the Soviet Union in 1991, the Russian Federation has redrafted its intellectual property laws to align them more closely with WIPO and TRIPs standards, and the Madrid Protocol, in an attempt to encourage foreign investment.[62] Russian law governing intellectual property, however, provides for the priority of national legislation over foreign legislation. As such, it recognizes only intellectual property that is directly specified in the Civil Code and international treaties to which Russia is a party.[63] Additionally, the first-come-first-served approach to Internet domain name availability in the RU zone has resulted in an explosion of cyber squatting, causing substantial concern and uncertainty for international trade-mark brand name owners.[64] Russia also boasts one of the highest intellectual prop-erty piracy and counterfeiting rates in the world.[65] Russia recently ranked 143 out of 179 countries on Transparency International's "2007 Corruption Perceptions In-dex."[66] Widespread bribery and collusion with police and lawmakers enables piracy there to continue largely uninterrupted.[67] During a November, 2003, interna-tional conference, the president of the Russian chamber of commerce estimated that "the shadow market of commodities in Russia amounts to 30 to 40 percent of the country's GDP."[68]

In fact, the FBI has predicted that counterfeiting and piracy will become "the crime of the 21st century,"[69] and the results thus far have been deadly! The Food and Drug Administration estimates that counterfeit drug sales account for 10 percent of all drugs sold in the United States. The Federal Aviation Administration estimates that 2 percent of the 26 million airline parts (approximately 520,000 parts) installed each year are counterfeit. In 2003, the Motor and Equipment Manufacturers Association cited safety violations due to the following counterfeit auto parts: brake linings made of compressed grass, sawdust, or cardboard; transmission fluid composed of dyed cheap oil; and oil filters using rags for the filter element.[70]

On February 26, 2003, in a joint operation between federal and local law enforcement, six people were charged in conjunction with an investigation of the illegal distribution of Symantec and Microsoft software, with more than $9 million worth of counterfeit software seized. The defendants were believed to have distrib-uted thousands of copies of counterfeit software and received an estimated $15 mil-lion over two years.[71]

Of greatest concern, however, is the increasing body of evidence connecting the ill-gotten proceeds from intellectual property piracy to acts of international ter-rorism. As far back as 1995, New York's Joint Terrorist Task Force believed that high-level players controlling a counterfeit T-shirt ring were using the proceeds to support terrorist groups such as the one that bombed the World Trade Center in 1993.[72] Indeed, in February 2000, an individual selling pirated music CDs, Sega, Sony, and Nintendo game discs to fund a Hezbollah-related organization was arrested for piracy and suspected fundraising for Hezbollah. Among the discs recovered were those containing images and short films of terrorist attacks and interviews with suicide bombers.[73] According to New York City Police Commis-sioner Raymond Kelly, the sale of pirated CDs was responsible for funding the 2004 bombing of a Madrid train—an incident of terror that resulted in the deaths of 191 people and injuries to countless more.[74] In the Congressional findings section for S. 522 (The Intellectual Property Rights Enforcement Act of 2007), specific find-ings were made that terrorist groups have used the funds generated from their sale of counterfeit goods and other intellectual property theft to finance their acts of terrorism.[75]

During his July 16, 2003 testimony before the U.S. House Committee on Interna-tional Relations, Ronald K. Noble, secretary general of Interpol, an organization responsible for coordinating information among law enforcement and security ser-vices in 181 countries, stated that "The link between organized crime groups and counterfeit goods is well established, but Interpol is sounding the alarm that intellec-tual property piracy crime is becoming the preferred method of funding a number of terrorist groups. There has been enough connection drawn already between orga-nized crime and intellectual property crime that we can no longer think of it as a victimless crime."[76] Trade in illegal products also ranged from counterfeit cigarette trafficking by Northern Ireland paramilitary groups to trade in fake computer soft-ware, shoes, and clothes connected to Chechen separatist terrorists in Kosovo.[77] In Kosovo alone, profits from traffic in counterfeit goods were estimated at $500,000 to $700,000 U.S. dollars per month.[78] The subsequent year, Interpol seized $1.2 million worth of counterfeit German brake pads. An ensuing investigation revealed that pro-ceeds were earmarked for Hezbollah supporters.[79]

Al-Qaeda has also been linked to the counterfeit industry through the sales of fake perfumes and shampoos.[80] In 2003, Danish customs intercepted a container filled with counterfeit shampoos, creams, colognes, and perfume allegedly sent from the United Arab Emirates by a member of al-Qaeda.[81] In fact, in 2005, John Newton, an Interpol officer specializing in intellectual property crime, stated that "North African radical fundamentalist groups in Europe, Al-Qaeda and Hezbollah all derive income from counterfeiting. This crime has the potential to become the preferred source of funding for terrorists."[82]

A 2009 RAND Corporation study, "Film Piracy, Organized Crime and Terror-ism,"[83] commissioned by the U.S. Motion Picture Association, found additional evi-dence of a connection between intellectual property piracy proceeds and international terrorist activities. It highlighted the case of two illegal CD plants in Pakistan that were being financed by Dawood Ibrahim, an Indian Muslim whom the U.S. Treasury Department had previously named a "specially designated global terrorist." Mr. Ibrahim has long been considered India's godfather of criminal gangs from Bangkok to Dubai, running the D-Company criminal gang since the 1980s. D Company has vertically integrated throughout the Indian film industry, forging a pirate monopoly over competitors in an effort to control the master copies of pirated Bollywood films.[84] Mr. Ibrahim is also wanted in India for the 1993 Bombay Exchange (Mumbai) bombings, and is known to have financed the activities of Lash-kar-e-Tayyiba (Army of the Righteous), a group the United States designated as a foreign terrorist organization in October 2001. The U.S. State Department believes that Ibrahim has found a common cause with al-Qaeda, sharing his smuggling routes with the terrorist network and funding attacks by Islamic extremists aimed at destabi-lizing the Indian government.[85]

A major roadblock to deterrence, however, is that counterfeiting on the inter-national level is often more profitable than drug trafficking, with one estimate placing the street value of a kilo of pirated CDs at 3,000 euros, while a kilo of can-nabis resin (marijuana) had a worth of approximately 1,000 euros."[86] In terms of the levels of risk involved, the penalties are generally low for selling counterfeit products as compared to those for illegal narcotic sales. Thus, the profit/risk ratio of counterfeiting is attractive to terrorist groups, as they can extract an illicit profit at each stage of the counterfeiting process from production to sale, thereby max-imizing their returns.[87] The International Anti-Counterfeiting Coalition (IACC) 2005 "White Paper" study echoed these findings of large profits available at low risks.[88] Consequently, new forms of policy, business, and technology solutions have be-gun to evolve in an attempt to combat the rising tide of international intellectual property theft.

Government and Corporate Responses to International Intellectual Property Theft: Nanotechnology to the Rescue?

As global levels of intellectual property piracy and criminal activity rise rapidly to unprecedented rates, it is becoming clear that a combined approach of government intervention and legislation, as well as innovative business responses to counterfeiters, and new technologies is desperately needed.[89] Governments are increasing customs enforcement and border patrols, and enacting new and targeted legislation. Businesses are exploring public awareness campaigns aimed at educating their customer bases, suppliers, and manufacturers to understand that intellectual property theft is not a victimless crime. At the same time, some corporate leaders are directly competing with pirates through the use of a variety of innovative processes, including faster product release, underpricing pirates, and improving efficiency in sales and distribution channels. In the technology area, nanotechnology, which is the study of matter on an atomic and molecular scale, offers significant promise for both law enforcement and businesses.

Government intervention is necessary to combat the organized crime elements involved in the global counterfeiting market, for as previously discussed, civil penalties are often viewed by intellectual property pirates and thieves as a "cost of doing business."[90] Additionally, the private sector is not equipped to deal with organized crime, nor is it industry's function to pursue and punish criminal activity.[91]

No longer viewing intellectual property as a victimless crime, the United States has recently enacted two pieces of legislation to further criminalize intellectual property crimes in the copyright arena: the "No Electronic Theft (NET) Act" and "The Money Laundering Act."[92] The NET Act,[93] which was promulgated in December 2007, modified criminal copyright statutes by doing away with showing any financial harm for those making illegal reproduction or distribution of their copyrighted materials. The Money Laundering statute, 18 U.S.C. § 1956, defines money laundering as "knowingly conducting a financial transaction affecting interstate commerce with the proceeds of some form of unlawful activity, designed in whole or in part to conceal or disguise the nature, location, source, ownership or control of the proceeds of the unlawful activity." Specified unlawful activities include the receipt of proceeds from trafficking in counterfeit goods or goods infringing on copyright ownership, thereby making this statute a powerful tool for law enforcement investigation and prosecution.[94]

European legislative approaches to combat rising intellectual property piracy have focused on confiscation, conviction-based laws, and extradition as enforcement mechanisms. The "United Nations Convention against Transnational Organized Crime,"[95] for example, assists signatories in streamlining the extradition process for those convicted of money laundering and other serious crimes affecting member nations. The treaty also encourages international law enforcement cooperation, technical assistance, and enforcement training. The "UK Proceeds of Crime Act 2002"[96] creates an asset recovery agency and "provides for confiscation orders in relation to persons who benefit from criminal conduct and for restraint orders to prohibit dealing with property." Upon identification, the assets obtained from counterfeiting activities can be seized, with bank accounts containing ill-gotten proceeds frozen.

Perhaps the most ambitious and wide-reaching attempt to date for establishing international standards on intellectual property rights enforcement has been the draft multinational agreement known as "The Anti-Counterfeiting Trade Agreement," (ACTA).[97] If enacted, ACTA will establish a new international institution apart from the World Trade Organization (WTO), the World Intellectual Property Organization (WIPO), and the United Nations. ACTA's stated components are "enforcement practices," "international cooperation," and a "legal framework for enforcement of intellectual property rights."

On April 20, 2010, an official version of the most recent draft treaty was leaked for public review before adoption by its initial participants.[98] The draft included a provision requiring Internet Service Providers ("ISPs") to provide information about suspected copyright infringers without first obtaining a warrant. While this would enable the record industry to sue music sharers more easily in overseas markets, critics, such as the Free Software Foundation, believe that this ACTA provision would ultimately create "a culture of surveillance and suspicion."[99]

Internet service providers would also be liable for infringing content disseminated on their networks in the new ACTA provision. Many technology providers are concerned that this lack of immunity may ultimately affect online companies hosting user-generated content.[100] Ed Black, president and CEO of the Computer and Communications Industry Association (CCIA), a trade group that includes Google, recently stated that "This agreement exports the strong penalties found in U.S. copyright law without also exporting those essential protections like fair use that provide much-needed balance."[101] The European Telecommunications Network Operators' Association also believes that "concerns regarding liability provisions remain."[102] The next and ninth round of ACTA negotiations is scheduled to take place in Geneva in early June, 2010. While more than 30 countries have been actively involved with the ACTA negotiation process, countries with high piracy such as China, Brazil, and Russia have not yet participated, thereby throwing into doubt ACTA's true long-term effectiveness.

Although great strides in the war against intellectual property piracy have been made by domestic and international legislation, it remains clear that businesses must take innovative additional steps, including monitoring and implementation of new technologies, if they are to remain ahead of the "pirate technology curve." During the May, 2004 meeting of the First Global Congress on Combating Counterfeiting held in Belgium, senior law enforcement, government, and business officials recommended a four part approach to combating global counterfeiting and intellectual property piracy: sanctions and other means of enforcing IPRs (intellectual property rights), administrative cooperation among the competent authorities, use of technical devices, and monitoring by the private sector.[103]

Technical devices designed to protect and authenticate products and services vary across industries, but generally include labels printed with invisible ink, radio frequency identification, product watermarking, and security hologram imprints.[104] Other ways to trace infringing sources more effectively are through the use of optical devices, chip cards, magnetic systems, biometric codes, and microscopic labels. Although technical devices act as a filter for the most obvious counterfeit or pirated goods, they generally do not defeat the more highly organized, well funded, and sophisticated infringers.[105] Thus, a blended approach using private sector monitoring techniques and strategic alliances is often the most effective battle plan in the war against piracy.

On an individual business or industry level, monitoring often consists of observing market trends and suspicious activities in order to detect acts of counterfeiting and piracy.[106] Other very effective non-technological solutions include implementing educational programs for online advertisers, financial payment services providers, and the general public to spread awareness of how IP piracy adversely affects everyone's interests.[107] Producers are also realizing that it is critical to tighten quality controls and supervision over every link of their supply and distribution chains, from supplier packing and machinery manufacturers, to distributors, retailers, and end user customers. Having consistent, well-documented distribution, labeling, and packaging standards, as well as the ability to trace every shipment's destination, lessens the opportunity for counterfeiters to insert fake products or divert products from the legitimate supply chain.[108] For the same reasons, manufacturers should attempt to establish standard procedures for customers' disposing of returned or damaged products to prevent their reentry into commerce.[109] In this way, legitimate producers can more successfully stem the short-term monetary losses and larger losses of brand integrity, which inevitably occur when customers lose confidence in the product names they have previously trusted as indicators of uniform quality and reliability.[110]

The different product sales and pricing strategies of Time Warner and Microsoft in piracy-ridden China illustrate how crucial it is for businesses to thoroughly analyze and adapt approaches to individual markets and consumers. Although Time Warner lowered its DVD prices to $3 apiece when it attempted to penetrate the Chinese consumer market several years ago, the majority of pirated DVDs there sold for less than a dollar each. Thus, even though Time Warner had lowered its prices far below American rates, the DVDs still remained uncompetitive. As there was no compelling reason for Chinese consumers to purchase the DVDs, Time Warner sustained significant losses, and was forced to retreat from that market. Microsoft, on the other hand, in addition to lowering prices, emphasized its product stability and security through its computer retailers there. The result? Chinese buyers began paying the higher prices for the legitimate and secure software, and Microsoft's market presence there is expanding. Microsoft has also wisely enlisted the Chinese local governmental agencies: Shanghai's tax bureau is requiring businesses to use legitimate Microsoft software on all computers in order to receive official tax receipts. Businesses can also buy the software, loaded on legitimate Hewlett Packard computers, directly from the tax bureau itself and deduct the cost all at once, rather than amortizing it as they would if they bought elsewhere.[111] Microsoft has also experienced considerable success in India, by emphasizing a consumer education and voluntary piracy reporting program in that market.[112]

International trade associations have proven to be effective advocates in lobbying governments to amend or enact legislation to provide more protection to intellectual property owners, and by assisting customs and border patrols in their enforcement activities. Three of the largest and most successful organizations have been The Coalition for Intellectual Property Rights, the International Chamber of Commerce and its Business Action to Stop Counterfeiting and Piracy (BASCAP) program,[113] and the Business Software Alliance (BSA).

The Coalition for Intellectual Property Rights (CIPR)[114] is an international development organization and think tank dedicated to increasing awareness of intellectual property as a tool for economic growth, particularly in developing countries. Offering policy and training workshops, the Coalition focuses on establishing constituencies of policy makers, business leaders, and judicial stakeholders in the developing world who view intellectual property rights protection as a tool for sustainable economic growth. In 2005, CIPR offered two training programs in Russia, jointly sponsored with the United States Patent and Trademark Office, entitled "U.S.–Russia Federation Workshop on the Border Enforcement of Intellectual Property Rights."[115]

Founded in 1978, the International Anti Counterfeiting Coalition (IACC) is a Washington, D.C. based nonprofit organization devoted solely to combating global intellectual property counterfeiting and piracy. With representatives from multinational pharmaceutical, software, and luxury good producers as members, IACC has been able to promote numerous regulations and directives. It recently published on its web site the publication "Business Action to Stop Counterfeiting and Piracy" (BASCAP), intended to provide businesses with practical steps to protect their IP-based products and services, and reduce the risk of unknowingly using counterfeit materials or infringing on other companies' IP rights. Those suggestions included establishing a corporate policy to conduct operations in compliance with IP laws and related best practices, acquiring only licensed copies of copyright and trademark protected material, taking reasonable steps to identify and protect the company's own IP, and designating a senior director or manager whose responsibility would include overseeing and enforcing the company's IP policies. Other recommendations of note were stressing employee, supplier, and customer education, and establishing adequate audit and security provisions to protect company intellectual property.

BASCAP also included a member completed "Survey Findings Report."[116] One of the most significant findings was that firms concentrated in mass production (e.g., music) considered spending on IP-related public education to be a far more effective means of combating counterfeiting and piracy, as compared to those firms concentrating on batch production or fast-moving consumer goods.

The Business Software Alliance (BSA)[117] focuses on protecting the software industry on a worldwide basis, and boasts members from more than 80 countries. BSA stresses educating corporations and consumers about the legal and digital security risks associated with unlicensed and pirated software use. For example, BSA recommends members use a basic software asset management (SAM) program that ensures that every computer in a company has been loaded only with licensed software, and that the software has been registered properly with the appropriate manufacturer. The BSA web site provides free tools and resources to help companies appraise software assets by conducting audits of their software licenses, and acquiring any licenses needed to be in full compliance.

Nanotechnology, however, may offer the brightest future promise for both businesses and law enforcement in the war against intellectual property piracy. Nanotechnology is a fundamental materials technology where structures are created and manipulated at the molecular level of 1to100 nanometers.[118] At that tiny size, properties of materials lend themselves to formulas of compounds and data that are so complex they are often impossible or incredibly time-consuming to replicate. As such, they offer a range of practical applications, from detecting counterfeiting in packaging to detecting it in pharmaceutical products.[119] For example, a laser nanometrology probe allows naturally occurring microscopic surface imperfections in products to be scanned and recorded at the nano level during production at the factory, thereby allowing an identity code to be rapidly built up from the surface of any item. "The code is unique, robust, cannot be copied or controllably modified and can be used for authentication or tracking," said Russell Cowburn, professor of nanotechnology at Imperial College, London. "You could say we are recording the 'DNA' of the package."[120]

The potential for nanotechnology solutions to consumer good and industrial product counterfeiting is astounding. Electrically coded radio tags, for example, can now link back to the legitimate manufacturer to detect point of sale falsification. Known as "organic and printed Radio Frequency Identification (RFID) tags," they include radio chips printed on thin and flexible foils, authenticity checks via cell phones equipped with radio frequency capability, and "smart packaging" that can link a product with its legitimate manufacturer and delivery chain at the point of sale as a substitute for standard optical bar codes, which are easily reproduced by counterfeiters.[121] Perhaps the most exciting and promising of the new technologies are the organic light emitting diodes (OLEDs) which provide automatic proof of opening a package or container. Unopened, an OLED surface in the package will light up when scanned. Once opened, a warning signal will appear. "A large problem with falsified products," Jani-Mikael Kuusisto, Business Development Manager at VTT Technical Research Center of Finland, explains, "is fraudulent re-use of opened packages."[122]

With counterfeit drug sales estimated to reach $75 billion by the end of 2010, pharmaceutical producers experience extensive monetary losses and brand value erosion by the fake inferior products, in addition to increased dangers to patient safety. Nanoencryption provides a new option for distinguishing between genuine and counterfeit goods by the use of RFID tags, invisible to the naked eye, to identify products at the package and individual tablet level. The authentication process would not destroy the tablet, which could be used as evidence of counterfeiting in a subsequent civil or criminal action.[123]

Nor is the value of nanotechnology limited to the private sector. Michigan State University recently launched the nation's first comprehensive research program studying product counterfeiting, known as the Anti-Counterfeiting and Product Protection Program (A-CAPP). Working directly with experts from the criminal justice, food safety, international business, engineering, public health, and communications areas, A-CAPP has created a database of U.S. product counterfeiting dating back to 2000. It also implements training programs for health and consumer goods protection though biosensors for the FBI as well as the departments of Homeland Security, Customs, and Border Protection.[124]

Nanotechnology is also being evaluated by researchers in an effort to protect the U.S. paper currency against counterfeiting attempts. Instead of being printed on paper, currency may be transformed to a very thin, high-tech machine. Another option being explored is manipulating molecules located within the bill itself, so that the texture and shape of the bill itself can be changed, and dynamic images inserted, thereby rendering the bill nearly impossible to illegally replicate.[125]

Indeed, the best way of characterizing the future promise of nanotechnology was stated by Professor Cowburn, who aptly characterized it as a "step change in the arms race between the good and bad guys. . . . It's the first time that anyone has tried to break the fundamental attack system."[126] In short, nanotechnology has the potential to transform business production systems, government operations, and virtually every aspect of our daily lives, as well as fight intellectual property pirates.

Conclusion

Intellectual property piracy is rampant and extends far beyond the borders of the original perpetrating countries. Its ill-gotten proceeds now have been traced to international terrorism funding, and the threat of cyber identity theft and cyber attacks is escalating on a daily basis. Although imperfect, international multinational treaties such as ACTA, as well as strategic alliances, trade associations, and individual business internal monitoring and compliance programs are all positive developments. Yet, as we pointed out in our previous chapter on this subject,[127] we stand at a critical juncture in the rapidly changing global economic climate. The financial ramifications of IP piracy deeply affect the analysis, and represent a critical test of the true scope and viability of individual nations' laws, as well as global treaties, to protect intellectual property rights.

Even multinational giant corporations such as Microsoft and Time Warner are struggling to compete with pirate businesses with substantially lower costs and higher profit margins, particularly in counties such as China, Brazil, and Russia, where IP piracy is skyrocketing. Legitimate producers' strategies of lowering product prices, creating customer loyalty and incentive programs, and launching education drives have had varying degrees of success. New technologies, such as nanotechnology, offer significant promise, yet are not panaceas. For example, questions such as whether, and to what extent, nano particles may interact with and affect our environment, still remain unanswered with this novel and unknown technology. The final outcome of this global economic struggle remains uncertain, yet it is a fight that governments and legitimate manufacturers cannot afford to lose.[128]

Notes

1. See also Joseph C. Gioconda and Joseph M. Forgione, "Controlling Counterfeiting," in *Intellectual Property Operations and Implementation for the 21st Century Corporation*, (forthcoming).

2. Robert Boyden Lamb and Randie Beth Rosen, "The New Role of Intellectual Property in Commercial Transactions," in Cumulative Supplement, *Global Piracy And Financial Valuation of Intellectual Property*, ed. Lanning Bryer and Melvin Simensky (New York: John Wiley & Sons, 1997).

3. Purchasing Power Parity (PPP) for measurement and comparison purposes, assumes similar costs for identical products and services located within different countries. Choong Khuat Hock, "China Surpasses Japan as the 2nd Largest World Economy," *The Star Online*, Business section, March 1, 2010.

4. "The Economic Benefits of Lowering PC Software Piracy," IDC Piracy Impact Study, Business Software Alliance, January, 2008, www.bsa.org.

5. David M. Dickson, "China Holds More U.S. Debt Than Indicated," www.washingtontimes.com, March 2, 2010.

6. Ibid.

7. John Markoff and David Barboza, "2 China Schools Said to Be Tied to Online Attacks," *New York Times,* Technology section, February 18, 2010.

8. James Hookway, "Cyberattacks Hit Vietnamese Dissident Blogs," *Wall Street Journal,* Asia Technology, March 31, 2010.

9. Steve Lohr, "Interview: Sergey Brin on Google's China Move," *New York Times* Bits blog, March 22, 2010.

10. An Android smart phone is a mobile device's operating system that uses a modified Linux code system that provides advanced capabilities, with PC-like functionality. See http://code.google.com/android/.

11. Murad Haddad, "Google Cancels Phone Launches in China," Business 2.0 Press, January 19, 2010.

12. Joe McDonald, "China without Google: 'a lose-lose scenario,'" *Lubbock Online*, March 16, 2010.

13. *"Google Exit Appears to Benefit Top China Rival, Baidu," New York Times,* Technology section (Reuters), April 29, 2010.

14. Alexa Olesen, "Google deals in doubt amid conflict with China's government," *Mercury News,* March 24, 2010.

15. Darren Murph, "China Unicom Won't Use Google's Search Engine on Android Phones," www.engadget.com, March 25, 2010.

16. Nick Mokey, "Motorola Abandons Google for Bing on Android Phones," *Digital Trends*, www.digitaltrends.com, March 11, 2010.

17. Dan Burrows, "Google's China Conflict Escalates, Making Shares A Screaming Good Buy," *Daily Finance*, March 22, 2010.

18. Rachel Donadio, "Larger Threat Is Seen in Google Case," *New York Times,* February 24, 2010.

19. Joe McDonald, "China without Google: 'a lose-lose scenario'" Lubbock Online, March 16, 2010.

20. Lucy Hornby and Alexei Oreskovic, "Some Yahoo e-mail accounts hacked in China, Taiwan," *Ottawa Citizen*, April 1, 2010.

21. Patrick Thibodeau, "Cyberattacks an 'existential threat' to U.S., FBI says," *Computerworld*, March 24, 2010.

22. Ibid.

23. Section 2, Congressional Findings, of S.1490 (Personal Data Privacy and Security Act of 2009), Senate Reports 111-10.

24. "Identity theft involves the fraudulent misuse of another's personal identifying information, usually to commit credit card, mortgage, or check fraud. Personal identifying information, such as name, Social Security number, date of birth, and bank account number is extremely valuable to an identity thief. With relatively little effort, an identity thief can use this information to take over existing credit accounts, create new accounts in the victim's name or even evade law enforcement after the commission of a violent crime." Federal Bureau of Investigation,

"Financial Crimes Report to the Public, Fiscal Year 2006," www.fbi.gov/publications/financial/fcs_report2006/financial_crime_2006.htm#Identity.

25. Federal Trade Commission, "Fighting Back About Identity Theft," 2010, www.ftc.gov/bcp/edu/microsites/idtheft/consumers/about-identity-theft.html.

26. Ibid. Dumpster diving is rummaging through the victim's trash to obtain papers with identifying information.

27. Ibid. With phishing, the perpetrator impersonates financial institutions via spam or pop-up messages to the victim.

28. Ibid. Pretexting employs false pretenses in an attempt to obtain personal information from financial institutions, telephone companies, and other sources.

29. Michael Isakoff, "Bernanke Victimized by Identity Fraud Ring," *Newsweek*, August 25, 2009.

30. Siobhan Gorman, "Hackers Stole IDs for Attacks," *Wall Street Journal*, August 17, 2009.

31. "Russian hackers: Cyber Gangs Infect 'More and More Computers,'" *Huffington Post*, September 25, 2009.

32. "Hackers Hit Dalai Lama, India," AP News, April 26, 2010, www.stuff.co.nz/technology/3553166/Hackers-hit-Dalai-Lama-India.

33. Danny Shea, "French Hackers Arrested in ASMALLWORLD Extortion Attempt," *Huffington Post*, September 17, 2009.

34. Sec. 2(2) of the Congressional Findings of the "Cybersecurity Act of 2009."

35. Ibid., Sec. 2(10).

36. Barack Obama, "Remarks by the President on Securing Our Nation's Cyber Infrastructure" (Washington, DC, May 29, 2009), www.whitehouse.gov/thelpressloffice/Remarks-by-the-President-on-Securing-Our-Nations-Cyber-Infrastructure/.

37. White House Executive Report, "Cyberspace Policy Review: Assuring a Trusted and Resilient Information and Communications Infrastructure," April 2009, www.whitehouse.gov/assets/documents/Cyberspace_Policy_Review_final.pdf.

38. Siobhan Gorman, "Security Cyber Czar Steps Down," *Wall Street Journal*, August 4, 2009, http://online.wsj.com/article/SB124932480886002237.html.

39. Sebastian Rotella, "Howard Schmidt named cyber-security czar," *Los Angeles Times*, December 23, 2009.

40. Susan Page, Thomas Frank, and Kevin Johnson, "What's our next terror threat?" *USA Today*, January 26, 2010, www.usatoday.com/NEWS/usaedition/2010-01-26-1Aterrordecade20_CV_U.htm.

41. "Justice Department Announces New Intellectual Property Task Force," The International Counterfeiting Coalition, February 12, 2010, www.iacc.org.

42. Chloe Albanesius, "House Bill Would Create Govt. Copyright Czar," *PC Magazine*, December 6, 2007.

43. Its companion bill in the House of Representatives, H.R. 3578, met with a similar fate.

44. Public Law 110-403, signed by the President on October 13, 2008. It is also known as the Enforcement of Intellectual Property Rights Act of 2008.

45. The Lanham Act, 15 U.S.C., §§1051 et. seq. See §1128 ("National Intellectual Property Law Enforcement Coordination Council") and §1129 ("Cyberpiracy Protections for Individuals": providing a safe harbor for copyright registrations containing inaccurate information).

46. The Copyright Act of 1976, as amended, 17 U.S.C. §§ 101 et. seq.

47. Mark Hachman, "Bill Asks Attorney General to Investigate Piracy," *PC Magazine*, July 24, 2008, www.pcmag.com/article2/0,2817,2326397,00.asp.

48. As of Dec. 19, 2010, S. 773: Cybersecurity Act of 2009 placed on Senate legislative calendar No. 707.

49. See the text of S. 773, http://thomas.loc.gov/cgi-bin/query/z?c111:S.773.

50. S. 778, Companion legislation aimed at creating a national cybersecurity advisor position, is currently pending before the Senate Committee on Homeland Security and Governmental Affairs. See also Elizabeth Montalbano, "Cybersecurity Bill Passes Senate Committee," *Information Week*, March 24, 2010.

51. See Sections 101 and 204 of S. 773, http://thomas.loc.gov/cgi-bin/query/z?c111:S.773:; see also Senator Jay Rockefeller, press release, March 25, 2010, http://rockefeller.senate.gov.

52. "Rockefeller/Snowe Demonstrate Strong Partnership with Private Sector in Crafting Cybersecurity Bill, but Work Remains to Address Specific Industry Technology Concerns," March 24, 2010, www.bsa.org.

53. Jay Rockefeller, press release, April 29, 2010, http://rockefeller.senate.gov.

54. "Get Real: The Truth About Counterfeiting," International Anti-Counterfeiting Coalition (IACC), 2010, www.iacc.org/counterfeiting/counterfeiting.php.

55. "Sixth Annual BSA and IDC Global Software Piracy Study," Business Software Alliance (BSA), 2008, http://global.bsa.org/globalpiracy2008/index.html.

56. "Global Financial Crisis Hits International Trademark Filings in 2009," WIPO, March 18, 2010, www.wipo.int/portal/en/news/2010/article_0009.html.

57. "Massive Piracy Industry in Brazil," BBC News, June 30, 2004, http://news.bbc.co.uk/2/hi/entertainment/3854261.stm.

58. Ibid.

59. China's trademark law was first adopted in 1982 and subsequently revised in 1993 and 2001. The new trademark law went into effect in October 2001, with implementing regulations taking effect on September 15, 2002, extending registration to collective marks, certification marks, and three-dimensional symbols, as required by TRIPs (the Trade Related Aspects of Intellectual Property Rights) of the WTO. "Protecting Your Intellectual Property Rights (IPR) in China: A Practical Guide for U.S. Companies," U.S. Department of Commerce International Trade Administration, January 2003, www.mac.doc.gov/China/Docs/businessguides/IntellectualPropertyRights.htm.

60. "Sixth Annual BSA and IDC Global Software Piracy Study," Business Software Alliance, 2008, http://global.bsa.org/globalpiracy2008/index.html.

61. Rogier Creemers, "The Effects of WTO Case DS.362 on Audiovisual Media Piracy in China" (July 16, 2009), *2009 European Intellectual Property Review*, Forthcoming.

62. See Part IV of the Civil Code of the Russian Federation, and the Law of the Russian Federation #3520-1 on Trademarks, Service Marks and Appellations of Origin of Goods, of September 23, 1992 (with changes and amendments introduced by the Federal Law # 166-FL on December 11, 2002, and entering into force on December 27, 2002).

63. See Clause 1231 of the Russian Civil Code. See also Victor Naumov and Anastasia Amosova, "Providers Liability," Innovation and Technology Issue 88, *AmCham News* (November 2009), 26.

64. Russian-American Chamber of Commerce in the USA, "Legal Protection of Intellectual Property," 2010, www.russianamericanchamber.com/en/business/legal/protection.htm.

65. "The Economic Impact of Counterfeiting and Piracy," OECD, 2006, www.iccwbo.org/uploadedFiles/BASCAP/(/OECD-FullReport.pdf.

66. "2007 Corruption Perceptions Index," Transparency International, September 29, 2008, www.transparency.org/policy_research/surveys_indices/cpi/2007.

67. "Film Piracy, Organized Crime and Terrorism," RAND, 2009, www.rand.org/pubs/monographs/2009/RAND_MG742.pdf.

68. See "Shadow Goods Market in Russia Makes Up 30–40% of GDP," Interfax News Agency, business report, November 13, 2003, and Hedi Nasheri, "Addressing Global Scope of IP Law," a research report submitted to the U.S. Department of Justice, January 2005, Document No. 208384, subsequently published as Hedieh Nasheri, *Addressing the Global Scope of Intellectual Property Crimes and Policy Initiatives in Combating Piracy*," ed. Jay S. Albanese (New Brunswick: Transaction Publishers, 2007, 2009).

69. Opening speech by Jean-René Fourtou, BASCAP meeting, November 26, 2004, ICC HQ, "Business Action to Stop Counterfeiting and Piracy," www.internationalcourtofarbitration.biz/id2249/index.html.

70. "Get Real: The Truth About Counterfeiting," IACC, 2010, www.iacc.org/counterfeiting/counterfeiting.php.

71. John G. Malcolm, Federal Document Clearing House, Congressional testimony, "The Internet, and Intellectual Property Committee on the House Judiciary, Copyright Piracy and Links to Crime and Terrorism," (March 13 2003), discussing the case of *United States v. Ke Pei Ma, et al.* (This unreported case was prosecuted by attorneys in the CHIP Unit in the Eastern District of New York.)

72. Roslyn A Mazer, "From T-Shirts to Terrorism: That Fake Nike Swoosh May Be Helping to Fund Bin Laden's Network," *New York Times*, September 30, 2001, B.02.

73. "The links between intellectual property crime and terrorist financing," Public testimony of Ronald K. Noble, Secretary General of Interpol Before the U.S. House Committee on International Relations One Hundred and Eighth Congress, July 16, 2003.

74. "Counterfeit goods are linked to terror groups," *International Herald Tribune*, February 12, 2007, www.iht.com/articles/2007/02/12/business/fake.php.

75. See findings 8 and 9 of S.522, "Intellectual Property Rights Enforcement Act," September 2007.

76. Ronald K. Noble, public testimony.

77. David Johnston, "Threats and Responses, the Money Trail," *New York Times*, Section A, p. 11, Column 2, July 16, 2003.

78. Ronald K. Noble public testimony.

79. Zachary Pollinger, "Counterfeit Goods and Their Potential Financing of International Terrorism." *Michigan Journal of Business* 1, no. 1 (January 2008), http://michiganjb.org/issues/1/article4.pdf.

80. See the International Anti-Counterfeiting Coalition web site, www.iacc.org.

81. "Al-Qaeda, Militants Turn to Crime to Fund Terrorism," *USA Today*, August 12, 2004, www.usatoday.com/news/world/2004-08-12-alqaeda-crime_x.htm.

82. Jon Ungoed-Thomas, "Designer Fakes 'are funding Al-Qaeda,'" *The Sunday Times*, March 20, 2005, www.timesonline.co.uk/tol/news/uk/article432410.ece.

83. "Film Piracy, Organized Crime and Terrorism," RAND, 2009, www.rand.org/pubs/monographs/2009/RAND_MG742.pdf.

84. Jeremy White, "With Pirated DVDs, U.S. Troops Unwittingly Fund Terrorism," *Huffington Post*, March 16, 2010, www.huffingtonpost.com/jeremy-white/are-us-troops-unwittingly_ b_501347.html.

85. Brooks Boliek, "Interpol Links Piracy To Terrorism Funding," *BillboardBiz*, June 10, 2004, www.allbusiness.com/retail-trade/miscellaneous-retail-retail-stores-not/4368051-1.html.

86. "La Contrefac̦on de CD Plus Rentable que le Trafic de Hasch," *Marianne*, 10th–16th December 2001.

87. "The links between intellectual property crime and terrorist financing," Public testimony of Ronald K. Noble, Secretary General of Interpol before the U.S. House Committee on International Relations. One hundred and eighth Congress, July 16 2003.

88. This paper was first released in June 2003 and was entitled "International/Global Intellectual Property Theft: Links to Terrorism and Terrorist Organizations"; it was updated and re-released in January 2005 as "The Negative Consequences of International Intellectual Property Theft: Economic Harm, Threats to the Public Health and Safety, and Links to Organized Crime and Terrorist Organizations," www.iacc.org/resources/IACC_WhitePaper .pdf.

89. See also David Rikkers, "Working with Government," in *Intellectual Property Operations and Implementation for the 21st Century Corporation*, (forthcoming).

90. C. Carr, J. Morton, and J. Furniss, "The Economic Espionage Act: Bear Trap or Mouse Trap?" *Texas Intellectual Property Law Journal* 8, 2000.

91. Nasheri, Hedi, "Addressing Global Scope of IP Law."

92. See L. Hsieh, J. McCarthy and E. Monkus, "Intellectual Property Crimes," American Criminal Law Review 35 (1998) and Hedi Nasheri, "Addressing Global Scope of IP Law."

93. No Electronic Theft (NET) Act of 1997, Pub. L. No. 105-147, 111 Stat. 2678 (1997).

94. See 18 U.S.C. § 1956(c)(7)(D) (2000 and Supp. 2001) (amended to insert section 1030, relating to computer fraud and abuse) and Hedi Nasheri, "Addressing Global Scope of IP Law."

95. Adopted by General Assembly resolution 55/25 on November 15, 2000, and entered into force on September 29, 2003.

96. PoCA 2002, Chapter 29, enacted on July 24, 2002.

97. See also en.wikipedia.org/wiki/Anti-Counterfeiting_Trade_Agreement.

98. See http://trade.ec.europa.eu/doclib/docs/2010/april/tradoc_146029.pdf. See also Jason Mick, (2010-04-21). "ACTA Draft: DRM Bypassing, Thought-Crime are Illegal, P2P Engine Development is Criminal," April 21, 2010, www.dailytech.com/ACTA+Draft+DRM+ Bypassing+ThoughtCrime+are+Illegal+P2P+Engine+Development+is+Criminal/article 18183.htm.

99. See the Free Software Foundation, "Speak Out against ACTA," www.fsf.org/campaigns/ acta/.

100. See Joelle Tessler, "Tech Companies Fear Implications of Trade Pact," Associated Press, April 20, 2010. www.google.com/hostednews/ap/article/ALeqM5jluxfDDkLXHU27Qbh RSTu_dmFS0AD9F6IM8O0.

101. Paul Mueller, "Counterfeiting Treaty, Now Public, Confirms Critics' Fears," *PCWorld*, April 21, 2010, www.pcworld.com/article/194698/counterfeiting_treaty_now_public_ confirms_critics_fears.html.

102. Ibid.

103. Interview conducted by author with Wolfgang Starein, Director, World Intellectual Property Organization, Geneva, Switzerland (2004). See also Hedi Nasheri, "Addressing Global Scope of IP Law," 92.

104. Kshitij Sharma, "Choosing the Right Anti-Counterfeiting Measures," IP Media Group: *World Trademark* Review, March 17, 2010, www.iam-magazine.com/reports/Detail.aspx? g=c07e6c17-8582-4901-a97b-7b00f26b48e5.

105. See Article 11 of the WIPO Copyright Treaty and Article 18 of the WIPO Performances and Phonograms Treaty. Both treaties were adopted by the Diplomatic Conference on Certain Copyright and Neighboring Rights Questions, which was convened under the auspices of WIPO in Geneva on December 20, 1996. See also Hedi Nasheri, "Addressing Global Scope of IP Law."

106. Hedi Nasheri, "Addressing Global Scope of IP Law."

107. Vilches, Jose, "RIAA, MPAA and Others Outline Anti-Piracy Plan," Tech Spot, April 16, 2010, www.techspot.com/news/38622-RIAA-MPAA-and-others-outline-antipiracy-plan.html.

108. Chris Catto-Smith, "Nanotechnology Is One Way to Combat the Counterfeit Supply Chain," *Nanowerk News*, June 1, 2007.

109. Kshitij Sharma, "Choosing the Right Anti-Counterfeiting Measures."

110. Chris Catto-Smith, "Nanotechnology Is One Way."

111. Shaun Rein, "How to Deal with Piracy in China" *Forbes,* October 15, 2009, www .forbes.com/2009/10/15/china-piracy-counterfeiting-leadership-managing-infringement .html.

112. "Microsoft Launches Consumer Education to Avert Piracy," Copyright United News of India, December 4, 2009, www.thefreelibrary.com.

113. See www.iccwbo.org.

114. See www.cipr.org:IP rights and www.cipr.org/activities/index.htm.

115. Ibid.

116. "Survey Findings Report," Global Survey on Counterfeiting and Piracy, BASCAP, January 29, 2007, 15–16 (Appendix 5, Table 2a), www.iccwbo.org/uploadedFiles/BASCAP/Pages/BAS-CAP%20Survey_%20Final%20Report_29%20January07.pdf.

117. See www.bsa.org and www.bsa.org/country/Tools%20and%20Resources.aspx.

118. Jeff Wacker, "Three Waves of Nanotechnology," HP Enterprise Services, January 14, 2008, http://h10134.www1.hp.com/news/features/4242/.

119. Mark Row, "Nanotechnology Offers Law Enforcement Tools to Fight Counterfeiting and Piracy," International News Services, March 1, 2007, www.internationalnewsservices .com/articles/36-archive/10868-nanotechnology-offers-law-enforcement-tools-to-fight-counterfeiting-and-piracy.

120. Ibid.

121. "Organic and Printed Electronics to Counter Product Piracy," March 17, 2010, www .nanotech-now.com/news.cgi?story_id=37279.

122. Ibid.

123. Laurie N.Jacques, "Nanotechnology: A New Weapon in the Battle Against Counterfeit Goods," Nanotechnology Law Report, June 1, 2007, www.nanolawreport.com/2007/06/ articles/nanotechnology-a-new-weapon-in-the-battle-against-counterfeit-goods/.

124. Alton Parrish, "Crime of the 21st Century is Counterfeiting, says FBI, Michigan State Opens First Anti-Counterfeiting Research and Training Program," *Nano Patents and Innovations*, February 9, 2010, http://nanopatentsandinnovations.blogspot.com/2010/02/crime-of-21st-century-is-counterfeiting.html.

125. Adam Davidson, "Nanotechnology Seen as Answer to Counterfeiters," NPR, February 27, 2007, www.npr.org/templates/story/story.php?storyId=7615643.

126. Mark Row, "Nanotechnology Offers Law Enforcement Tools."

127. Robert Boyden Lamb, and Randie Beth Rosen, *The New Role of Intellectual Property in Commercial Transactions*.

CHAPTER 8

When to Litigate: Rise of the Trolls

Raymond DiPerna
Ladas & Parry LLP

Jack Hobaugh[*]
Blank Rome LLP

There exists a class of patent holders who do not practice their patented invention. Nonpracticing patent holders are also referred to by many as patent trolls, or in short, simply trolls. To some, the term *troll* evokes an emotional response because the term is seen as unfairly disparaging—conjuring up an image of a medieval creature jumping out of nowhere, demanding a costly fare to allow passage. For the purposes of this chapter, we will refer to an entity that holds and enforces a patent without practicing the patent by the neutral term, nonpracticing entity (NPE). We do not render a verdict here as to whether NPEs are good or bad for society. The focus of this chapter is primarily to provide context and discuss the legal options available to a company for defending against an NPE. Many of the concepts would also apply toward a practicing competitor. Our goal is to help you and your company make a sound business decision based on prudent legal options and an awareness of the scope of the NPE issue.

Let's start with a brief hypothetical. Suppose your company has a great new product or service—for the purposes of this chapter we'll call it product X. Product X is about to be released, or has already been released, to great reviews. You, your staff, or your outside counsel have already done the homework in an attempt to identify any potential land mines that may interfere with the manufacture or sale of Product X. Those potential land mines would include issued patents or patents that are about to be issued to competitors or to an NPE that might read on your new Product X. An analysis has been completed determining whether your product would infringe a particular patent. A business decision has been made to move forward based on either a determination that there would likely be no infringement or that the risk of being

---

[*] The views expressed are those of the authors and not necessarily those of Blank Rome LLP or Ladas & Parry LLP.

called to task would be worth it. That analysis and decision-making process is fairly straightforward because those patents are on your radar screen. But there are other categories of potential land mines. One such category would be those patents that are still under the confidential veil of the United States Patent and Trademark Office (PTO) because they have not yet issued, nor have they been published by the PTO. Yet another category would be those patent applications that were published only to become abandoned and then revived at a later date, perhaps years later. Making this even more difficult is the notion that if a patent or published application is not held by your direct competitor, it may not be on your radar.

The bottom line is that you will never be able to tell your CEO with 100 percent confidence that a patent will not emerge that will not read on Product X. For the purposes of this discussion, we assume that just such a patent has emerged—or if not a patent that reads on Product X, a patent that is at least potentially dangerous as being close enough to be brought as a nonfrivolous infringement claim. We will further assume that this patent is being asserted against your company by an NPE. In the end, the action or nonaction you take will be a business decision. This chapter addresses those areas of analysis necessary to make that business decision.

What Is a Non-Practicing Entity?

As the Internet rapidly expanded during the mid to late 1990s, gaining increasing popularity and fostering significant commercial growth, a group of new Internet-based companies took form. These companies became known as dot-coms, and were characterized by doing most of their business on the Internet, usually through a web site having a top-level domain name ending in ".com," short for "commercial." For a time a number of dot-com companies enjoyed greatly rising stock valuations and a rapid ascent to success; however, much of the euphoria and good fortune eventually began to dissipate, and, starting in 1999 and continuing into the early 2000s, the so-called dot-com bubble burst.

In the aftermath of the burst of the dot-com bubble, many dot-coms went bankrupt, and their intellectual property rights came onto the market. The big corporations for the most part failed to get into the act of buying up these rights and so fell prey to entrepreneurs who did act. Such entrepreneurs mostly took the form of a relatively new kind of business entity that became more and more prevalent during this time period. This kind of business entity had a peculiar business model: purchasing patents from others and using licensing and the threat of litigation to realize monetary value from those patents, with no intention of ever manufacturing any product. This kind of business entity, and variations thereof, quickly became known as patent trolls.

The term *patent troll* was coined in the late 1990s by Peter Detkin, who was then the assistant general counsel of Intel Corp. During that time period, Intel found itself under heavy aggression from patent infringement lawsuits. Detkin initially labeled such plaintiffs "patent extortionists." However, as told by Detkin in 2001: "We were sued for libel for the use of the term 'patent extortionists' so I came up with 'patent trolls.'"[1] Detkin defined a patent troll as "somebody who tries to make a lot of money off a patent that they are not practicing and have no intention of practicing and in most cases never practiced."[2] Accordingly, rather than attempting to commercialize the patented invention, these kinds of business entities sought to generate income through aggressive licensing and litigation of their patent portfolios.

Although the term patent troll began to gain widespread usage, many people, including commentators, judges, and patent lawyers, quickly resisted using that term, as it was—and still is—often seen as being unfairly disparaging to the kinds of business entities that would qualify under one interpretation or another of the term. Patent trolls have been designated with various monikers over the years, such as:

- Nonpracticing entity, or NPE
- Patent aggregator
- Patent marketer[3]
- Nonmanufacturing entity or nonmanufacturing patentee
- Patent dealer[4]
- Patent enforcer or patent enforcement specialist[5]
- Patent pirates
- Patent litigation firm

As noted at the beginning of this chapter, the term nonpracticing entity or NPE is used herein.

Precisely what defines an NPE varies. There is no singular definition; rather, there are a number of factors typically exhibited by NPEs. In one respect, NPEs are seen as "one of a class of patent owners who do not provide end products or services themselves, but who do demand royalties as a price for authorizing the work of others."[6] An NPE often has no significant assets other than patents and has attorneys as its most significant employees. NPEs could include: (1) individual inventors or patent owners who do not make a product but seek to assert their patents against large corporations; (2) small think tanks who exist to think up ideas for inventions, patent them, and then assert or license them; (3) companies that seek solely to acquire patents for the purpose of asserting them and enforcing them in the courts if necessary; (4) universities and other academic institutions; (5) government research organizations; and (6) contract research companies. However, even some companies that do manufacture products nevertheless adopt a "patent factory" approach and acquire patents covering products they are *not* manufacturing. Also, it should be noted that some entities do attempt to commercialize their patented inventions, but fail for various reasons, such as lack of funding.

Critics of NPEs typically view such entities as opportunists who, rather than attempting to practice the patented invention, have acquired the patent "on the cheap" in order to exploit the rights under the patent, exclusively for financial gain. The effect, critics argue, is to do harm by forcing threatened companies to invest in licensing rather than research and development, thereby stifling innovation. Another complaint is that NPEs attempt to enforce patents that are generally of questionable validity, spawning unnecessary litigation and tying up the legal system with lawsuits that are without merit.

Supporters, on the other hand, see NPEs as providing a valuable function in the patent system, in that NPEs create a market for intellectual property (IP) rights, which can be inherently difficult to value. The rise of patent auctions and the growth of Ocean Tomo LLC, an IP brokerage,[7] provide evidence for the value of a market for

IP rights, one that did not exist before the rise of NPEs. Supporters argue that establishing a market value for patents causes patents to become more liquid, which in turn allows inventors to more readily be compensated for their patents. Additional capital for inventors helps reward inventors for their efforts and provides a source of revenue leading to new innovation and more patents by the inventors.[8] It is also argued that the actions of NPEs stir further innovation and competition by prompting threatened companies to decide to design around the technology at issue. Moreover, it is argued, the greater the value of a patented invention, the greater the incentive for others to innovate in the particular technology area.

Supporters also see NPEs as being an important weapon for use by small inventors against powerful corporations, helping prevent such corporations from free riding; the rationale is that NPEs afford inventors leverage in licensing negotiations by providing the sizeable amount of capital that is needed to create a serious threat of litigation.[9]

Regardless of how one views NPEs and their role in the patent system, the fact remains that NPEs exist and pose a potentially serious threat to corporations, a threat that corporations must be aware of and must be prepared to deal with. This chapter lays out strategies for doing so.

Why Do You Believe Your Company May Be at Risk?

One key to being aware of potential threats to your company from NPEs is to be vigilant as to the activity occurring in your industry. While companies often attempt to monitor the patent filings, publications, and issuances of their competitors, it can be more difficult to monitor patents acquired by NPEs. However, one action your company can take is to watch for any problems your competitors may be having with NPEs. This can be done by keeping abreast of patent litigation in your industry or area of technology, since patent litigation that others in your field are involved in could be a harbinger of potential problems to your company posed by NPEs.

One technique sometimes practiced by companies is defensive patent aggregation. This technique consists of acquiring patents from inventors and from patent holders to prevent those patents from falling into the hands of NPEs. In fact, there are entities that exist solely to provide this service.

If an NPE has requested a meeting, or has inquired as to whether your company has any interest in licensing a patented technology that the NPE owns, then clearly by that point you should be aware that a patent exists that could potentially be asserted against you. The way such behavior from the NPE typically is initiated is that the NPE will often approach a company with a letter inviting a discussion as to whether the company infringes a particular patent or patents in the NPE's portfolio. The company will be asked to accept a license fee at that time or face the unenviable prospect of litigation down the road.

Often an NPE will go even further, requesting product material to determine infringement, sending a letter that meets the notice requirement of 35 U.S.C. § 287 accusing a company of infringement, or actually filing an infringement lawsuit. If a patent is indeed identified as potentially being troublesome to your company, you should without delay initiate the process of analyzing the patent to determine its scope, whether it may cover your product, and whether it may be invalid.

What Are Your Defenses?

An assessment of possible defenses is an essential step in determining whether to litigate. The first question to ask is: Does my product infringe? Perhaps that question has already been asked, and outside counsel has already created an opinion paper as to whether your product infringes the patent. If so and the opinion paper was objective and dispositive on the subject of infringement, such work may not need to be redone. However, if the opinion paper was written for the sole purpose of avoiding willful infringement, the opinion paper may not actually be that helpful in determining a realistic litigation outcome. For the purposes of this chapter, we are assuming that such an opinion paper does not exist.

The best defense to an infringement claim is to be able to confidently state that your product does not infringe the patent. Of course, a public statement of non-infringement may be different from what the corporation realistically believes. Therefore, for these purposes, we are not talking about what is portrayed to the public, to the patent holder, and to the court but what the reality is as can best be determined. The first step is gathering all the pertinent materials for deciding the likelihood of infringement. Those materials include the issued patent, the file prosecution history (also called the file wrapper), and a team of knowledgeable attorneys and subject matter experts.

For a finding of infringement, the patent holder must prove that every element of a single claim is found in your product. First, however, any ambiguous claim elements must be construed. The patent and file history will be considered to be "intrinsic" evidence in any future construction. Such construction is normally provided by court order after full briefing by both parties and a Markman hearing. Usually, at least some of the claim terms are argued to be ambiguous and offered to the court for construction. If a plain meaning for the term exists, the court will usually accept that plain meaning. However, if no such plain meaning exists, the court will first look to the intrinsic evidence found in the patent application specification, claims, and file history and will then look to outside information, known as extrinsic evidence. The bottom line is that intrinsic evidence trumps "extrinsic" evidence. And file history intrinsic evidence carries less weight than the claims and specification intrinsic evidence. Normally, the patent can be found on Google/Patents or on the PTO web site. Further, the file history may be available for downloading through the PTO Patent Application Image Retrieval (PAIR) web site. In the event that the file history is not available on PAIR, it can be ordered through a service provider.

The next step is to build a claim chart. This may seem like an overwhelming task, especially if you are staring at 50 or more claims. The good news is that we only need to look at the independent claims, that is, those claims that do not refer to any other claim. The independent claims are typically circled in the patent and copied to the claim chart. The claim chart should be composed of five columns: Claim, Language, Terms and Constructions, Support for Construction, and Position. The Claim column is the number of the claim. The Language column contains the elements of a section of the claim. The Terms and Constructions column contains each element of the Language column broken out by element. Along with each broken-out element is the proposed construction, or "plain and ordinary meaning." Plain and ordinary meaning is simply another way of stating that the term does not have to be construed because it is not ambiguous. The Support for Construction column contains the location of the support for each proposed construction. Finally, the Position column is the argument for why your product does not infringe under the proposed construction.

Now that we have our columns with claim elements broken out, we can read the patent and the file history to determine the realistic construction of each element. This must be a conservative and objective approach. This is not the time to argue a claim construction that is unrealistic and has little chance of being adopted by the court. Also keep in mind that this is attorney work product and should always be marked as such. Do not do anything that would make this material discoverable. Notice that there are no discussions with experts at this stage. This is also not a step that you want to skimp on or try to do on the cheap. This step requires experienced attorneys who know patent claim construction law, and ideally have knowledge of the subject matter. Basically, what we are looking for at this stage is to determine where the inventor has limited the scope of any element. The inventor may have limited the possible scope through the acknowledgement of prior art, in the specification and claim language, or in responding to a PTO rejection. The file history will tell a story of how and where the inventor gave up claim breadth to the PTO.

The next step is to compare the alleged infringing product against the claim construction. This is best done with someone knowledgeable of the product, i.e., the in-house expert. Make sure that these communications are protected under the attorney-client relationship. It is likely that the patent holder has also created a similar claim comparison chart to determine whether your product infringes. Also helpful at this point is determining whether the claims have been construed by a court in another action. In other words, is the patent battle tested? Although a different court in a new action does not have to adopt the previous court's construction, such a construction will provide valuable insight into how the patent holder views its patent and what sort of evidence the patent holder will bring to the table to support its construction. After construing the claims and comparing the claims to the product you should have a rough idea of whether the product infringes. If it is determined that the product might infringe, not all is lost because other defenses may exist that could save the day.

The bad news is that defenses that are not non-infringement defenses will likely not dissuade NPEs from enforcing their patent against your company. Basically, NPEs, and probably most patent enforcers, believe that they can withstand these other defenses, or at least get into a good settlement position based on infringement. They understand that most companies do not want to roll the dice on these other defenses if the company is indeed infringing. The good news is that defenses are a legitimate option, and with proper evidentiary support are worth pursuing. Also, most NPEs and enforcers are not focused on countering these defenses. Their resources tend to be focused on proving infringement, although that is not to say that the patent holder will not be wary or unconcerned about these other defenses.

In order to evaluate the strength of these defenses, it is helpful to understand the history of any litigation involving the patent. Has the patent been litigation tested? If so, what defenses were raised and what were the associated rulings? What was the evidence presented in support of these defenses? In other words, just how battle-hardened is this patent? And if it is litigation tested, is there any new evidence that can be discovered that might change the momentum?

We start with a look at invalidity or validity—depending on your view. A patent claim can be found to be invalid either because it is anticipated by a single source containing all the elements of the claim or through the combination of sources that contain all the elements. Prior to the ruling in *KSR Int'l Co. v. Teleflex Inc.*, 550 U.S. 398 (2007), to find obviousness, at least one of the sources must have contained a teaching, suggestion, or motivation to combine those sources or they could not be combined to find obviousness. *KSR* removed the strict application of the teaching, suggestion, or motivation rule and replaced it with the question of whether it would have been reasonable for one skilled in the art to combine those elements. Basically, this allows judges and juries to look back in time and make a determination with the aid of expert testimony of whether it would have been reasonable to combine those elements at the time of the invention. *KSR* therefore swung the pendulum for how to determine obviousness to the side of the defendants. Thus, a patent claim that might not have been found valid because the prior art did not contain the magic teaching, suggestion, or motivation in a case prior to *KSR* might today be found to be invalid under the new *KSR* reasonable approach. Later in this chapter we discuss whether to file a request for reexamination with the PTO against the patent. *KSR* will also be applied in such a reexamination. Accordingly, *KSR* can be a powerful tool in these inquiries.

Inequitable conduct is another defense that if found by the court would render the patent unenforceable, thus ending the case. This defense is based on the requirement that those involved with the prosecution of the patent are obligated to maintain a duty of candor with the PTO during prosecution of the patent. The materiality and intent factors are balanced to determine whether the duty of candor has been breached. If this duty has been breached, the patent is held to be unenforceable.

Prosecution estoppel also exists as a useful and potentially powerful defense in the construction of claims. If during prosecution the patentee gave up a position and narrowed the claims due to that position, then during claim construction the patentee cannot reclaim that material in an attempt to broaden the scope of the claim. Also helpful may be any reasons for allowance provided by the PTO examiner in the prosecution history. These can also limit the scope of the claims.

Laches occurs when the patent holder waits too long to take action against an alleged infringer. Basically, if an NPE makes noise that your product may be infringing its patent, but then does not take any action to back that up for several years, one would assume that the product was safe from such action or that it was just a bluff, that is, that maybe the product really didn't infringe at all and the behavior by the NPE was just a ploy to get licensing royalties. At some point in time it is reasonable to assume that your product does not infringe, based on inaction by the NPE.

We are assuming for the purposes of this chapter that NPEs do not have a product in the marketplace, that is, that the NPE does not have its own product that requires marking with the patent number. However, the NPE might still be required to prove marking for damages. If the NPE has licensed the patent to other entities, then the NPE is responsible for enforcing marking to warn the public that the product is being produced under a patent. If a licensee is producing a product without the patent number on the product, or in some cases, on the package if the product is too small or for other good reason, then it is the same as if NPE had produced a product without marking. A quick way to check whether the NPE has indeed required marking by its licensees would be to ask for their license agreements and check for the marking clause. Another quick way is to ask who else has a license and then find out whether their products are being marked. If there are products on the market through licensing but without marking, damages will only be available from the notice of infringement from the NPE. Further, the courts have also found that such notice must be a specific notice of infringement. And, of course, such a specific notice would probably give the company grounds to open a declaratory action—something the NPE might not want to experience. Otherwise, damages would only start from the actual filing of the complaint.

Another possible defense is that of patent exhaustion. The U.S. Supreme Court recently ruled on patent exhaustion in *Quanta Computer, Inc. v. LG Electronics, Inc.* The doctrine of patent exhaustion basically states that "the initial authorized sale of a patented item terminates all patent rights to that item."[10] The doctrine also applies in certain cases where the apparatus that has been sold also embodies the accompanying method claims.

Take Action or Wait?

Your infringement and defense positions are now understood. You have met with the other side have and discussed either settlement or licensing. You have done your homework and know how many times the patent at issue has been in court and whether it has become battle-hardened. You also know whether the patent has been reissued or reexamined before the PTO and the prior art involved. Perhaps you have decided that there is no hope left for a settlement, or there is no desire on the part of your company to license the technology. Three general options may be available: File a declaratory judgment (DJ) action; file a patent reexamination request with the PTO; or do nothing.

If the threat of action by the patent holder meets the proper threshold, you may be able to bring a DJ action. Opening a DJ action turns the tables on the patent holder who is about to start an action against your company. First, a DJ action will be brought in the court of your choice versus that of the patent holder. It is well known that some districts are better for the patent holder than others. The Eastern District of Texas is one such district. Often the best place for the action to be brought is in your own back yard. Here, the jurors may provide a "home field advantage," especially if the patent holder will be perceived as a bully trying to pick on a local industry supporting local jobs. An action closer to home may also provide cheaper resources and lower costs.

If you have outside counsel who has represented your company in other infringement actions, they will also be able to suggest a venue preference. There is value in operating in a district where the patent rules are known and where there has been past success. In theory, attorneys' fees should be somewhat reduced because counsel should already be familiar with the district's local rules and therefore need less time for research. Other cost factors to consider when choosing a district are the add-on costs, such as tutorials and technical advisors if required by a particular district.

Another factor in pursuing a DJ action is the ability to take the fight to the patent holder before the patent holder is ready for the fight. Although the patent holder should have been ready to litigate after notifying your company of infringement, perhaps the patent holder does not have all its logistics worked out and there is an advantage to be gained by pushing the timetable. Of course, a safer assumption would be that the patent holder is ready to litigate.

Taking the offensive in the form of a DJ action can also send a strong message to the NPE community that your company is not afraid of litigation and that an NPE that waves its patent on your doorstep might not get the license it is looking for, but instead a long and costly court action—something an NPE and its contingency-based counsel may not want. Also, thanks to a recent Federal Circuit case, *Hewlett-Packard Co. v. Acceleron LLC,* 587 F.3d 1358 (Fed. Cir. 2009), the threshold for pursuing a DJ action is not that high. Basically, "conduct that can be reasonably inferred as demonstrating intent to enforce a patent can create declaratory judgment jurisdiction."[11]

This next thought may be considered obvious but it is worth mentioning: Bringing a DJ action would not fit well with any sort of delaying tactic, such as a request for staying the action in conjunction with a request for reexamination before the PTO.

An action with the PTO can also be pursued, either by itself or in conjunction with a DJ action. A request for patent reexamination may be filed anonymously. PTO statistics have shown that a high percentage of patent reexamination requests are granted. The fees involved are relatively low when compared to a court action. To succeed in having a request for reexamination granted, the requester need only show a substantial new question of patentability. Meeting the substantial new question of patentability has proven in many cases to be a relatively low threshold. The material submitted with the request must be limited to prior patents and publications. If the PTO finds the submitted matter to be material, such a finding could also support an inequitable conduct claim later raised in district court. The key here is the strength of the prior art. The last thing you want to do at this stage is to submit weak prior art that is just good enough to meet the substantial new question of patentability threshold but is so weak that all of the claims emerge unscathed and strengthened by a second trip through the PTO. The reexamination request can be for either an *ex parte* or an *inter partes* reexamination. For an *inter partes* reexamination, the patent being brandished as a sword against your product must have an application filed on or after November 29, 1999.

Both *ex parte* and *inter partes* reexaminations are limited to the question of invalidity based on anticipation (35 U.S.C. § 102) or obviousness (35 U.S.C. § 103). However, the standard for proving invalidity before the PTO is only a preponderance of the evidence, whereas the standard for proving invalidity in a district court is clear and convincing evidence. Also, there is no presumption of validity in the PTO, while a patent holder enjoys a presumption of validity in district court. If no claims survive the reexamination, then it is game-over for the patent holder and the requester also wins in the parallel district court action. Or if the claims are narrowed, then intervening rights will apply.

Intervening rights occur at the point in time when the claims change. With a reexamination this would be at the time of the certificate of reexamination. There are two types of intervening rights: statutory and equity. Statutory intervening rights (35 U.S.C. § 307(b)) restart the damages clock, wiping away all previous damages. Equitable intervening rights can be applied at the court's discretion to future damages based on the fairness of applying the narrowed claims to a company that would be unfairly attacked by the narrowed claims.

A byproduct of the reexamination process is the creation of more prosecution history. Prosecution history is generally viewed as something that can be used against the patent holder in a later court action. The prosecution history can become a gold mine for admissions and prosecution history estoppel for the doctrine of equivalents. The history, although considered weaker than the claims and specification, is intrinsic evidence that can be used in a future Markman hearing.

Also worth noting is that multiple reexamination requests may be filed against the same patent before the first reexamination is completed. The follow-on reexamination requests may be directed toward amended claims pending in the prosecution file. This method has two effects. First, it allows the requester to almost act as a participant in the first reexamination. Second, it increases the costs for the firm representing the NPE. In many cases that representation is contingency-based. This sends a message early on that there is a long and protracted fight ahead and may be demoralizing for the firm looking for a big and quick paycheck leading to a quicker and reduced settlement. The PTO may at its discretion merge these related reexaminations.

Although an *inter partes* reexamination is more expensive than an *ex parte* reexamination, the *inter partes* reexamination has the advantage of allowing the requesting party to participate in the proceeding, while the *ex parte* reexamination does not allow requesting party participation. Depending on the stage of a parallel district court action, the district court is more likely to stay a proceeding to wait for the conclusion of an *inter partes* action because both parties are involved before the PTO. Of course, this attitude may be changing, as *inter partes* actions can take four to six years to complete and the courts are catching on to the fact that many litigants use reexaminations as a delaying tactic.

Although a reexamination before the PTO does offer many advantages, there is always the risk that the patent will emerge unscathed and stronger. Also, with the *inter partes* reexamination before the PTO, the court will not allow the defendant to retry the defense of invalidity after a final ruling from the PTO. The defendant is estopped from reusing the same prior art for invalidity in the district court. Of course, the other defenses remain intact in the district court. Although this is fair because both parties participate in the *inter partes* action, it should be noted that district courts are much better suited to handle complex evidentiary issues than the PTO. Input from experienced counsel is crucial in making this decision.

Doing nothing may be appropriate when no advantage exists for taking action. Perhaps it is unclear whether the patent holder will follow through with a suit. Perhaps there are no advantages to a different forum or to seeking to invalidate the patent. If the NPE is a nonproducing entity, there is likely a reduced risk of a preliminary injunction because the NPE may not be able to meet the irreparable harm factor. Basically, to meet the irreparable harm factor, the plaintiff must be able to show that it cannot be made whole by damages determined at trial. Because the NPE does not have a competing product in the marketplace, it can be argued that the NPE is not being irreparably harmed by losing market share or goodwill and can be made whole by the awarding of damages.

Doing nothing may delay any public action against the company. Perhaps your company is right in the middle of a marketing campaign and does not want public notice of any sort of action. Or, on the contrary, perhaps a DJ action putting the company on the offense will look better to the shareholders and consumers. There is no one answer that fits all: Each situation will have to be analyzed to determine the best path. It will ultimately be a business decision, informed by the legal landscape.

License or Litigate?[12]

Sometimes a culture for dealing with threats from NPEs may emerge within a company. Some companies or company heads may hold the philosophy of "We never give in—we want to send a message to trolls." Others may be more willing to negotiate and accept a license where they feel it is appropriate. Still others seek to avoid litigation at all costs, preferring a license over litigation.

In actuality, the best approach to dealing with threats posed by NPEs is to treat each situation on a case-by-case basis, taking into account all of the facts and circumstances involved in the threat. No single approach to dealing with NPEs should be adopted to the exclusion of all other approaches, since no "one size fits all" solution exists.

At some point early on in the process, your company should ask itself how much of a license fee the company would be comfortable paying. This calculation should be an informed decision, made in light of an analysis including whether the patent in question may cover your company's product and whether there is a good argument that the patent is invalid. The calculation should also be made in light of an assessment as to how feasible it might be for your company to design around or invent around the problem, particularly if some of the potentially infringing products are still being developed. The cost of licensing should be balanced against the potential cost and likelihood of success of litigation or reexamination. Of course, even if litigation is initiated by the NPE, the option of settling and accepting a license will usually still remain on the table.

Accepting a license can be beneficial because it provides certainty in both cost and outcome. It may also ultimately cost only a fraction of the amount of proceeding with litigation. In contrast, the outcome of litigation is, of course, not certain and the threat of a substantial monetary judgment, or even of a debilitating injunction, hangs overhead. According to the American Intellectual Property Lawyers Association (AIPLA) Economic Survey, in 2009 the median litigation costs for a defendant in a patent suit with between $1 million and $25 million at risk was about $1.5 million through the end of discovery, and about $2.5 million inclusive of all costs.

A crucial factor in assessing whether to license or litigate is the matter of an injunction. An injunction, if granted, would empower the NPE to immediately stop an accused infringer from carrying out its allegedly prohibited activities. This can be crucial because such activities typically comprise a significant subset of the company's business. The threat can be particularly acute when dealing with an NPE because there is no risk in return that the same would happen to the NPE, given that NPEs do not manufacture the patented product. Thus, there is no threat to the NPE of a counterclaim of patent infringement by the accused infringer through defensive use of the accused infringer's patent portfolio, as may occur in a more typical patent litigation. Moreover, the accused infringer cannot "paper to death" the NPE in a litigation by way of a costly and sustained attack of document requests, interrogatories, depositions, and the like, because the NPE typically has only patents as assets, a small number of employees, and few documents to search that relate to the patent in question. Also, the cost of litigation tends to be borne by the company, but the NPE typically has an attorney who has taken the case on a contingency fee basis.

It is clear that the threat of an injunction could potentially provide the NPE with significant leverage with which to initiate licensing negotiations and obtain a favorable licensing fee. If, however, an injunction is not a likely outcome (or the accused infringer is not still producing the product in question or is not intending to continue producing the product for much longer), the accused infringer may not take the threat of an injunction posed by the NPE as seriously.

An important case considering the ability of a plaintiff to obtain an injunction is *eBay Inc. v. MercExchange, L.L.C.*[13] In *eBay*, the U.S. Supreme Court considered the question of injunctions in a case in which the plaintiff, MercExchange L.L.C., was an entity that could classify as an NPE. The Supreme Court invalidated the Federal Circuit's "general rule that courts will issue permanent injunctions against patent infringement absent exceptional circumstances."[14] More specifically, the Supreme Court ruled that the traditional four-factor test applies to the question of whether a plaintiff should be granted a permanent injunction, regardless of what kind of entity the plaintiff is. According to that test, the plaintiff must demonstrate: (1) that it has suffered an irreparable injury; (2) that the remedies available at law, such as monetary damages, are inadequate to compensate for that injury; (3) that, considering the balance of hardships between the plaintiff and defendant, a remedy in equity is warranted; and (4) that the public interest would not be disserved by a permanent injunction. The Supreme Court made it clear that the decision to grant or deny permanent injunctive relief is an act of equitable discretion by the district court, reviewable on appeal for abuse of discretion.

Accordingly, the Supreme Court, in one respect, rejected an invitation to replace traditional equitable considerations with a rule that categorically *denied* injunctive relief to plaintiffs or to a particular class of patent holders. The Supreme Court also rejected an invitation to categorically *grant* injunctive relief to plaintiffs or to a particular class of patent holders. However, a concurring opinion authored by Justice Kennedy, with whom Justices Stevens, Souter, and Breyer joined, came out against injunctions for NPEs, and took the position that damages alone may well be sufficient to compensate an NPE for infringement. The Kennedy concurrence highlighted considerations that were "unlike earlier cases," specifically noting, for example, that "[a]n industry has developed in which firms use patents not as a basis for producing and selling goods but, instead, primarily for obtaining licensing fees." Justice Kennedy cautioned the following:

For these firms, an injunction, and the potentially serious sanctions arising from its violation, can be employed as a bargaining tool to charge exorbitant fees to companies that seek to buy licenses to practice the patent . . . When the patented invention is but a small component of the product the companies seek to produce and the threat of an injunction is employed simply for undue leverage in negoti-ations, legal damages may well be sufficient to compensate for the infringement and an injunction may not serve the public interest. In addition, injunctive re-lief may have different consequences for the burgeoning number of patents over business methods, which were not of much economic and legal significance in earlier times. The potential vagueness and suspect validity of some of these pat-ents may affect the calculus under the four-factor test.[15]

In the aftermath of *eBay*, it has generally been difficult for NPEs to secure perma-nent injunctions. A defendant can potentially argue against an injunction by arguing, for example, (1) that the patented invention is only a small component of the prod-uct (see Justice Kennedy's concurrence); (2) that the NPE's lack of commercial activ-ity in practicing its patent establishes that the NPE would not suffer irreparable harm if an injunction did not issue (see the first factor of the above-noted test); (3) that the NPEs offer of a license shows that monetary damages as a remedy would be ade-quate (see the first and second factors of the test); (4) that the threat of an injunction has been employed by the NPE simply for undue leverage in negotiations (see again Justice Kennedy's concurrence); (5) that the balance of hardships weighs in favor of the defendant since the cost of designing around the technology would be prohibi-tive (see the third factor of the test); and (6) that the public interest would be dis-served by an injunction since the defendant's customers rely greatly on the defendant's product and would suffer significantly if an injunction were granted (see the fourth factor of the test).

In determining whether an NPE might be successful in securing an injunction, it would also be wise for a company to determine whether the NPE did in fact take *some* steps, even if cursory ones, toward manufacturing the patented technology in an attempt to set itself apart from pure NPEs, in light of the *eBay* decision. If this occurred, the NPE may have a greater chance of obtaining a permanent injunction.

A case that illustrates a rare post-*eBay* grant of a permanent injunction in favor of an NPE is *Commonwealth Scientific and Indus. Research Org. v. Buffalo Tech. Inc.*[16] Commonwealth Scientific and Industrial Research Organisation (CSIRO) is the princi-pal research arm of the Australian government, and exists as a noncompeting, non-manufacturing patent holder—essentially, an NPE. CSIRO has regularly generated revenue through licensing schemes relating to its patented wireless technology. In its case against Buffalo, CSIRO secured a permanent injunction against Buffalo at the district court level. Despite its status as an NPE, the district court granted the perma-nent injunction, viewing CSIRO as primarily a research-based entity and not a tradi-tional patent troll. Under the district court's rationale, "because the work of research institutions such as CSIRO is often fundamental to scientific advancement, [CSIRO] merit[ed] strong patent protection."[17] The Federal Circuit ended up vacating the in-junction, but did so on the basis of patent validity, thereby avoiding the propriety of the district court's rationale in granting the injunction.

Nevertheless, since in the wake of *eBay* it has generally been difficult for NPEs to secure permanent injunctions, a substantial amount of leverage previously possessed by NPEs has been taken away. With a lesser threat of an injunction, an accused infringer has less of an incentive to negotiate a license. One reason for this is that even if the litigation were to result in a reasonable royalty being determined against the infringer, such may in effect be similar in cost to a licensing fee (although the cost of litigation and potential damages must be factored in as well).[18]

With further regard to royalties, some case law suggests that different royalty rates are appropriate before and after a finding of infringement; that is, courts have recognized a difference between a negotiated royalty rate and a continuing royalty, the latter being imposed if the court denies injunctive relief. For instance, in *Paice LLC v. Toyota Motors Corp.*[19] the court found that different pre- and post-judgment royalty rates were warranted, given the changes in the parties' legal relationship and other economic factors. On return to the district court, the continuing royalty rate imposed was significantly higher than that which had been used to calculate the pre-judgment infringement damages.

NPEs commonly bring litigation, when initiated, in the U.S. District Court for the Eastern District of Texas. That venue has been seen as being favorable to plaintiffs since it has special expertise in patent actions: judges in the Eastern District of Texas are typically familiar with patent cases. Furthermore, many litigators feel that eastern Texas has a less sophisticated jury pool and that this weighs in a plaintiff's favor in a complex infringement case. Given such considerations, the first priority for defendants who are sued in the Eastern District of Texas is to move to get the suit out of the Eastern District of Texas. If the defendant is successful in doing so, it can be an easier task to show the patent to be invalid, especially if the patent in question is trivial or overly broad.

A company threatened by an NPE should understand what the interests of the NPE are so that the company can use what leverage it does have over the NPE to its advantage in negotiations. For example, if the accused infringer seeks reexamination of the patent or challenges the patent's validity in court and the patent is held to be invalid, such outcome would be devastating to the NPE, as the NPE would lose its ability to assert the patent, which of course would affect other licensing opportunities as well. Therefore, an NPE is determined to avoid this disastrous outcome and as such may not go to extreme lengths to vigorously assert a vulnerable patent and demand exorbitant licensing fees. Also, it should be recognized that the NPE wishes to receive as much money as possible from a patent, while using as little time and expense as it can to procure such monies. On the other hand, it should also be recognized that some of the usual strategies for dealing with demands to take a license don't work; for example, the threatened company cannot offer the NPE a cross license since the NPE doesn't produce any product.

Something else the threatened company should attempt to learn is the number of licenses the NPE has for the patent. To the extent this information is available, it can be an indication of how strongly other companies view the patent, and how firm the NPE believes its position is. If it is still early in the process and the NPE has not yet secured any licensees, the NPE may not have confidence in the strength of its position, and therefore the threatened company may be able to successfully negotiate a less expensive licensing fee. Another bargaining chip the threatened company may have at its disposal is to offer to allow the NPE the opportunity to make public the fact that the company will become a licensee, in exchange for a lower licensing fee.

For a threatened company, when not accepting a license there is uncertainty as to outcome and damages, there is at least the threat of an injunction, and there is uncertainty as to the cost and ability to design around. Among the options a threatened company has are to (1) accept a license, (2) engineer or design around the patent in question, (3) purchase alternative technologies, (4) proceed to reexamination, (5) initiate a declaratory judgment action, or (6) assess the available defenses and continue to use the patented technology without permission, thereby accepting the risk of litigation

Conclusion

In conclusion, each threat posed by NPEs will present a number of important issues that will call for a careful consideration of all the facts and circumstances involved so that the threatened company may devise a sound strategy for response.

Companies and corporations manage risks every day. Risks are part of doing business, and the NPE is a manageable risk. The first step is to identify the specific risk or risks posed by an NPE. The second step is to understand the available defenses in light of the potentially asserted patent(s) and the potentially accused products. Only then can management make an informed decision with regard to taking action or waiting. Such action could include licensing the patent to avoid all risk immediately or taking offensive action in the form of a declaratory action in the district court of choice, or a reexamination request before the United States Patent and Trademark Office, or both. There is no "one size fits all" solution.

Notes

1. Brenda Sandburg, "You May Not Have a Choice. Trolling for Dollars," *The Recorder* (July 30, 2001): 1.

2. Ibid.

3. Katherine E. White, "Preserving the Patent Process to Incentivize Innovation in Global Economy," *Syracuse Science and Technology Law Reporter* (2005), 11.

4. James F. McDonough III, "The Myth of the Patent Troll: An Alternative View of the Function of Patent Dealers in an Idea Economy," *Emory Law Journal* 56 (2006): 189; Emory Public Law Research Paper No. 07-6; Emory Law and Economics Research Paper No. 07-7.

5. Sandburg, "You May Not Have a Choice," 2.

6. John M. Golden, "'Patent Trolls' and Patent Remedies," *Texas Law Review* 85, (2007): 2110–2161, 2112.

7. See Chapter 5 for commentary from a principal of Ocean Tomo, LLC.

8. See, e.g., Miranda Jones, "Permanent Injunction, A Remedy By Any Other Name Is Patently Not the Same: How Ebay v. MercExchange Affects the Patent Right of Non-Practicing Entities," *George Mason Law Review* 14-4 (2007), 1035, 1047.

9. See, e.g., Susan Walmsley Graf, "Improving Patent Quality Through Identification of Relevant Prior Art: Approaches to Increase Information Flow to the Patent Office," *Lewis & Clark Law Review* 11 (2007), 498.

10. Ibid.

11. Ibid., 1363.

12. See also James Markarian, "Strategic and Legal View of Licensing Patents," in *Intellectual Property Operations and Implementation for the 21st Century Corporation*, (forthcoming).

13. *eBay Inc. v. MercExchange, L.L.C.,* 126 S. Ct. 1837, 1842 (2006).

14. Ibid.

15. Ibid.

16. *Commonwealth Scientific and Indus. Research Org. v. Buffalo Tech. Inc.*, 492 F. Supp. 2d 600 (E.D. Tex. 2007).

17. Ibid., 607.

18. It is noted that an NPE would not qualify for damages in the form of lost profits, since the NPE does not manufacture anything.

19. *Paice LLC v. Toyota Motors Corp.*, 85 USPQ2d 1001 (Fed. Cir. 2007).

CHAPTER 9

Using Insurance to Manage Intellectual Property Risk

Kimberly Cauthorn[*]
Duff & Phelps

Leib Dodell
ThinkRisk Underwriting Agency LLC

H istorically, the insurance industry has approached intellectual property (IP) risk in a highly fragmented way. For certain specialized industry segments, such as media and technology companies, the insurance industry has created specialty insurance products that attempt to solve some of the IP risks faced by these businesses—although generally not patent-related risks. For the rest of the commercial marketplace, the insurance industry has attempted to provide some limited coverage as a component of the Commercial General Liability (CGL) policy, with generally poor results. As to patent infringement risk specifically, some insurance companies have attempted to create stand-alone insurance solutions, but the marketplace remains extremely small and highly inefficient.

This is not an effective approach to twenty-first century IP risks. Thought leaders in the insurance community have begun to recognize that IP-related exposures permeate the entire commercial marketplace, as opposed to being limited to narrow industry segments like media and technology. Virtually all businesses now face some degree of IP risk arising out of their business practices, whether that risk primarily relates to copyright, trademark, patent, or other areas. Current insurance structures, however, do not allow for the delivery of IP-related insurance solutions to the Main Street commercial marketplace in an efficient manner.

To illustrate this problem, we have developed two hypothetical businesses: Bob's Bike Shop and Blaze Telecommunications. The first is a relatively straightforward "Main Street" commercial business venture, representative of the tens of

---

[*] Special thanks to Soha Bhardwaj and Ted Barlow for their invaluable assistance in the writing of this chapter.

thousands of small businesses across multiple industry segments. The second is a more sophisticated technology-related enterprise. The following section outlines the two business models, discusses the various IP and related exposures generated by the two companies' business practices, and then analyzes the potential insurance solutions available.

Case Study—Bob's Bike Shop

Bob opened his first bike shop in Kansas City in 1999. Due to Bob's business acumen and passion for cycling—and the serendipity of opening his shop the year Lance Armstrong won his first of seven consecutive Tours de France—the business grew rapidly. By 2009, Bob owned and operated 10 stores throughout the Midwest, with annual revenues of around $50 million, and was considering additional locations around the country.

In 2002, Bob launched the company's web site, www.bobsbikeshop.com. The web site began as little more than a brochure for the shop. However, Bob aggressively added new functionalities to the site. The web site now includes: news and information about cycling; a training program that allows cyclists to monitor their training schedule, track their fitness level, and predict their peak racing periods; and a chat room where cyclists can communicate about gear, upcoming races, and so forth. The web site makes frequent use of images of famous cyclists and prominent races like the Tour de France. Bob has not bothered to license these images, figuring he is making fair use of publicly available material. Bob also launched a paper catalog containing many of the same images that he mails quarterly to the customers on his mailing list. He obtains information about customers through the web site, which collects personal information about all visitors. He put his catalog online in 2007 so customers could buy bikes and cycling-related products directly from the web site using e-commerce software he found on the Internet.

In 2004, Bob, working with a friend who is a software engineer, developed a proprietary software program to allow him to track cycling inventory in each of his shops. Because they are friends, they did not execute any kind of contract for the provision of the software engineer's services. The software was so effective that Bob, ever the entrepreneur, decided to package the software and make it commercially available. He now sells CD-ROMs, containing the software, to other small business owners in his community, and is considering offering it nationwide.

Bob began his business purely as a retailer, selling bikes and cycling-related products made by other manufacturers. However, Bob has always loved tinkering with bikes and bike components. In 2009, Bob and his friends developed what they believe to be a revolutionary new design in bike frame geometry. Working in Bob's garage, they have begun to manufacture a very small number of Bobbikes, selling them in Bob's Bike Shops alongside more famous brands like Trek and Cannondale.

A friend mentioned to Bob that he ought to consider obtaining a patent for this new technology. Bob has met with a patent lawyer, who is currently preparing a patent application for the Bobbike.

In 2005, Bob's success generated some unwanted attention. Bob received a letter from an attorney for another, much smaller bike shop in Seattle also named Bob's

Bike Shop. The letter stated that the Seattle company holds a federally registered trademark for "Bob's Bike Shop," and instructed Bob to cease and desist from using the name. Bob has received other letters similar to this in the years since, though no legal action has yet been taken. A little research indicated that there are at least three other "Bob's Bike Shops" operating in the United States.

In fact, Bob has been receiving a lot of mail. Bob recently received a letter from Diamondback stating that his Bobbike infringes on a patent owned by Diamondback. And, he received an "offer to license" letter from Patent Pain regarding the e-commerce software used to sell product from his web site.

Case Study—Blaze Telecommunications

Ryan Blaze demonstrated a gift for engineering from a young age when he attempted to build a working "Star Trek" communicator with components from a local electronics store. Today, he is the founder and CEO of Blaze Telecommunications, a major designer, manufacturer, and marketer of cellular phones and smart phones. Blaze succeeded where established telecommunications firms failed by hiring the brightest engineering talent and concentrating relentlessly on innovation.

Today, Blaze is a multibillion-dollar firm with a full line of cell phone and smart phone products, a large patent portfolio, and a team of internal counsel to assist with intellectual property matters. Blaze's large R&D budget and engineering-focused culture makes it a hotbed of technological innovation. Ryan has repeatedly stated it is Blaze's policy to apply for patents based on any technology arising from Blaze's R&D, especially on any innovation covering key commercial differentiators that give Blaze's products a competitive edge in the marketplace.

Blaze also earns millions of dollars a year from licensing out its patents to other technology companies, including its competitors. In addition, while Blaze gives developers free programming tools to develop applications that work with the Blaze operating system, it collects a toll on any sales of those applications to Blaze customers.

Blaze must license in a thicket of patents in order to sell operational phones. Communications companies need to agree on common standards in order to successfully operate. If cellular phone towers and cell phones do not communicate in the same frequency band using the same codes, cell phones are not very useful. Standards such as CMA, CDMA, and 802.11 are generally created by organizations such as the Institute of Electrical and Electronics Engineers (IEEE). Use of these common standards makes networks much more valuable to consumers and firms.

These standards can require hundreds of patents to practice. Generally speaking, the standards-setting organizations try to ensure they have license agreements to all necessary patents bundled in a patent pool. However, they cannot prevent patent holders who are not part of the pool from asserting that their patents are necessary to practice the standard.

Blaze learned the risks of patent litigation the hard way. In 2004, Blaze faced a litigant who sought an injunction against Blaze, based on an accusation of infringement of the litigant's patent on an aspect of a communications standard practiced by several of Blaze's cell phone lines. Blaze believed it could design around the accused technology, but saw its stock price and sales plummet in the face of the threat of an injunction that could cripple the firm. Blaze eventually paid a settlement worth hundreds of millions of dollars. While threats of injunctions have since been eased somewhat by the *eBay* decision, Blaze faces enough "offer to license" letters from potential litigants to keep several staff attorneys busy.

Ryan is wary of the conflicts and dangers involved in organizing a joint defense. Blaze recently settled an infringement claim brought by an independent inventor who asserted broad claims against a number of smart phone manufacturers and marketers. Blaze's co-defendants included both its direct competitors and several of its distributors. The lawsuit turned out to be a significant distraction for Blaze's leadership. Although Blaze's confidential information was shielded by a protective order, the potential risks inherent in sharing the company's financials, costs, and profits with its competitors' attorneys and experts loomed large over Blaze's strategy. Blaze's settlement was motivated in part by a desire to maintain the confidentiality of its pricing, profits, know-how, and other sensitive information.

Ryan also worries that Blaze faces the threat of infringement accusations based on the components that it purchases and incorporates into its products. The chips, batteries, cameras, processors, and other components each represent a bundle of technologies that are potentially vulnerable to infringement claims. Although Blaze generally seeks indemnification from its suppliers, Ryan knows that its smaller suppliers cannot afford to defend themselves as well as their customers. In the event of a successful damages claim, he is concerned that these indemnification clauses will not be worth the paper on which they're printed. Ryan also foresees a furious round of finger-pointing among the various suppliers regarding whether they are obligated to indemnify Blaze and, if so, which parties are obligated to indemnify Blaze and to what extent.[1]

Recently, Blaze introduced a new brand of consumer smart phone, the FireStarter. Blaze's advertising agency created a television advertisement scored to a song by a popular alternative rock musician. Blaze was able to license the rights to the musical composition itself, but when the singer refused to grant the right to a specific recording of the song, the agency re-recorded the song using a different singer with a similar voice. It wasn't long before both Blaze and the agency were notified by the original musician of a right of publicity lawsuit. Although Blaze's attorneys assure Ryan the assertion is baseless, the publicity surrounding the case has done damage to Blaze's image.

The new FireStarter is designed to compete in the increasingly popular category of touch screen phones. Before designing the FireStarter, Blaze commissioned a series of focus groups with touch screen phone users to explore why they found the touch screen interface appealing, and how they used it. Blaze's product manager attempted to use this feedback to create a list of the most popular features of competitors' phones. Luckily, before Blaze invested too much time on reverse engineering these features, their attorneys stripped the list of the features protected by competitors' business process patents. When Ryan was informed of this process, he wondered anew how a company could ever fully protect itself from IP lawsuits if something as simple as a method of touching a phone could potentially be infringing.

Issues Raised by the Case Studies

These case studies show that both standard commercial Main Street businesses like Bob's Bikes, as well as large complex technology enterprises like Blaze, face a daunting array of IP-related exposures. While Bob's efforts have met with success, like many businesspeople, his lack of familiarity with intellectual property risk has created several problems. Moreover, if Bob's Bikes has not purchased any insurance beyond the standard commercial insurance package, the company probably does not have coverage for most of these exposures. Similarly, Ryan's example shows that even indemnification clauses and a team of attorneys cannot fully protect a successful high technology firm from intellectual property risk. A description of several of these issues follows.

Trademark Exposures

Bob faces a potential claim of trademark infringement by Bob's Bike Shop of Seattle, among other possible claimants. The growth of the Internet has made it more likely that ordinary commercial businesses will face trademark claims such as this. Prior to the Internet, similarly named small businesses could operate in separate geographic regions for many years—possibly forever—without running into one another. However, only one company can own the domain bobbikeshop.com, making it much more likely multiple companies using the same name would run into one another sooner rather than later.

In addition, one does not need to provide proof of trademark ownership in order to register a new domain, increasing the likelihood that a business could be using a particular domain name without realizing there is a prior owner of the mark. Of course, a prudent business owner would conduct a trademark search before registering a domain, but many small business owners either do not have the resources to conduct such a search or are not savvy enough about intellectual property issues to recognize the potential problem.[2]

In response to this claim, Bob will have to demonstrate that either the Seattle shop's federal trademark is invalid or his mark is non-infringing. Bob has been using his mark Bob's Bike Shop for 10 years, but he has never filed a federal trademark application to protect his intellectual property. Bob has been on notice for some time and he has avoided taking legal action to defend his intellectual property. This oversight may prove costly.

However, there potentially are three factors in Bob's favor. First, Bob may be eligible for a Kansas state-based trademark, or trademark protection within the Midwestern region, if he, with the help of his trademark attorney, can demonstrate that the Seattle shop has not yet entered his zone of expansion. Second, given that Bob has been using his mark for over 10 years, it is likely to be a strong mark that has garnered an associated distinctiveness. Bob may be able to argue that the Seattle mark is not widely used in commerce and lacks distinctiveness. Third, if Bob can demonstrate that the Seattle shop has not aggressively policed its mark, then this may weaken its trademark infringement argument against him.

In addition to the Bob's Bike Shop name, Bob may face other trademark issues. For example, the Tour de France is a very valuable trademark, and to the extent

Bob's uses it to help market its business, it risks a claim of infringement. Indeed, the organizers of the Tour de France brought a trademark claim against the promoters of a women's bike race that they billed as the "Women's Tour de France."

Even if Bob has successful legal defenses to the claims, the impact of a trademark infringement suit on a business such as Bob's could be significant. Win or lose, legal expenses can be high, and if Bob's loses the case it could be required to pay damages to the prior owner of the mark. If the Seattle shop's trademark is federally registered, such damages could be based on Bob's profits, any actual damages sustained by the Seattle company, the Seattle company's costs for bringing the action, including its attorney's fees, and trebling of actual damages.[3] In addition, Bob's could be ordered to cease and desist from using the mark, which would require the company to rebrand itself, and result in loss of use of all marketing materials bearing the prior brand.

It is unlikely the trademark infringement suit would be a covered claim under Bob's commercial general liability (CGL) policy[4] because the current version of the standard ISO form contains an exclusion for "'personal and advertising injury' arising out of the infringement of . . . trademark."[5] The CGL form is occurrence-based (discussed later in this chapter), so it may be Bob's could rely on an earlier form of the CGL that was in effect at the time the alleged infringement began. However, he likely would become embroiled in coverage litigation with his CGL carrier over the existence of a duty to defend, since the question of whether earlier versions of the CGL cover trademark infringement has vexed courts for decades.[6] Although there are specialty insurance products available that would protect Bob from this sort of litigation, it is unlikely that Bob was aware of the existence of such insurance products given that Bob's local agent is likely to be unfamiliar with specialty insurance products.

Developed Software Exposures

Bob's sales of the inventory tracking software expose him to several issues. As software programs are literary works, they are in the same category of copyrightable works as novels, letters, and magazine articles. Bob is likely to face a claim of authorship from his software engineer friend on the software he is selling because an author owns a copyright even if he does not federally register the copyright.

Moreover, with respect to the sale of the software to purchasers, in the eyes of the law Bob's is now a professional service provider and is potentially subject to liability if its software does not meet expectations and causes losses to users. This is a pure errors and omissions (E&O) exposure, similar to the malpractice exposure faced by any other provider of professional services. Most professional service firms, however, purchase E&O insurance that is tailored to the services that they provide. Specific industries, such as medicine, law, and accounting, have specialized E&O programs designed to address the specific risks faced by these businesses. The same is true for technology service providers, who generally purchase a specialized product known as Technology E&O. Other services providers that do not fit into one of these well-defined categories generally purchase miscellaneous professional liability (MPL) insurance, a generic form of E&O that can be customized to suit virtually any service provider.

Once again, Bob's standard commercial insurance coverages generally would not respond to a claim alleging either financial loss as a result of the failure of the software to function as promised, or a claim involving ownership of the software itself. In order to protect itself against such claims, Bob's would need to purchase specialty professional liability insurance. In most cases like this, companies like Bob's Bikes do not think of themselves as professional service firms, and therefore never explore the possibility of these specialized coverages.

As a vendor of a sophisticated product with built-in software applications often developed by outside developers and as a communications network provider where third party apps are sold, Blaze is vulnerable to software copyright infringement claims. Blaze attempts to limit its exposure by purchasing technology E&O insurance. However, the scope of coverage could be limited to software developed by Blaze, so Blaze will want to review its policy. Blaze typically does not require such coverage from its outside developers, which are often small shops or individuals.

As already mentioned, Blaze requires the suppliers of its product components, which often include both hardware and software, to indemnify it against claims of IP infringement. However, such suppliers may not be able financially to honor such indemnification obligations. One potential solution is for Blaze to require its outside developers and component suppliers to purchase IP infringement liability coverage from a vendor insurance program set up by Blaze solely for its suppliers. Such coverage could be offered for a more reasonable premium to its suppliers and could cover Blaze as well.

Media Exposures

Bob's decision to use images of Lance Armstrong on his web site and in his print catalog creates additional problems. This is because the law in most states allows individuals to prevent others from capitalizing on the popularity of their own names or likenesses. Bob's Bikes might view the image on the web site as standard and no different than putting up a poster in its shop. In reality; however, with the addition of online sales and product marketing, his web site has transitioned to a commercial venue—not to mention the practical fact that posting the image online makes it much more likely the use will be detected.

Again, the only insurance Bob's likely has in order to address this claim is the CGL policy, but the words "misappropriation" or "right of publicity" do not appear anywhere in the definition of "personal or advertising injury." Some insurance forms will cover publication of material that violates a person's right of privacy and because the right of publicity is often considered to be part of the right of privacy, the argument can be made by the insured that such claims are covered by the CGL. However, such an argument is not likely to be accepted by the carrier.

Bob's issues do not end here. He has exposed himself to other media risks as well. He may face a domain name dispute with other Bob's Bike Shops in the future, and may need to seek the application of the Uniform Domain Name Dispute Resolution Policy through an attorney. By activating a chat room on his site, he potentially is exposing himself to defamation and product disparagement claims. Current CGL policy forms do not cover such claims.

Blaze's advertising firm presumably knew enough not to use the song in the ad for the FireStarter without licensing the lyrics and music in order to avoid a copyright infringement claim. However, they are not necessarily in the clear by using a different singer to record the song. Singer Bette Midler successfully sued Ford Motor Company for hiring a sound-alike who had been told to sound as much as possible like Bette Midler. The court found that Ford had wrongfully appropriated an attribute of her identity, and that therefore Ford had misappropriated her "right of publicity." If Blaze did not instruct the singer to sound like the original singer, or if the company indicated in the advertisement that celebrity voices were impersonated, they might be in the clear on the right of publicity claim.

If the ad campaign was produced by an outside advertising firm, then the ad firm is likely to have specific media insurance. If the ad was produced by Blaze's in-house marketing team, it is far less clear whether Blaze would have coverage. Blaze likely has a technology E&O policy, but that policy may not extend to claims arising out of the advertising of Blaze's technology products. As discussed further below some carriers have developed advertiser's liability policies for non-media companies geared toward damages or liability resulting from the content of advertisement.

Privacy Exposures

Furthermore, Bob's Bikes' activities in the harvesting and use of information obtained online from consumers and web site participants could expose it to liability. Over the past decade, the law concerning the maintenance of personal data in the electronic age has developed and grown. Most states now have consumer protection legislation setting forth specific actions businesses like Bob's must take if their web site experiences a breach of network security that results in a third party gaining access to personal information about Bob's customers or employees. These statutes generally require the business to notify every consumer whose data may have been compromised and offer credit monitoring and other tools to mitigate any potential consequences. Compliance with such requirements can be costly. In addition, affected consumers and banks could sue Bob's for damages caused by the breach. Regulatory agencies such as the Federal Trade Commission and the various state attorney general offices have become increasingly active in this arena, and regularly bring enforcement actions arising out of data privacy violations. Bob's CGL policy likely would not respond to any of these situations because the newest CGL ISO form eliminates coverage for personal and advertising injury arising out of violation of a statute, ordinance or regulation limiting the sending, transmitting, communicating, or distributing of material or information.

Patent Exposures

Bob's patent risk falls into three categories: ownership, validity, and infringement. As Bob developed his product with the help of others, they most likely need to be named as co-inventors on the patent. If he fails to do so, he could be faced with an inventorship or ownership issue. Under U.S. patent law, co-inventors are co-owners. Therefore, the unnamed co-inventors could make a claim on all sales of the Bobbikes made after the patent issues.

Of course, the patent application must be filed and a patent must be issued before the co-inventors would have a claim, and if Bob does not get his application filed within one year of the first Bobbike sale, then he most likely will lose his one-year grace period under 35 USC § 102(b) to apply for a patent on his bike frame invention. Speaking of applying for a patent, Bob is now on notice by Diamondback of a patent it claims is being infringed by his Bobbike. Aside from the threat of an infringement suit, Bob is now potentially faced with the threat of relevant prior art if Diamondback's patent covers the same bike frame invention. This could prevent him from obtaining a patent; so instead of protecting his own invention, he may at best be paying royalties to Diamondback to continue selling his Bobbike or, at worst, no longer be able to sell his Bobbike.

Patent Pain has delivered an offer to license letter to Bob's for the e-commerce software. Because anyone who makes, uses, sells, offers to sell, or imports an infringing device is a direct infringer, Bob could be facing a patent infringement lawsuit even though he did not himself develop the e-commerce software. Litigation costs to defend against a patent infringement suit can easily run into the millions. Bob might want to go back and look at the terms of the license to determine whether the software licensor agreed to indemnify him for IP infringement claims. At the very least, there may be an implied warranty of non-infringement under UCC § 2-312.[7]

A firm like Blaze is relatively unlikely to face ownership disputes. A typical Blaze engineer's contract would allow the engineers who developed a patentable technology to obtain inventor or co-inventor credit. At the same time, it would require him to assign any ensuing patent rights, as well as the rights to any other work product developed as a Blaze employee, to Blaze. Also, Blaze typically licenses in patents covering the components provided by its suppliers and rarely jointly develops intellectual property with its suppliers.

However, Blaze faces the risk that any of its patents could be legally challenged. Invalidity or unenforceability of patents covering key commercial advantages of the products and technology Blaze sells or patents from which Blaze derives substantial royalties could cause Blaze to lose revenue. Blaze might want to explore purchasing coverage to insure against this risk; Liberty and Kiln, a Lloyd's syndicate, both offer this type of coverage.[8] As a large high-tech company, Blaze is vulnerable to patent infringement claims from competitors and nonpracticing entities. It attempts to minimize its infringement risk through a combination of licensing, standards, and indemnification. However, these measures sometimes create challenges of their own. For example, suppliers may claim the component or technology they provide does not infringe or contribute to the infringement, or they may claim even if the supplied component or technology contributes to the infringement, the supplier should only indemnify up to its pro rata contribution. For example, Sprint was sued for patent infringement by Digital Technology Licensing. When Sprint turned to its digital cellular product suppliers for indemnification, a dispute arose between Sprint and the suppliers over the scope and extent of their patent infringement liability indemnification obligations. As a result, Sprint brought the suppliers into the patent infringement suit as third party defendants.[9]

Blaze has attempted to de-escalate potentially expensive patent wars by entering into cross licenses with many of its competitors. In these agreements, Blaze willingly licenses out its patents in exchange for a similar license from a competitor. Any licensing fee exchanged is generally minimal, as these licenses exist primarily as a way to declare *détente*. In addition, Blaze, like many in the industry, has avoided infringement suits by licensing in communication standards at well-known rates.

Of course, some parties, especially nonpracticing entities, are not interested in cross licenses. In the past, Blaze has sought patent infringement liability insurance against such situations. These policies generally cover legal defense costs, damages, and/or settlement up to a stated amount. Unfortunately, Blaze's size and visibility make it a likely target for litigation. As a result, Blaze has not found an insurer willing to take on a portion of its potential liability for an affordable premium. Accordingly, Blaze must self-insure. One avenue Blaze is considering is membership in an entity such as RPX. In return for an annual membership fee, Blaze will have a license to RPX's growing patent portfolio and if a nonpracticing entity asserts a patent against Blaze, RPX may be able to negotiate the purchase of the patent as an alternative way to resolve the litigation.

Managing the Risks

Even a relatively simple business like Bob's Bike Shop faces many intellectual property and related exposures that fall outside the scope of the standard CGL policy. However, before shopping for other types of insurance that can address these gaps in coverage, Bob needs to develop a good risk management plan. Of course, step one of that plan should be hiring attorneys so he can determine whether he has a patentable invention, negotiate an agreement with his software engineer friend, better protect his mark, decide whether to challenge Seattle Bob, determine the best strategy for responding (or not) to Patent Pain and Diamondback's letters, and either obtain the appropriate licenses or pull the problematic images off the web site and halt further printing of the catalog. Step two of the plan should be an IT risk assessment and putting the proper policies and procedures in place to protect customers' information. Step three of the plan should be the development and implementation of an IP risk management plan. By taking into account all IP-related facets of business risk, including legal, financial, and traditional risk management, an IP risk profile can be developed so Bob's Bike Shop can effectively identify and proactively manage its IP risks. Although related to step three, step four should be investigating types of insurance available to address these risk issues.

Blaze Telecommunications would not be able to survive without a reasonable understanding of intellectual property exposures and the skills and manpower to deal with them. Blaze's attorneys seem to have developed and implemented an IP risk management plan. As we have seen, this plan has several components:

- A policy of seeking IP infringement liability indemnification from its suppliers
- A standard contract for Blaze engineers and inventors spelling out Blaze's rights to their work product and inventions
- A program of cross licensing with competitors and licensing-in of technological standards
- Insurance tailored to several of its IP exposures

However, as has already been illustrated, there are limitations to each of these risk management tools. For a company the size and complexity of Blaze with commensurate IP risks, more sophisticated risk management tools are required. Such tools could include not only membership in an entity such as RPX, but also some combination of the following:

- Development of a vendor insurance program
- Formation of its own captive insurance company
- Requiring its vendors to add it as an insured on their insurance policies or to schedule their contractual indemnification obligation to their insurance policies
- Purchasing a modular policy to more efficiently address most of its IP exposure areas

Why Buy Insurance to Cover Intellectual Property Risk?

If Bob's Bike Shop is like most other Main Street commercial businesses, it probably has a standard package of commercial insurance products: general liability, property, crime, worker's compensation, auto, and possibly Directors and Officers (D&O). However, the case study illustrates that businesses like Bob's are faced with serious exposures mostly likely not covered by this standard package.

A firm like Blaze will almost certainly have the same types of coverage with higher limits, along with technology E&O insurance, and possibly media liability coverage. Blaze would have difficulty obtaining patent liability coverage, even though patent infringement is one of its major exposure areas.

That Was Then: Development of Insurance Policies Covering Intellectual Property-Related Risks

General liability policies have been construed broadly in many jurisdictions to recognize a duty to defend copyright, trademark, and in rare cases patent infringement claims. However, in recent years carriers have been modifying their general liability forms in an effort to eliminate or narrow such coverage. This generally has been done by narrowing the personal and advertising injury coverage sections by modifying definitions of advertising, requiring a closer nexus between advertising and the damage or injury, and in many cases inserting restrictive intellectual property exclusions.[10]

Shoe-horning infringement coverage into "advertising injury" is not the ideal way to address IP infringement liability risk.[11] Generally, the large commercial insurance companies that provide general liability coverage do not have the underwriting and claims-handling expertise to manage these risks. As alternatives, insurers have either added IP coverage to policies that cover related exposures, such as E&O, media, and cyber liability policies, or developed policy forms solely addressing IP risk.[12]

This Is Now: Types of Insurance Policies Responsive to Intellectual Property-Related Risks

While there are more insurance options available to cover IP-related exposures, there is a good deal of variation in underwriting process, form, availability, and coverage. Some insurance products address both IP and non-IP-related exposures but do not include coverage for any type of patent risk. Before examining types of policies that address patent risk, we will review potential options for Bob's Bike Shop and Blaze Telecommunications to consider in order to address some of the risk areas previously identified. In addition, Table 9.1 provides a list of insurance providers offering IP-related coverage.[13]

TABLE 9.1 IP Insurance Providers

Provider	Product	IP-Related Coverage
Allied World/Darwin www.darwinpro.com	Media Liability	Coverage for advertising, media and entertainment companies for wrongful acts including: defamation, invasion of privacy, copyright infringement, breach of confidentiality, and deceptive trade practices
Allied World/Darwin www.darwinpro.com	Tech E&O	False advertising, unfair competition, coverage for cyber and Internet-related exposures, coverage for tech E&O exposures, patent infringement liability coverage by endorsement
Ambridge MGA Partners www.ambridgepartners.com	Transactional & Litigation Risk Insurance	IP reps and warranties, coverage for IP infringement indemnification in licensing deals, IP litigation appeal risk, IP contingencies such as proper assignments
Axis Pro www.mediaprof.com	Axis Pro Media Liability	Cyber/technology E&O including TM and © infringement
Beazley www.beazley.com	Technology, Media & Business Services: Media Tech	TM and © infringement, domain name, trade secret misappropriation
Beazley www.beazley.com	Information Security & Privacy & Beazley Breach Response	TM and © infringement, domain name, improper deep-linking or framing
CFC Underwriting www.cfcunderwriting.com	Tech	Modular policy targeting key professional liability exposures for technology companies with specific coverage for TM and © infringement

Provider	Product	IP-Related Coverage

Chartis
  www.chartisinsurance.com
	Patent Infringement
	  Liability
		Patent indemnity for companies
		  domiciled in the United States

Chubb
  www.chubb.com
	Internet Liability	Cyber security and Internet
		  liability for Internet exposures,
		  defamation, © and TM
		  infringement, denial of service,
		  e-threats, e-vandalism

Chubb
  www.chubb.com
	MediaGuard	Third party liability protection
		  against defamation, invasion
		  of privacy, © and TM
		  infringement, and
		  misappropriation for media-
		  related companies

CNA
  www.cna.com
	Tech E&O	Includes software copyright
		  infringement, third party loss of
		  use, and unauthorized access

CNA
  www.cna.com
	NetProtect	Covers information risks
		  including network security,
		  media liability, and privacy
		  liability

Euclid Managers
  www.euclidmanagers.com
	Internet, Tech, Media,
	  Manufacturers, MPL
		TM and © infringement, misuse
		  and piracy

HISCOX
  www.hiscox.com
	Technology E&O,
	  Technology Media
	  Telecom Policies,
	  Hacker Insurance
		TM and © infringement, cyber
		  squatting violations, moral
		  rights violations, any act of
		  passing off

IPISC: Intellectual Property
  Insurance Services
  Corporation
  www.ipisc.com
	Defense Cost
	  Reimbursement
	  Insurance
		Damages and defense costs
		  for TM, patent and
		  © infringement actions

IPISC: Intellectual Property
  Insurance Services
  Corporation
  www.ipisc.com
	Intellectual Property
	  Infringement
	  Abatement Insurance
		Litigation expenses to enforce IP
		  rights in TM, patent, and
		  © with worldwide geographic
		  cover available

IPISC: Intellectual Property
  Insurance Services
  Corporation
  www.ipisc.com
	Multi-Peril IP Insurance,
	  Reimbursement
	  Insurance (MPIP)
		First party coverage for loss of IP
		  value due to named legal
		  event or lost income due to
		  imposition of injunction for
		  infringement

IPISC: Intellectual Property
  Insurance Services
  Corporation
  www.ipisc.com
	Asset-Backed IP
	  Insurance Policy
	  (ABIPI)
		Financial performance insurance
		  for third parties with a
		  financial interest in IP assets

Kiln
  www.kilngroup.com
	4Thought	Insurance against loss of IP value
		  due to certain legal events
		  such as a finding of invalidity

Liberty
  www.libertyiu.com
	Intellectual Property
	  Infringement Insurance
		Damages and defense costs
		  for TM, patent, and
		  © infringement actions

(*continued*)

TABLE 9.1 (*Continued*)

Provider	Product	IP-Related Coverage
Liberty www.libertyiu.com	Intellectual Property Value Insurance	Loss of revenue/value resulting from invalidity or government action
Munich Re/MARP www.marp.com/MARP	IP Infringement Liability Insurance	Patent, TM, © infringement liability coverage
One Beacon/First Media www.onebeaconpro.com	Media Liability	Covers range of IP-related exposures for media-related companies
Safeonline www.safeonline.com	SafeEnterprise	TM and © infringement, domain name, technology errors and omissions, network security liability and media liability risks
Safeonline www.safeonline.com	SafeCommerce	See above but also protects a company's reputation and the privacy of its customers' information
SAMIAN (Subsidiary of Safeonline) www .samian-underwriting.com	IPGuard	TM, Patent, © infringement liability coverage
SAMIAN (Subsidiary of Safeonline) www .samian-underwriting.com	RepSure	IP reps and warranties coverage
Swiss Re www.swissre.com	Appeal Risk	For existing policy holders, may offer a bond type of coverage to protect a company from failing as a result of a patent infringement judgment
ThinkRisk Underwriting www.thinkriskins.com	Converging Risk Liability Coverage	Media, tech, ad, privacy and network security risks, including TM and © infringement

Media

One form of insurance that might provide a partial solution to the gaps in Bob's insurance program is media liability insurance. This form of specialty insurance has existed for a number of decades, primarily to protect traditional media companies—newspaper and book publishers, broadcasters, and so forth—from claims arising out of the distribution of content. More recently, some carriers have taken the basic media platform and developed "advertiser's liability" policies designed for non-media companies.

This form of coverage has some important limitations, however. First, some advertiser's liability policies specifically exclude claims alleging trademark infringement, which, as we have seen, is among the more serious potential exposures that

Bob's faces. Second, these advertiser's policies are geared exclusively toward content. This means that the policy, unless significantly expanded by endorsement, would not cover E&O claims arising out of Bob's software package or the development of the Bobbike or other similar products. Nor would it respond to network security claims involving unauthorized access to personal information.

Technology E&O

Some E&O policies, especially for technology and software companies, provide coverage for some classes of IP infringement liability. At least one carrier will go so far as to include limited patent infringement coverage by endorsement. However, these claims must arise out of the policy holder's professional services activities, and the limits for patent infringement liability are generally in the $1 million range. A technology E&O policy, therefore, generally would not respond to an IP claim arising out of the insured's advertising activities because such a claim would not relate directly to the services provided by the insured. Nor would Blaze's tech E&O policy likely cover patent infringement liability risk because Darwin, the one carrier currently offering such coverage by endorsement, would not be inclined to offer such coverage to a company like Blaze.

Cyber[14]

In the late 1990s, when it became apparent the Internet was here to stay, some insurance companies created Internet liability, or cyber liability, policies to address the new exposures that businesses faced in an online environment. Such a policy could provide a partial solution to Bob's liability issues. There is very little standardization across these different policy forms—each carrier's program has evolved differently depending on the carrier's underwriting expertise and loss experience. Therefore, it is important to study the language of each policy carefully; Bob's relatively small online operation might find its needs met by a standard form policy, while Blaze's integration with a number of telecommunications networks would require a custom policy.

However, some generalizations can be made about the type of coverage these companies are likely to find in an Internet liability policy. First, just as media policies are geared toward content, cyber liability policies are geared toward Internet-related activities. Thus, while these policies might provide coverage for Bob's web site and related operations, they may not cover Bob's offline activities, such as print advertising, brochures, and catalog. Similarly, the policies may not extend to Bob's software development initiative, and almost certainly would not cover Bob's product development activities. Finally, these policies do not provide any patent-related coverage.

Privacy/Network Security Policies

A related type of policy that has emerged in recent years is privacy/network security coverage. These policies generally provide coverage for risks associated with the maintenance of confidential data by the insured. Again, there is little standardization across these policy forms. Some provide liability coverage for claims associated with data privacy; others provide "first-party" coverage for costs incurred by the insured in responding to a data breach, such as the cost of notifying potentially impacted consumers.

Carriers offering these policies have differing appetites. Some will offer coverage to banks and other financial institutions; some will insure hospitals and other health care businesses; and others prefer retailers and other Main Street commercial companies. Many of these policies now include regulatory coverage—coverage for the insured's costs of defending a regulatory action brought by the FTC and/or state/local law enforcement bodies. Often this coverage is provided with a sublimit of liability. Some policies even go so far as to state that they cover civil fines or penalties imposed by such regulatory bodies, although it is unclear whether such coverage is void as it's against public policy.

While these policies can provide an effective solution to the data privacy issues faced by Bob's and Blaze, they would not address any of the media or E&O issues previously discussed.

Modular Policies

Very recently, some carriers have recognized that none of the policies described provide a comprehensive solution to the myriad liability issues faced by companies in today's information and technology economy. These carriers have developed modular policies that contain a menu of coverages from which the insured can select depending on its business activities and the types of exposures it faces. For example, many of these modular policies contain opportunities for the insured to purchase, in one form or another, media liability, technology E&O, network security, and other coverages, occasionally with different deductibles and limits of liability applicable to each coverage section.

There are about as many variations of these modular forms as there are exposures, so once again it is important for insurance purchasers and their insurance agents to carefully study the forms to ensure they are purchasing the correct portfolio of coverages. However, these modular forms are a step forward to providing a comprehensive solution to the new liability challenges faced by today's commercial businesses, and plugging the gaps in most CGL policies.

Policies Covering Patent Risks

The development of insurance for patent risk has been ongoing since at least the early 1980s. The Lloyd's of London insurance market has been underwriting patent risk for non-U.S. companies since the early 1980s and has been in and out of the U.S. market since 1998. Intellectual Property Insurance Services Corporation (IPISC), a managing general agency based in Louisville, Kentucky, has been offering patent coverage in the United States since 1990. Some large carriers and reinsurers have, on a one-off basis, provided catastrophic coverage for patent infringement liability risk or provided excess coverage where patent infringement liability risk coverage is part of an integrated risk program. In addition, there are several carriers offering patent coverage in specific European Union (EU) countries. For a survey report of available IP insurance coverage, including patent, go to www.betterley.com. Betterley normally performs an IP insurance market survey every other year with policy synopses, contact information, trends, and product comparisons. Its most recent 2010 Intellectual Property and Media Liability Insurance Market Survey was published in April 2010.[15]

Currently, there are a limited number of carriers that insure patent risks. Insurable patent risks are as follows:

- From the first party patent ownership perspective, some of the potentially insurable risks include:
  - The legal costs of protecting and enforcing patent rights
  - The loss or diminished value of the patent as an asset, or diminished licensing or product revenues, as a result of legal findings of invalidity, unenforceability, or non-infringement, some other type of governmental action, or challenges to title or ownership
- From the third party patent infringement liability perspective, some of the potentially insurable risks include:
  - The legal costs to defend against a patent infringement suit
  - Any resulting settlement or damages paid to a third party for past infringement of the third party's patent
  - Patent infringement indemnification obligations to indemnitees such as distributors, customers, and licensees
- From a first party direct or consequential loss perspective, the following also may be insurable:
  - Design-around costs to avoid infringement of a third party's patent
  - Lost revenue due to an injunction imposed as a remedy for infringing a third party's patent

Most insurers provide such coverage through a monoline, or specialty line, coverage form that covers only IP-specific risk. Some will insure patent-related exposures for non-U.S., but not U.S., companies; they will insure first party but not third party risks; or they will provide coverage only above a high retention point or only to companies below a certain size or will exclude companies in certain industries. For example, Blaze may be too large to fit within the size parameters of carriers that offer patent infringement liability coverage. Therefore, patent insurance buyers must stay abreast not only of the different types of coverage available, but also of what the different insurance providers offer, to whom, and on what terms.

PATENT INFRINGEMENT LIABILITY   Insurance policies that cover the third party risk of the policy holder being accused of patent infringement are usually referred to as defensive or infringement liability policies. This type of policy will cover legal defense costs and/or damages and settlement. However, these are typically claims-made policies in which defense costs are included within the policy limits. This means if you purchase a $4 million policy and spend $4 million in defense costs, you will have nothing left in the policy to cover damages/settlement. These policies can be broadened to cover trademark and copyright infringement liability risk as well. In addition, some carriers allow endorsements to these policies that cover the insured's contractual patent infringement liability indemnification obligations to customers and others. At least one technology E&O insurance carrier, Allied World/Darwin, offers a $1 million patent infringement liability endorsement, but on a very selective basis. Since Bob's Bike Shop is a U.S.-based company, its only current options for insurance against claims of patent infringement are IPISC and Allied/World. However, Liberty, through its international unit, is expected to begin offering IP infringement liability policies in the United States beginning in 2011. Lloyd's, through SAMIAN (now part of Safeonline), is expected to reenter the U.S. market by 2011 as well. According to the Betterley Report, Chartis is now offering patent infringement liability coverage, too.

Regardless of who the carrier is, Bob's would need to disclose the two letters it has received. Also, without an issued patent or federally registered trademarks or copyrights protecting its products, services, and brands, these insurance providers could either decline to offer coverage or increase the cost of the coverage. Also, as noted, Blaze is likely too large to be eligible for patent infringement liability coverage, but some of its suppliers may be eligible to purchase the coverage and to add an endorsement to such a policy to cover their indemnity obligations to Blaze. Another option would be for Blaze to approach one of the patent insurance providers about developing a vendor IP insurance program.[16] Finally, if Blaze is sued for patent infringement, loses, and appeals the verdict, then it could purchase appeal risk insurance offered by providers such as Ambridge Partners.

PATENT ENFORCEMENT   Insurance policies that cover the first party risk of incurring litigation expenses to enforce the policy holder's own patent are usually referred to as legal expenses, offensive, abatement, or enforcement policies. In effect, the policy funds the insured's/patent holder's enforcement effort. Such coverage can be extended to include enforcement of trademarks and copyrights as well. Until Bob's Bike Shop obtains a patent or trademark, this coverage is not yet relevant. Because Blaze is so large, and because it has the financial wherewithal to cover its own enforcement costs, such insurance is not as useful to it.

PATENT ASSET VALUE AND REVENUE PROTECTION   Insurance policies also can be obtained to protect against the first party financial loss of the insured caused by a legal finding of invalidity or unenforceability of the covered patent(s). On the flip side, insurance policies can be obtained that cover the insured's consequential loss of investment and/or revenue due to imposition of an injunction for infringement.[17] Variations of this coverage have been offered as a way to protect third parties having a financial interest in the patent, such as investors and lenders, with limited success.[18] While Bob's Bike Shop does not yet have any patents to protect, coverage to protect against its consequential loss should an injunction be imposed against it could be useful. However, injunctions resulting from lawsuits brought by the bike shop in Seattle and Patent Pain likely would be excluded, as Bob's Bikes already is aware of those potential issues. In the case of Blaze, such coverage would have at least partially protected it against revenue loss if an injunction had been granted in the 2004 case.[19]

REPRESENTATIONS AND WARRANTIES AND OTHER M&A-RELATED COVERAGE[20]   In certain mergers and acquisitions (M&A) transactions where representations and warranties insurance is required in order for the transaction to close, carriers sometimes will cover the IP-related reps and warranties, including representations and warranties regarding no knowledge of infringement, validity/enforceability, and title. Alternatively, a separate IP reps and warranties policy may be purchased. Such insurance covers legal expenses and damages/settlement associated with the breach of IP-related reps and warranties made in the context of the sale of a business, products, technology, or intellectual property. In the event Bob's Bikes were approached about a possible acquisition, this coverage might be available to help mitigate any concerns about the software sales or development of the Bobbike, and might help facilitate the sale. Such coverage also might be useful for acquisitions Blaze seeks to make. Ambridge Partners and SAMIAN (through Safeonline) offer IP-focused deal-facilitation insurance coverage.

The Details: Process, Paperwork, Pricing, and Getting Claims Paid

Much of the following section focuses on the process for obtaining stand-alone IP insurance coverage, especially patent insurance coverage. It is meant as a high-level guide to the submission, underwriting, pricing, placement, and claims process. It also provides guidance about policy terms, conditions, and exclusions.

Submission Process

To understand the submission process, it helps to first understand the insurance supply chain, as shown in Figure 9.1. Companies typically have a risk manager or someone else within the company responsible for purchasing insurance on the company's behalf. The person responsible usually retains insurance brokers to access insurance products offered by insurance providers. In the United States, each state has its own insurance laws and regulations; therefore, insurance brokers and insurance carriers must be separately licensed in each state where they wish to transact insurance business. Examples of large, global commercial brokers include Marsh, Aon, Willis, Lockton, and Arthur J. Gallagher. Some of the larger, better known U.S. commercial retail brokers include Daniel & Henry, AH&T, Barney & Barney, Woodruff Sawyer, William

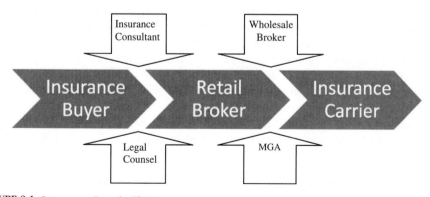

FIGURE 9.1 Insurance Supply Chain

Gallagher, IMA, Hays Companies, HUB, and Frank Crystal. Banks such as Wells Fargo have taken over smaller regional brokers and consolidated them under the bank's name in a separate retail insurance unit. There are also strong regional insurance brokerage firms such as AH&T, Barney & Barney, Woodruff Sawyer, William Gallagher, and Wortham.

U.S. retail brokers that do not have wholesale or surplus lines licenses or sufficient technical expertise in a specific insurance area will sometimes work with wholesale brokers to gain access to insurance products. Some of the larger wholesale commercial brokers include Swett & Crawford, Crump, and AmWINS. Also, U.S. surplus lines brokers may be required to access the Lloyd's insurance market.

Authorized brokers communicate with specialist underwriting agencies or managing general agencies (MGA) or directly with carriers to access insurance products backed by capacity provided by one or several insurance carriers. For example, IPISC is an MGA with Gotham and other insurance carriers providing its supporting capacity. Countries outside the United States operate somewhat differently but the same supply chain system applies.

Not all insurance brokers, regardless of size or geographic reach, have the necessary expertise in the area of intellectual property-related risks. Therefore, when investigating any type of IP-related insurance coverage, either select a retail insurance broker with specific expertise in IP insurance, use a consultant to work with your usual insurance broker, or ask your retail broker to use a knowledgeable wholesale broker. Regardless, stay involved in the process. And, if confidential information must be divulged as part of the submission process, ensure legal counsel is involved in the process as well. In the case of Bob's Bike Shop, it is likely the insurance broker that helped it obtain its CGL coverage does not have the necessary knowledge or expertise to assist Bob's with obtaining insurance to address its IP risks. Otherwise, Bob's would have purchased more than CGL coverage. A major firm like Blaze would likely have a more sophisticated insurance broker. However, even the most sophisticated and experienced brokers do not necessarily have sufficient knowledge placing IP insurance products, especially patent insurance.

The IP insurance submission process is not standardized (see Figure 9.2). However, generally speaking, the seven steps in the placement process are as follows:

1. Submit completed application or at least sufficient information in order for the insurance provider to indicate whether it is interested in receiving a submission.
2. Receive indication of interest (or not) from the insurance provider; the indication may provide premium and limit of indemnity ranges.[21]
3. Provide detailed submission/presentation via a completed insurance application with information about the company and what the company seeks to insure, as well as requested exposures to be covered and limits. For patent insurance some insurers require legal opinions and patent searches, and some insurers require payment of an underwriting fee. Insurers are generally cooperative about executing confidentiality agreements before receiving a submission that contains confidential or potentially legally privileged information. However, note that separate agreements between the applicant and its broker and the applicant and the insurance markets may need to be executed.
4. Allow the provider to conduct its due diligence and underwriting analysis.

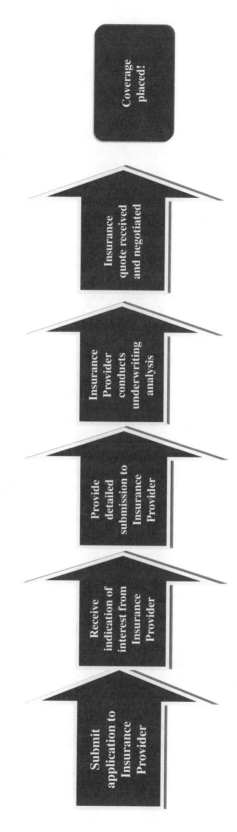

FIGURE 9.2 Submission Process

5. Receive terms and conditions from the underwriter.
6. Negotiate quote, terms, and conditions.
7. Place the coverage.

Failure to make full and accurate disclosure of relevant information is not an option. This includes information about offer to license letters and past IP-related litigation, including how much such disputes cost the applicant and how any such disputes were handled. If the policy is placed and it is subsequently determined that relevant information was not provided to the carrier, then the coverage can be voided. And, if a circumstance leading to a claim is not divulged prior to placement and the circumstance matures into a claim, the insurer has grounds to deny the claim. In the case of Bob's Bike Shop, the letters from Patent Pain and the Seattle bike shop would need to be disclosed. In the case of Blaze, the potential insurer would want to know not only about offers to license, but also about the settlement amounts, verdict amounts, and defense costs for prior patent cases.

Underwriting Process

One of the reasons insurance for patent risk, especially patent infringement liability risk, has not developed more quickly is lack of available loss data. Because it is difficult to obtain litigation cost and settlement data, patent insurance underwriting models are determinative, not actuarial. These determinative models vary by carrier, and the carriers and managing general underwriters hold such models very close to the vest.

While there is not yet a uniform underwriting process or model for patent insurance, applicants should expect insurance underwriters to focus on the following categories of information: relevant patents held by the applicant and how such patents were developed and/or obtained, relevant products made or sold by the applicant, the applicant's financial information, the applicant's patent risk management policies and practices, and the applicant's patent dispute history. Most carriers view the following to be red flags:

- Applicant is unable to provide a full inventory of its IP.
- Applicant has no patents of its own and has not in-licensed patents to protect its products' key market differentiators.
- Applicant has received several offer to license or warning letters.
- Applicant already has been involved in patent litigation (this can also be viewed as a positive).
- Applicant is in a high-risk industry such as medical device, tech and telecom, consumer, or pharmaceutical.
- Applicant is a threat to the market leader and has no patents on its products and the market leader owns a large patent portfolio.
- Applicant cannot identify its competitors.
- Applicant does not monitor patent activity in its technology space.

The results of the insurer's underwriting analysis typically are not shared with the applicant. The submission and underwriting process rarely takes less than two weeks and usually takes four to six weeks.

Pricing

Premiums for media, cyber, and technology E&O insurance have decreased as more carriers have entered the market, more loss data is available, more premium is put on the carriers' books, and loss histories are established. Premiums for stand-alone IP policies, especially patent infringement liability policies, continue to be relatively expensive, especially in the United States. However, pricing has moderated and will decrease as more carriers enter and stay in the market and vie for market share. The base premium usually is calculated on a rate-on-line basis with typical percentages ranging from 1 to 10 percent per million in limits and the percentage decreasing with each million dollars of coverage. By way of example, a patent infringement policy with a $1 million limit of indemnity priced at 2 percent rate-on-line would cost $20,000. The base premium is then modified by the underwriter based on a multitude of factors relating to the underwriter's appraisal of the specific risks presented. Most specialty line IP policies include a self-insured retention (SIR) and co-insurance. The SIR works like a deductible but does not count against the policy limit. The co-insurance counts against the policy limit and can be anywhere from 5 to 20 percent. This is the portion of each legal expense or damages that must be paid by the insured. In addition to other factors, the premium is priced against the SIR and the coinsurance percentage. If the applicant is willing to retain more risk (higher SIR), the premium typically will decrease. Likewise, if the applicant is willing to share more risk with the carrier, the premium typically will decrease.

Policy Form, Conditions and Exclusions

Just as underwriting models vary, so do policy forms. Even identical terms may have different meanings, depending on the carrier. Conditions, especially claims submission and management, are not uniform and can make a major difference in how the coverage works. Also, it is not unusual for carriers to endorse additional exclusions to their standard exclusions on patent infringement liability policy forms. Therefore, it is necessary to carefully read the policy form.

POLICY FORM   Policy forms vary but are often written on an aggregate limit of indemnity basis rather than any one claim, using claims-made forms as opposed to occurrence forms. This means that for there to be coverage, the claim must be made during the policy period. Because policy forms are not standardized and because there is only a certain amount of negotiating of specific terms and conditions in which carriers are willing to engage, care should be taken to understand the key parts of the insurance contract:

- Scope of the insuring agreement
- Definition of terms
- Exclusions
- Conditions, especially regarding the claims approval and management process[22]

SCOPE, DEFINITIONS, AND CONDITIONS   Applicants should take care to apply for the appropriate type of coverage and should therefore be clear about what they want to cover. The increasing use of modular policy forms makes it more effective and efficient for insurance purchasers to identify and select the coverages that best fit the purchaser's business activities and best address the types of exposures the insurance buyer faces. However, until more of such forms include patent risk in their menus of coverage, patent insurance buyers will have to purchase stand-alone policies. In such cases, the buyer must have a clear understanding of the patent risk it seeks to cover. For example, if the applicant is interested in enforcement coverage, does it want to cover all its patents or just a subset? If the applicant is interested in infringement liability coverage, does it want to protect all its products against claims of infringement of just certain products? Does the applicant want coverage for both defense costs and damages or just damages?

Applicants also should be clear about who they want covered. For example, it is becoming more common for customers to require their vendors/suppliers to carry patent insurance. Another increasingly common situation is where one company contractually agrees to indemnify another company against claims of IP infringement and the indemnitor seeks insurance to stand behind that indemnification obligation. While the cost of the insurance weighed against the value of the contract may be high, the company providing the indemnification can spread that cost by purchasing a policy that covers any claims of IP infringement against it with an endorsement that extends the coverage to any entity it contractually agrees to indemnify. In some situations, the indemnitee or the party requiring the insurance may even share the cost of the premium.[23]

Special attention should be paid to geographic scope of coverage. Even those insurers who will not provide insurance to U.S.-based companies will provide worldwide coverage, including the United States. This means if an Australian company is sued for infringement in the United States, it will have coverage under its IP infringement liability policy. If a company is applying for infringement liability coverage, it typically should seek geographic coverage in every country where it makes, uses, sells, offers to sell, or imports product. The temporal scope of coverage is typically one year, but IP reps and warranties and loss of value/revenue coverage can have longer terms.

The amount of limits purchased is critical for several reasons. One, most IP policy forms include litigation costs inside the limit of indemnity purchased so the applicant must ensure he is purchasing limits sufficient to cover litigation costs and damages/settlement. Two, if the applicant is purchasing a policy to insure against events impacting IP value, then some type of valuation must be conducted. Three, if the coverage is for contractual liabilities and the limit of liability is capped, then coverage should only be purchased up to that amount. Different carriers offer different limits of indemnity. If, for example, the applicant seeks to purchase a $20 million limit of indemnity policy, it may have to go to several carriers and purchase excess coverage to build sufficient limits. An excess policy generally follows the form of the underlying primary policy, and allows the insured to build higher limits and spread the risk among multiple carriers. Unfortunately, because there are relatively few players in the patent infringement marketplace, it can be difficult for larger companies to build meaningful towers of patent-related coverage.

Policy definitions vary among carriers. For example, "claim" may be defined to require initiated legal action in one policy form but only the threat of legal action in another policy form. "Covered patents" may include related patent applications and continuations and divisionals in one but not another. "Prior acts" may be defined such that if a claim is made against the insured for infringement that allegedly began two years before the policy inception date, then the claim either will be denied or the carrier will not cover any damages accruing prior to the policy inception date. Some policies also require a waiting period before any claim can be brought.

A company may seek to purchase a modular policy that covers it against Internet exposures, defamation, privacy claims, data breaches, technology E&O, and copyright and trademark infringement, along with a stand-alone policy that covers it against claims of both trademark and patent infringement. It should compare policy forms to ensure both policies do not say they sit excess if other coverage exists to avoid a situation where the company is sued in a single action for trademark and patent infringement and the carriers dispute which policy goes first.

EXCLUSIONS   As would be expected, IP policies typically will not provide coverage for fraudulent, willful, dishonest, or criminal acts. However, read the exclusions carefully. While damages for willful infringement may not be covered, litigation costs to defend against such allegations may be available. If settlement is in the form of a paid-up license, then the portion of the paid-up license that represents the going-forward license typically will not be covered. Some causes of action, such as unfair competition, brought in addition to causes of action for patent infringement may be excluded. There also may be a number of exclusions relating to which patents will be covered by an enforcement policy and which products may be covered by an infringement liability policy.

Claims Process

Make sure you understand policy requirements for claims approval and claims management. For example, for enforcement policies, the insured's counsel may need to provide claim charts, and the insurer may require some type of evaluation of the claim. For defensive/infringement liability policies, the insurer may require a legal opinion of non-infringement. A financial valuation of the claim may be required for first party IP policies that protect against loss of IP asset value due to events such as a legal finding of invalidity.

Where the policies are not duty to defend forms, the insured may select counsel. However, selection may be limited to selection from a list of approved counsel or to counsel meeting certain criteria or counsel may be subject to insurer approval. The insured and its counsel are typically required to communicate with the insurer on a regular basis, including the provision of written reports. Settlement typically requires the insurer's consent.

Conclusion: Why IP Insurance Is No Longer Optional

Today's economy is driven by technology and is globalized, whether you are a bike shop or a Fortune 500 media and telecommunications company. The value of intellectual property continues to increase, the amount of intellectual property continues to increase, and companies are aggressively protecting and enforcing their intellectual property rights. Further, because of the perceived increased value of IP, the IP marketplace is growing and dynamic. A dynamic IP marketplace, together with IP owners more aggressively protecting the value of their assets, means increased uncertainty about who owns IP and who may be asserting their rights against you. With this increased uncertainty comes a greater interest in ways to decrease risk and ways to decrease the costs of managing risk. Insurance offers a way to manage that risk.

Notes

1. See Amended Answer, Affirmative Defenses, Third-Party Complaint and Jury Demand of Sprint, *Digital Technology Licensing LLC v. Sprint Nextel Corporation*, and *Sprint Spectrum L.P. and Sprint Spectrum Equipment Company, L.P. v. Sanyo North America Corporation, Kyocera Communications Inc., and Palm, Inc.*, Civil Action No. 07-5432 (SRC/MAS) (D. N.J. May 18, 2010).

2. See also Dennis Prahl and Elliot Lipins, "Domain Names," in *Intellectual Property Operations and Implementation for the 21st Century Corporation*, (forthcoming).

3. Section 35(a) of the Lanham Act, 15 U.S.C. § 1117(a).

4. See Development of Insurance Policies, Section D, page 13, for a discussion of general commercial liability insurance.

5. ISO insurance forms, including the current commercial general liability form, can be purchased at www.iso.com.

6. E.g., *General Casualty Co. of Wisconsin v. Wozniak Travel Inc.*, 762 N.W.2d 572 (Minn. 2009).

7. UCC § 2-312 (2004)("(2) Unless otherwise agreed, a seller . . . warrants that the goods shall be delivered free of the rightful claim of any third person by way of infringement or the like but a buyer that furnishes specifications to the seller must hold the seller harmless against any such claim that arises out of compliance with the specifications.").

8. See table of insurance providers.

9. See Amended Answer, Affirmative Defenses, Third-Party Complaint and Jury Demand of *Sprint, Digital Technology Licensing LLC v. Sprint Nextel Corporation*, and *Sprint Spectrum L.P. and Sprint Spectrum Equipment Company, L.P. v. Sanyo North America Corporation, Kyocera Communications Inc., and Palm, Inc.*, Civil Action No. 07-5432 (SRC/MAS) (D. N.J. May 18, 2010); see also Samuel Howard, "Sprint Sues Palm, Sanyo, Kyocera For DTL Defense," *IPLaw360* (May 19, 2010), http://ip.law360.com/articles/169574.

10. For a comprehensive and informative article discussing the progressive narrowing of the advertising injury clause, see William F. Campbell, "New Policies, Less Coverage: Insurance Coverage for Intellectual Property Claims," *IPL Newsletter* 22, no. 3 (Spring 2004).

11. See David Henry, "Insurance Coverage for Intellectual Property Claims," *The Briefs* 77, no. 6 (2009).

12. For a more in-depth discussion of legal issues arising from insurance coverage of IP risks, see David A. Gauntlett, *Insurance Coverage of Intellectual Property Assets* (Aspen Publishers 2010).

13. This table does not list Ambridge Partners (www.ambridgepartners.com) or Concord Specialty (www.concordspecialtyrisk.com); however, these managing general underwriters will entertain submissions for IP reps and warranties and contingent liability coverage.

14. See also Steve Mortinger, "The Brave New World of Web 2.0 and the 3-D Internet," in *Intellectual Property Strategies for the 21st Century Corporation.*

15. An executive summary to the Betterley Risk Consultants report, "Intellectual Property and Media Liability Insurance Market Survey—2010," is available at http://betterley.com/samples/ipims10_nt.pdf. The report can be purchased for $50.

16. For a discussion of the interplay between IP infringement liability indemnification and insurance, see Kimberly Cauthorn, Thomas Britven, and Tamara Turek, "Sharing the Risk: Patent Infringement Liability Indemnification and Insurance," *ABA IP Litigation Committee of the ABA Section of Litigation Newsletter* 21, no. 3 (Spring 2010).

17. For example, IPISC offers a multiperil IP reimbursement rider to its IP Defense Cost Reimbursement Insurance.

18. The most recent iteration of IP asset protection insurance is IPISC's ABIPI product.

19. IPISC offers multiperil reimbursement insurance that covers losses resulting from unsuccessful attempts to enforce IP or to defend against claims of IP infringement. IPISC requires the policyholder to carry IP enforcement and/or IP infringement liability insurance as well. Liberty is now offering a first party loss of value insurance product to U.S. companies.

20. See also Diane R. Meyers, "Growth through Acquisition or Merger," in *Intellectual Property Strategies for the 21st Century Corporation.*

21. This initial step is more common when applying for patent insurance. Otherwise, insurers typically prefer to receive a fully completed application as a first step.

22. For an informative discussion of different types of policy forms, see Robert D. Chesler, "Intellectual Property and Cyber-Insurance Issues under General Liability Policies," AIPLA Annual Conference (2009); see also Tod I. Zuckerman, Robert D. Chesler, Christopher Keegan, *Assets and Finance: Insurance Coverage for Intellectual Property and Cyber Claims* (West 2010).

23. See Kimberly Cauthorn, Thomas Britven, and Tamara Turek, "Sharing the Risk: Patent Infringement Liability Indemnification and Insurance," *ABA IP Litigation Committee of the ABA Section of Litigation Newsletter* 21, no. 3 (Spring 2010).

CHAPTER **10**

Exploring Alternative Dispute Resolution

Alicia Lloreda
Jose Lloreda Camacho & Co.

Why ADR Is Relevant

Alternative dispute resolution (ADR) is and will always be relevant because its purpose is to speed up conflict resolution and provide parties with tools to avoid conflicts before they even flourish.

The worldwide economy requests players to remain profitable in spite of short budgets and difficult atmosphere in the marketplace. Every cost-saving tool comes into consideration. ADR provides cost savings and that is what businesses are focusing on today. Companies may avoid disputes or diminish their length and costs by using ADR and be able to use their budget for economic growth.

The world is certainly different now than it was 10 years ago. The Internet[1] has changed how we think and how business is done around the world. It is not necessary to be physically present in any one place anymore to conduct business. Today the world is global. Businesses have no time to stop and deal with conflicts in different jurisdictions and different laws and approaches. There is a need for one solution, tool, or mechanism that may deal with a problem in a faster and cost-effective way. This solution is ADR. ADR will play a major role due in part to the new pace of the economy, the importance of the Internet, and the new ways of doing business globally.

ADR tools used in negotiations, contracts, and deals can certainly keep up with the new pace of doing business. Companies cannot stop and deal with long and cumbersome litigation in various jurisdictions that may have different outcomes. By using mediation or other ADR techniques, companies are opting to have a fast and integral solution to a conflict that could add value to a deal, contract, or negotiation.

Businesses and law firms recruit people who are open-minded, trained in ADR techniques, and who are willing to solve conflicts faster so that business is not interrupted. Success is not possible if at the arrival of a conflict the players (businesspeople and lawyers) are not aware of the benefits and options of ADR and are unwilling to consider it.

In this chapter we explore the methods of using ADR, the different types, the benefits and disadvantages of ADR as seen by the author, mediation, and what to look for when choosing a mediator. The process normally used in mediation is explained and the reader is provided with tips for a successful mediation as well as an attempt to predict the future of mediation in the IP field.

Exploring the Use of ADR Methods

The incremental cost of intellectual property (IP) litigation around the world, the general lack of knowledge on IP laws by the courts, and the varied results regularly obtained after lengthy litigation, have made clients and lawyers look closely at alternatives to litigation.[2]

The results of a survey conducted in 2006 by the Panel of Neutrals of the International Trademark Association[3] showed that costs with respect to intellectual property in litigation matters are considered to be high.[4]

Additionally, it is commonplace that the judges presiding over IP disputes have very little knowledge of IP law and practice.[5] Only a few developed economies, such as Germany and France, have specialized IP courts or specialized panels of judges. Generally, in most countries, courts that review the trademark, patent, and copyright cases also deal with a huge variety of commercial and civil disputes that have no relation to IP. IP is a specialized area of the law studied only by the attorneys interested in practicing or writing about it. When judges do not have sufficient knowledge of IP matters, there is certainly a risk for the parties if, regardless of the merits, the outcome of a case could be unpredictable.

Moreover, if the court is not knowledgeable in intellectual property matters, the case could last a longer time. The Panel of Neutrals survey showed that in most countries, trademark infringement cases take more than 20 months to be resolved.[6]

For these reasons, ADR is not only becoming more attractive for the IP owners but perhaps a necessity in the world today. IP owners, both individuals and corporations, need less expensive, faster, and more creative solutions.

ADR is known for providing solutions to the issues just discussed. Often, it is known to be the best resolution to a conflict. Many types of ADR are explained later in this chapter. The ideal type of ADR for a particular IP dispute should be selected on a case by case basis or depending on certain characteristics of the matter. This is discussed more fully in the chapter when choosing which form of ADR is the most appropriate is addressed.

Types of ADR

There are many types or models of alternative dispute resolution and they vary from country to country. The most used types worldwide are negotiation, mediation, and arbitration. There are also hybrids of the these three types as well as other forms of ADR used in some developed systems.[7]

What all ADR methods have in common is that they are an alternative to litigation, though they vary in other ways. Some are private, some promoted by governments, and some promoted or mandated by a court. Likewise, some are voluntary, when parties decide to use them, and some are mandatory as a consequence of the law establishing them as part of a judicial process or as a requisite to start a process. For example, in some countries, legislation requires parties to go through mediation before starting a civil court proceeding when no injunctions will take place.[8]

The result obtained by using an ADR form is sometimes binding in the case of arbitration and sometimes nonbinding in the case of mediation, unless the parties agree that it is to be binding.

Definitions of the most common forms of ADR follow.

Negotiation

Negotiation is the process by which the parties explore the possibilities of reaching an agreement to resolve their dispute. This process does not include a facilitator. Negotiation could be the first step before going to litigation or exploring an ADR form. For negotiation to succeed, there should be a willingness to settle by all parties.[9]

Mediation

Mediation is a voluntary process by which the parties select a neutral person, or mediator, to assist them in resolving their dispute. The parties choose the mediator, the process they are going to use, and the rules. The mediator has no power to reach a solution; the mediator is and must be neutral and his mission is to assist the parties in trying to reach an agreement. The mediator helps the parties to identify the issues of their dispute and the interests of each party. Following a process agreed to by the parties, which normally consists of giving the parties equal time to express themselves and time to explore all possible solutions, the mediator then aids them in trying to reach an agreement that could be much more beneficial to them than what they could get in a court through litigation.[10]

There are many styles of mediators and various techniques they can use to help the parties reach a mutual beneficial agreement. These different techniques are explained later in this chapter.

Arbitration

Arbitration is when the parties submit their conflict to a neutral individual (arbitrator) or to a panel of neutrals (arbitrators), for her or them to reach a binding decision. The arbitrator is not a judge, but more likely an expert in the matter. The parties normally pick the arbitrator, unless they have agreed otherwise.

The arbitrator imposes a decision (the award) by which the parties have agreed to be bound. Arbitration is more widely used in commercial disputes and technical matters as the parties can choose arbitrators with an appropriate degree of expertise. The parties cannot choose a judge. The process has its own rules, which can vary slightly depending on the entity under whose rules the parties agree to arbitrate a controversy.

Arbitration is similar to litigation, but more flexible. It is also, on average, faster than litigation in most courts. Arbitration awards are often confidential, unless all parties agree to make them public. By contrast, decisions from courts are usually made public.[11] Court proceedings are limited by jurisdiction. Arbitrations can cover international disputes. An example of a successful arbitration in an IP case is the following case resolved by the World Intellectual Property Organization (WIPO) Arbitration Center.

> *A North American software developer had registered a trademark for communication software in the United States and Canada. A manufacturer of computer hardware based elsewhere registered an almost identical mark for computer hardware in a number of Asian countries. Both parties had been engaged in legal proceedings in various jurisdictions concerning the registration and use of their marks. Each party had effectively prevented the other from registering or using its mark in the jurisdictions in which it held prior rights. In order to facilitate the use and registration of their respective marks worldwide, the parties entered into a coexistence agreement that contained a WIPO arbitration clause. When the North American company tried to register its trademark in a particular Asian country, the application was refused because of a risk of confusion with the prior mark held by the other party. The North American company requested that the other party undertake efforts to enable it to register its mark in that Asian country and, when the other party refused, initiated arbitration proceedings.[12]*
>
> *Following proposals made by the Center, the parties appointed a leading IP lawyer as sole arbitrator. In an interim award, the sole arbitrator gave effect to the consensual solution suggested by the parties, which provided for the granting by the hardware manufacturer of a license on appropriate terms to the North American company, including an obligation to provide periodic reports to the other party.*

As mentioned previously, there are other forms of ADR used in a variety of countries, such as the Early Neutral Evaluation, which is a way to obtain an independent view of the conflict by a third party and can serve to facilitate negotiation and settlement.

Med-Arb is a combination of both mediation and arbitration. The parties try to solve the conflict using mediation until they reach an impasse, then the mediator is authorized to issue a binding decision. Following is an example of this combination of alternative dispute resolution methods. This case was also handled by the WIPO Arbitration Center:

> *A publishing house entered into a contract with a software company for the development of a new Web presence. The project had to be completed within one year and included a clause submitting disputes to WIPO mediation and, if settlement could not be reached within 60 days, to WIPO expedited arbitration. After 18 months, the publishing house was not satisfied with the services delivered by the developer, refused to pay, threatened rescission of the contract, and asked for damages. The publishing house filed a request for mediation. While the parties failed to reach a settlement, the mediation enabled them to focus on the issues that were addressed in the ensuing expedited arbitration proceeding.*

Following the termination of the mediation, the publishing house initiated expedited arbitration proceedings. The Center appointed a practicing judge who had been agreed on by the parties as sole arbitrator. The arbitrator conducted a one-day hearing in Hamburg (Germany), in the course of which the parties expressed their desire to settle their case, asking the arbitrator to prepare a settlement proposal. The parties accepted the arbitrator's proposal and requested the arbitrator to issue a consent award. In addition to confirming the terms of the settlement, the consent award made reference to a press release to be published by the parties announcing the settlement of their dispute.[13]

Another type of ADR is the mini-trial, which is a mock trial where parties present their respective arguments and evidence and where the parties could choose to have a mock jury or not. This process encourages the parties to facilitate a later settlement.

There are also summary jury trials, where there is a short presentation by each party so an impartial jury can reach a verdict that eventually helps the parties to negotiate.

Benefits of ADR

One way to predict which ADR form will prevail in the future is to examine the benefits of each method. Generally, people agree that ADR methods have the benefits summarized in this section.

Confidentiality

One of the most valuable benefits of ADR is that it is confidential. Sometimes, companies fear that their conflicts with others may be publicized in the media. ADR is not only private in the sense that it takes place in a private room to which the public has no access, but also that the information disclosed is confidential and the parties agree that the information cannot be used for another purpose. Entering into confidentiality agreements is customary when using ADR, although parties should be aware of the scope of the agreement and the local regulations.[14]

Expense

There are many discussions as to whether ADR is less costly than litigation. This is mainly because arbitration fees are considered to be high in most countries, so some claim that at its conclusion, an arbitration case could cost as much as litigation. The main argument is that the parties have to pay for the privilege of a "judge," since they have to pay the arbitrator(s) fees.[15]

Nevertheless, many studies show that arbitrations cost less than litigation. Surveys conducted by organizations like Ernst and Young and the American Bar Association state that trial lawyers and in-house lawyers believe that the costs of arbitration are lower than the costs of litigation.[16]

Mediation is definitely less costly than litigation. A case submitted to mediation can be resolved in days or a few months and the cost involves the fees of the mediator and the fees of the center.[17]

In an article written by Dr. Karl Mackie, Barrister and Chief Executive of CEDR and Tony Allen, Solicitor and a Director of CEDR in 2007, it is argued that surveys in the United Kingdom demonstrate that cases that have been solved through mediation that otherwise would have been handled by litigation, have saved U.K. business in excess of £1 billion a year in wasted management time, damaged relationships, lost productivity, and legal fees.[18]

These low costs are certainly a benefit for today's world, when businesspeople are faced with conflicts routinely and the budget for dealing with them plays a major role in a corporation's expenses. The cost of litigation not only involves legal fees, but also the damage that occurs to the business as a consequence of the dispute being made public. For this reason alone, ADR should be considered by every businessperson.

Outcome

As mentioned before, parties in litigation know their best and worst case scenarios. The best case always has limitations under law on what the judge can decide. A winning party can get a decision in its favor, legal costs, and damages.

In some forms of ADR, such as mediation, there exists a possibility for an unexpected positive outcome, as the decision reached by the parties relates not necessarily to the relevant law but to the interests of the parties. The parties can resolve the conflict and also end up with new business possibilities.

Mediation then can be a means to add value to an old conflicting business relationship. A clear example of this is a case recently mediated at the WIPO Arbitration and Mediation Center.

> *A European airline entered into an agreement with a U.S. software company concerning the development of a worldwide platform for the management of ticket sales. This was followed by a professional services agreement, which contained a more detailed description of the project as well as the support services to be delivered by the software company. The latter agreement included a WIPO mediation followed by WIPO expedited arbitration clause. The airline paid several million USD for the application. Some years later, the airline terminated the agreement. In response, the software company asserted that, with the termination, the airline's rights in the application had lapsed and requested the software to be returned. The airline was of the opinion that it was entitled to retain the software application and initiated mediation.[19] The result of the mediation was a new license between the parties.*

Fast

In most countries, IP litigation takes many years. A survey conducted by the ADR Committee of the International Trademark Association (INTA) in 2006 showed that trademark infringement cases take from two to four years on average to reach the first decision.[20] Alternative dispute resolution methods are much faster. Mediation could be the fastest. As mentioned before, through mediation a case can be resolved in a matter of days or, at the maximum, a few months. Some argue that mediation needs the complete attention and presence of the parties, but compared to many years of litigation, it seems worthwhile to try it.

Expertise

Judges around the world deal with a large variety of cases relating to many different aspects. Another benefit of ADR is that the conflict is handled by an expert in the matter. The parties choose the neutral mediator or arbitrator on the basis of his or her expertise in the subject matter. According to the survey conducted by the ADR Committee of the International Trademark Association in 2006, lawyers consider that courts have no real expertise in trademark matters in most countries.[21] IP matters require specific knowledge; in the case of patents, a specific technical background is often required and the same can apply to many cases of copyrights. ADR methods offer the benefit of allowing the parties to choose the neutral arbitrator or mediator with a specific background or education so as to facilitate understanding of the particular issue and assistance in resolving it.

Preserve Relationships

Parties can cultivate their interests and realize during the mediation that not only is it worthwhile to try to solve the conflict, but also that a new business opportunity may arise. Many parties sometimes want or need to preserve their relationship, such as that between licensor and licensee, franchisor and franchisee, or supplier and distributor. For these cases, mediation is an excellent solution. Therefore, it is true that some forms of alternative dispute resolutions methods can be beneficial when the relationship with the other party is or could be important.

Preserve Client-Attorney Relationships

Not only can alternative dispute resolution methods benefit the relationships between parties, but they can also help the relationship between the client and the attorney. As litigation is cumbersome, lengthy, and costly, it could damage the relationship between the client and the attorney.

ADR, however, can benefit the relationship between the businessperson who has to manage a conflict, and the attorney who can offer an expedited and less costly way of resolving the conflict. Moreover, the fact that the businessperson can actively participate in the resolution of the conflict and can be creative with respect to the outcome, which is the case in mediation, certainly helps the relationship between client and attorney.

Solve International Disputes

Courts have limited jurisdictions; therefore, solving an international dispute is not easy. Using alternative dispute resolution methods is the best way to solve an international conflict, as the parties may agree on what rules to apply. In the case of IP conflicts, this is a very important issue because in many cases the dispute between parties involves rights in foreign countries. An example of this is the following.

A Dutch company concluded a copyright license with a French company regarding the publication of a technical publication. The license agreement included a WIPO mediation clause. The licensee became insolvent and defaulted on the payment of royalties due under the license. When the licensor requested the mediation procedure, the Center, after consultation with the parties, and with approval of the court-appointed liquidator, appointed an intellectual property specialist as the mediator. Following two meetings between the parties and the mediator, a settlement agreement was concluded.[22]

Control

One important advantage that some types of ADR like mediation or negotiation can offer, as opposed to litigation, is control.

Businesspeople cannot control a litigation or arbitration: Once the matter is in the hands of a court or even an arbitrator, the parties cannot control the outcome. In mediation, the parties have control of the outcome.

Michael Leathes, an international authority on mediation, and director of the International Mediation Institute, stated recently in an article, "Whether the resolution requires negotiation, mediation or some other process, taking direct control over the potential outcome and the process to reach it requires strong doses of leadership, vision, determination, innovation and, often, courage."[23]

Disadvantages of ADR

Here we will examine what critics point out to be the major disadvantages of ADR.

No Guaranteed Resolution

Alternative dispute resolution methods may not always lead to an outcome. Only in the case of arbitration do the parties know that they will obtain a decision. In the case of a mediation, since the parties have the decision-making power in their hands, a full or final decision is not always reached. Notwithstanding this fact, some see this characteristic as a benefit, since control over the decision is one of the advantages of mediation.

No Appeals

Decisions reached by alternative dispute resolutions are generally definite and only some types can be subject to an appeal. In some countries, decisions reached by arbitrators can be the subject of an appeal.

In the case of a mediation, this is not applicable. As the parties control the decision, they are satisfied with the agreement that they have negotiated, so having the opportunity to appeal is not important or necessary. On the contrary, the parties want the decision to be final.

Time and Attention Required of Management

Some critics point out that managers have no time to sit for two or three days with full attention to resolving a conflict. This is true; mediation certainly requires the complete attention of the parties as opposed to that of their attorneys. As mediation does not necessarily entail solving the conflict with respect to the applicable law, but solving the conflict with respect to the parties' interests, the complete attention from the parties is necessary for the mediation to succeed. However, this should not be seen as a disadvantage, but as a benefit. It is an opportunity for managers to add value by concentrating on the interests of the company. The outcome could be much more than expected when analyzing it against the best case scenario of litigation.

Perceived as a Weakness

This is a common criticism, mainly of mediation, though, in my opinion, it has no basis in fact. The fact that a party realizes that it is better to try alternative dispute resolution methods in an effort to settle a case, incurring costs and having the possibility of obtaining a fast decision cannot be a weakness. On the contrary, if the mediation fails, the parties are free to go to court. The brightest strategy could be to try mediation first at a lower cost, and try to reach a decision that could be more beneficial than one obtained in a court of law.

Rosemary Jackson, in an article for Keating Chambers, expressed:

> *Experience shows, however that parties who feel coerced into mediation, or indeed who are ordered by the Courts to mediate, do nonetheless engage in the process and often achieve a settlement.* "I'm only here so that you can't accuse me later of refusing to mediate" *often precedes a settlement.*[24]

Mediation is not a sign of weakness. On the contrary, it could be an opportunity for the parties to realize how strong their cases are and whether it is worthwhile or risky to pursue litigation.

Mediation Is the Best Option for IP Conflicts

All the benefits previously mentioned also apply to mediation. Since it is a nonbinding process during which parties have control and autonomy as well as the help of a neutral mediator who is an expert in the matter, it is a very good tool to consider when facing an IP conflict.

It is easy to agree that conflicts involving intellectual property rights require a knowledgeable person to understand them. Judges seldom are aware of the laws that deal with patents, trademarks, and copyrights and of their complexity. As discussed earlier in this chapter, IP attorneys believe that international courts do not have adequate knowledge on IP.[25] In many countries, parties are often afraid of the outcome of a case, due to their concern that the judge probably would not easily understand the conflict and in many cases that the judge would not have the time and resources to study it.

During litigation, the party having the most convincing expert to testify in its favor, or the most costly survey, may be the one ending up with a favorable result based on this fact exclusively.

IP conflicts regularly involve long-lasting relationships, such as the relationship of the licensor and licensee of a particular trademark. For whatever reason, when a conflict between the parties develops, litigation cannot be the solution, as there is an interest in the parties rebuilding their relationship. For this reason, mediation should be considered. The parties can walk away from mediation, not only solving the conflict but entering into a renewed business relationship.

A perfect illustration of this circumstance is the WIPO case mentioned previously in which a European airline entered into an agreement with a U.S. software company concerning the development of a worldwide platform for the management of ticket sales. The agreement was terminated and the case went to mediation since the agreement had a mediation clause. The result of the mediation was a new agreement.[26]

This result would not have been possible in litigation.

Another matter to consider is that often the parties involved in the controversy are corporations that need to protect their image and reputation. A trademark owner has to be very careful with respect to its image projected to consumers. A publicized conflict can certainly hurt a company's reputation and its trademarks.

Considering mediation can be a smart choice in order to preserve a company's reputation and image and to keep its conflicts with competitors confidential and private.

Cost is another big issue for corporation managers who constantly measure how efficiently they spend their budgets. Companies in the past few years, due to the difficult economic times, started looking more carefully at legal fees and litigation costs. Mediation certainly is a very low cost option for resolving conflicts. Companies can achieve a good result, with no risk involved, when undergoing mediation as the first step to solve their IP conflicts.

Companies have to think of their best interests and what they need to protect. Having a favorable decision is less important than saving costs, resolving the conflict fast, and having no exposure of a major conflict. Moreover, as explained before, in many cases, the parties add value to the mediation by not limiting the agreement to the legal issues, but to their business interests.

Mediation can be appropriate to solve many intellectual property disputes,[27] such as:

- Trademark and service mark infringement
- Opposition and cancellation proceedings before patent and trademark offices
- Trademark license and other contract disputes
- International trademark disputes[28]
- False advertising and trade disparagement
- Unfair competition proceedings
- Consumer protection proceedings
- Disputes involving domain names, corporate names, and other trade names
- Right of privacy and right of publicity
- Misappropriation

Because mediation is a nonbinding process, it is a very attractive alternative for IP disputes. If, after trying to solve a conflict with a neutral expert in IP, the parties are not able to reach a solution, they can stop the mediation and go to litigation or to an alternative resolution method such as arbitration.

Mediation for IP matters has more benefits than arbitration: The costs are lower, the proceedings are faster and the parties have control over the decision. Moreover, if the mediator helps the parties to explore their interests and focus on them, the solution reached can often be better than the best outcome in a court or arbitration and can generate new value to the parties.

The Best Mediator

A good mediator is a key to a successful mediation. There are important factors to consider when choosing a mediator: One is the style of mediation he or she follows.[29]

Some mediators follow the evaluative style. These mediators often provide their analysis of the case and state in private caucuses the strengths and weaknesses of their case to each party. This style is followed normally by judges who, by law, have to conduct mediations during proceedings or by former judges who act as mediators when they retire. This style is used to encourage the parties to reach a resolution. But it does not comply with one of the most important benefits of the mediation, which is to focus on the interests of the parties, not only which party is right or wrong according to the law.

Other mediators follow the transformative style, which focuses basically on the relationship of the parties. The mediator meets with the parties together and works hard to understand the relationships and the emotions of the parties. After the parties disclose their emotions and issues, the mediator evaluates the interests of the parties. This style is more commonly used in family disputes but is also used in commercial disputes. This style is frequently used in Latin American countries, especially in Argentina and Colombia, where mediation is mandatory in civil proceedings.[30]

The most common and frequently used, and perhaps more beneficial style, is when the mediator acts as a facilitator. The mediator makes clear to the parties at the beginning of the session that the solution to the problem is in their hands. The mediator does not render his opinion on the case. The mediator makes certain that the parties reach a decision on the basis of agreed upon facts which have been submitted. The mediator assists the parties with questions in identifying the issues and helps the parties to focus on their interests. The mediator helps the parties to brainstorm a solution. This can be done with both parties together or by having private sessions with each party (caucusing). It is important to point out that having caucus meetings depends on whether the parties agreed to do so at the beginning of the mediation.

Zema Zumeta, in her article, *Styles of Mediation: Facilitative, Evaluative, and Transformative Mediation*, clearly explains:

> *There seem to be more concerns about evaluative and transformative mediation than facilitative mediation. Facilitative mediation seems acceptable to almost everyone, although some find it less useful or more time consuming. However, much criticism has been leveled against evaluative mediation as being coercive, top-down, heavy-handed and not impartial. Transformative mediation is*

criticized for being too idealistic, not focused enough, and not useful for business or court matters. Evaluative and transformative mediators, of course, would challenge these characterizations. Sam Imperati, for example, sees evaluative mediation as ranging from soft to hard: from raising options, to playing devil's advocate, to raising legal issues or defenses, to offering opinions or advice on outcomes. He therefore believes that it is not appropriate to assume that evaluative mediation is necessarily heavy-handed. Folger and Bush, on the other side of the discussion, see transformative mediation as ultimately flexible and suited to all types of disputes.[31]

There are other factors to consider when choosing a mediator. Certainly, not everybody has the necessary skills or experience to mediate. Some argue that mediators are naturally skilled and are born, not made.[32] They have to be social, good listeners, and patient. Others argue that the skills depend of the cultural background and on their education; they believe that anyone can become a good mediator by studying and practicing.[33]

The best approach is probably a combination of both. A mediator needs natural skills and education. Good mediators have to be good listeners. Mediators have to listen to what the party is saying and try to read what the party is not saying.[34] It is important too that the mediator verifies whether the parties are listening. If there is a misunderstanding, the mediator has to clarify.

The mediator has to be able to create empathy so that the parties feel that the mediator understands their problems and is interested in what the parties have to say.[35]

It is widely accepted that a required talent of a good mediator is being able to diminish stress and tension levels during a mediation session.

It is very common in a mediation session that emotions like anger, sadness, revenge, and impatience emerge. The mediator has to know how to deal with these emotions. The mediator has to read the parties, identify their negative emotions as soon as they arise, and be able to deal with them. The mediator has to be attentive if emotions like fear, sadness, surprise, guilt, shame, and so on, surface.[36]

Learning how to deal with an impasse is essential to being a good mediator. Impasses in mediations are more usual than commonly believed. A good mediator deals with an impasse by bringing the matter to the table for discussion by all parties. If the mediator chooses to ignore it, it is probable that the issue will arise later, or the mediation will fail.

Another talent to consider is communication skills. A good mediator has to know how to communicate with the parties. He has to recognize when it is important to rephrase something that a party has said and to know how to rephrase it. He has to know how to ask the right questions and when to ask them. The mediator not only has to understand the emotions, but also help the parties to understand their emotions.

Some desirable talents of a good mediator are:[37]

- Art of listening
- Art of talking
- Power of persuasion
- Sense of humor

- Tact
- Diplomacy
- Consideration
- Facilitation

A good mediator also has to identify whether there are cultural differences, and respect them,[38]

Additionally, the mediator is in charge of leveling the differences of the parties. In case there is a very powerful party at the table, the mediator is in charge, without forgetting that he or she is a neutral, of making the less powerful party feel that the mediator is impartial and not biased in favor of the powerful party.

The only way to evaluate whether the mediator has the above-mentioned skills is to find previous references. Referrals of the parties who have used a mediator help others to know if the mediator is the right person to choose. Did the counsel report that the mediation showed credibility? Did the parties feel that the mediator was neutral? Was it easy for him or her to deal with an impasse?

The mediator has to have a very good reputation.[39]

Process and Tips

There is not one set procedure to follow and if the parties agree to the details, they may amend the procedure with the mediator. INTA has a complete set of guidelines on mediation translated in several languages that are very useful for IP cases.[40] Mediations normally are conducted following some stages.

Agreement to Mediate

Mediation can arise because (1) parties include a mediation clause in a contract,[41] (2) one party suggests it to the other, or (3) it is necessary to initiate a judicial action and mediation is a necessary stage in the proceedings in a court or before or during arbitration.

The Role of the Mediator

As mentioned before, it is important to choose the right mediator. For this purpose, parties can agree on a particular list of mediators to guarantee the necessary qualifications of the mediators.[42] After being chosen, the mediator should contact the parties to request necessary documentation from them. The mediator needs to establish with them the process, location, and fees.

The mediator needs to prepare the mediation. He has to be sure that he has clarity on the facts and that he has in his hands all the relevant documents. Before starting the process, it is important that the mediator verify that the parties are the decision makers, and that they are empowered to reach a decision.

At the first meeting, the mediator explains the process, and establishes the ground rules.[43] The mediator agrees with the parties on whether everyone is to attend all the meetings, or if the mediator may have separate meetings (caucuses) with each party. In this first meeting, the parties execute the corresponding confidentiality agreements.

The mediator starts gathering information. He gives each party the opportunity to tell the story without interruptions. The mediator starts asking open-ended questions and may repeat ideas to make sure the parties heard everything said. The mediator should take notes to be able to summarize.

Afterward, the mediator can help the parties brainstorm, and look for options to solve their conflict. If the mediator finds common goals, he should memorialize them in order to verify that both parties agree. The mediator can conduct the brainstorming with both parties together or using caucus (private sessions with each party).[44]

Depending on the complexity of the meeting, the mediation could last some days or months.

If the parties reach a settlement, the mediator reduces it to writing. If no settlement is reached, the mediator could propose other alternatives such as arbitration or litigation and will terminate the session.

Some tips for having a successful mediation are:

- Be familiar with the proceedings. Read the rules before attending the mediation.
- Ask yourself these questions:
  - What background knowledge do you want the mediator to have?
  - Does the mediator have experience in IP matters? Does he have a good reputation?
  - How much will the mediation cost?
  - What style does the mediator have or use?
  - What information will be exchanged in advance?
  - Will the information provided be confidential? Can the other party use it if the mediation fails?
- Be aware of your and the other party's strengths and weaknesses.
- Be aware of time, costs, and exposure of litigation.
- Concentrate on your business interests, not on the legal position or the law.
- Use the mediator. Brainstorm the mediator in caucus.
- Be prepared to negotiate.
- Be creative.
- Be flexible.
- Be open-minded. Mediation works.

International Mediation (Cultural Differences)

One of the benefits of the mediation is that it can solve international disputes. Often, intellectual property matters involve parties from different countries and different jurisdictions with varied rights.

In contrast to litigation, mediation can include parties from various countries with rights in several countries as well. The mediator, at the same time, could be from a different country. As the procedure is agreed on previously by the parties, they can agree on a location that is neutral to both parties and establish a proceeding that serves both parties' interests.

For these cases, it is very important to choose a mediator with international experience as there are important cultural differences to take into consideration.

The misunderstanding of a cultural practice can lead to the failure of the mediation.

Communication is different around the world. Some cultures are straightforward and others are more reserved. Interrupting conversation in some cultures is not only accepted, but expected.[45]

Josefina Rendon, in her article, *When You Can't Get Through Them: Cultural Diversity In Mediation,* which defined well the differences between the Latin and the Anglo-Saxon culture, states:

> *People from predominantly expressive cultures touch often, maintain long intense eye contact and feel comfortable with those who maintain the same tactile and visual demeanor. In fact they may distrust those who do not look at them "in the eye" or who respond uncomfortably to their touch.*
>
> *Conversely, people who are more restrained or neutral tend to be more poker-faced. Their speech, rather than fluid and dramatic, is more monotonic. They are uncomfortable with too much touching or intense eye contact. Although they may feel just as emotional or tense, these people tend to hide these emotions. They generally value stoicism in others and think little of those who are openly emotional.[46]*

Cultures shift and are dynamic. It is dangerous to make culture generalizations. People are influenced by different cultures, so if people come from a different culture it does not mean that they are going to act in a certain way.[47]

Being aware of cultural differences is an important tool for any mediator in order to be able to deal with impasses and obstacles that can arise during the sessions and to be able to make the parties comfortable from the beginning of the process.

The Future of Mediation

Companies hate conflicts. Having a way of resolving them at a low cost and in an expeditious manner is the perfect solution. That is the exact definition of mediation. Mediation is a tool for resolving conflict in a fast and inexpensive manner without losing control over the process. Companies wish to have control over their conflicts. For reasons relating to budgets, timing and reputation, companies need to be certain that they can control their conflicts.

Fast resolution at a lower cost is not only positive for companies but is also beneficial for courts. Courts worldwide have many more cases than they are able to deal with in an efficient manner. If mediation is widely used, people will bring fewer cases to the courts.

So now it is necessary to ask the question: If mediation is so worthwhile, why isn't everybody using it? Why are some companies reluctant to try it? Why do some companies still blindly pursue litigation before trying to resolve the conflict through mediation? Is it due to ignorance?

Mediation advocates argue that once you try mediation you will recommend it. James Melamed in his article, *A View of Mediation in the Future,* states:

> *Even among those that do not reach agreement in mediation, over 90% still recommend the process to a friend in a similar situation. Mediation has rapidly become the "day in court" we perhaps never really had.[48]*

It seems that the problem is that there is not enough convincing education about mediation worldwide. Law schools throughout the world should make changes to the benefit of the profession and orient their curriculum more to alternative dispute resolution methods than litigation.

In the same manner, business schools around the world should be more aware of the needs of corporations and include in their curriculum a thorough understanding of alternative dispute resolution and mediation training for future managers. By doing so, future managers would be more likely committed to utilizing mediation when facing conflicts.

Conclusion

It seems easy to conclude that given the current economic situation, the new pace of the world economy, the constant advances in technology and how the Internet is present in every business, ways of conducting business are changing and this will likely lead to more conflicts.

Conflicts will keep arising and we need a fast, cost-effective way to handle them. ADR is a compelling answer. Young generations of businesspeople and lawyers should not cope with a system that is lengthy, limited (to a jurisdiction), and costly such as litigation. ADR techniques and tools are serving and will continue to serve these new needs of the business world.

We have entered into a new world where there is a terrific need to speed up the way we manage conflicts. Businesses are requiring lawyers to be creative and solve their problems faster and more cost-efficiently. ADR is the right alternative to make available.

Notes

1. See also Steve Mortinger, "The Brave New World of Web 2.0 and the 3-D Internet," in *Intellectual Property Strategies for the 21st Century Corporation.*

2. See also Raymond DiPerna and Jack L. Hobaugh Jr., "When to Litigate: The Rise of the Trolls," in *Intellectual Property Strategies for the 21st Century Corporation.*

3. INTA, 2006, Survey at www.inta.org.

4. Ibid.

5. Ibid.

6. Ibid.

7. Some examples are the early neutral evaluation, the mini trial, the summary jury trial, and the mediation-arbitration.

8. In Argentina and Colombia it is mandatory to attend mediation before going to civil court if no injunction is requested. Alirio Galvis Padilla, "Análisis Comparativo de la Legislación de Mediación Colombo Argentina," www.cejamericas.org/doc/documentos/ARTICULO_COLOMBO_ARGENTINA.pdf.

9. www.mindtools.com/CommSkll/NegotiationSkills.htm.

10. www.inta.org/index.php?option=com_content&task=view&id=683&Itemid=222& getcontent=4.

11. www.wipo.int/amc/en/arbitration/why-is-arb.html.

12. www.wipo.int/amc/en/arbitration/case-example.html.

13. Ibid.

14. www.morganlewis.com/pubs/C6681EF0-0952-4BD0-ABD4ACE191D88B1A_Publication.pdf.

15. www.startribune.com/business/11763816.html.

16. Robert S. Haydock, "Arbitration v. Litigation," November, 2007, at www.startribune.com/business/11763816.html.

17. An example of the fees is the 2010 tariff established by WIPO Mediation Center. There is an administration fee of 10 percent of the value of the mediation subject to a maximum of $10,000 and the mediator fees which are from US$300 to US$600 per hour, or US$1,500 a US$3,500 per day. See: www.wipo.int/amc/en/mediation/fees/.

18. "The Costs Crisis—Mediation as a Solution?" CEDR's submission to the Jackson Inquiry into legal costs, www.cedr.com/index.php?location=/library/articles/20091221_273.htm.

19. www.wipo.int/amc/en/mediation/case-example.html#m9.

20. "What Is the Approximate Time for the First Decision (Months)?," www.inta.org/images/stories/downloads/2006adrsurvey.ppt#266, 10.

21. "Do Courts in Your Country Have Sufficient Knowledge of Trademark Law?," www.inta.org/images/stories/downloads/2006adrsurvey.ppt#268, 12.

22. Case mediated at WIPO Arbitration and Mediation Center, www.wipo.int/amc/en/mediation/case-example.html#m9.

23. Michael Leathes, "Conflict Leadership," September, 2009, www.imimediation.org/conflict-leadership.html.

24. Rosemary Jackson Q.C., "Mediation: Some Do's and Some Dont's," 2005, www.keatingchambers.co.uk/resources/publications/rj_mediation_dos_and_donts.aspx.

25. Survey conducted by the ADR Committee of the International Trademark Association in 2006, www.inta.org/images/stories/downloads/2006adrsurvey.ppt.

26. www.wipo.int/amc/en/mediation/case-example.html#m9.

27. INTA, "Resolution through Mediation" brochure at www.inta.org/images/stories/downloads/adr_brochure2005.pdf.

28. See also Robert Lamb and Randie Beth Rosen, "Global Piracy and Financial Valuation of Intellectual Property Revisited: Threats, Challenges, and Responses," in *Intellectual Property Strategies for the 21st Century Corporation.*

29. Zena Zumenta, *Styles of Mediation: Facilitative, Evaluative, and Transformative Mediation,* September 2000, www.mediate.com/articles/zumeta.cfm.

30. Ley 24573 de 1995, Mediación y Conciliación Obligatoria, República de Argentina; Ley 640 de 2001, Conciliación Obligatoria, República de Colombia.

31. Zena Zumenta, *Styles of Mediation.*

32. "Alternative Dispute Resolution: Training and Accreditation of Mediators," discussion paper 21 (1989), www.lawlink.nsw.gov.au/lrc.nsf/pages/DP21CHP3.

33. Tammy Lenski, Alice Estey and Susanne Terry, "The Value of Extended, Integrated Mediator Education," 2007, www.mediate.com/articles/LenskiTbl20100208.cfm.

34. G. R. Thomas, "Mediator Skills," 2004, www.nadr.co.uk/articles/published/mediation/Mediator%20Skills%20Thomas%202004.pdf.

35. "Through empathic listening the listener lets the speaker know, 'I understand your problem and how you feel about it, I am interested in what you are saying and I am not judging you.' The listener unmistakably conveys this message through words and non-

verbal behaviors, including body language. In so doing, the listener encourages the speaker to fully express herself or himself free of interruption, criticism or being told what to do. It is neither advisable nor necessary for a mediator to agree with the speaker, even when asked to do so. It is usually sufficient to let the speaker know, 'I understand you and I am interested in being a resource to help you resolve this problem.'" Salem, Richard. "Empathic Listening." *Beyond Intractability*. Eds. Guy Burgess and Heidi Burgess. Conflict Research Consortium, University of Colorado, Boulder. Posted: July 2003, www.beyondintractability.org/essay/empathic_listening.

36. Jaidivi Nuñez, Alfredo Revelo, and Jose Octavio Zuluaga. "Manual Practico de Mediación," *ASIPI-LEGIS* (2008).

37. Ibid.

38. M. Hecht, L. Larkey, and J. Johnson, "African American and European American Perceptions of Problematic Issues in Interethnic Communication Effectiveness." *Human Communication Research* 19, 209–236 (1992). Ling Chen, "Perceptions of Intercultural Interaction and Communications and Satisfaction: A Study of Initial Encounters," *Communication Reports*, 15 (1992).

   Alessandra Sgubini, "Mediation and Culture: How different cultural backgrounds can affect the way people negotiate and resolve disputes," March 2006, Bridge Mediation LLC 2005.

39. Eric Van Ginkel, "Door Number One? Door Number Two? Or Door Number Three?: Choosing the Right Mediator Part II," March 2010, www.ipadrblog.com/2010/03/articles/authors/eric-van-ginkel-1/door-number-one-door-number-two-or-door-number-three-part-ii.

40. Mediation Guidelines and Agreements, Intenational Trademark Association, www.inta.org/index.php?option=com_content&task=view&id=1700&Itemid=261&getcontent=4.

41. Ibid.

42. There are lists of mediators specialized in Intellectual Property matters. See: INTA Panel of Neutrals at www.inta.org/index.php?option=com_content&task=view&id=684&Itemid= 223&getcontent=4; also see WIPO Domain Name Panelists at www.wipo.int/amc/en/domains/panel/panelists.html.

43. See: Mediation Rules of the International Trademark Association, www.inta.org/downloads/adr_NA_MediationRules.pdf.

44. Caucuses are meetings that mediators hold separately with each side of a dispute. They can be called by the mediator or by one of the parties to work out problems that occur during the mediation process. Brad Spangler, "Caucus," in *Beyond Intractability.*, ed. Guy Burgess and Heidi Burgess. Conflict Research Consortium, University of Colorado, Boulder. Posted: June 2003, www.beyondintractability.org/essay/caucus.

45. "In some cultures, interrupting others is not rude but expected. Interruption often means attention and participation in the conversation rather than rudeness. Interruption is in some cultures a type of "active listening" and quiet passive listening may be a sign of lack of interest or attention." Josefina Rendon, "When You Can't Get Through To Them: Cultural Diversity In Mediation," www.mediate.com/articles/rendon.cfm.

46. Ibid.

47. LeBaron, Michelle, "Culture and Conflict," in *Beyond Intractability*, ed. Guy Burgess and Heidi Burgess. Conflict Research Consortium, University of Colorado, Boulder. Posted: July 2003, www.beyondintractability.org/essay/culture_conflict.

48. James Relamed, *A View of Mediation in the Future*, June 2009, www.mediate.com/articles/on_mediation_in_the_future.cfm.

CHAPTER 11

Outsourcing and Offshoring of IP Legal Work

Olga M. Nedeltscheff
Limited Brands, Inc.

Thirty years ago or so, the term *outsourcing*[1] conjured up images of delegating work to outside counsel—to a trusted firm, where the lawyers worked in tandem with internal corporate staff to achieve the goals of the clients. This arrangement consisted of internal staff comprised of legally trained personnel or paraprofessionals relaying instructions or interpreting corporate wishes to the attorneys in private practice, who then communicated with local counsel or agents in jurisdictions throughout the world.[2]

Outside counsel corresponded with the world at large, received the information, sifted through the voluminous requirements and minutiae, and summarized for the benefit of the corporate liaison. Frequently, the liaison would simply forward the communication drafted by the external lawyer directly to the businessperson, having successfully outlined the requirements of such communication.

Reality Check

Today "outsourcing" evokes a different image: offshore execution, complex communication, instantaneous responses—all possible as a result of advancements in technology from e-mail to virtual realities. If years ago communication from one country to another took the time a call could be placed on a frequently unreliable telephone line, through connections by trunk lines, today fiber optics, cable, and mobile equipment erase the factor of delay. By the time a telex was transmitted, first having been typed into the hole-punched tape, and then received and interpreted on the other side, some time would pass. Facsimiles increased the speed of the exchanges by allowing entire documents to be transmitted through telephone lines. And today instant messaging sends the note within seconds of being composed.

With the increase in tempo there came increased flexibility: One could work anywhere, keep in touch by means of a plethora of mobile communication devices, and raise productivity and results. But do increased productivity and results really ensue?

The change in speed of communication also enabled the "virtual workforce": It does not matter where people are located physically; it only matters whether the work can get done and delivered to the client.

As an extension of these virtual workplaces, and as it no longer matters where the work is done, working offshore—where expenses are lower and the work product is just as good as "homegrown"—became more attractive. And the quantity and quality of work continues to increase, with lessons learned. For outsourcing to different locations to be successful, surveys in India indicate that management of teamwork is paramount in the success of such endeavors.[3] For companies and law firms in the United Kingdom and the United States, outsourcing has been a practice for decades, while offshoring is becoming an alternative model since the turn of the century. With the ease of communication, increased reliability of data exchanges, availability of educated and English-speaking local professionals, work is increasingly sent to countries outside the client's center of operations.

Outsourcing is frequently thought of primarily for repetitive or low-level activities. Software support, call centers, and customer service are most often candidates for being delegated outside an enterprise. Initially, these offshore delegations were seen as a way to enhance American productivity and growth, and create new, higher value, higher paid technical jobs.[4]

As late as 2006, there was the perception that "lower paying jobs are being outsourced while the more skilled ones are being kept here" (in the United States).[5] But in recent publications, the prognostication is that U.S. companies will outsource over 200,000 service jobs each year, totaling 3.3 million jobs by the year 2015.[6] This prediction may have included 50,000 U.S. legal jobs.[7] Even then it was recognized that labor costs are only one of the factors to consider. Proximity to vendors and customers, and reliable power supplies were also seen as important in determining whether service jobs were to be outsourced.[8]

With time and budget constraints weighing even greater on corporate departments,[9] "outsourcing [was] here to stay."[10] While companies in the United States continued (and continue) to announce layoffs of thousands of employees, some of the biggest companies continue to invest in India.[11] Hewlett Packard and McKinsey, among others who have sent legal work outside of the United States, and particularly to India, claim significant cost savings.[12] For example, in 2003, chief operating officer Bruce Masterson of Socrates Media was disappointed with outside counsel's estimate of $400,000 to customize a residential lease, and sent the work to Jurislex in Hyderabad, India, to do the work for $45,000.[13] Other attorneys agree that "India has very talented attorneys" but believe that it is a misconception to think the work can just be sent over and gets done: "You need proper supervision and security."[14]

Having assignments and projects completed outside the core business or firm may have its proponents, but some work can be fraught with complications. Even delegating this work to an outside firm results in certain loss of control and communication gaffes; imagine the potential discrepancies where there is tenuous common ground, where the cultures are different, and expectations are not clearly defined.

Another example of outsourcing and offshoring to India has been the Rio Tinto project with CPA Global.[15] Tasks that were delegated to the team of lawyers in India included document review, contract drafting, and legal research in the expectation that such outsourcing would reduce the Rio Tinto "annual legal budget by 20 percent" and would be "seven times cheaper than simply using its own lawyers in London."[16]

Microsoft has offshored its patent operation to India in recent years,[17] following the outsourcing lead of Texas Instruments and General Electric. Texas Instruments is a veteran, having begun in the late 1980s.[18]

Microsoft has also offshored its internal technical support services to India,[19] which Microsoft says "will not impact [their] internal resources." Microsoft's associate general counsel and director of worldwide IP operations, Martin Shively, has even moved to New Delhi, India, with his family as part of legal processing outsourcing through Microsoft's "Realizing India's Potential" program.[20] By Shively's estimates, Microsoft will spend about $3 million on patent services in India:

> *If you estimate that work at US pricing, that's $9.5 million worth of work at about $6.5 million cost savings. For a company the size of Microsoft that may seem negligible, but for our department, that's a significant sum of money.*[21]

In surveys conducted in December 2009,[22] about 5,200 legal processing outsourcing professionals in India and the Philippines were providing services such as electronic document management, electronic discovery, intellectual property, and associate level activities. The intellectual property work included prior art searching for patents, preliminary screenings of trademarks, proofreading, and docket maintenance. The belief is that 90 percent of such work is being directly outsourced by in-house counsels or on behalf of such internal attorneys.[23]

India is not the sole center for outsourcing or off-shoring. Arguments have been made for other jurisdictions, including South Africa.[24] Trademark work, from searching and clearance work, to filing, prosecution, and even enforcement, along with assignment and licensing, renewal management, and maintenance tasks, due diligence projects, trademark surveillance—all appear to be possible candidates for outsourcing. At every level of outside firm involvement, there is a cost to the internal resource. The cost is not only in expense, but also in time and effort in relaying the instructions and information to the outside counsel, following up, maintaining internal records, and advising corporate management.

Law firms themselves outsource legal work[25] to other specialty or smaller firms, or offshore work, where such action may lead to efficiencies and centralization of certain functions.[26] In some cases, the outsourcing is to a less costly center in the United States, as WilmerHale is said to have done recently, in moving certain office functions to Dayton, Ohio.[27]

But costs are not the sole factor in making the decision to outsource to other countries. Vendors use terms such as *partners*, and qualitative measures are becoming as important as quantitative (i.e., customer satisfaction versus cost savings).[28]

There is even an emerging trend where offshoring may result in a project being based in the United States.[29]

In fact, some in-house counsel are reevaluating this type of decision as is the American Bar Association (ABA).[30] Concerns of varying degrees include confidentiality, privilege, conflicts of interest, competence, and even billing.[31]

Outsourcing or Offshoring in the IP Context

While much has been has been said about the act of sending work to outside counsel, overseas firms, and legal support vendors, it is important to define the type of subject matter in the field of intellectual property that is most suitable and likely to be delegated.

For patents, unless the client has an internal attorney or patent agent skilled in describing the patentable object or process, performing priority searches and filing relevant applications, it is prudent to avail oneself of the expert services of an attorney, preferably specializing not only in patents generally, but in the specific field, such as chemistry or mechanical engineering, depending on the circumstances. Maintenance of the ensuing registration—which may be annual in many jurisdictions—is also easily handled by such firms.

For trademark matters, searching, clearing, and acquiring trademark protection benefits greatly from the advice of knowledgeable and experienced attorneys. In addition, trademark watch services alleviate the burden of policing the marks, alerting the owners to possible conflicts and filing oppositions or cancellations, as appropriate to enforce the trademark.

As for copyright, registration is not mandatory in many jurisdictions, and in fact not even possible. In the United States, after adherence to the Berne Convention, registration of copyright is advantageous for statutory damages in infringement cases.

And most of all, few clients have the manpower or resources to conduct litigation completely internally, given the complexity of the proceedings in each state or district, and the bane of discovery in the United States.

Accordingly, the preceding is a mere outline of the myriad of possible tasks or functions that could be sent to outside counsel or legal support groups.

Conflicts of Interest[32]

Conflicts of interest are not solely an offshoring concern.[33] Before a matter may be undertaken by an outside firm, the attorney must verify whether the attorney or firm being hired have had or have at present any clients or matters that may create a conflict of interest. A conflict of interest is a potential bar to the project being handled by the firm that has work "for the adversaries of their clients on the same or substantially related matters;" in such an instance, the outsourcing lawyer could choose another provider.[34] If there is any possibility that the attorney entrusted with the project would be limited in his or her representation of the incoming client or would be in an adverse position, the attorney should not accept the assignment, unless there is full disclosure to the incoming client, and a waiver by such client.

In some U.S. jurisdictions, the law firm is also required to maintain meticulous records of prior engagements and to have a system for checking proposed engagements against current and prior engagements.[35] "As a threshold matter, the outsourcing . . . lawyer should ask the intermediary, which employs or engages the overseas non-lawyer, about its conflict-checking procedures and about how it tracks work performed for clients."[36] It is also recommended that the outsourcing party pursue further investigations as required, and remind the intermediary and non-lawyer of the need to safeguard confidences and secrets of their other former and current clients.[37]

It has been suggested that when dealing with an outsourcing firm, the client's identity may be camouflaged by using only reference numbers or pseudonyms. While this may be acceptable in certain situations, such camouflaging may also inadvertently expose the client to loss of confidentiality and conflicts nevertheless, because the client's identity could be deduced from substantive information that is transmitted in the course of the work.

For example, if offshoring trademark searches, it is possible for the "vendor" to be conducting searches for many clients, some of whom are competitors. If the vendor is also providing an opinion regarding use and registration, the clients need to be aware that the vendor is also acting for adversaries. If the client is incognito, the investigation for conflicts can only be superficial and in relation to criteria provided by the outsourcing attorney. But will that be sufficient?

In usual cases of conflicts, both clients are advised that the firm or attorney represent the other party. Unless there is a waiver or agreement by the clients, the most prudent course of action for the attorney or firm is to represent neither party in the matter. This scenario is especially troublesome in any litigation or contentious case.

Meticulous record keeping of the outsourced attorneys (and perhaps even paraprofessional staff in the intellectual property context) could alleviate some concern. While onerous in itself—imagine having to keep track of every professional who is working on the litigation case—the consequences of not investigating or clearing personnel could be devastating to the client.

Confidentiality[38]

Similarly, maintaining confidentiality of the client's matters is the responsibility of the lawyer, unless the client gives informed consent.[39] In most U.S. jurisdictions, ethical rules require that the lawyer preserve information as a "confidence" which may be protected by attorney-client privilege[40] and "secret" as other information "gained in the professional relationship that the client has requested be held inviolate or the disclosure of which would be embarrassing or would be likely to be detrimental to the client."[41] The rules also place an obligation on the lawyer to exercise reasonable care that employees, associates, and others whose services are utilized by the lawyer do not disclose such confidences or secrets.[42]

The conclusion drawn by the Association of the Bar of the City of New York in its Opinion 2006-3 with regard to disclosure of such confidences in the course of an outsourcing assignment is that the lawyer should obtain the client's consent to outsource in advance.[43] One of the ways to safeguard such information is to have contractual confidentiality agreements or clauses in writing between the U.S. attorney and the outsourcing company/intermediary which include remedies for breach.[44] From the client's perspective, there needs to be informed consent when legal services are outsourced on the client's behalf.[45]

The next section deals with the more practical aspects of enforcing the conflict checks and maintaining the client's confidentiality when offshoring legal work.

Supervision and Competence of Those Being Supervised

In 2008, the American Bar Association released an opinion that appeared to address the increase in potential outsourcing.[46] Primarily, the duty to supervise and the competence of those being supervised were addressed. Outsourcing to a foreign country would require ascertaining whether the legal training in those countries is comparable to that in the United States, and whether the legal professionals share ethical principles with legal professionals in the United States, and whether there is an effective disciplinary system for transgressors.

In engaging a vendor for legal services overseas, it is highly recommended that reference checks be conducted, and to interview and investigate the background of lawyers and non-lawyers, as well as any non-lawyer intermediary. In outsourcing, there remains the direct responsibility of the U.S. attorney to interview those working on the project or assignment[47] and to understand the roles of principal non-lawyers. If Opinion 08-451 is to be interpreted strictly, such review is required at the outset of each outsourced project.

In addition to verifying the credentials of the individuals providing the legal support service, the attorney is required to adequately supervise the work of the partners, associates, and non-lawyers.[48]

The ABA Committee also suggested that the U.S. attorney investigate the security of the provider's premises, its computer network, and perhaps even recycling and refuse procedures. All of these factors may affect the ability of the legal services provider to protect confidentiality and integrity of the client's matters.

While it is clear that ethical rules require that the lawyer visit the premises and inspect personally employees and premises, one of the most powerful drivers of offshoring is cost reduction. But when one is dealing with different time zones, such as between the United States and India, and with differences in culture, there are limits to the accessibility and credibility of such information. Repeated trips to vendor offices can become costly and inconvenient, which diminishes the value of outsourcing. While it is understood that there is the requirement to spend time and money verifying staff and procedures, it becomes onerous if the goal is to conserve resources.

It may be suggested that large-scale off-shoring may work for those with large portfolios and commensurate internal staff to liaise with the legal support vendor. Optimally, there is a dedicated team or certain staff who remain on the project, thereby reducing or eliminating the need to screen personnel anew. It does not, however, remove the necessity to supervise, to be vigilant and creative in discharging this duty.[49] As previously noted, U.S. lawyers generally outsource to vendors located in countries with common law systems. Education in such countries, aside from probably being in English, is also possibly comparable in philosophy. But differences remain, which may mean that the work must be scrutinized even more.

Direct supervisory authority over the non-lawyer "shall make reasonable efforts to ensure that the person's conduct is compatible with the professional obligations of the lawyer."[50]

Attorney-Client Privilege and the Practice of Law

In the context of outsourcing and offshoring, there are also concerns over the unauthorized practice of law in multiple jurisdictions in violation of the regulation of the legal profession in the respective jurisdiction.[51]

It soon became clear that the ABA Ethical Opinion of 2008[52] did not mollify the concerns of many practitioners. The ABA Commission on Ethics 20/20 Legal Process Outsourcing (Domestic and International) has called for comments[53] in preparation to both expand and update the 2008 opinion. The questions calling for comments cover topics such as who are the decision makers to outsource, whether the choice includes outsourcing outside the United States, and what issues, besides price, were considered in the decision.[54]

An additional concern is the controversy and confusion over attorney-client privilege.

The purpose of the attorney-client privilege is to facilitate full and frank communication between a client and its attorney.[55] However, the concept and the privilege vary greatly in multinational situations. Generally, the privilege is recognized only on a national level. In the midst of outsourcing legal work with intermediaries and lawyers, and non-lawyers located in several jurisdictions, which country's law will apply?

Attorney-client privilege laws vary, especially between common law and civil law jurisdictions. Even U.S. courts do not apply rule consistently. And the failure of counsel to understand the degrees of protection may inadvertently jeopardize the client's position by waiving the attorney-client privilege or disclosing confidential information.

In the United States, each state has its own privilege rules, and a federal court must apply the rules of federal common law of privilege.[56] Where cases include both federal and state claims, such as the Lanham Act, and unfair competition, or copyright and state moral rights, a combination of privilege rules may apply.

There are also differences in privilege as applied to trademark and patent agents, vis-a-vis attorneys admitted to the practice of law. In the United States, patent agents are licensed by the United States Patent and Trademark Office, and privilege has been extended to patent agents.

However, trademark agents are not licensed in most jurisdictions,[57] including the United States. While U.S. courts have found the prosecution of patent and trademark applications to be analogous to each other,[58] to the extent communications could be privileged, they appear to be limited to the specific application. The privilege is likely to terminate at issuance of the registration.[59]

There is division of opinion on whether and how privilege affects communication with foreign patent agents.[60] A further step removed is the application of privilege to non-U.S. IP advisers.

Since foreign attorneys and patent or trademark agents are not U.S. attorneys, nor members of the bar, the "no privilege" rule applies. Under the "touch base" test, if communication with a foreign IP advisor (attorney or agent) "touches base" with the United States, U.S. law will be used to determine whether privilege applies. This standard has been relevant since the *Duplan* case in 1975.[61]

However, even application of the touch base standard is fraught with inconsistencies since courts have rendered decisions closely based on the facts in each of such cases to determine whether such communications are privileged and should remain so.[62]

Mindful of differences in privilege rule, just copying in an attorney does not insulate communication from disclosure.[63] Foreign privilege protection is usually restricted to privilege standards of the country and application for which the non-U.S. patent agents provided substantive assistance,[64] but will be denied if the foreign agent is merely a conduit.[65]

Communications between an American attorney and a foreign agent could be protected as communication between attorney and non-attorney working under the supervision of the U.S. attorney[66]—or, if rendering substantive legal advice on foreign matter, the same privileges as between co-counsel could be relevant.[67]

One caveat to the preceding discussion: Many countries do not recognize attorney-client privilege for in-house counsel.[68]

Billing

In offshoring work, where the non-lawyer is performing legal support services is not, by definition, performing legal services. Accordingly, it is inappropriate for the lawyer to include the cost of outsourcing in the lawyer's fees.[69]

> *Absent a specific agreement to the contrary, the lawyer should charge the client no more than the direct cost associated with outsourcing, plus reasonable allocation of overhead expenses directly associated with providing the service.*[70]

In the traditional outsourcing scenario, in sending work to a law firm, fee arrangements can be more flexible than hourly rates by position in the hierarchy. During the recent recession, payment schedules have been negotiated between clients and attorneys in the best interest of both parties.

Flat fee agreements are becoming more acceptable, and appropriate in certain situations. These may include predictable expense assignments such as trademark searching and clearance (x for the search conducted + y for the attorney's opinion), the filing of applications, and oppositions. To reduce costs and waste, there may be an agreement to report only problems to the client. For example, for a flat fee prosecution arrangement, unless there are significant issues requiring company management decisions, the client receives information confirming the filing of the application, and then the certificate of registration. All prosecution information is retained by outside counsel. While these templates are not new, the reduction of paper and duplication of efforts, along with reduced corporate staffing, have been instrumental in making such relationships more popular.

Status Quo

As some have discovered, outsourcing/offshoring can complicate life for in-house attorneys.[71] A number of companies have decided to refrain from offshoring at this time and instead send their more routine and administrative work to smaller regional or local firms.[72] And with currency fluctuations affecting the value of the U.S. dollar, domestic firms may provide similar cost savings, geographic proximity, and minimal cultural adjustment.

Additional concerns about the quality of certain assignments have resulted in second thoughts about offshoring.[73] Nevertheless, in the appropriate circumstance, it may be the right decision to use an outsourcing legal process vendor whose staff is located offshore.[74] Many factors influence such decisions: Is there sufficient staff to accomplish the task in a professional and efficient manner? Would it be better to deploy the internal resources available for the project? What are the budget and time constraints? Is the portfolio large enough (or too small) to justify the outsourcing and/or offshoring?

Conclusion

As we have already seen, the virtual workplace is becoming a reality on many different levels. A common manifestation is the telecommuter staying at home or a place of choice, and completing assignments outside the office. And legal work, including intellectual property work, can be accomplished in places outside a traditional office space.

Some companies no longer allocate office space dedicated to particular staff but provide temporary, or fluid, workspace, or part-time cubicles. Already many workers seek arrangements to accommodate family and personal needs, from flexible work schedules, to temporary assignments by projects and type of work.

If the appropriate infrastructure exists, it is feasible to access the information needed from distant locations, and complete the work off-site. For example, companies are already creating digitized or scanned libraries and file rooms of important or core documents. Certificates of registration are suitable for storage as electronic records so that the images are accessible for evidentiary purposes and transfer to outside firms—even those in international jurisdictions.

Already today litigation documentation and application filing is electronic in many countries.[75] In the future, the entire process could be conducted from multiple locations without the need to appear in person. And since it can be done anywhere, the question is then again: Why not in the United States?

Why must the outsourcing be to a different country? Why not to an enterprising smaller company or service provider in the United States or the local client? What prevents outsourcing to smaller, more agile, and responsive law firms?

The recent economic downturn has led to the reassessment of billing practices. Close attention is being paid to getting value for the expense. The agility and responsiveness at lower cost is what the vendors have advertised. Exceptions abound for staff that is located in different countries and cannot provide certain legal services. It is still not appropriate to get a legal opinion about clearing a trademark for registration and use in the United States from a practitioner located abroad, nor for that matter, in the United Kingdom, or Canada, or a multitude of other countries from attorneys located outside of those respective jurisdictions. Notwithstanding EU movement of workers concepts, each jurisdiction requires examinations and extensive knowledge not only of the law, but of the practice in such jurisdiction. An attorney admitted to the bar in the State of New York, and not in India, may not practice law in India. The corollary remains valid.

In the future, it may become possible to render legal opinions from anywhere, provided the legal professional has knowledge and is admitted to practice in the respective jurisdiction of the subject matter.

In the future, the ethical and confidentiality issues may be different. Even these matters may be accommodated by the promulgation of, adherence to, and enforcement of multi-jurisdictional codes of conduct. Under such regime, if you are an attorney in China, your values and behavior would be governed by the same rules as an attorney in Calgary, Canada.

In the meantime, the service or work can be accomplished by workers within the clients' base country. The legal intellectual property work may not necessarily be done by attorneys and staff located in great metropolitan centers but in areas where the cost of living is lower, as many corporations have already seen by moving to suburban areas.[76] Employment of skilled personnel in exurban regions of the United States could reap many benefits—from the obvious, such as lower costs of wages resulting in lower expenses, to the more subtle factors, such as language and culture in common. The first aspect appeals to the budget-conscious; the second and third factors help foster efficiency in communication and execution.

Circumstances and goals of the clients should dictate whether IP legal work is outsourced, offshored, or completed internally. Whatever the choice, it is important to recognize how varied and flexible the landscape can be. In order to aid readers in considering the important issues involved with outsourcing of IP legal work before proceeding with it, a non-exhaustive checklist is included here.

Basic Checklist for Outsourcing

Are there adequate internal resources to achieve a timely and professional result?
Who is the vendor or provider of legal support services?
Where is the staff that will perform the work located?

Does the vendor firm make the staff accessible?
Is the same group dedicated to a project or client's work?

Has the client consented to the work being outsourced or delegated?
How is confidentiality maintained—through clearly defined procedures?

Are there "Chinese walls" in place?

Are conflicts of interest reported?

What is the procedure in the event the vendor represents or works for two known competitors or adverse parties?

In the country/countries where the outsourced staff is located, is there attorney-client privilege?

If so, what are the rules and exceptions?

How does the vendor firm deal with cross border transactions?

Given the in-house work that must be done in preparation and the duration of the project or legal task, is it cost effective?

Notes

1. Outsourcing refers to work contracted to an outside firm; offshoring is the shift of work abroad.

2. See also Marilyn Primiano, "Intellectual Property Legal Process Outsourcing," in *Intellectual Property Strategies for the 21st Century Corporation.*

3. Kannan Srikanth and Phanish Puranam, "Advice for Outsourcers: Think Bigger," *Wall Street Journal*, January 25, 2010, R7.

4. Virginia Postrel, "Economic Scene; A Researcher Sees an Upside in the Outsourcing of Programming Jobs," *New York Times,* January 29, 2004.

5. "Why Outsourcing May Lose its Power as a Scare Word," *New York Times,* August 13, 2006.

6. Daniel Gross, "Surfing the Next Wave of Outsourcing: The Ethics of Sending Domestic *Legal* Work to Foreign Countries," *NY City Opinion 2006-3.*

7. Forrester Research in Boston, MA; *New York Times,* August 21, 2007, Business section.

8. Ibid.

9. Ibid.

10. Heather Timmons, "India Feels Less Vulnerable as Outsourcing Presses On," *New York Times,* June 2, 2009.

11. Ibid.

12. Bruce Masterson, *New York Times,* August 21, 2007 Business section.

13. Ibid.

14. Ibid., quoting Janine Dascenzo of GE.

15. Alex Aldridge, "Global In-House, A Package to India," *Corporate Counsel,* September 1, 2009.

16. Ibid.

17. David Hechler, "Passage to India," *Corporate Counsel,* January 1, 2009.

18. Ibid.

19. Nick Wingfield, "Microsoft, Too, Calls India for Tech Support," *Wall Street Journal,* April 14, 2010, p. B6.

20. CPA Global.com/download centre, case studies.

21. Ibid.

22. "LPO and the Great Recession," IP Frontline PatentCafe, Evalueserve, April 27, 2010. Article includes extensive statistical data by category and time periods of outsourced and offshored legal work in the United States and United Kingdom and current trends.

23. Ibid.

24. Darren Olivier, *Supplement-Africa IP Focus 2009 South Africa's IP Outsourcing Advantage,* Managingip.com, Oct 1, 2009.

25. Debra Cassens Weiss, "Are Top US Law Firms Outsourcing Some Legal Work? 83 Percent Won't Say,*"* www.abajournal.com, posted July 7, 2010.

26. Virginia Harrison, "Low-Level Legal Wok Goes Offshore but It's Still In-House," *The Australian,* April 23, 2010; www.theaustralian.com.au/legal-affairs/low-level-work-goes-offshore.

27. www.integreon.com/blog/2010/04/wilmerhale-reduces-its-middle-office-costs.html.

28. "Old assumptions are being challenged as the outsourcing industry matures," *The Economist,* July 26, 2007, External Affairs.

29. Ibid. Wipro close to reaching agreement with Tata Consultancy to set up software development centers in one of three American cities.

30. ABA Formal Ethics Opinion 88-356, Temporary Lawyers (1988).

31. See Steven C. Bennett, "The Ethics of Legal Outsourcing," *N. Ky L. Rev.* 36, no. 4:479, 484-487.

32. See also Michael Downey, "Satisfying Ethical Obligations When Outsourcing Legal Work Overseas," in *Intellectual Property Strategies for the 21st Century Corporation.*

33. "A concurrent conflict of interest exists if the representation of one client will be directly adverse to another client or there is a significant risk that the representation of one or more clients will be materially limited by lawyer's responsibility to another client, a former client or a third person." ABA Model Rules.

34. ABA Committee On Ethics and Professional Conduct, Formal Opinion 08-451 (2008).

35. Association of the Bar of the City of New York, Committee on Professional and Judicial Ethics, Formal Opinion 2006-3, August 2006, in referring to DR 5-105 (E) ("Formal Opinion 2006-3").

36. Formal Opinion 2006-3, re "Duty to Check Conflicts When Outsourcing Overseas."

37. Formal Opinion 2006-3.

38. See also Michael Downey, "Satisfying Ethical Obligations When Outsourcing Legal Work Overseas," in *Intellectual Property Strategies for the 21st Century Corporation.*

39. Model Rules of Professional Conduct 1.6 (a) (2007). See also Formal Opinion 2006-3, "The Duty to Obtain Advance Client Consent to Outsourcing Overseas" and "The Duty to Preserve the Client's Confidences and Secrets When Outsourcing Overseas."

40. For example, see NY Rule DR 4-101 and discussion in Formal Opinion 2006-3.

41. NY DR 4-101(A).

42. NY DR 4-101(D).

43. Formal Opinion 2006-3.

44. Liquidated damages for such breaches can be an incentive not to breach.

45. Ibid.

46. Formal Opinion 08-451, "Lawyer's Obligations When Outsourcing Legal and Nonlegal Support Services."

47. ABA Formal Opinion 08-451, "Lawyer's Obligations When Outsourcing Legal and Nonlegal Support Services."

48. Formal Opinion 2006-3, re "Duty to Supervise and to Represent a Client Competently When Outsourcing Overseas."

49. Formal Opinion 2006-3.

50. Model Rules of Professional Conduct 5.3.(b) (2007).

51. Ibid. Rule 5.5, Unauthorized Practice of Law.

52. See www.abanet.org/ethics2020/speakers.pdf.

53. At this writing, see www.abanet.org and veran@staff.abanet.org.

54. Commission Questionnaire at www.abanet.org/ethics2020/pdfs/outsourcing_questionnaire.pdf

55. WIPO opinion, *The Client Attorney Privilege*, World Intellectual Property Organization, Standing Committee on the Law of Patents, 13th Session, at 5 (March 23 to 27, 2009), www.wipo.int/edocs/mdocs/scp/en/scp_13/scp_13_4.doc.

56. Fed R Evidence 501.

57. Exceptions include Australia, Canada, and the United Kingdom.

58. *Advertising to Women Inc. v. Gianni Versace S.p.A.,* No 98 C 1553, 1999 WL 608711 at *2-4 (N.D. Cal Nov. 18, 1997).

59. *John Labatt Limited et al. v. Molson Breweries et al.,* 898 F. Supp. 471, 475 (E.D. Mich. 1995).

60. Ibid.

61. *Duplan Corp. v. Deering Milliken,* 397 Fed Supp 1146 (D.S.C. 1975).

62. See *Status Time Corp. v. Sharp Electronics Corp.,* 95 F.R.D. 27 (S.D. N.Y. 1982); *Golden Trade S.R.L. v. Lee Apparel Co.,* 143 F.RD 512 (SDNY 1992) (looking to Norwegian, German, and Israeli law for guidance as to whether privilege extended to foreign patent agents).

63. *Rice v. Honeywell* 2007 WL 865687 (E.D. Tex. March 15, 2007) at *3. A communication will not be excluded from disclosure only on the basis that in-house counsel, or an outside attorney, are shown as being recipients of the communications.

64. Willemijn Houdstermaatschaapij 707 F Supp 1429; see also In re *Rivastigimine Patent Litigation,* 237 FRD 69, 74 (S.D.N.Y. 2006) for extensive discussion regarding the privilege laws in 39 countries, and their application to communications between clients and their foreign patent agents and attorneys in connection with patent applications in the respective jurisdictions. *Id.* At 78. and Robert J. Anello, *Preserving the Corporate Attorney-Client Privilege: Here and Abroad,* 27 Penn St. Int'l L. Rev. 291, Fall 2008; and Joel R. Merkin, "Litigating Outsourced Patents: How Offshoring May Affect the Attorney Client Privilege," *Journal of Law,* Technology & Policy Vol 2006 215, 220-226.

65. *Detection Systems, Inc v. Pittway Corp.,* 96 FRD 152, 156 (W.D.N.Y. 1982).

66. *Baxter Healthcare Corp. v. Fresenius Medical Care Holding, Inc.* C07-1359, 2009 WL 533126 at *1 (N.D.Cal. March 3, 2009).

67. *Mitts & Merrill, Inc. v. Shred Pax Corp.,* 112 F.R.D. 349, 352 (N.D. Ill. 1986).

68. See Robert J. Anello supra n. 61. See also *Akzo Nobel Chemicals Ltd and Akcros Chemicals Ltd v. Commission* (C-550/07 P) April 29, 2010 decision where internal communications with in-house lawyers do not enjoy protection under privilege under EU law, confirming the judgment of the ECJ in *AM&S v. Commission* (case 155/79).

69. Formal Opinion 2006-3, "The Duty to Bill Appropriately for Outsourcing Overseas."

70. ABA Formal Opinion 93-379 (1993).

71. Alex Aldridge, "Out of Sight, Out of Oversight? Security, quality, location: Let us count the concerns over outsourcing," *Corporate Counsel,* March 1, 2010.

72. Ibid.

73. Debra Cassens Weiss, "Deposition Company Ended Overseas Outsourcing Over Quality Problems," www.abajournal.com/news/article/ posted May 18, 2010, 8:19 A.M. DT. See also Saritha Rai, "Security Breaches Worry Outsourcing Industry," *New York Times,* October 5, 2006.

74. For the sake of fairness, there will be no recommendations for any particular companies specializing in outsourcing or offshoring of legal work. There are numerous resources on the Internet, and web sites advertising and proposing various services, including intellectual property processing. It may also be beneficial to consult with colleagues who have used such services for their perspectives on the efficacy and quality of the results.

75. In the United States, federal court filings are electronic in many courts, and applications can be filed online in Canada (www.cipo.ic.gc.ca/eic/site/cipointernet-internetopic.nsf/eng/h_wr00002.html), the United Kingdom (www.ipo.gov.uk/tm.htm) and the United States (www.uspto.gov).

76. See Note 26 re Wilmer Hale office in Dayton, Ohio.

CHAPTER 12

Intellectual Property Legal Process Outsourcing

Marilyn O. Primiano
Vice President, Legal Services (Europe),
Pangea3 LLC, a Thomson Reuters company

This chapter provides expert insight into outsourcing as an intellectual property strategy for the twenty-first century corporation. It considers the current state of the industry, provides recommendations and considerations for successful IP outsourcing, and concludes with a forward look at where things are headed.

History

Offshore outsourcing is evolving, but it is by no means new. Companies have been forming global strategic partnerships for hundreds of years, dating back to the commission of inexpensively manufactured textiles and jewelry from Asia and Africa in lieu of having them manufactured in Europe or the New World. Traditionally, such relationships hinged on goods over services, and this continued through the 1970s and 1980s when American automobile and information technology (IT) companies looked to China, Japan, Taiwan, and even Mexico for the manufacturing of car parts and chips, sometimes closing U.S. plants and moving their own operations abroad in an attempt to leverage the stronger dollar. With advances in communication technologies, however, came freer exchanges of information and, in turn, the sourcing of business process services, knowledge process services, and, eventually, legal process services. And so modern offshore outsourcing was born.

Thought of as back office tasks, early business process outsourcing (BPO) included billing, human resources functions, and other non-core competency jobs (i.e., business support functions). Businesses got leaner and often more profitable, but anti-outsourcing predilections among workers intensified as jobs and sometimes entire departments were dissolved with the work sent overseas. India's early out-sourcing hub lent its name to English lexicon, with office workers fearful of being "Bangalored."

In spite of outcry and concern from certain individuals, unions, and politicians, companies were learning that the quality of BPO services performed overseas was good enough to get the job done—and the cheaper price tag was the kicker. By way of evolution, companies began entrusting higher level functions to overseas profes-sionals. No longer were foreign workers charged with simply hitting the "generate report" button and mailing invoices; they were now making strategic decisions, such as completing tax returns and opting for the most beneficial elections, customized for each client. This maturation from BPO was dubbed "Knowledge Process Outsourc-ing," or KPO, and from it the performance of general legal and delicate intellectual property work was just a hop away.

Statistics on the Intellectual Property Outsourcing Market and India's Leading Role

Today, even the most complex of patent analytics such as invalidity searches, free-dom to operate searches, infringement analysis, and landscaping are performed by overseas professionals for some of the world's largest companies. Valuenotes, a well established research firm known for pioneer surveying of world markets, speculated that the total IP market, both tapped and untapped by legal process outsourcing (LPO), was $2.2 billion back in 2007, and it is also estimated that the revenue into India alone for just IP LPO work will reach $206 million by December 2012.[1] Within this ever growing market, the projection is that 60 percent of the IP work getting offshored to India comes from U.S.-origin companies.[2]

India's leading role in the IP LPO market is largely ascribed to its potential to scale. The number of India-based professionals working in LPO is expected to jump from 15,400 in 2010 to 26,000 by 2014,[3] and surely few (if any) other countries could generate the English-speaking legal talent to fill the vacancies.

Although the accuracy of these projections are anyone's guess, assuming that they are within the ballpark, the outsourcing of IP services to foreign professionals is still in the nascent stages, and industry leaders are poised to see tremendous aggran-dizement, driven by "growth in worldwide patent markets, increased offshoring of Research and Development (R&D) activity, lack of onshore manpower and the impact of the US Patent Reform Act of 2007."[4] If recent trends are indicative, it won't be surprising if growth actually exceeds the predictions.

Motivators, Consumers, and Critics of IP LPO

Out of corporations, law firms, and individual inventors, the corporations have tradi-tionally been the driving force behind most IP LPO initiatives. Faced with tightened budgets and often pressed for time and human resources, sending work to lower cost, highly qualified professionals is a logical corporate legal team venture. For many IP support services, such as prior art searches or invalidity reports, in-house attorneys, working at times with their R&D groups, tend to send work directly to LPOs and often develop working relationships such that the foreign professionals ostensibly become a geographically displaced extension of the company itself. For large and complex IP services with a heavier accent on law, such as complex IP litigation document review, corporate groups often mandate that their outside counsel work with an LPO to minimize costs. How law firms and outside counsel react to these mandates varies.[5]

With the exception of a few progressive visionaries, law firms traditionally viewed LPOs as threats—either skeptical of work quality or fearful of potential revenue loss. Many firms, however, are increasingly standing behind LPO as an attractive alternative to more traditional work models. A chief reason for this is the growing acceptance of LPO practice. With more companies and firms admitting to working with offshore providers and willing to discuss their experiences as references, fear, uncertainty, and doubt are being dispelled. Not wanting to go first is being replaced by not wanting to miss the boat, and firms are increasingly realizing that, by championing outsourcing, they can be seen as offering more holistic counseling to their clients. Compound this with the recent financial crunch which has driven more companies to give less-strategic IP work to onshore staffing companies such that firms aren't receiving that revenue anyway, and the walls of resistance to LPO utilization crumble.

Ironically, many law firms are able to generate more revenue by having their IP clients go offshore than by using onshore providers since many clients will ultimately spend up to a budget, especially in areas such as patent drafting, prior art searches, invalidity reports, or claim chart preparation. A lower cost provider will leave more of that budget in the coffers of the firm. Another surprise for many firms is that often they feel greater control over projects sent overseas than projects outsourced onshore. It can be theorized that because the overseas providers are aware of the skepticism toward their quality and aware of concerns over communications based on time zones or language, they work harder to overcome these perceived barriers. In any case, the traditional law firm critic is increasingly playing the role of advocate, contingent only on his or her satisfaction with the quality of the provider.

Aside from corporations and firms, other groups that often try to have a stake in offshoring IP work are the individuals looking to avoid heavy IP attorney fees and boutique IP firms interested in taking on more work without the costs associated with full-time hiring. While the first group is not often a good fit for LPO since no legitimate LPO provider will deliver work product to someone other than a licensed U.S. attorney, the second group stands to benefit greatly in terms of being able to take on more work without the heavy overhead.

It also merits mention that consultancy groups are often the ultimate gatekeepers of outsourced IP, so it is crucial to ensure that those consultants have the background necessary to perform thorough due diligence on providers. While some aspects of IP LPO, such as IP litigation document review, might be generally understood by a consultant, other tasks such as patent monetization, white space/gap analysis, or patent portfolio analysis can be of such specialized, technical nature that it would be easy for a nonexpert to miss the subtle differences in qualification or experience that might separate the most able provider from the rest. Nonetheless, the right consultants can prove priceless in objectively screening providers against client needs and by fairly playing both critic and cheerleader.

Data Exchange Risks and Protection Issues

Quality concerns may be the most common offshore inhibitor, but for certain projects, concerns over privacy, confidentiality, privilege, and export control issues, if founded, may prove seriously consequential.

Privacy, Confidentiality, and Privilege

When working with leading LPO providers, security breaches can be less of a threat offshore than onshore thanks to preventative measures. Restrictions on cell phones and cameras, biometric (finger scan) access, closed circuit video monitoring, prohibitions against external media drives, restrictions on printing, and employee background checks are just some of the techniques used offshore to safeguard data from falling into unauthorized hands. Security at top U.S. law firms, ironically, is typically far more lax. The issue thus really becomes one of conducting proper due diligence on potential providers and then comparing that security with the security currently afforded to data by in-house, law firm, or onshore providers. Once you are convinced that the opportunity and likelihood of breach is equal to or less than that of your current provider, concerns over security should cease to be prohibitive in your quest for economical IP support alternatives.[6]

Qualms about losing protection from the attorney client privilege or work product doctrine can be easily put to rest with the right provider. As mentioned elsewhere in this chapter, legitimate offshore legal providers will not deliver work product to nonrepresented parties,[7] and they therefore work at the direction of counsel. Akin to hiring a detective or having a non-barred paralegal or law intern perform work at a firm, the privilege and doctrine extend to the work performed by foreign professionals since it is at the direction of counsel, that is, the foreign professional is acting as counsel's agent.[8] Additionally, foreign attorneys trained in common law, such as those trained in India, are likely to already understand the protections afforded to certain communications or work product, whereas "[e]nsuring the preservation of confidential information by foreign professionals is more difficult where the foreign professions operate under different laws and traditions regarding the confidentiality of information learned from clients."[9]

Export Control

While concerns over privacy, confidentiality, and privilege might weigh evenly across litigation, corporate, and intellectual property LPO channels, export control issues bias IP LPO given the heavy technology content.[10] Prior to sending any technology overseas, a party must confirm that export control laws are not implicated. The easiest test for this is a two prong application of the origin test and the dual use test, that is, (1) Is the transmittal information originating in the United States?[11] and (2) Does the information have both commercial and military or proliferation applications? In rare circumstances, items without obvious military uses or proliferation applications might be subject to export controls but this dual prong test is a safe way of clearing the bulk of technologies sent overseas for LPO services, provided intelligent foresight of possible uses is applied.

When it appears that an export control license might be required, a proper categorization and classification of all items under consideration for export from the United States to a foreign destination must be made. The Bureau of Industry and Security (BIS) is responsible for implementing and enforcing the Export Administration Regulations (EAR), which require an export license depending on an item's technical characteristics, the destination, the end user, and the end use.[12] Once classified, the exporter must determine whether the item intended for export has a specific export control classification number (ECCN) (an alpha-numeric code, e.g., 3A001). All ECCNs are listed in the Commerce Control List (CCL), which provides a clear and detailed delineation of technologies (www.access.gpo.gov/bis/ear/ear_data.html#ccl). Cross-reference of the ECCN with the Commerce Country Chart (www.access.gpo.gov/bis/ear/pdf/738spir.pdf) should determine whether the exporter needs an export license based on the "reasons for control" of the item and the country of ultimate destination, though final care must be taken that the controlled item is not exported to a restricted person (a "Denied Person") or entity (a "Denied Entity") identified by the BIS in conjunction with other federal agencies.

In closing the discussion on export control issues, clarification about United States Patent and Trademark Office (USPTO) foreign filing licenses, which are distinct from export control licenses issued by the U.S. Department of Commerce, is appurtenant. Although often confused as an impediment to offshoring IP work, material requiring a foreign filing license is simply limited to use for the filing of foreign patent applications, and there are no further restrictions imposed on sending the material offshore. Moreover, any export that is not subject to a foreign filing license (or other special license) remains unqualified and its uses are not limited. As is the case with material subject to export control license, the type of data typically outsourced to IP legal providers is infrequently subject to special licenses and is therefore not frequently restricted. Nonetheless, parties should heed potential limitations and licensing requirements.

Outsourcing Economics

The idea behind outsourcing is simple enough: Leverage cheaper foreign economies and pass the cost savings to clients. The general enthusiasm over cheaper overseas labor and business expenses, however, must be tempered by foreign professionals' ability to deliver a work product comparable to that of their U.S. counterparts. This is often referred to as "U.S. quality," but it actually goes a step beyond mere quality. The integrity of data and the legal accuracy of a report may be flawless, and thus of good technical quality, but if the presentation or language is such that it must be reprocessed and sandpapered by the U.S. client before that work product is usable, some value is lost.

Consumers must be careful that they know what they are being offered and expectations must be aligned. While one overseas company may be able to deliver a fully drafted patent application ready for filing, another might be capable of providing only a draft because employees lack the language expertise to take the project to the finish line. Pricing weighed against both quality and an American-style product will yield the true value proposition.[13]

Modernized Price Models

Historically, IP, corporate, and litigation LPO were each structured like large law firms: An hourly rate was applied to time sheet entries and bills were generated. Over the past year, there has been a divergence from this traditional billing, with damnations and accusations, such as "hourly billing masks inefficiencies," being thrown at the familiar billable hour.

Traditionalists, perhaps rightly, maintain that the billable hour will never be abolished. For complex or unusual projects where even experts can't foresee time or complexity commitments, billable hours will likely remain the only real pricing option. For other projects, however, alternative price structures are viable and units other than hours, such as per patent application or per prior art search, are becoming more common offerings. The attraction to such structures is obvious: upfront cost assurances whereby the provider, rather than the client, bears the brunt of project inefficiencies. If providers staff junior (read: less efficient) resources on a per unit project, the client is not financially penalized for the learning curve. An added bonus to per unit pricing is that it can convey a company's expertise and confidence in that companies are not going to commit to a flat price if they don't know exactly what to expect on a project.

The current state of the LPO industry, largely driven by economic pressures that have caused clients to demand customized service and billing options, thus now offers more pricing options than existed in the past, and clients are wise to explore alternative arrangements to the billable hour as the industry continues to evolve and while clients are empowered to help craft its evolution.

Upfront Investments into a New Employee versus an LPO Relationship and Return on Investment (ROI)

The mutual goal of any in-house counsel and LPO company is to integrate the LPO team into the general counsel's legal department in much the same way that a new associate or group of associates might be integrated. On day one, any IP lawyer will join an IP group with his or her own preferences, objectives, styles, and priorities. Conforming to the group's established preferences and positions requires an investment of time and effort both from the standpoint of the new employee and from the senior reporting lawyers. Initially, the output of work product from that new attorney is relatively low, regardless of his or her prior experience. Over time, however, after reviewing legacy materials, interacting with senior attorneys, and obtaining feedback on how things are done differently within the particular company's in-house legal department, the new in-house team member begins to deliver work product at a pace and level consistent with departmental peers.

The nature of upfront investment and the evolution in pace and consistency of work product from a team of IP lawyers and professionals in an overseas LPO is much the same. At the outset of the relationship, the company's in-house legal group must invest time and resources to impart to the LPO the company-centric and industry-centric know-how, processes, and preferences. How does this company view its IP relative to its peers in the market? How does the company's IP translate into its product portfolio? Is the company strategically focused on building an

IP portfolio that blocks peers in the marketplace, fills white space in the industry, enhances licensing opportunities, and/or ensures a competitive lead for its own products? What is the general counsel's posture toward relevant prior art and how does this legal department prefer to document prior art? What is this team's view of an exhaustive versus adequate search for prior art?

This is the kind of knowledge and experience that requires substantial investment of time and money from in-house experienced team members as well as the new participants—whether they are new associates or an LPO team working to integrate with the in-house counsel team. The ramp activity and ramp time in the LPO context, however, is more concentrated and focused. LPOs do not have the luxury that an onsite employee has knowing that he or she can stop by a senior attorney's office to ask questions as they arise real time. Consequently, the LPOs execute specific engagement launch activities and processes aimed at ensuring that upfront learnings are completed comprehensively and are well documented so that, in the future, those answers *are* available in as close to real time as possible. Documented processes also enable an LPO to onboard new team members onto a client engagement team at any point in time, whether to increase the size of the team or to replace a leaving team member. As compared to the typical in-house employee situation where a senior in-house attorney will be required to incur considerable time and effort in recruiting and ramping up a new employee replacement, the LPO's ability to take over this responsibility and perform the ramp up function independently represents, in and of itself, a huge return on the initial investment that far exceeds the benefits associated with a traditional in-house employee. See Figure 12.2 ("New Attorney Onboarding") and the corresponding text for additional explanation.

Once the ramp-up and integration related learning times level off and once the LPO team starts to function as would an integrated in-house employee, the LPO team can start to draw on its specialized experience generating process efficiencies (such as the incorporation of Six Sigma tools and methodologies) to focus on process improvement and efficiency gains. See Figure 12.1 ("New Project Start-Up") and the corresponding text for additional explanation. In task-based fee arrangements, the client thus benefits from consistent work product and reduced turnaround times. In hourly rate relationships, the client reaps these benefits plus reduced bills. In spite of a potentially higher initial cost/time expense in the LPO scenario, these opportunities for higher return rates as compared to in-house or in-firm hiring justifies the investment.

Figure 12.1 demonstrates the upfront investment versus return on investment relationship in both a traditional legal hire (in-house/in-firm) scenario and in a new LPO engagement.[14] Initially, the LPO attorney may require a higher investment of client resources (shown on the Y-axis) but, depending on the project complexity, will eventually match a new in-house or in-firm hire in terms of cost and output (this occurs at Month 6 on the diagram). The LPO, as demonstrated by the dotted portion of the diagram, will then be able to implement process improvements such as Six Sigma methodology, based on unique process expertise which characterizes leading LPOs and distinguishes them from many law firms or in-house groups. This will improve efficiencies and consistency and, combined with the lower cost of offshore services, will result in value add and savings that exceed the initial higher expenditures.

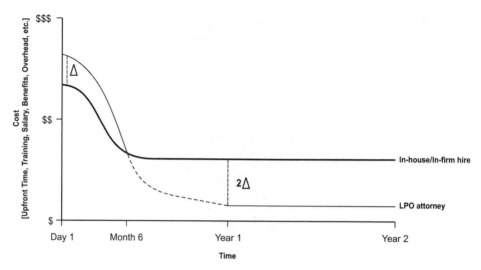

FIGURE 12.1 New Project Start-Up

The value proposition would show greater exaggeration over time if the newly trained in-house or in-firm attorney left her position (even temporarily) or if new attorneys were onboarded to grow the team, thus requiring the company/firm to train yet another hire. In comparison, in the case of replacing an LPO attorney or upsizing the LPO team, the LPO would invest in the new attorney selection and up-skilling rather than draining the clients' resources. This scenario might be visually depicted as shown in Figure 12.2.

Figure 12.2 considers cost and ROI incurred from onboarding a new attorney at the one year mark (indicated by the two Xs) to replace a departure (indicated by two Os). Although any new attorney will start off less efficient than a trained team

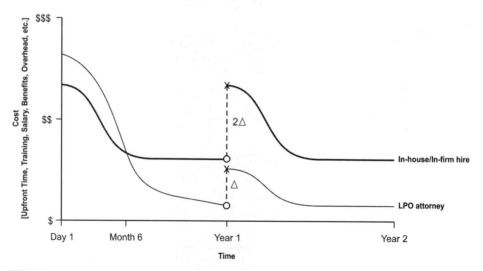

FIGURE 12.2 New Attorney Onboarding

member, thus costing the client something in terms of productivity and bang for the buck, in the LPO scenario, it is the LPO itself that invests time in onboarding and up-skilling, thus saving the client much of the upfront cost investment.[15] A new hire in-firm or in-house will comparatively require a cost investment that is comparable to the original cost investment from day one.

If the legal work involved in the project is highly redundant or not stimulating, it is also likely that the in-house group/law firm will see more departures than an LPO, which might be able to better retain talent thanks to the lure to foreign counsel of performing U.S. legal work. The cost savings associated with one LPO attorney turnover compared to multiple in-house or in-firm attorney turnovers over several months or years is self-evident and, even absent turnover, for the right project, the ROI on an LPO relationship can be extremely compelling.

Selecting Projects and Providers: What Is Outsourcable and Who Can Do It?

The suitability and success of outsourcing IP work depends largely on project and provider selection. You stand to lose not only time but potentially the very rights you seek to protect, not to mention your reputation for championing a project that ultimately flops. Upfront due diligence and sound investments in project design are indispensible components of the outsourcing process.

The Right Project

Very few projects are of such complexity that a properly selected offshore IP professional will be incapable of performing them. Projects that fit poorly into the outsourcing model, rather, are projects that require too much of an initial time investment to result in savings. A first foray into outsourcing should involve a discrete task that is large enough or repeated at a proper volume to overcome the initial time investment required to integrate the offshore provider into your business.[16] A project that is too small can require all the upfront preparation of a bigger project, but not yield as bountiful a return. Although each potential project should be subject to its own cost-benefit analysis, general guidelines can be suggested.

Recurrent tasks on the less specialized end of the IP spectrum, such as patent/ trademark violation monitoring and drafting or tracking cease and desist letters, are great for outsourcing. For a company that invests, say, three to 15 or more hours weekly into such tasks, the benefits of having their skilled employees freed to perform other tasks or the savings over hiring a new onshore resource to perform the task can result in significant overall benefits to the company.

IP document review is another commonly outsourced project type. The affordability of offshore subject experts (e.g., attorneys, specialized engineers and scientists, technologists) allows employment of a dream team, which might be economically impractical onshore. Determining the tipping point at which a review is large enough to outsource, though, can be tricky. A simple IP review with 10 or 20 issues, privilege and confidentiality review, and involving light technology might be taught to a bright team in half a day or less, thus justifying a review as small as

15,000 or 20,000 documents, perhaps fewer. Complicated reviews will require more case examination, perhaps necessitating one to two weeks of preparation followed by intense client commitment to discussing the disposition of unusual documents. So as not to invest more time in project setup than would be invested to perform the work in-house, a larger review of perhaps upward of 100,000 or 150,000 documents is warranted. Similarly, other types of IP litigation support, such as assistance in Markman hearings and expert report analyses, should be weighed on a case-by-case basis, and often an offshore provider can help you make this analysis.

More specialized IP projects are also outsourced regularly, but it is clients who send multiple projects overseas that reap the most benefit in terms of time invested versus overall time and cost savings. Examples of projects requiring more skilled professionals that are successfully outsourced with frequency include patent application drafting, office action responses, patentability/novelty searches, freedom to operate/right to use clearance reports, invalidity analyses, prior art searches, general patent portfolio management services (such as identification of patents for abandonment or for licensing opportunities, identification of critical/strategic patents, etc.), and landscaping reports.

Highly specialized projects can be outsourced as a one-off project, but better known providers, often having the most qualified personnel, may decline *small* one-off engagements in furtherance of a business modeled on repeat work from long-term clients. Moreover, such one-off projects can lose profitably if substantial start-up efforts cannot be parlayed into a longer running, and thus overall time and cost saving, project.[17] Additionally, providers will undoubtedly face an unsatisfied client if the client could have completed the project in the time it takes them to integrate the offshore resources into it. This is not to say that small, one-off projects cannot find highly qualified, lower cost, offshore takers, but it might require some searching and more rigorous diligence on the professionals offering to perform the service, especially if the subject matter is nuanced.

With upfront discussion aligning expectations about project startup time investment and estimated hours at peak efficiencies, a company should be able to determine whether outsourcing a particular project or projects can save time and money and thus whether it is a good project to outsource, and the right provider will be able to complete such projects within all science and engineering disciplines with stunning accuracy and smart cost savings.

The Right Provider

Depending on the suite of services offered by an LPO, there are instances where an LPO is not best suited to perform certain projects. A reputable LPO will decline undertaking work if it has no prior relevant experience or subject experts on staff, if the work is a significant departure from the services it provides, or if it anticipates a learning curve that runs afoul of the client's expectations in terms of time line or quality.[18] Best practices dictate that an LPO be candid about its competence, but it is ultimately the client's burden to select the right provider.

In Ethics Opinion 08-451, the American Bar Association (ABA) suggests a framework for diligence when selecting an outsourcing company. In consideration of this framework, the following considerations and analyses are advisable:

- Are the professionals you are hiring qualified to perform the work?

  Understand the education and prior experience of the attorneys, engineers, scientists, or technologists who would be staffed on your project.

  Short of terminology and language, the sciences will be the same around the world, so a review of credentials and prior experience should translate into a solid understanding of whether there is a skill set match for the work to be performed. Request resumes for the professionals who will be staffed to your project, and if you need context (a school ranking or U.S. degree equivalent, for example) take to the Internet and also ask the provider. For a large or sensitive project, it's entirely acceptable to ask to speak to the proposed team of professionals to ensure your comfort with them. In doing so, however, do not allow the red herring of foreign speech fool you. It's possible to have a brilliant mind and write clear and grammatical English, yet still speak using colloquialisms or with intense accents. Consider, too, that the mind that resolves scientific or technological intricacies may not belong to the same individual who drafts the final project report. Your provider should be forthcoming about team members' credentials as well as their roles.

  Should your project be based more in, or equally in, law than science, ascertaining credentials can involve more diligence. In addition to the investigation suggested in the foregoing paragraph, find out whether schooling is comparable to U. S. legal training. The Indian legal system, for example, is based on common law. Legal training and IP practice are, arguably, similar to that in the UnitedStates, but such is not the case for all foreign jurisdictions where outsourcing is offered. It will likely take more training time and expense, and possibly result in poor quality or product usability, if your outsourced team does not share a similar educational foundation with a U.S. provider. Ask providers how local schooling is like the U.S. educational system—and also ask how it is different. Ask in the context of the work you are requesting, as well as generally. Be wary of answers denying any differences and be wary of a company that cannot tell you what the differences are.

  Your understanding of the capabilities and limitations of a proposed project team will align expectations and ensure that your work is entrusted to a qualified provider.
- Will your project receive adequate supervision from a member of the U.S. patent bar or other appropriate mentor?

  Surprising as it may sound, not all offshore companies offering intellectual property support have on-staff members of the USPTO or even onsite U.S. attorneys. For obvious reasons, it's important to clarify the chain of command on each project and, ultimately, to ensure that someone with relevant practice experience is at the head of that command. As a rule of thumb, that person should have education and experience comparable to a person in the UnitedStates who would be charged with a similar project.
- Is confidentiality protected and is data secure?

  As discussed later in this chapter, confidentiality and data security are cardinal concerns over whether work is done onshore or offshore. Don't be hesitant to ask a service provider for details such as:
  - How it ensures data safety and monitors physical security
  - Whether it has had breaches in security, what its policies are in the event of breach, and what type of background checks it performs on hires

- How it avoids conflicts of interest, what type of conflict check database is used, and whether you can have a copy of their conflict check procedure
- What international security certifications they have received, whether the certification is for the whole facility or only designated portions (and in which portion will your work be performed), and what the requirements are for maintaining certification

    Ask whether you can visit the facilities. If you don't have time for a visit, ask for pictures and ask to speak with clients who have visited. A great company will be proud of its operations, and will gladly show prospects or existing clients around.

- Check references.

    The best assurances are from your peers. Don't be shy about calling references and asking them why they continue to use their offshore provider. Ask what they know now that they would have liked to have known before outsourcing. Many top companies and law firms outsource work on a regular basis; take advantage of their experience.

    As a final suggestion, take your time collecting information, ask follow-up questions, and become comfortable with your contacts. Careful selection of a provider will avoid most or all the risk and hassle sometimes experienced on projects, and a successful project will be good payoff for your due diligence efforts.

Case Studies

The following case studies illustrate some of the ideas presented in this chapter.

Case Study #1: Cost and Efficiency Savings to Client-Enable a Project That Could Not Be Done Onshore

A Fortune 50 client, a prominent engineering company, was incurring significant spend-on activities such as prior art searches, clearance searches, and state-of-the-art searches. The R&D divisions frequently came up with many ideas that needed a quick search, but the client's in-house team was struggling to keep up with the flow and the client was forced to send these searches to external search firms. Furthermore, for searches in similar technology areas, the searchers would often end up repeatedly reviewing and reporting the same references in different searches.

    The client knew that building a patenting landscape of the technology areas in which they operated and searching ways to reduce such redundancies and control their search costs would save them both time and fees. Unfortunately, the R&D projects spanned a vast number of technology fields, some of which were extremely crowded, so building a landscape of the patenting activity in these fields and conducting even a simple analysis of the relevant patents was cost prohibitive in the United States.

    Pangea3 solved the client's problem by building a structured database of the client's patents as well as patents owned by their competitors. It provided a comprehensive internal resource that accurately and dynamically captured patenting activity in the technology areas of interest to the client (e.g., filing trends, filing velocity, jurisdictions of interest, prolific inventors, etc.), with an eye toward determining areas of relative strengths and weaknesses. Pangea3 delivered this database in a format that allowed the client to leverage the analysis to conduct the quick searches in a fraction of the time they would usually spend.

Ultimately, Pangea3 prepared and maintained structured databases for the client's top ten R&D projects, and the client uses them regularly to assess the direction of its patenting activities and to guide future development. In addition, the client's IP department is able to quickly assess the likely outcome of clearance searches by inexpensively running a first cut clearance search in the database, thereby only pursuing a full-blown clearance search in limited instances. Moreover, periodic updating of the resource database keeps the client aware of all relevant patents in the industry (including those held by the client itself), and leads to identification of important patents for licensing/acquisition.

The client thus has increased capabilities, at time and cost savings via a project which was not possible onshore.

Case Study #2: Company's Demand That Outside Counsel Work with LPO Results in Significant Benefits to Company, and Outside Counsel Becomes a Proponent of Offshoring

Client, a leading global financial services company, was incurring significant costs building its patent portfolio. Its various business units would frequently come up with innovative ideas that would be potential differentiators from products/services offered by competing financial services companies. Client wanted to protect these ideas by securing patents in the underlying methodologies and systems, but the outside counsel costs associated with preparing and prosecuting these applications was an impediment. Client therefore sought to outsource the work and requested that outside counsel from several firms provide high level oversight.

Outside counsel was, understandably, initially concerned and cited both negative past experiences with LPOs as well as a general lack of confidence in offshore provider quality. Pangea3 appreciated all these concerns and recognized that part of its job was to win over outside firms. By the first joint meeting, Pangea3 had already used the Patent Application Information Retrieval (PAIR) USPTO database to review the prior filings of each of Client's engaged law firms and had studied the drafting preferences of individual attorneys. The LPO was thus able to finalize project guidelines with a working knowledge of outside counsels' styles, and it was agreed that the law firms would share redlined feedback throughout the early days of the project to fine tune the LPO work and, thereafter, would review the filings at a senior-most level. To further assuage lingering concerns, Pangea3 provided each outside firm with an open invitation to visit its offices and to conduct workshops with the team, which was also made available via video and telephone conferencing.

It was just a matter of weeks before the law firms began viewing the Pangea3 team as a geographically displaced extension of their own team and, pleased with the quality of the work, have since referred unrelated clients to the LPO. A pivotal turning point in the LPO-law firm relationship was outside counsels' realization that their time was being better spent on the highest level review and on sophisticated aspects of patent prosecution than on performing the more junior project tasks, and that without the more cost-effective alternative of offshoring, Client was unlikely to pursue as many patents. This, combined with security in the quality of the LPO work, resulted in a win-win for all parties.

Case Study #3: Project Where Volume *Was Not* Sufficient to Justify Outsourcing Ramp-Up Costs

A globally recognized top U.S. university approached leading LPO Pangea3 to: (1) conduct research directed toward identifying genes that could be potential thera- peutic targets; (2) identify the corresponding drug candidates; and (3) identify the status of the clinical trials for each identified drug candidate. The work was very interesting and fell squarely within Pangea3's expertise.

As with most projects, the Pangea3 team scheduled a call with the university's scientists to further discuss the proposed methodology and other parameters attend- ant to the project. During the call, the LPO team sought to align the client's expect- ation with that of the team and to determine the best methodology, associated fee, and time line.

Upon discussion, it became apparent that the most comprehensive approach to the project would be to search using a very specific subscription-fee based database. Pangea3, however, did not have a license to said database. Moreover, the university was not in a position to renegotiate its license agreement to include Pangea3, even for a limited period. When the LPO investigated the cost associated with procuring a license, it found that the license fee to the database was over five times the project fee. Being that the project was a one-off request in a narrow scientific field, it made little pragmatic sense to proceed and the project did not move forward. Had there been volume rather than a one-off request, however, with time the license fee could have been justified by the offshore savings accumulated on each repeat project/task.

Case Study #4: Project Where Volume *Was* Sufficient to Justify Outsourcing Ramp-Up Costs

A leading electronics manufacturing company had a significantly large patent portfo- lio and hoped to have it reviewed from a licensing (monetization) perspective. The involved technology was complex and required thorough knowledge of the state of the art in disparate domains. The two in-house options available to the client were either indefinitely delaying its monetization efforts or increasing head count to support the project. Neither were deemed palatable, and Client looked to LPO for a solution.

Pangea3's proposed LPO solution involved an initial investment of substantial time to first understand the state of the art and the patents in Client's portfolio using an agreed-on set of guidelines. The client had to appreciate that it would not be seeing any tangible results while ostensibly paying for services for weeks while the Pangea3 team was getting familiar with the state of the art and developing a sound understanding of the client's patent portfolio. However, once the Pangea3 team gained the required know-how, it would be reviewing the thousands of patents in the client's portfolio at a rate that was unachievable if the client were to do this in-house.

Per the project plan, the Pangea3 team devoted substantial time to reading and understanding significant volumes of technical literature and to developing an understanding of the functioning/implementation of products and solutions available in the market. Once the team was adept at the technology and the state of the art, the team turned its attention to evaluating Client's patent portfolio.

Ultimately, the time invested by the Pangea3 team in developing an understanding of the state of the art and Client's patent portfolio materially reduced the time it took the team to evaluate the patents from a licensing perspective. The client thus benefited not only from having a reliable source with abundant bandwidth review its patent portfolio, but also from cost savings realized by the efficiencies developed from the initial investment in time.

The foregoing wouldn't have been a viable solution if the client's patent portfolio were small—for example, 10 patents. However, where the portfolio is large or there is repeat volume, an initial investment of time goes a long way in creating efficiencies that translate into direct cost savings for the client, without delaying important initiatives or increasing internal head count to achieve them.

Case Study #5: A Project Not Initially Suited to LPO, Disclosure to the Client, and a Solution

Client, a leading semiconductor manufacturer with an extensive patent portfolio, approached LPO, Pangea3, to conduct infringement analysis on a chip that required reverse engineering. Pangea3 assured Client that it could digest technical documents and data sheets in furtherance of analysis, claim chart creation, and mapping infringing product parts to corresponding claim elements, but warned that, like all LPOs, it lacked a reverse engineering lab with scientific equipment such as oscilloscopes, X-ray machines, and electron microscopes, which would be required to perform the required engineering. The project was therefore not a good fit for legal outsourcing as it was originally contemplated.

Looking for a work around, Pangea3 and Client decided to engage a reverse engineering firm that would share its findings with the LPO team. The team could then undertake the infringement analysis based on information that was not publicly available and was only ascertainable through reverse engineering, and Client ultimately received the best in business service at every step of the engagement.

Conclusion

The best way to conclude a look at IP legal outsourcing is to turn to where the industry is heading. While it is impossible to accurately predict the future, the following musings can certainly find support in both historic and recent outsourcing and legal trends.

- Legal outsourcing is here to stay. More companies and firms are using it with increasing frequency and scales, while players previously on the sidelines are now trying it enthusiastically, with faster adoption rates. In turn, with increased buzz about outsourcing and with companies and firms being willing to discuss publicly their experiences, new companies and firms are, each day, sending first projects overseas and beginning what often will turn into long term relationships spanning many projects.
- The legal billing bubble has burst. Lower prices and alternative billing models available overseas are forcing firms to take a look at their own efficiencies, and the current economy has clients demanding that firms lower their prices, enter into alternative billing arrangements, and find new ways of providing services in a cost-effective manner, including using offshore providers and resources. The cost alternative provided by LPO will, along with client demand, serve as a check and balance on firm prices, and as an enabler of alternative billing arrangements. Billing rates will likely never again inflate as they did in the past.
- Early adopters of LPO have reaped cost savings ahead of the pack and are now scaling their use of LPO. As with counterpart early adopters in business process outsourcing (BPO) and IT outsourcing (ITO), the projects outsourced have grown dramatically in size and scope. Likewise, the early adopters have now grown their use of LPO such that a company that may have originally outsourced only one type of work (i.e., IP, litigation, or corporate) now outsources work spanning several legal departments and disciplines. These industry leaders better understand risks and payoffs, and their learning curve paved the way for a self-trajectory toward larger savings. As was the case with other types of outsourcing, it is likely that companies new to outsourcing will ultimately catch up and, over perhaps the next five years, level the field. It is therefore possible that visionary companies, the earliest adopters of LPO, will eventually push the envelope again, sending even more complex, higher cost projects overseas to maintain the advantage.

Notes

1. "Offshoring Patent Services to India," Valuenotes (June 2008), 4.

2. Ibid. at 6.

3. "Legal Process Outsourcing: Crisis Creates New Opportunities for LPO," Valuenotes (Nov. 2009).

4. "Offshoring Patent Services to India," 6.

5. A case study looking at a company's demand that outside counsel work with an LPO and counsels' reaction thereto is included as Case Study #2 at the end of this chapter.

6. More discussion on how to evaluate a provider's confidentiality and data security provisions is to be found in this chapter under the head, "Selecting Projects and Providers: What Is Outsourcable and Who Can Do It?"

7. Clients should always have representation by a qualified U.S. barred attorney.

8. As set forth in Restatement (Third) of the Law Governing Lawyers, §70 (2000), "[p]rivileged persons are . . . the client's lawyer . . . and agents of the lawyer who facilitate the representation." Comment g to this section expounds: A lawyer may disclose privileged communications to other office lawyers and appropriate non-lawyer staff. . . . The privilege also extends to communications to and from the client that are disclosed to independent contractors retained by a lawyer, such as an accountant or a physician retained by the lawyer to assist in providing legal services to the client.

9. Association of the Bar of the City of New York Committee on Professional Responsibility, *Report On the Outsourcing of Legal Services Overseas* (August 2009).

10. See also Michael Downey, "Satisfying Ethical Obligations When Outsourcing Legal Work Overseas," in *Intellectual Property Strategies for the 21st Century Corporation.*

11. It is often the case with multi-national companies that the technology is itself developed offshore, and U.S. export control laws and regulations are not thus not implicated by sending such technology to common IP LPO locales such as India or the Philippines.

12. "Introduction to the U.S. Commerce Department Export Controls" from BIS provides additional guidance on the categorization and classification of items. www.bis.doc.gov/licensing/exportingbasics.htm.

13. See "Selecting Projects and Providers: What Is Outsourcable and Who Can Do It?" in this chapter, for guidance on ascertaining a company's capabilities.

14. For demonstrative purposes, Figure 12.1 assumes a more complex project that may take longer to run the full course of the value proposition than one of lesser complexity, which could achieve maximum efficiencies in as little as one or two weeks.

15. It is assumed that the LPO would not charge the client for the time required to replace a departing team member, and most leading LPOs will stipulate to this in contracts of engagement.

16. It should be noted that this upfront time investment is not basic legal training. A good provider will have professionals from multiple disciplines already experienced in IP practice. Rather, you will need to customize the provider's work style to reflect the preferences of your organization and nuances of the project. This may include generating reports in a proprietary format, learning to work with a proprietary technology, or simply taking time to discuss expectations and technical aspects of the particular project.

17. For an in-depth look at projects where the volume was not and was sufficient to justify outsourcing ramp-up costs, see Case Studies #3 and #4 at the end of this chapter.

18. A demonstration of this scenario is included in Case Study #5 at the end of this chapter.

CHAPTER 13

Satisfying Ethical Obligations When Outsourcing Legal Work Overseas

Michael Downey
Hinshaw & Culbertson LLP

For some corporations, outsourcing legal work—in particular to legal process outsourcing (LPO) providers in foreign countries—offers a way to maintain or even improve legal service delivery while reducing costs. A 2010 study by a global research and analytics firm, Evalueserve, reports the LPO sector grew by almost 40 percent per year during the so-called Great Recession, and that revenue growth for LPOs is expected to be 26 percent between 2010 and 2015. Virtually all this outsourcing is being sent from the United States and United Kingdom, with approximately 90 percent coming directly or indirectly from corporations. Corporations that have recently announced they were significantly using or increasing LPO activity include Microsoft and mining giant Rio Tinto.

As the use of LPO providers has increased, a number of bar associations have opined that offshore outsourcing (i.e., outsourcing to lawyers in foreign countries) is permissible, as long as certain ethics concerns are properly addressed. Those opinions, however, tend to provide little practical guidance regarding how in-house or outside counsel should address those ethical concerns. This chapter seeks to remedy such shortcomings by integrating the guidance of the recent ethics opinions on offshore outsourcing[1] with practical advice for corporate counsel seeking to satisfy ethical and risk management considerations while outsourcing.

Permissibility of Outsourcing

Each bar group that has considered offshore outsourcing has found it permissible under the applicable rules of professional conduct. American Bar Association (ABA) Formal Opinion 08-451, for example, pronounces, "There is nothing unethical about a lawyer outsourcing legal . . . services, provided the outsourcing lawyer renders legal services to the client with the 'legal knowledge, skill, thoroughness and preparation reasonably necessary for the representation,' as required by [Model] Rule 1.1.'" North Carolina (NC) Formal Ethics Opinion 12 (2007) makes the point even stronger: "[A]s long as the lawyer's use of the nonlawyer assistant's services is in accordance with the Rules of Professional Conduct, the location of the nonlawyer assistant is irrelevant." (The foreign lawyer is called a "nonlawyer assistant" because that person is not admitted to practice in North Carolina.)

ABA Opinion 08-451 even extols potential benefits that legal outsourcing may offer to clients:

> *Outsourcing affords lawyers the ability to reduce their costs and often the cost to the client to the extent that the individuals or entities providing the outsourced services can do so at lower rates than the lawyer's own staff. In addition, the availability of lawyers and nonlawyers to perform discrete tasks may, in some circumstances, allow for the provision of labor-intensive legal services by lawyers who do not otherwise maintain the needed human resources on an ongoing basis.*

Although each existing ethics opinion permits offshore outsourcing, each requires that the lawyer comply with other ethical requirements when retaining and using an offshore LPO provider. Most ethics opinions are written to guide outside counsel at law firms, and thus contain discussion regarding whether a client should receive notice of the outsourcing and how the law firm can charge its clients for LPO provider services. These concerns are less important here, because it is presumed that corporate counsel will discuss the outsourcing with their business managers and that payments will generally flow directly from the corporation to the LPO provider. The major concerns addressed here, therefore, relate to the duties of corporate counsel to investigate and supervise potential nonlawyer assistants such as LPO providers.

Need for Heightened Investigation and Supervision

ABA Model Rules 5.1 and 5.3, as adopted by the relevant jurisdiction (normally the corporate counsel's home jurisdiction), are the starting points to determine ethical obligations for corporate counsel seeking to outsource legal work offshore. Model Rules 5.1 and 5.3 require that a supervising lawyer establish reasonable safeguards and then make reasonable efforts to supervise subordinate lawyers (Rule 5.1) and nonlawyer assistants (Rule 5.3) within such a framework of those safeguards. The supervising lawyer must "ensure that tasks are delegated to individuals who are competent to perform them, and then to oversee the execution of the project adequately and appropriately."[2] This obligation to supervise applies even when a nonlawyer assistant is not working directly with the lawyer. "Outsourcing does not alter the attorney's obligations to the client, even though outsourcing may help the attorney discharge those obligations at lower cost."[3]

The impact of these two rules—in particular Rule 5.3, which covers nonlawyers "employed or retained by or associated with the lawyer"—on offshore outsourcing is quite significant because the various bar committees are concerned that distance, language issues, and differing legal environments and traditions may give rise to unique concerns for clients when offshore LPO providers are used. Each relevant ethics opinion reflects that the obligation to supervise becomes difficult to satisfy when the subordinates are physically separated by thousands of miles and a time difference of several hours.[4] Electronic communications may "close the gap to some degree," but such communications also may "not be sufficient to allow the lawyer to monitor the work of the lawyers and nonlawyers working for her in an effective manner."[5] "Given [the special] considerations and given the hurdles imposed by the physical separation between the [domestic] lawyer and the overseas non-lawyer, the [domestic] lawyer must be both vigilant and creative in discharging the duty to supervise."[6]

A lawyer considering outsourcing must believe the difficulties posed by distance, language, and legal culture can be overcome before outsourcing legal work to individuals trained in another country. "If physical separation, language barriers, differences in time zones, or inadequate communication channels do not allow a reasonable and adequate level of supervision to be maintained over the foreign assistant's work, the lawyer should not retain the foreign assistant to provide services."[7]

Issues relating to distance, language, and different legal cultures must therefore be considered and resolved when corporate counsel is considering referring work to overseas LPO providers. A lawyer considering outsourcing should undertake particular care in vetting the project and LPO provider, and directing and overseeing the work.

Evaluating the Project

To address the ethical concerns in offshore outsourcing, corporate counsel should first evaluate the project that the foreign contract lawyers or nonlawyers (hereinafter "contract lawyers") will handle to ensure the project is appropriate to outsource overseas. One frequent mistake outsourcing lawyers make is to handle all projects or aspects of projects the same way. Once an offshore LPO provider is vetted, for example, an outsourcing lawyer may use that provider for an entire project or group of projects. Yet some of the specific projects or a portion of a larger project may give rise to special concerns. For example, just as in-house counsel would not automatically retain its patent prosecution firm to handle major IP litigation, in-house counsel should not automatically assume that an LPO provider selected to draft patent applications or search for prior art would also be ideally situated to conduct massive document review for patent infringement litigation.

The nature of specific information at issue in a matter may make it inappropriate to send certain work to overseas LPO providers. It may be more suitable to have overseas contract lawyers review and organize electronically stored information provided in disclosures by a litigation adversary, for example, than to have those same contract lawyers handle the client's own sensitive materials. In addition, some information may be too sensitive to send overseas. A company may hesitate before sharing a particularly novel, important set of patent applications with anyone outside the company, and balk in particular at sharing such innovations effectively with strangers located halfway around the world. Or the legal work may be subject to particular limitations regarding its use and distribution, such as import-export controls like the

International Traffic in Arms Regulations (ITAR) that prohibit certain defense and military related technologies from being shared with non-U.S. individuals and corporations. Corporate counsel considering using outsourcing should assess whether the corporate client is willing to send the information to relative strangers overseas, or whether instead they want or need to keep that information closer, perhaps using domestic outsourcing partners or even keeping the project completely in-house.

Evaluating the Potential Provider

Once a project has been deemed suitable for outsourcing, whether domestic or offshore, the LPO provider and contract lawyers who will be providing the work should be evaluated. Ethics opinions reviewing the propriety of using outsource providers advise conducting investigations of LPO providers on two levels. First, the lawyer must conduct an investigation into the LPO provider itself, to ensure that the LPO provider has in place adequate safeguards to protect client interests. Second, at least some authorities suggest an outsourcing lawyer should also conduct an investigation into the individuals who will actually be serving as contract lawyers and working on the project.

ABA Formal Opinion 08-451 does not take a clear position whether the due-diligence investigation should be at the entity or individual contract lawyer level. Rather, ABA Formal Opinion 08-451 blurs the line, stating:

> [A] lawyer outsourcing services for ultimate provision to a client should consider conducting reference checks and investigating the background of the lawyer or nonlawyer providing the services as well as any nonlawyer intermediary involved, such as a placement agency or service provider. The lawyer also might consider interviewing the principal lawyers, if any, involved in the project, among other things assessing their educational background. When dealing with an intermediary, the lawyer may wish to inquire into its hiring practices to evaluate the quality and character of the employees likely to have access to client information.

A full evaluation of an LPO provider will often constitute a four-step process. First, corporate counsel should familiarize itself with the legal culture of the company where the LPO provider will provide the services. This will generally require the outsourcing lawyer to assess the legal education system and environment in the country where contract lawyers will be used. Counsel should seek to ensure that the country's legal education system will provide people with skills and abilities adequate to handle the project competently. In addition, corporate counsel should consider whether the country's legal system will provide adequate protection for privileged and confidential information, as well as adequate means for recourse if, for example, the LPO provider does not provide competent services or threatens to or engages in other misconduct, such as seeking to ransom or employ intellectual property for its own benefit. (San Diego Ethics Opinion 2007-1 references an outsource provider who threatened to disclose patient health information if the hospital client did not help secure overdue payment from a third-party intermediary.)

Second, corporate counsel should evaluate the LPO provider itself, both through personal investigation and through communications with past clients. This review should ensure the LPO provider itself has a strong, positive reputation and financial foundation, that it is a well-governed entity and understands its role and legal obligations, and that the LPO provider selects and retains good workers. The LPO provider assessment should evaluate the sophistication and strength of LPO management, availability of management (including communications and whether the LPO provider has domestic operations), compliance controls, financial resources, and availability of applicable insurance or bonding.

Corporate counsel may also consider what control the LPO provider will grant corporate counsel over the contract lawyers, including whether corporate counsel will have the ability to review, evaluate, and reward or exclude contract lawyers based on their performance. Corporate counsel should ensure that an LPO provider has the necessary resources, for example, an adequate automated docketing system for managing maintenance of the company's intellectual property. Corporate counsel should also be comfortable with questions involving possible worst case scenarios, such as what will happen if communications are lost or the LPO provider files for bankruptcy.

In many instances, corporate counsel should also assess the protections for confidential information, including reviewing physical (premise) security and network security. This assessment may necessarily be quite thorough and address issues such as receipt, retention, and disposal of client information. As ABA Opinion 08-451 notes, "In some instances, it may be prudent to pay a personal visit to the [LPO provider's] facility, regardless of its location or the difficulty of travel, to get a firsthand sense of its operation and the professionalism of the lawyers and nonlawyers it is procuring." Such investigation seems particularly important where the information shared will be intellectual property assets whose value would largely be lost if confidentiality were breached.

In conducting this review, corporate counsel should remember that not all LPO providers are established or operate the same. Some are affiliated with United States or other law firms, or have established relationships with United States or international lawyers or clients. Others employ U.S.-trained lawyers as project managers or in other roles, including sometimes having such personnel in a U.S. office. Corporate counsel should shop around enough to ensure they are comfortable with the framework and operations of the LPO provider.

For example, an outsourcing lawyer may meet with representatives of the LPO provider in person, and speak with people at the offshore location before entrusting that offshore site with client-related information. In some circumstances, it may even be appropriate for the outsourcing lawyers to visit the LPO provider's staff and facilities where the work will be performed. Where confidentiality or protection of confidences are particularly important, for example, where the outsourced work will involve important intellectual property assets, many LPO providers can provide facilities where only the lawyers and nonlawyers working on the client matter will have access to the areas where that work will be performed. Further, all other employees, even officers of the LPO provider, may be unable to access computers and other communications equipment dedicated to a client's work.

While evaluating the LPO provider, corporate counsel will likely also start the third step: investigating the individual contract lawyers who will be designated to work on corporate counsel's project. In the best circumstances, the LPO provider will be prepared to establish a dedicated team to serve a client or work on a project. Corporate counsel may then request resumes and writing samples and assess the background and ability of each contract lawyer. This may include conducting in-person, telephone, or web camera interviews. The review may also include verifying information on the contract lawyer's resume, and investigating the contract lawyer's licensure status and disciplinary history. Corporate counsel may even want to learn how contract lawyers will be compensated, including whether the compensation may be adjusted for good or bad performance.

Finally, corporate counsel should ensure that written documents governing the outsourced project spell out and secure the necessary warranties and commitments regarding the review just conducted. This may include specific statements regarding how the LPO provider will conduct its business, what network and other security will be used, how staffing or changes in staffing will be handled, and the availability of insurance or other financial protections. I am aware of at least one situation in which an overseas provider tendered one group of individuals for telephone interviews, but used another group of individuals to perform the actual (non-legal) project. Specifying in writing the qualifications or identities of individuals who will work on a project should reduce the risk of such problems. Further, corporate counsel may secure written commitments to avoid conflicts and preserve confidentiality. All such desired commitments should be secured before corporate counsel sends any information to the LPO provider.

Ensure Absence of Conflicts[8]

Once the provider has been selected, corporate counsel should ensure that the LPO provider and the contract lawyers themselves do not have any conflicts of interest. Depending on the nature of the legal profession in the country at issue as well as the sophistication of the LPO provider, this may be a very simple process, or it may require considerable involvement from corporate counsel because the LPO provider may not fully appreciate what legal and business conflicts the corporate client will consider problematic. Without some familiarity with how a conflict check was conducted, corporate counsel should not simply rely upon a simple statement that "No conflicts were identified."

Where the anticipated projects are quite large or sensitive (such as the outsourcing of significant patent drafting and prosecution work) corporate counsel may benefit from securing an LPO provider who warrants it will not handle other projects on the same topic or in the same industry, or who will use a particular facility or portion of a facility for corporate counsel's project. This is consistent with advice in ABA Formal Opinion 08-451 that, "to minimize the risk of potentially wrongful disclosure, the outsourcing lawyer should verify that the outside service provider does not also do work for adversaries of their clients on the same or substantially related matters; in such an instance, the outsourcing lawyer could choose another provider."

Of course, where such warranties regarding the absence of conflicts are sought and secured, they should be memorialized in the agreement between the LPO provider and client. Also, some LPO providers have indicated they will only agree to an industry-exclusive arrangement where the industry is relatively limited or the work offered is quite extensive and lucrative.

Providing Initial Direction and Ongoing Supervision

Sometimes corporate or outside counsel conduct considerable due diligence when selecting and retaining an LPO provider, but then simply dump the project on the LPO provider with no additional information or guidance. This may result in major problems with the quality of the services provided. Legal outsourcing is one field that demonstrates the maxim, "Garbage in, garbage out."

To avoid this problem, corporate counsel should ensure that the contract lawyers working on a project receive the information and guidance necessary to carry out the project properly. Ethics opinions emphasize the critical importance of good communication between the supervising and contract lawyers. Often establishing such good communication begins before the project is outsourced. The lawyers or business leaders in charge of a project may need to sit down before the project commences and lay out the necessary background and instructions for the project. Then this information should be communicated to the contract lawyers in a manner that will ensure they receive and understand it. Often this requires personal involvement of a supervisor with sufficient knowledge of the project and strong communication skills. Normally the presentation should be in person or at least in real time (i.e., by telephone or video conference). The presenter must be mindful of differences in the legal systems at issue, and also account for varying fluency and ability levels among the contract lawyers.

Contract lawyers and the supervising team then should continue strong communications throughout the project. In a large document review, for example, the supervising lawyer may need to review an initial unit of each contract lawyer's review to ensure that the contract lawyer is applying the proper standards to the project, and then provide periodic communication and review to ensure the contract lawyer's work remains appropriate and that any questions that arise are addressed. Likewise, a company outsourcing intellectual property work such as investigations of prior art or preparation of new patents must provide adequate information to ensure the LPO provider's work will result in meaningful review and analysis. In the best situations, supervising counsel will treat contract lawyers as valued members of the team, and this team mentality improves the services and dedication the contract lawyers provide.

Avoiding the Unauthorized Practice of Law

ABA Model Rule 5.5(a) prevents a lawyer from assisting another person in practicing law in a jurisdiction where that other person is not permitted to do so. Thus, the lawyer who retains an outsource provider must ensure that contract lawyers (and nonlawyers) under the lawyer's supervision do not engage in the unauthorized practice of law. The type of services outsource lawyers typically provide would generally limit such risks; however, the risk to the lawyer as well as the client advise corporate counsel to monitor what tasks the contract lawyers are permitted to perform, and the level of supervision they receive on such projects.

Protecting Confidences

Throughout the engagement, corporate counsel should take steps to ensure that adequate protections for confidences remain in place. ABA Model Rule 1.6 and related fiduciary obligations impose a burden on lawyers to take reasonable steps to protect client confidences While addressing obligations regarding disclosure for metadata, for example, N.Y. State Bar Op. 782 warns, "It is the sending lawyer's obligation to take reasonable steps to safeguard the confidentiality of all communications sent by electronic means to other lawyers and third parties and to protect from other lawyers and third parties all confidential information."

To protect confidences in the LPO setting, this would generally include an initial assessment of the network and procedures the LPO provider uses to transfer and handle client information, including whether the LPO provider creates and operates a specific secure facility for a client's project. During a project, corporate counsel may also need to monitor the LPO provider's staffing of a project, as well as the network, physical, and other confidentiality protections established for the project to ensure they remain in place. Corporate counsel may want to remind contract lawyers periodically and through multiple media of the need for confidentiality, confirm that new staff execute personal acknowledgements of the confidentiality agreement, and communicate with contract lawyers to make sure they understand and continue satisfying their confidentiality obligations.

Corporate counsel should also seriously consider having any LPO provider execute a confidentiality agreement that requires the LPO provider to have and maintain adequate safeguards for information, to notify corporate counsel if a problem occurs with such safeguards, and to maintain the confidentiality of all client-related information that the LPO provider receives, regardless of the source. Such agreements should also make clear how the LPO provider should handle information at the end of the engagement, including if the engagement ends due to payment or performance problems of either party. FL Bar Opinion 07-02 explains: "Attorney should require sufficient and specific assurances (together with an outline of relevant policies and processes) that the data, once used for the service requested, will be irretrievably destroyed, and not sold, used, or otherwise be capable of access after the provision of the contracted-for service." Such an agreement should also provide for periodic auditing, and corporate counsel should periodically conduct such an audit to ensure adequate safeguards are being employed.

Payment for Outsourced Services

As noted, corporate counsel may and often will arrange and pay directly for outsourced services to better monitor and control costs—and to retain leverage in the case of billing or other disputes. Some have suggested that it would be unfair to as-cribe the full supervisory responsibilities to outside counsel where corporate counsel has selected the LPO provider, but I have not yet seen authority that supports such a distinction. In fact, although not much information on such arrangements exists, the anecdotal evidence I have heard support that, where a corporation has made arrangements with an LPO provider, its outside counsel has coordinated with that LPO provider without significant resistance.

Where corporate counsel instead elects to use a law firm as an intermediary, cor-porate counsel may want to obtain assurances from the law firm intermediary regard-ing how the corporation will be billed for the LPO provider's services. Corporate counsel may also want to ensure that the corporation is specified as a third-party beneficiary on all contracts and insurance arrangements with the LPO provider, so the corporation would have standing to enforce such rights independently in case problems arise with the law firm or LPO provider.

Regarding billing by outside firms for LPO services, ABA Formal Opinion 08-451 provides that there are two ways a law firm may bill for outsourced legal services. First, the law firm may bill for the legal services through the firm, as the firm does other legal services, and add a reasonable surcharge as appropriate to account for additional costs incurred because of the outside lawyer. Absent the client's agree-ment to the contrary, ABA Formal Opinion 08-451 indicates this surcharge should include only the law firm's "actual cost plus a reasonable allocation of associated overhead, such as the amount the lawyer spent on any office space, support staff, equipment, and supplies for the individuals under contract." The opinion also notes that in the outsourcing context normally such additional overhead costs would be "minimal or nonexistent," thus limiting the surcharge.

Alternatively, the law firm may bill for the contract lawyer as if the contract law-yer were an expense, and simply pass through the cost of the outside lawyer. "If the firm decides to pass those costs through to the client as a disbursement . . . no markup is permitted."[9]

Corporate counsel may want to take a proactive approach to ensuring that its law firms handle use and billing for contract lawyers, whether at an LPO provider or elsewhere, in a manner corporate counsel deems appropriate. Specifically, corporate counsel may insist that a law firm give written notice when it will use nonemployees to provide legal services to the corporation, and that such notice indicate how much the contract lawyer or LPO provider will be paid—and what markup or surcharge will be assessed by the law firm. Such disclosures should allow corporate counsel to limit unnecessary expenses, particularly as law firms are generally reluctant to im-pose a large surcharge and then tell the client about that surcharge.

Insurance[10]

Finally, a client whose work is outsourced may face difficulties in recovering should the outsourced work be mishandled. When an intermediary law firm is used, the law firm's insurance policy may include temporary or contract attorneys within the defi-nition of an insured. But the policy language, or the nature of the outsourcing rela-tionship (for example, that the outsourced service providers are located outside a law firm office and overseas or employed for lengthy periods) may exclude contract lawyers' actions from coverage. Further, that the service providers may be located overseas, and may have limited assets, may effectively render them judgment proof. Corporate counsel may therefore wish to ensure—probably in writing—that professional liability insurance or other funds are available, or consider the absence of such funds when deciding whether to outsource or what outsource provider to use.

Conclusion

Therefore, as noted at the outset, the ethics rules generally permit lawyers to outsource legal work, including to overseas legal process outsourcing (LPO) providers. But lawyers, both in-house and at law firms, should take care to ensure that the specific tasks are appropriate to outsource, that the LPO provider is appropriate to receive client information and complete the desired tasks, and that the work is completed in a suitable manner. Only then should a lawyer believe that he or she has satisfied the ethical obligations that accompany legal outsourcing.

Notes

1. The ethics opinions on offshore outsourcing that serve as the foundation for this chapter are ABA Formal Opinion 08-451, Colorado State Bar Opinion 121 (2008), Los Angeles County Ethics Opinion 518 (2006), New York City Bar Opinion 2006-3, North Carolina Formal Ethics Opinion 12 (2007), Ohio Supreme Court Bd. of Commissioners on Grievances and Discipline, Opinion 2009-6, and San Diego Bar Association Opinion 2007-1. In August 2009, the New York City Bar issued a further report on offshore outsourcing titled "Report on the Outsourcing of Legal Services Overseas," available at www.nycbar.org/pdf/report/uploads/20071813-ReportontheOutsourcingofLegalServicesOverseas.pdf. Each of these opinion analysis varies, sometimes in a material way. Therefore, where a particular ethics opinion governs conduct, it should be consulted in addition to this chapter.

2. ABA Formal Opinion 08-451.

3. San Diego Bar Association Opinion 2007-1.

4. ABA Formal Opinion 08-451; see also Florida (FL) Bar Opinion 07-02 ("Attorneys who use overseas legal outsourcing companies should recognize that providing adequate supervision may be difficult when dealing with employees who are in a different country.").

5. ABA Formal Opinion 08-451.

6. New York City (NYC) Bar Opinion 2006.

7. NC Formal Ethics Opinion 2007-12.

8. See also Olga Nedeltscheff, "Outsourcing and Offshoring of IP Legal Work," in *Intellectual Property Strategies for the 21st Century Corporation*.

9. ABA Formal Opinion 08-451.

10. See also Kimberly Klein Cauthorn and Leib Dodell, "Using Insurance to Manage Intellectual Property Risk," in *Intellectual Property Strategies for the 21st Century Corporation*.

CHAPTER 14

The Brave New World of Web 2.0 and the 3-D Internet

How to Prepare Your Company to Participate

Steve Mortinger
International Business Machines Corp.

I magine picking up the newspaper to read that your company's CEO has been anonymously blogging about significant company matters on a third party financial web site. Imagine further that you learn your company's employees are creating and selling virtual Rolex watches in a virtual world site while they sit at their desks in your workplace. How is this possible? What can you as the company's lawyer do to address—or, even better—to prevent this?

As the press regularly reports, the new era of the Internet is being ushered in by social media web sites (or Web 2.0 sites). At the same time, there is also an emerging set of virtual world sites sometimes referred to as the three-dimensional Internet (or the 3-D Internet). Much of the attention these sites get is focused on the personal or social aspect of this evolution in the Internet. People are not only shopping online and sending e-mails; they are interacting across the world, in real time. The traditional media looks to short bursts of text, from average people, in remote or war torn areas to gather real-time information for news stories.[1] Additionally, there are people living a simulated online existence through web sites providing them (and their online personas called "avatars") a virtual world where they can be someone or something very different from their real world personas.[2] All this activity could easily be dismissed as frivolous and even irrelevant by busy lawyers focused on the day-to-day business needs of their corporate clients. However, that would be a mistake.

This chapter provides an overview of these emerging Internet areas and discusses their relevance to legal practitioners supporting corporate clients, especially with regard to potential pitfalls involving intellectual property. This chapter also

---

The views expressed in this chapter are those of the author alone and do not necessarily express the views of IBM Corporation.

discusses best practices that could be employed to prepare corporate clients to intelligently participate in these online arenas.

Background: The Internet

As shown in Figure 14.1, the Internet is not a static environment. In its brief history, the Internet has had at least three overlapping phases. This section briefly looks at recent developments in the Internet.

From the Internet to Web 2.0

The Internet initially emerged as a less than interactive experience. In the early days of the Internet typically only sophisticated users would go onto the Internet itself.[3] Other users could go onto proprietary portals, like Prodigy or America Online, which acted as on-ramps to the Internet. In either case, if the users were not doing programming work,[4] they were using the Internet or the Internet portal to find information or to send e-mail. Portals, like Prodigy, offered features providing news, data on trip planning, weather forecasts, online encyclopedias, and the like.[5] The typical user had little or no direct interaction with the Internet itself or with others on the Internet, other than through use of e-mail. Data flowed out to the user in a manner akin to a person reading an encyclopedia. No commercial uses were even officially permitted on the Internet until the mid-1990s.[6]

Over time, more interactive elements began to appear on the Internet. The key characteristic of today's Web 2.0 is an Internet that acts as a platform for interactive and collaborative activities among its participants.[7] The Internet has become a forum for users sharing information, commenting on information, and even creating information in real time. This latter point is evidenced by the rise of sites like the online, user generated encyclopedia called Wikipedia. Wikipedia relies on the efforts of

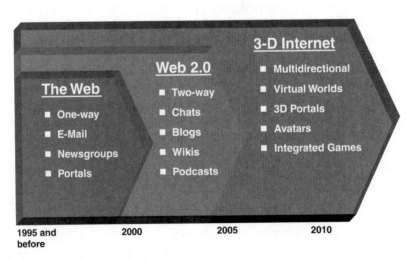

FIGURE 14.1 The Evolution of the Internet

thousands (even millions) of volunteers to collaboratively create, post, edit, and also police content.[8] Other classic examples of Web 2.0 sites include YouTube (a web-based video sharing site), Facebook (a social networking site), and Twitter (a site for social networking that also allows for micro weblogs (blogs) of text-based messages not to exceed 140 characters).[9]

The 3-D Internet

Even as Web 2.0 has gained in prominence, the development of what may be the next phase of the Internet has begun. Virtual world sites are the primary example of this development. Virtual worlds are proprietary sites accessed through the Internet and in which users operate characters and personal representatives, called avatars. Some virtual worlds are massively multiplayer, online, role-playing games (MMORPGs), with objectives like completing certain tasks to gain points or status. Others do not have a game element, per se. Those sites are more like the popular "The Sims" computer game series, where users engage in activities similar to every-day life. By recent estimates, which vary widely, there are as many as 300 million active users of virtual worlds.[10] Possibly the best known of these worlds is Second Life, operated by Linden Lab. But there are other virtual worlds, including Disney's Club Penguin for children.

Virtual worlds offer users an interactive, immersive 3-D Internet experience. While these sites have not achieved anywhere near the financial return of Web 2.0 sites like Facebook,[11] they do offer users the potential to make real money. For example, the owner of a virtual space station in Second Life was able to develop it and then sell it for $100,000.[12]

How Do Businesses Participate in Web 2.0 and Beyond?

While many companies are tentatively or even aggressively participating in the Web 2.0 environment as a part of a considered business strategy, others are unintentional participants. Whether companies with a significant number of employees know it or not, they are likely participating in Web 2.0 or the 3-D Internet. This may be based solely on the actions of their employees as these employees click through the terms of service (TOS) of social media sites while they sit at their desks.[13] For the purposes of this section, we focus on some of the intentional company uses of Web 2.0 sites.

Most of the widely known uses of Web 2.0 sites by companies are in the context of trying to reach and/or sell to targeted groups of consumers. As of August 2009, for example, Facebook had reached around 300 million registered users.[14] This is equivalent to the total population of the United States, which obviously makes this site and its users a significant and attractive target for consumer-oriented companies. Likewise, because registration is required on these sites, age data for site users can readily be obtained in a manner that allows companies to choose the site that best reaches their targeted customer set. For example, as of August 2009, Twitter users could be separated by age group as shown in Figure 14.2.[15]

Many companies today choose to maintain an Internet presence both on a traditional web site and on Web 2.0 sites like Twitter and Facebook. Top consumer

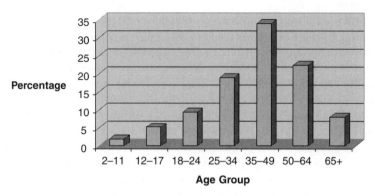

FIGURE 14.2 Twitter Users by Age Group—August 2009

brands use Twitter, for example, to post information on existing products and new products and to answer questions from customers and potential customers in real time. Perhaps most importantly, for some, these sites are also being used as a tool to promptly and visibly address (i.e., confirm or debunk) rumors and media stories about their products and brand.[16]

As mentioned, the mainstream press now also regularly uses Twitter as a source of information and for gathering facts for stories.[17]

The Facebook site is likewise used by consumer-oriented companies. A recent study by the interactive marketing agency Rosetta found that 59 percent of 100 leading U.S. retailers have a Facebook page.[18] Like Twitter, the majority of business-oriented uses are to generate brand interest and loyalty as well as to answer customer questions.[19]

A perhaps more controversial use of Web 2.0 sites by employers has been in the human relations/employment context. According to the job search web site Career-Builder, in an August 2009 survey of employers, 45 percent reported using social network web sites to research the background of job candidates.[20] There is the now well-known example of the prospective employee who, on completion of an interview with Cisco, posted on Twitter:

> *Cisco just offered me a job! Now I have to weigh the utility of a fatty paycheck against the daily commute to San Jose and hating the work.*[21]

Reportedly Cisco tracked this "tweet"[22] back to the creator and the job offer was withdrawn.[23]

Another now widely-reported example of an employment-related use of Facebook occurred in Switzerland. A woman there told her employer she was unable to come to work due to a medical condition that required her to lie down in the dark, and it was painful for her to look at light—such as that on a back-lit computer screen. Her employer, an insurance company, fired her when they discovered that she was chatting on Facebook while she was out of the office taking her sick day.[24]

Of course, employers have also used or attempted to use negative comments made by an employee about the employer or about a manager on the employee's Facebook page (or other social media site) as the basis for an adverse job action, such as a firing.[25] These employment-related uses of social media sites do generate controversy and are not universally accepted.[26]

Companies use virtual world sites for many of the same purposes as they do social media sites. While there may be fewer companies that have adopted the use of 3-D Internet sites like Second Life when compared to Web 2.0 sites, there are nonetheless Fortune 500 companies making active use of these sites. They do so to build the interest of potential customers in their brand as well as to answer questions and, in some cases, even to handle the first steps in the sales process.[27]

Perhaps the most interesting aspect of the 3-D Internet for major companies arises out of the personal attachment users of these sites have for each other and for the environment itself. This enables companies to use the sites to replace traditionally live events with virtual events. During the worldwide economic downturn, companies and universities turned to holding meetings in virtual worlds using avatars to not only cut costs but also to retain some sense of personal contact.[28] Users appear to stay longer and interact more at these virtual world events as compared to similar events held via teleconference.

Virtual world sites additionally allow for simulation, in a highly controlled manner, of disaster sites and emergency situations that can provide an ideal setting for training of lifesaving personnel and other first responders in a relatively low cost manner.[29]

With the foregoing understanding of what Web 2.0 and 3-D Internet sites are and how companies are using them, this chapter next considers some of the risks and issues associated with the use of these sites. This includes an exploration of matters that companies should be aware of in planning for their employees' participation, intentional or not, in these sites.

Risks and Issues to Consider in Web 2.0 and Beyond

This section explores some of the typical issues that have arisen or may arise when companies or their employees participate in Web 2.0 and the 3-D Internet. Understanding these issues prior to or contemporaneous with participation better allows companies to plan and to participate thoughtfully.

The Terms of Service/Use or End User License Agreement

Whenever a company's employees click through the online terms of use for a Web 2.0 site while conducting company business, they are binding their company to those terms. Most users, when acting in their personal capacity, view these terms as little more than an annoyance. However, when users accept these terms of service (TOS) on behalf of a corporation, with assets and potentially with intellectual property rights that need to be protected, it becomes important to understand what these terms say and what they mean for the company.

As one commentator aptly wrote in the context of the TOS for online games:

> *There are gods, and they are capricious, and [they] have way more than ten commandments. Nobody knows how many because everyone clicked past them.*[30]

While there may be any number of unexpected terms in the TOS for Web 2.0 sites, there do seem to be some consistent and potentially problematic terms related to intellectual property.

Since posting of content is a key feature of Web 2.0 sites, it is quite common for those sites to address rights regarding this content in their TOS. While it is not common for Web 2.0 sites to claim ownership of the content posted by a user, a few TOS have the user grant a broad copyright license to any posted content back to the site's operators.[31] In some cases, these rights continue even after the posted content has been pulled off the site.[32] By contrast, on a number of social media sites, users are specifically prohibited from collecting and using the data on or content of other users.[33]

It is more common on Web 2.0 sites to have users grant the site the right to make derivative works from the content the users post.[34] Some sites have the user grant the site a broad license to make derivative works of user content only so long as that content is on their site.[35] In the sample set of Web 2.0 site TOS that were reviewed for this chapter,[36] the sites' owners more frequently had the user grant them a right to make derivative works that continued for some lengthy period, sometimes forever, and such grant persisted even after the content had been deleted from the site.[37] Notably, on the SlideShare site, the user grants not only the site's operators but also all other users of the site the right to make derivative works of posted content. This right continues even after the content has been deleted. This right is further extended to the related LinkedIn site by the users of Slide Share.[38]

More broadly, most social media sites require their users to make a representation of non-infringement regarding any content posted by the user. This is accompanied by an indemnity against intellectual property claims against the site due to content posted by the user and there is rarely any cap or limitation on these indemnities.[39]

In many cases, the TOS of Web 2.0 sites are silent on patent rights. But, in at least one TOS for a 3-D Internet site, by just accepting the TOS the user of the virtual world (and arguably her or his employer) grants a patent license to any patents he or she creates or uses on the site to the platform provider and to all other users for in-world use.[40]

Finally, it is important to mention that the TOS may contain other restrictions or limitations on commercial activity. If a company's user is accessing these Web 2.0 sites for business use, he or she should be aware that in some instances framing of or linking to these sites is prohibited.[41] Additionally, in the case of the MySpace site, posting an advertisement or solicitation on the site as content is prohibited.[42]

Actions on Behalf of the Company versus Personal Actions

Whether an employee is accepting the TOS of a social media site or interacting with others on that site, the question of which actions of an employee are personal and which actions are taken on behalf of the company can be crucial. As previously noted, a click through by an employee on the TOS of certain sites can grant valuable intellectual property rights to the owners of that site as well as, in some cases, to other users.[43] Also, a company can be not only liable for the blog posts of its employees and agents, but can further be liable for any failure by its employees or agents to identify their relationship with the company in making these posts.[44]

It is the informality and seeming anonymity of Web 2.0 and 3-D Internet sites that can contribute to employees' confusion as to when they are acting on their own and when their actions are on behalf of or can be attributed to their employer. Fundamentally, the legal principle of respondeat superior defines when someone is acting on behalf of or as an employee of a company. However, the common law standard for determining when someone is acting as an employee focuses only on the general identification of indicators of an employment relationship. This standard is recited in the Restatement of Employment Law as:

1. Unless otherwise provided by law or by § 1.02 or § 1.03, an individual renders services as an employee of an employer if
   a. the individual acts, at least in part, to serve the interests of the employer,
   b. the employer consents to receive the individual's services, and
   c. the employer precludes the individual from rendering the services as part of an independent business.[45]

This does not, however, anticipate determining employer liability for the actions of, for example, an avatar on the Second Life site. Such an avatar may hold itself out as an authorized representative of a company; it may even have a name or group affiliation tag that indicates affiliation with a company. However, the avatar's operator may not actually be authorized, at least in the company's view, to act on behalf of the company.[46]

Likewise, an employee may perform internal product analysis of the benefits of its company's products verses those of the competitor's products during his workday without likely incurring any liability for the company. However, upon posting this type of data on a third party social media site, over the weekend and even on the employee's personal time, the employee may have committed an action that will be attributed to the company and that may cause liability for the company.[47]

An understanding of respondeat superior does not alone address the fact that, in some cases, people who are clearly employees of a company may be acting in ways that are beyond the scope of their actual authorization. However, these actions may nonetheless bind the company.

Disclosure Issues

Employers may well remember a time when the exposure to and risks associated with broad, public disclosures of data were relatively small. However, social networking sites thrive on enabling broad, worldwide disclosures and on providing instant access to data to millions of people worldwide. This obviously heightens disclosure concerns for employers.

CONFIDENTIALITY AND EXPORT   Given the broad scope of access to content that is provided by Web 2.0 sites and the informal/casual style of communications that they encourage, the typical concern of employers would be that employees would inadvertently disclose sensitive and confidential information of their company or their company's customers and/or partners. Employee disclosure of, or provision of, access to the company's valuable intellectual property would be a closely related concern of employers.

Under the Uniform Trade Secrets Act, as amended in 1985, the owner of a trade secret is required to make "efforts that are reasonable under the circumstances to maintain its secrecy."[48] It may not be entirely clear in the Web 2.0 era what these reasonable efforts would entail. However, simultaneous worldwide exposure of a company's key intellectual property, especially without a strong showing that it was done in express violation of company policy, would not be a good place for a company to start in a subsequent attempt to enforce its intellectual property rights. This is not a concern that is unique to Web 2.0—but it is certainly enhanced by it.

Likewise, it is important to be aware of the worldwide scope of the Internet. Information that is subject to export controls or to International Traffic in Arms Regulations (ITAR) restrictions[49] likely can never be disclosed on social media sites, even in so-called secure areas. Such sites may have system monitors with access to all areas of the site. These monitors may be of any nationality and may further be located anywhere in the world.[50] So, while an employee of a company sitting at her desk in the United States may not be thinking of export implications related to her use of a social media site, they exist. When an employee using a social media site discloses export controlled and/or ITAR controlled information and it is viewed by another user or a system monitor who is (1) a foreign national sitting in the United States or (2) sitting in a country subject to export controls, in either case, a restricted disclosure has occurred. [51]

ANONYMOUS POSTS BY INSIDERS   The disclosure of intellectual property or export controlled data is not the only disclosure concern related to Web 2.0 sites. As shown by the chief executive officer for Whole Foods, John Mackey, the blog posts of a company's employees (particularly senior level employees) can be problematic in certain circumstances. To start, it is important to realize that blog posts made by employees can and sometimes will be attributed to the company itself. Mackey, for example, used an official Whole Foods blog to express his professional opinions. He additionally posted blog entries regularly over a seven-year period on a Yahoo! blog under the pseudonym Rahodeb (a variation of his wife's name spelled backward).[52] Under this persona, Mackey made what he later characterized as personal posts about his company, his competitor the Wild Oats grocery stores, and ultimately about a U.S. Federal Trade Commission (FTC) investigation into a proposed merger between Whole Foods and Wild Oats.[53]

Ultimately, these postings were included as part of the analysis done by the FTC into whether the acquisition of Wild Oats should be approved.[54] Additionally, this anonymous blogging activity led to an investigation by the Securities and Exchange Commission (SEC) in the United States. The SEC investigation did not lead to sanctions. However, Mackey's first post on the official Whole Foods blog after the matter closed, expressed a new realization of the power of this forum and the consequences of his actions as he stated:

> *The main reason I began posting on Yahoo! was because I enjoy and learn from online community interactions. I also like to express my viewpoints and I like to argue and debate. . . . My mistake here was one of judgment—not ethics. I*

didn't realize posting under a screen name in an online community such as Yahoo! would be so controversial and would cause so many people to be upset. That was a mistake in judgment on my part and one that I deeply regret.[55]

Certainly, these actions seem to be at odds with the SEC's clear view that employees of a company blogging on a third party web site on an authorized basis cannot claim to be doing this in their individual capacity. The question is whether the CEO of a company can claim this type of activity was not authorized blogging. It is clear that the SEC does not allow for such employees to simply post a disclaimer that no investment decisions should be made based on their blogging and/or that the company is not liable for any investments made based on the blogging activity.[56]

IDENTIFICATION OF THE AFFILIATION OF BLOG POSTERS Even when the identity of the blog poster is accurately stated and the blogger is authorized to make posts, companies still need to be aware of potential liability that may arise if the company's official or unofficial posters on blogs and microblogs do not disclose their affiliation with the company. The U.S. Federal Trade Commission's (FTC) guidelines generally require that companies do not have their employees or affiliates act in a manner that is deceptive or unfair.[57] More detail is provided on how this general requirement would likely be applied to blogging on behalf of a company in the FTC's recently revised Guides Concerning the Use of Endorsements and Testimonials in Advertising.[58] Under these guidelines, when employees or other people are making a statement that is "sponsored" by the company, then the blog poster must fully disclose that affiliation.[59] Such sponsorship could include payment, or even receipt of free products—assuming the value of the product received is relatively high or, in the alternative, that the blogger is a frequent recipient of free products from the company.[60]

Additionally, whether an individual making a blog post has or has not disclosed an affiliation with a company, the blog posts can lead to liability for the company. Under state law principles of respondeat superior as previously described, the actions of an employee acting in an official capacity will be attributed to the employer company.[61] This state law principle has been adopted and expanded in the FTC guidelines. The FTC clearly holds *both* the blogger and the company responsible for the actions of the "sponsored" blogger whether the blogger is an employee or not and whether the relationship is disclosed or not. The guidelines state that both the company and the blogger are "subject to liability for false or unsubstantiated statements made through [such] endorsements, or for failing to disclose material connections between themselves."[62]

Content and Posting

For an intellectual property practitioner, misuse of third party intellectual property by company employees may already be a daily concern. Certainly, the Web 2.0 and 3-D Internet environments do not lessen this concern.

Users, especially in the early days of Internet content/file sharing sites like the music download sites Napster and Grokster, seemed to feel impervious to copyright laws.[63] Those content sharing sites enabled and even encouraged users to share files with one another (i.e., peer-to-peer file sharing). Sites, like Grokster, provided the tools and the forum for file sharing—although the actual sharing of the content file was set up to be performed at the user level.[64] Over time, and as file-sharing sites were found to have contributory liability for intellectual property violations due to their active participation in establishing and even encouraging the environment, this form of Internet service largely disappeared.[65]

Today's social media sites are much more likely to expressly prohibit (in their TOS, among other things) posting of infringing content.[66] Likewise, to avoid liability for the content posted by users, the providers of social media sites will follow the requirements of the Digital Millennium Copyright Act's safe harbor provisions including by "taking down" content alleged to be infringing by a third party following the safe harbor take-down process.[67] Even with precautions and this heightened awareness, users still frequently post infringing content on social media sites like Facebook and YouTube.[68]

Given the large amount of copyright infringement and other violations of intellectual property rights going on in Web 2.0 sites, it is reasonable to assume that if a company's employees are participating in these sites, they may also be participating in such activity. There are no protections against liability available for employers that are analogous to the Digital Millennium Copyright Act's safe harbor provisions, as these provisions are only available to online service providers, such as the hosts of the social media sites. So, this is a significant potential liability exposure for companies with employees participating on these sites.

It is also worth noting that a company's employees could be a valuable asset in enabling the company to track down violations of its intellectual property on social media sites if those employees were made aware of the importance of spotting such violations.

In the emerging 3-D Internet space, the potential for copyright infringement by users may be even more likely. Many virtual worlds sell open space on their sites. On the popular virtual world site, Second Life, the open space is called an Island.[69] When users acquire such space, it is empty. In the rush to establish a quick and compelling presence on such Islands and to drive "eyeballs" to a company's space, a company's programmers or the contractors a company may hire to create the programming and content may be tempted to shortcut the process by using already existing third party code or content. This temptation to profit from the content of others in virtual worlds is far from uncommon. In fact, the majority of lawsuits arising from the emerging activity in virtual worlds to date have been in some way related to claims of theft of content.[70]

How to Address the Risks and Issues of Participation in Web 2.0 and the 3-D Internet

The focus of this chapter has been on not only understanding what social media and virtual world sites are and how they are used by businesses, but also on helping lawyers supporting companies participating on these sites to be aware of the potential liability and risks associated with participation. Importantly, this analysis was not intended to advise against use of or participation in these sites. Rather, this analysis was intended to lay the groundwork for thoughtful participation. The next section of the chapter considers how a company can encourage and create an acceptable framework for employee participation in social media and virtual world sites.

Engage

The starting point for participation in social media and virtual world sites is to engage. This refers to encouraging your company's employees to engage in these sites in an acceptable and thoughtful manner. Employees should understand the purpose of their participation: Are they authorized to transact business, are they there to observe, are they permitted (or required) to comment/act as an advocate of the company? Of course, your company's employees will not know what types of participation and behaviors on social media and virtual worlds sites are acceptable to the company unless they receive some guidance.

In providing guidance, a company should first have a business strategy for engaging in social media and virtual worlds. The company will want to decide what its expectations are for participation (e.g., to sell products, to promote brand awareness, to answer customer questions, etc.). Having this knowledge will help provide the groundwork for describing acceptable participation. It is also important to ensure that senior management of the company understands what these sites are and that there are risks associated with their use. Likewise, the company's senior management should have a realistic understanding of what the potential benefits of the company's participation in these sites can be. There is no better way to do this than to sit down with management, log into some of the sites, and explore them together (focusing particularly on the activities of the company's competition, if possible).

The company can then use its strategy to develop guidance for those employees who are permitted to participate on behalf of the company. This should be clearly communicated as soon as possible.

How to Create the Guidance

An important part of preparing for a company's participation in social media and virtual world sites is to reach out to the employees who are already participating in these sites, whether in an official capacity or on a personal basis. These employees can be a valuable resource. With them, you will want to understand the norms of behavior in these Web 2.0 and 3-D Internet sites. They can also assist you in understanding what the current reputation of your company is, if there is one, in these sites. This can help with determining whether the company will want to reinforce that view—or work to change it.

PROCESS FOR CREATION   The biggest mistake a company could make in entering into social media sites and in attempting to give guidance to employees for participation would be for a group of lawyers in a conference room, who had never actively participated in these sites, to set forth a collection of "things not to do."[71] When IBM created its well-regarded Virtual World Guidelines in late 2005, as an adjunct to its Social Computing Guidelines, it started by "virtually" convening a broad group of people from within IBM. That group included human resources professionals, communications experts, lawyers, and heavy users of virtual worlds environments. IBM utilized a wiki to begin discussions of what it wanted to communicate to employees about virtual worlds. The first order of business was not for management to tell employees what they should not be doing in virtual worlds. Rather, the focus was on how the company could encourage employees' use and exploration of the 3-D Internet's virtual world environments as IBM's chairman had requested.

The most basic way to do this was to make it clear to employees that common sense should prevail. There was also a strong interest in having employees realize that the normal business conduct guidelines of the company would continue to apply and that they still had the same obligations in the Web 2.0 and 3-D Internet environment that they have while interacting in the real world.

ADDRESSING THE ISSUES AND RISKS   The approach IBM used to create guidelines seems to have been adopted by others in the corporate world. In reviewing the guidance on participation in social media sites from various companies,[72] there seems to be a common theme addressed that is oriented toward encouraging good and meaningful participation. This is coupled with a reminder to employees to comply with the law and to use their common sense. The themes of these guidelines, not surprisingly, address the concerns we have explored. They also try to set a tone for the company's participation.

Some of the issues with employees participating in social media and virtual world sites and potential themes for social media guidelines that can help to address them with employees follow.

Issue 1:
- Ensuring the company's employees will both understand your company policy on participation in social media and act in the company's best interests.

Guideline theme for Issue 1:
- Socialize guidelines encouraging meaningful participation but reinforcing use of common sense.

Issue 2:
- Ensuring employees know whether and in what circumstances they are authorized to act or speak on behalf of the company in social media sites (i.e., knowing the "metes and bounds" of their authority).

Guideline themes for Issue 2:
- Reinforce that only those specifically identified by the right level of management[73] are authorized to do business on behalf of the company. Others may still be encouraged to explore (while still getting their day-to-day work accomplished).
- Make sure employees think about their personal responsibility for their actions on social media sites.

Issue 3 (a), (b), and (c):
- (a) Ensuring employees can distinguish between their personal and corporate roles on social media sites.
- (b) Making sure employees/affiliates identify themselves and their affiliation with the company when acting in an official capacity.

- (c) Making sure employees/affiliates use a disclaimer when speaking about the company in their personal capacity.

Guideline themes for Issue 3 (a), (b) and (c):

- Encourage employees to think about their anticipated role each time *before* they participate on a Web 2.0 or 3-D Internet site and whether that role is consistent with their authorization.
- Encourage employees to always identify themselves and their company affiliation on Web 2.0 or 3-D Internet sites when acting in an official capacity.
- Require employees to use a disclaimer when speaking in their personal capacity about (but not on behalf of) the company or to consider refraining from such activity.
- Reinforce the importance of complying with your company's code of conduct and with applicable laws whether speaking on behalf of the company (authorized) or just speaking in an acceptable manner about the company (personal capacity).

    To the extent there are topics that should always be avoided in discussions on sites especially when acting on a personal basis (e.g., company financials, competitors, acquisitions), outline them for employees.

Issue 4:

- Ensure that employees protect the confidential information of your company and its customers and/or partners. Ensure that employees do not discuss export controlled information.

Guideline theme for Issue 4:

- Educate employees about the fact that there is no protection on Web 2.0 or 3-D Internet sites for confidential information or export controlled information. Any disclosure should be considered a disclosure to the entire world. The normal rules for protection and control of this type of information apply.

Issue 5:

- Ensuring employees respect the intellectual property rights of the company and of others.

Guideline themes for Issue 5:

- Educate employees about the ongoing importance of respecting and protecting intellectual property. Although these environments are new and exciting, the rules about respecting intellectual property are the same.
- Encourage thoughtful review and consideration of intellectual property provisions in the TOS of Web 2.0 or 3-D Internet sites *prior to* posting company intellectual property on such sites to understand how the company's intellectual property can be used by the site host and others.

Other guideline themes worth including:

- Help employees to consider what to do when they make a mistake on Web 2.0 or 3-D Internet sites.
- Remind employees that they can "walk away" from unacceptable behaviors in the environment (i.e., they can always log off).

Some, but not all, of the social media guidelines currently available also detail the consequences or potential consequences of violating the guidelines.[74] Some, of course, contain reminders to not forget that social media is only a portion of the employee's work responsibilities (i.e., don't forget your "day job").

Notably, of the guidelines reviewed, none started with "*do not participate except . . . .*"

In a final form these guidelines can look like the IBM Social Computing Guidelines listed here. These guidelines try to strike a balance between legal/human resource concerns and ensuring that the company's employees are actually participating in a meaningful way in the social media environment and are adding value to that community.

IBM Social computing guidelines: Executive Summary[75]

1. Know and follow IBM's Business Conduct Guidelines.
2. IBMers are personally responsible for the content they publish on blogs, wikis or any other form of user-generated media. Be mindful that what you publish will be public for a long time—protect your privacy.
3. Identify yourself—name and, when relevant, role at IBM—when you discuss IBM or IBM-related matters. And write in the first person. You must make it clear that you are speaking for yourself and not on behalf of IBM.
4. If you publish content to any web site outside of IBM and it has something to do with work you do or subjects associated with IBM, use a disclaimer such as this: "The postings on this site are my own and don't necessarily represent IBM's positions, strategies or opinions."
5. Respect copyright, fair use and financial disclosure laws.
6. Don't provide IBM's or another's confidential or other proprietary information. Ask permission to publish or report on conversations that are meant to be private or internal to IBM.
7. Don't cite or reference clients, partners or suppliers without their approval. When you do make a reference, where possible link back to the source.
8. Respect your audience. Don't use ethnic slurs, personal insults, obscenity, or engage in any conduct that would not be acceptable in IBM's workplace. You should also show proper consideration for others' privacy and for topics that may be considered objectionable or inflammatory—such as politics and religion.
9. Find out who else is blogging or publishing on the topic, and cite them.
10. Be aware of your association with IBM in online social networks. If you identify yourself as an IBMer, ensure your profile and related content is consistent with how you wish to present yourself with colleagues and clients.
11. Don't pick fights, be the first to correct your own mistakes, and don't alter previous posts without indicating that you have done so.
12. Try to add value. Provide worthwhile information and perspective. IBM's brand is best represented by its people and what you publish may reflect on IBM's brand.

CHECK UP ON COMPANY ACTIVITY AND COMPANY GUIDELINES   Finally, a company's social media participation and its guidelines should not be set and forgotten. It is important to understand what is being said by and about the company and its employees on social media sites. Given that this is a continuous and real-time environment, it is worth investing in some of the tools and services that are available to companies to help with monitoring such activity.[76] In fact, in light of the new FTC Guidelines discussed above, this type of monitoring may become more and more of a requirement for companies to ensure their compliance.[77]

Likewise, for any social media guidelines to be meaningful on an ongoing basis, they should be reviewed and revised on a regular timetable (i.e., annually, if not more frequently). One potential option is to allow users to have access to an unofficial version of the social media guidelines on an internal wiki. This would allow them to be informally revised and re-revised continuously. Once the company was ready to do its formal annual review of the guidelines, the wiki version would provide, at the very least, a starting point for the review.

Conclusion

The Internet has evolved and continues to evolve into an environment that is increasingly attractive for use by companies. As explored in this chapter, whether companies officially embrace and plan for use of Web 2.0 and the 3-D Internet or they do not, it is likely that their employees will use these tools to keep up with the company's competition. While there are certainly risks and issues that will come along with participation in these new Internet frontiers, the risks should not have to outweigh the benefits. By planning for a company's participation in these emerging Internet areas and by working with the company's employees to create a strategy and guidelines for participation, companies can enable participation while establishing clear ground rules to guide that participation.

Notes

1. "Tweetdeck Infiltrates the News Room," http://mashable.com/2010/01/07/sky-news-tweetdeck (accessed January 10, 2010).

2. "Second Life Frees Disabled from Restrictions of Everyday Life," VOANews.com, September 17, 2008, www1.voanews.com/english/news/american-life/a-13-2008-09-17-voa24.html (accessed January 24, 2010).

3. Walt Howe, "A Brief History of the Internet," www.walthowe.com/navnet/history.html (accessed December 30, 2009).

4. Ibid.

5. Prodigy Communications Corporation, www.fundinguniverse.com/company-histories/prodigy-communications-company-history.html (accessed September 27, 2010).

6. Walt Howe, "A Brief History of the Internet."

7. Tim O'Reilly, "What Is Web 2.0?" http://oreilly.com/pub/a/web2/archive/what-is-web-20 .html?page=3 (accessed December 30, 2009).

8. http://en.wikipedia.org/wiki/Wikipedia (accessed December 30, 2009).

9. In May of 2009, Knowledge Networks attempted to list the 27 sites that then defined social media or Web 2.0. These sites were: Bebo.com, Blackplanet.com, Cafemom.com, Classmates .com, ClubPenguin.com, Del.icio.us.com, Digg.com, Facebook.com, Flickr.com, Flixster.com, Friendster.com, Hi5.com, Imeem.com, Last.fm, Live.com, LinkedIn.com, Livejournal.com,

Myspace.com, Myyearbook.com, Ning.com, Picasa.com. Plaxo.com, Reddit.com, Reunion.com, Tagged.com, Twitter.com, and YouTube.com. Knowledge Networks Press Release, May 2009. www.knowledgenetworks.com/news/releases/2009/052009_social-media.html (accessed February 4, 2010).

10. "K-Zero: More than 300 Million People are Registered on Virtual World Sites," www.metaversejournal.com/2008/06/02/k-zero-more-than-300-million-registered-for-virtual-worlds (accessed December 2, 2009).

11. It is estimated that Facebook's annual revenue was US$550 million in 2009. The Business Insider: Silicon Valley Insider, "Everything You Wanted to Know About Facebook's Revenue But Didn't Know Who to Ask," Nicholas Carlson, posted July 2, 2009, www.businessinsider.com/breaking-down-facebooks-revenues-2009-7.

12. Dean Irvine, "Virtual Worlds, Real Money," March 12, 2007, CNN.com (accessed December 21, 2009).

13. An IDC survey of 4,710 U.S. workers in October 2009 found that 34 percent use consumer social networks like Facebook and LinkedIn for business purposes, and 9 percent use micro-blogging sites like Twitter for business purposes. Jon Brodkin, "Facebook, Twitter Becoming Business Tools, but CIOs Remain Wary," *Network World*, January 7, 2010, www.sfgate.com/cgi-bin/article.cgi?f=/g/a/2010/01/07/urnidgns852573C400693880002576A40062146B.DTL .Read more at www.sfgate.com/cgi-bin/article.cgi?f=/g/a/2010/01/07/urnidgns852573C400693 880002576A40062146B.DTL#ixzz0cF8pg9M7].

14. BNET, " Where Your Customers Are: How Facebook, Twitter and Others Break Down by Age," www.bnet.com/2403-13237_23-366331.html?tag=content;col2 (accessed January 4, 2010).

15. Ibid.

16. Jennifer Van Grove, "40 of the Best Twitter Brands and the People Behind Them," http://mashable.com/2009/01/21/best-twitter-brands/ (accessed January 10, 2010). When accessing the Toyota USA page on Twitter on 2/5/10, the author found the page filled with responses from Jim Lentz, President and COO of Toyota Motor Sales, USA to concerns about the just-announced brake problems with the popular Toyota Prius. http://twitter.com/TOYOTA (accessed February 5, 2010).

17. See note 1 above.

18. "Social Media Study Shows 59 Percent of Retailers Now Using Facebook," http://news.prnewswire.com/ViewContent.aspx?ACCT=109&STORY=/www/story/01-09-2009/00049521 55&EDATE= (accessed January 13, 2010). Facebook encourages such business use and has directions on its site showing companies how to establish a presence on their site. See: www.facebook.com/advertising/?pages (accessed January 12, 2010).

19. Brodkin, "Facebook, Twitter becoming business tools," (accessed January 13, 2010).

20. "45% Employers Use Facebook-Twitter to Screen Job Candidates," August 24, 2009, http://oregonbusinessreport.com/2009/08/45-employers-use-facebook-twitter-to-screen-job-candidates/ (accessed January 13, 2010).

21. "Lose Your Job in a Single Tweet," Josh Smith posted March 19, 2009, www.walletpop.com/blog/2009/03/19/lose-your-job-in-a-single-tweet/ (accessed January 13, 2010).

22. *Tweet* is the term commonly used to refer to individual posts on Twitter.

23. See note 21.

24. CityNews.ca Staff, "Woman Fired for Using Facebook While Off Sick," April 27, 2009, www.citytv.com/toronto/citynews/life/money/article/9857--woman-fired-for-using-facebook-while-off-sick.

25. Arjun Ramachandran, "Maroney to Probe Facebook Six Case," November 9, 2009, www.smh.com.au/national/maroney-to-probe-facebook-six-case-20091109-i48h.html. Also see Note 26.

26. "Students Love Social-Networking Sites—and So Do Employers," posted August 31, 2006 by Christina Cuesta, www.foxnews.com/story/0,2933,208175,00.html (accessed January 24, 2010). See also *Pietrylo v. Hillstone Restaurant Group.* Slip Copy, 2009 WL 3128420, 29 IER Cases 1438, D.N.J., September 25, 2009 (NO. CIV.06-5754(FSH)). In this unpublished case, an employer gained uninvited access to a private, password protected MySpace chat session hosted by its employees in their personal time. The employer used information it obtained from such access to terminate the employment of the blog posters. New Jersey's Federal District Court confirmed a jury's judgment that repeated, unauthorized access to the site constituted a violation of the federal Stored Communications Act, among other things, and as a result could subject the employer to payment of punitive damages for its actions.

27. "Manpower Inc. and the World of Virtual Work: Manpower Inc. Convenes Avatar Thought Leaders in Second Life to Discuss Virtual Workforce of the Future," press release, www.manpower.com/press/secondlife.cfm?mode=secondlife (accessed Janaury 24, 2010).

28. "Success Stories Case Study: IBM A virtual event at one fifth the cost and no jetlag," posted February, 2009, http://work.secondlife.com/en-US/successstories/case/ibm/.

29. "Second Life Helps Save, Improve Lives: Chicago's Children's Memorial Hospital uses the virtual world for disaster preparedness training, while disabled people turn to it for peer support," InformationWeek, posted by Mitch Wagner, October 1, 2009, www.information week.com/news/healthcare/patient/showArticle.jhtml?articleID=220300671&pgno=1&query Text=&isPrev=.

30. Ralph Koster, "What Are the Lessons of MMORPGs Today?" posting to Ralph Koster's web site, February 24, 2006, www.raphkoster.com/2006/02/24/what-are-the-lessons-of-mmorpgs-today, (accessed March 3, 2008). Also cited in David P. Sheldon, "Comment, Claiming Ownership, But Getting Owned: Contractual Limitations on Asserting Property Interests in Virtual Goods," 54 UCLA L. Rev. 751, 751 (2007).

31. Facebook.com Terms of Service, www.facebook.com/terms.php (accessed January 24, 2010).; Digg.com Terms of Use, http://about.digg.com/tou (accessed January 24, 2010); Slideshare.com Terms of Service, www.slideshare.net/terms (accessed January 24, 2010).; Twitter.com Terms of Service, https://twitter.com/tos (accessed January 24, 2010). Twitter can also sublicense these rights.

32. Digg.com Terms of Use, http://about.digg.com/tou (accessed January 24, 2010).

33. See Facebook.com TOS at note 31 above; LinkedIn.com User Agreement, www.linkedin .com/static?key=user_agreement (accessed January 24, 2010). MySpace.com Terms of Use Agreement, www.myspace.com/index.cfm?fuseaction=misc.terms (accessed January 24, 2010).

34. AddThis.com Terms of Service, www.addthis.com/tos (accessed January 24, 2010). See note 31 above for Digg.com TOS, see note 30 for Slide Share.com and Facebook.com TOS. See note 32 for LinkedIn.com and MySpace.com TOS. YouTube.com Terms of Service, www.youtube.com/static?gl=US&template=terms (accessed January 24, 2010).

35. See note 30 for Facebook TOS, and note 32 for MySpace TOS.

36. The review of TOS conducted for this section included those from MySpace.com, Facebook.com, Digg.com, SlideShare.com, Twitter.com, AddThis.com, LinkedIn.com, YouTube.com, Delicious.com, and Second Life (secondlife.com).

37. See note 34 above for AddThis TOS and YouTube TOS; see note 31 above for Digg TOS and Slideshare TOS; see note 33 above for LinkedIn TOS; In the YouTube TOS the rights granted to YouTube by users continue for "a reasonable period" after deletion of the content.

38. See note 31 for SlideShare TOS.

39. See note 33 above for MySpace TOS and LinkedIn TOS; see note 31 above for Twitter TOS and Slideshare TOS; see note 34 for AddThis TOS and YouTube TOS; see note 31 for Facebook TOS and Digg TOS. Users are likewise required to make the same broad indemnity to many sites for any breach by them of the TOS and, again, there are rarely any limitations of liability applicable to these indemnities for the user.

40. Second Life Terms of Service Section 3.2, http://secondlife.com/corporate/tos.php (accessed January 24, 2010).

41. This is true, for example, on MySpace. See note 33.

42. Ibid.

43. See notes 31–39 above.

44. See note 59 below.

45. REST 3d EMPL § 1.01 (T.D. No. 2, 2009).

46. Some companies and associations, anticipating the liability, confusion, or embarrassment these affiliation tags could cause in certain circumstances, actually instruct users as to how they can be turned on and off in certain circumstances. OCCDLA In Second Life (Blog) SL Tip, "Explore freely without showing group affiliation." Posted February 10, 2009, http://slorcc .blogspot.com/2009/02/sl-tip-explore-freely-without-showing.html (accessed January 20, 2010).

47. See note 58.

48. Unif. Trade Secrets Act, 14 U.L.A. 437, et seq. (1985).

49. 22 CFR 120-130.

50. Second Life TOS at Section 6.2, http://secondlife.com/corporate/tos.php (accessed January 25, 2010).

51. Under the U.S. Export Administration Regulations (EAR), an export of technology is deemed to take place, even when the act takes place in the United States, if the technology is released to a foreign national. See §734.2(b)(2)(ii) of the EAR.

52. "Whole Foods Executive Used Alias," *New York Times,* www.nytimes.com/2007/07/12/business/12foods.html, posted July 12, 2007, (accessed January 3, 2010).

53. Ibid.

54. Ibid at 52.

55. Douglas Quenqua, "SEC Investigation Behind Him, Whole Foods CEO Returns to Blogging," ClickZ. Posted May 28, 2008, www.clickz.com/3629669 (accessed January 3, 2010).

56. 17 CFR sec 241, 271 (II)(B)(4).

57. Deceptive Trade Practices Act at section 5 of FTC Act—15 USC sections 41 et seq.

58. 16 CFR sec. 255, December 1, 2009.

59. 16 CFR sec. 255, December 1, 2009 Notice of Adoption.

60. Ibid. and see also 16 CFR 255 example 8 and 16 CFR 255.5 example 7.

61. Liisa M. Thomas, "Blogomania—User Generated Content and the New Media Revolution?" Paper presented at ABA Annual Meeting, 2009.

62. See note 56.

63. John Borland, staff writer, CNET News, "Metallica Fingers 335,435 Napster Users," May 1, 2007, http://news.cnet.com/2100-1023-239956.html (accessed January 21, 2010).

64. *Metro-Goldwyn-Mayer Studios Inc. v. Grokster, Ltd.* 545 U.S. 913, 125 S.Ct. 2764 U.S., 2005. June 27, 2005.

65. Ibid. Liability for contributory copyright infringement is a well-established legal concept. Perhaps the seminal case describing this concept was the so-called Sony Betamax case. While the Supreme Court did not find Sony liable for contributory infringement in that case, it clearly affirmed that the vicarious liability concept for contributory infringement existed and could be applied. *Sony Corp. of Am. v. Universal City Studios, Inc.* 464 U.S. 417 (1984).

66. Greg Sandoval, "YouTube's No Friend to Copyright Violators," CNET News, posted October 21, 2006, http://news.cnet.com/YouTubes-no-friend-to-copyright-violators/2100-1030_3-6128252.html?tag=mncol (accessed January 21, 2010).

67. 17 U.SC. § 512(c)(2) allows a service provider to receive the safe harbor benefit where it designates an agent to receive notifications of claimed infringement by notifying users and the public "including on its website in a location accessible to the public" the name, address, phone number, and electronic mail address of the agent or other appropriate contact information with whom a request to take down content viewed to be infringing can be filed.

68. Miguel Helft and Geraldine Fabrikant, "WhoseTube? Viacom Sues Google Over Video Clips," *New York Times*, posted March 14, 2007, www.clickz.com/3629669 (accessed January 21, 2010). www.nytimes.com/2007/03/14/technology/14viacom.html?_r=5&ei=5087%0A&em=&en=bcb5e08ab1d3227c&ex=1174017600&pagewanted=all

69. Linden Lab, the owner of the Second Life virtual world site, describes the concept of an "Island" or "Private Island" at http://wiki.secondlife.com/wiki/Private_Island (accessed February 8, 2010).

70. See, for example, *Eros, LLC v. Doe*, No. 8:07-CV-01158 (M.D. Fla. filed July 3, 2007) (alleging, among other things, copyright infringement, unfair competition, and false description of origin).

71. "Terra Nova: A Weblog about Virtual Worlds," http://terranova.blogs.com/terra_nova/2007/08/ibms-virtual-wo.html (accessed January 22, 2010).

72. Intel's Social Media Guidelines are at www.intel.com/sites/sitewide/en_US/social-media.htm; Cisco's Internet Postings Policy is at http://blogs.cisco.com/news/comments/ciscos_internet_postings_policy/ (accessed February 9, 2010). IBM's Social Computing Guidelines are at www.ibm.com/blogs/zz/en/guidelines.html (accessed February 9, 2010).

73. IBM, for example, created Frequently Asked Questions (FAQs) addressing participation in third party social media sites and specifically addressed the question of "When am I authorized to speak on behalf of IBM?"

74. See note 72.

75. The more detailed version of these guidelines with commentary is at www.ibm.com/blogs/zz/en/guidelines.html (accessed February 9, 2010).

76. "There are tools: sysomos.com, buzzstream.com, and Biz360.com—and services: Custom-Scoop.com, EchoSonar.com, and SentimentMetrics.com—available in the marketplace to help." Douglas J. Wood, corporate counsel, "5 Steps to Manage Social Media Risks," posted January 15, 2010, www.law.com/jsp/article.jsp?id=1202438328710&rss=newswire (accessed January 22, 2010).

77. See note 58.

CHAPTER 15

Managing Green Intellectual Property

Larry Greenemeier
Scientific American (a division of Nature, Inc.)

This chapter introduces the issue of green intellectual property (IP), an area that will increase in relevance as investments are made in the development of technology that creates renewable energy and serves to lower the carbon footprint of existing technologies. Of particular interest is the U.S. patent and trademark office's 2010 initiative to speed the evaluation process for applications pertaining to "environmental quality, energy conservation, development of renewable energy resources or greenhouse gas emission reduction."

Technology that improves our ability to harness energy from renewable resources—including the winds that sweep across Earth's surface, the oceans that cover most of the planet, and the sun that provides us with warmth and light—may not necessarily be new, but the demand for it has grown sharply in recent years thanks to more concerted efforts by some to wean society from its dependence on coal, oil, and other fossil fuels. Advances in the efficiency of solar cells and wind turbines, not to mention promising experiments to generate electricity from the motion of waves and tides, have made the underlying technology (and the companies that produce it) appealing investments for the government as well as private firms.

As a result, the intellectual property that defines so-called green technology is gaining prominence, both in long-established companies looking to move in a more environmentally friendly direction and in start-up businesses where green intellectual property constitutes the crown jewels. The U.S. Patent and Trademark Office (USPTO) knows this well, and, in late 2009, initiated an effort to help shepherd green innovations through its patenting process, with mixed results.[1]

Protecting the intellectual property created during the green gold rush has turned out to be a complicated matter, and one to which businesses across a wide swath of markets (automotive, information technology, and communications, to name just a few), should pay attention. The USPTO has more or less defined what green technology does, but it is much harder to define what constitutes a patentable invention in this area. If a car company, for example, develops a newer, lighter type of aluminum that makes its vehicles more fuel efficient, is this green IP or just greenwashing?[2]

Green IP Fast Track

That question has become a significant one, particularly with the launch of the USPTO's Green Technology Pilot Program to fast-track the evaluation of patent applications qualifying as green technology. The test program, launched in December 2009 for a year-long trial but later extended through the end of 2011, got off to a slow start. At the start of 2011, only 993 of the 2101 petitions submitted to the program had qualified to jump to the front of the patent examination line. This has led to mixed reviews from technology companies and even the USPTO itself.[3]

The new program was announced on December 7, 2009, days before the United Nations Climate Change Conference in Copenhagen, Denmark. It was designed such that up to 3,000 new products would receive patent protection more quickly so as to encourage the brightest innovators to invest needed resources in developing new technologies and help bring those technologies to market more quickly.[4] The rationale: Every day an important green technology innovation is hindered from coming to market is another day we harm our planet and another day lost in creating green businesses and green jobs. Applications in this pilot program will see significant savings in pendency, which will help bring green innovations to market more quickly.[5]

The program's initial acceptance rate was about one-third of petitions, less than expected as applicants had been aggressive in their hopes of taking advantage of the patent evaluation fast-track program without necessarily meeting the program's requirements.[6] The USPTO defined these requirements in the December 8, 2009, Federal Register, in which it stated it is looking for inventions that fit into a number of broad buckets, such as environmental quality, energy conservation, development of renewable energy, and greenhouse gas emission reduction.

In addition to these broad categories, the Federal Register listed 79 very specific classifications for the program, stating, "In order to be eligible for the Green Technology Pilot Program, the application must be classified in one of the U.S. Patent Classifications [USPCs] listed below at the time of examination." These classifications covered a large swath of categories: alternative energy production (in particular biofuels, fuel cells, and solar cells); energy conservation (such as hydrogen or other alternative power vehicles); environmentally friendly farming (like fertilizer alternatives); and environmental purification, protection, or remediation (including environmentally friendly coolants). However, given the office was approving only one-third of applications, it decided to eliminate the class and subclass designations to open up the definition for green tech.[7]

As originally defined, the program would have rejected an application from a car company touting a new way of joining aluminum that makes its cars lighter and improves gas mileage, although this could change over time as the office continues to study what constitutes a green technology innovation and what is needed for the program to be successful.[8]

Most of the technology being developed to improve (or at least not harm) the environment is little more than an incremental change in devices already in use.

In reality, the program has been received tepidly by the industry. Whereas anything that creates energy and reduces reliance on fossil fuels could be considered green, the actual technology that does this often draws on an interdisciplinary set of components from other areas.[9]

The USPTO revised the program on May 21, 2010, to allow more categories of technology to be eligible for expedited processing under the program. Initially, the program was limited to inventions in certain classifications to help the office balance the additional workload for its evaluators and gauge the resources needed for the program, according to the USPTO.[10] The USPTO concluded that the classification requirement was unnecessary because Green Technology Pilot Program petitions were not adding much workload, and the requirement was causing the denial of petitions for a number of green technology applications that would have otherwise qualified for the program. The acceptance rate has since risen closer to about 50 percent.

The program to fast track green patents will not have a big impact on the development of green technology, some say, because so many of these technologies have already been patented. As a result, it is important not to oversell the importance of the green patent fast track. The technologies that companies are trying to patent as green are typically only a small part of a larger process or project that may cut fossil fuel consumption or otherwise help the environment. There will never be something like a killer application in clean technology that stands completely on its own.[11]

This is not to say there is not still a lot of incentive to do research and development, but companies might consider managing their patent portfolios differently. The intellectual property might be really valuable, but it needs a complementary technology to make it work. An example of this would be the software, networking, and hardware that enable a "smart" electrical grid to automatically generate and distribute more or less power, depending on demand. Given that much of the technology to do this already exists, it is unlikely that a lot of patents in the smart grid space will be very meaningful.[12]

Companies will need to pay close attention to how intellectual property in the green space is being treated both by the USPTO and the courts. A March 31, 2010 ruling by U.S. District Court judge Robert Sweet invalidated patents on two genes commonly tested to determine risk for breast and ovarian cancers, and brought to a head a lively debate on what is and is not patentable in biotech.[13] Sweet's ruling later prompted the U.S. government to evaluate its own policy and ultimately agree that human and other genes should not be eligible for patents.

The question of whether genes can be patented may have some impact on a key area of green technology: biofuel development. Many biofuel and bioplastics producers rely on gene patents in developing their products. Regulators and judges have generally acknowledged that the work identifying gene sequences and functions is expensive and risky and have allowed patents intended to compensate universities and companies that invest in such risks supposedly for the greater good. The courts have also ruled, however, that naturally occurring genes cannot be patented, since they are discoveries as opposed to inventions.[14]

Although Judge Robert Sweet's March 31, 2010 ruling does not sit well with some biotech companies and universities, researchers from the Duke Institute for Genome Sciences & Policy agreed with Sweet that broad patent claims such as those made by the patent holders in this case, that is, Myriad Genetics and the University of Utah Research Foundation, do more to block competition and discourage promising new technologies than to spur innovation.[15]

What's a Patent Worth?[16]

Others believe the USPTO's program could turn out to be very valuable, particularly for startup companies. Patent examiners normally evaluate patent applications in the order they are filed, a process that takes as long as 40 months before a final decision is rendered on their validity. The pilot program promises to shave about a year off of that time frame for the first 3,000 eligible applications.[17]

The problem with a young company is that because it generally takes so long for patentable intellectual property to be recognized, usually the company is already down the road before it has protection, if that protection is obtained at all. To a new industry, removing that uncertainty is extremely valuable. For a young company to have a beachhead of patents is of paramount importance.[18] On May 6, 2010, Skyline Solar became one of the first companies to receive patent approval under the USPTO's Green Technology Pilot Program. The company received a Notice of Allowance on its application slightly more than two months after acceptance into the program. The patent (number 7,709,730), titled "Dual Trough Concentrating Solar Photovoltaic Module," covers fundamental aspects of Skyline's high-gain solar architecture.

Although Skyline Solar's technology is constructed of solar cells, panels, and reflectors made by other companies, Skyline holds five patents for its manufacturing technology, processes, and system for cooling the solar cells, among others. The ability to say that a technology is fast-tracked means that something is interesting there. This certainly makes investors more comfortable, which means a startup is able to get financing at lower interest rates and can spend less time raising that money.[19]

A clean technology patent superhighway that would expedite consideration is the way to go. Having a patent approved or even under consideration by the USPTO helps startup companies attract investors. If a company has a better sense of when it might know the USPTO's decision on a patent claim, and there is a good chance it will get approval, it has a much better chance of attracting venture capital than does a company developing a technology that is in limbo. The patent office already offers a way to expedite consideration of a patent, but to do this, inventors have to do more research into prior art, as opposed to having the patent office do it. This is a pretty high bar, and most people choose to not jump over it.[20]

To Patent or Not to Patent

In some ways, the voracious demand for technology that delivers renewable energy resources, particularly to remote regions of the planet, also complicates a company's decision to seek intellectual property protection via the USPTO. Although the Green Technology Pilot Program promises to cut a year from the patent approval process, the mediocre response to the program indicates some inventors may be concerned that if their technology is granted a patent, they may be compelled to license the technology inexpensively to developing countries.[21]

A parallel can be drawn between the worldwide demand for renewable energy and a similar demand for a new drug, such as a compound that prevents or treats human immunodeficiency virus (HIV). Under World Trade Organization rules, if a drug is deemed beneficial to the public health of a developing country, the owner of a patent on that drug can be compelled to license it at a fee that is lower than fair market value to licensees in developing countries. Developing countries and others are now lobbying for similar rules applying to clean technology. In addition to devaluing the intellectual property, selling into developing countries could be tricky because that is where the technology is most likely to be counterfeited.[22]

An alternative to putting the details of intellectual property out in the open by filing with the USPTO is to sidestep the patent process entirely. Some companies and researchers developing green technologies could instead rely on trade secret agreements and contract law to protect the core components of their intellectual property.[23]

Another reason for companies to avoid the patent process at this time is because their technology is not fully hatched. Being the first to have your patent examined is not always the best way for a company to do things. Filing a patent application is something that most companies do early on to put their marker on something, but entering into examination too early might straightjacket their flexibility. Of course, this depends on the business. Larger, more established companies see advantages to having some mention of their technology on file, in the event a smaller firm later files an intellectual property infringement case.[24]

The Old Guard: Feeling the Winds of Change

General Motors has increased its interest in patents over the past five years or so, primarily because the nature of the automobile itself is changing so drastically. GM has basically entered an era that is reinventing the vehicle. The vehicle was invented in the early 1900s and by twenty years into it, the DNA of the vehicle had settled down. Now there are hardly any components of the vehicle that are not being reinvented.[25] When Alan Taub arrived at General Motors in 2000, the company was filing about 100 patents a year; in 2009, the company filed approximately 1,300 patents in the United States, more than half of which (670) could be considered green.

General Motors, by way of example, seeks to patent ways of using a material called Shape Memory Alloy (SMA), which changes shape when it is heated, and to build a recovery device that would convert waste heat from a vehicle's engine into electricity to power auxiliary equipment, such as the radio or interior accent lighting. What is so green about this? General Motors claims that such a device made from SMA could help to further improve the fuel economy of its cars, while also making next-generation hybrids more efficient. General Motors' attraction to SMA also provides an example of how the IP picture can quickly get muddied, particularly when an emerging technology is at the center. The company does not claim to have developed SMA; in fact it is working with Dynalloy, Inc., a Tustin, California-based manufacturer of SMAs that are specially made to be used as actuators, and with the Smart Materials Collaborative Research Lab at the University of Michigan.[26] Of course, SMA is a material that a number of scientists are trying to perfect, including Yuuki Tanaka and other researchers at Japan's Tohoku University. The Tohoku researchers reported, in a March 2010 issue of the journal *Science*, having discovered an iron-based shape metal alloy that shows an almost full recovery of shape change even when subjected to nearly twice the strain levels endured by shape metal alloys currently used in some cellular antennas, eyeglass frames, and medical devices.[27] The researchers report their alloy's strength is comparable with that of high-strength industry alloys.

The energy and environmental agenda has dominated the auto industry for the past two decades. Nearly half or two-thirds of the budget pie now goes into green. Whereas this share started with catalysts and exhaust treatment, it now relates to electrification and batteries.[28]

The turnaround on patent decisions has lengthened a bit, making it more difficult for the car company to legally establish new intellectual property and collaborate with business partners. The USPTO's main problem has been a lack of resources, in particular examiners themselves. It is pretty clear that they are recognizing that they have become more of a bottleneck as the world is becoming more technological.[29]

The USPTO, which has struggled in the past to keep up with the growing volume and diversity of patent claims, has not hired additional patent examiners as part of its green technology program. A lot of green technology is made up of existing technologies in which the office's 6,200 examiners already have expertise.[30] Commissioner of Patents Robert Stoll has indicated that he would like to hire 1,000 more examiners in 2011 and another 1,000 in 2012, but none of them would be devoted exclusively to green technology as a category.

IBM is another established company with an impressive list of patents that plans to test out the Patent Office's pilot program. More U.S. patents have been issued to it in the past 17 years than to any other company. IBM takes a look at most of the USPTO's pilot programs, if for no other reason than to understand how they work. It is surprising that so many applications filed for the program have been rejected, and also unfortunate because several patent attorneys and the USPTO spent a lot of time on things that do not come to fruition.[31]

IBM, along with Nokia, Pitney Bowes, and Sony, launched the Eco-Patent Commons in 2008 as a way of keeping the growing number of green patents from being an impediment to future development. Through the Commons, members can pledge not to assert their patents as long as they are used for green purposes because they want to promote green technology and generate more positive publicity for themselves.[32] These patents generally relate to technology that is not core to a company, but rather is tangential to their business.

Despite criticism of patents as creating a drag on innovation, the fact is that patents are provided for in the U.S. Constitution.[33] They were of prime importance to our founding fathers and the idea is to offer legal protection that frees up an applicant to share the information about its invention without fear of that information being reused without proper licensing. Patents also serve as a basis of scientific growth by providing this information to the public.[34]

In the end, the USPTO will measure the pilot program's success in a number of ways. According to Commissioner of Patents Robert Stoll, these include how enthusiastic inventors are about using the program (the number of applications would be a strong indicator), how well inventors adhere to the program's predefined categories (filing legitimate green technology applications), and the public's perception of the program. Adds Stoll, "I read the blogs every day."[35]

Conclusion

The intellectual property at the heart of the technology in demand to harness renewable energy from the wind, sun, and seas (not to mention a variety of other inventions designed to cut our carbon footprint), must be managed in a way that protects the inventors' interests—this is no different from any other investment made in IP. The USPTO tried to facilitate that effort throughout 2010 with a program that promised to fast track patent claims that fell into the realm of green IP. Of course, we're still in the early stages of thinking about IP in terms of its impact on the environment, which has led to loose interpretations of what, exactly, can be considered green. One thing is definite—companies big and small, new and old, are staking their claims in the field of environmentally friendly technology and processes, and the competition only becomes fiercer when government money and USPTO assistance is at stake. As these developments unfold, it's best to care for your green investments as though they were gold.

Notes

1. See also Maureen Beacom Gorman, "The Future's So Green, I Gotta Wear Shades: Maximizing Green Brand Exposure and Minimizing Perceptions of Greenwashing," in *Intellectual Property Operations and Implementation for the 21st Century Corporation*, (forthcoming).

2. Greenwashing is defined as "expressions of environmentalist concerns especially as a cover for products, policies, or activities," Merriam Webster Dictionary web site, www.merriam webster.com/dictionary/greenwashing?show=o&t=1299184183.

3. USPTO web site, www.uspto.gov/patents/init_events/green_tech.jsp.

4. Gary Locke, U.S. Secretary of Commerce, press release of statement announcing the Green Technology Pilot Program, Dec. 7, 2009.

5. David Kappos, U.S. Undersecretary of Commerce and director of the USPTO, press release of statement announcing the Green Technology Pilot Program, Dec. 7, 2009.

6. Robert Stoll, U.S. Commissioner for Patents, personal communication, April 15, 2010.

7. Robert Stoll, personal communication.

8. Robert Stoll, personal communication.

9. Eric Raciti, partner at the law firm of Finnegan, Henderson, Farabow, Garrett & Dunner, LLP in Cambridge, Massachusetts, and former patent examiner in medical device arts at the USPTO, Personal communication, April 14, 2010.

10. Press release, May 21, 2010, www.uspto.gov/news/pr/2010/10_21.jsp.

11. Mark Bünger, research director at Lux Research Inc., a technology consulting firm in New York City, personal communication, April 9, 2010.

12. Mark Bünger, personal communication.

13. *Association for Molecular Pathology, et al. v. United States Patent and Trademark Office, et al.*, *Financial Times*, May 11, 2010, www.ft.com/cms/s/0/1d850e76-5c8c-11df-bb38-00144 feab49a.html.

14. *Association for Molecular Pathology v. U.S. Patent and Trademark Office*, no. 09-cv-4515, 94 USPQ2d 1683 (S.D.N.Y. March 29, 2010).

15. Robert Cook-Deegan and Christopher Heaney, "Gene patents and licensing: Case studies prepared for the Secretary's Advisory Committee on Genetics, Health, and Society," *Genetics in Medicine*, no. 4: S1–S2. (April 14, 2009).

16. See also David Blackburn and Bryan Ray, "Intellectual Property Valuation Techniques and Issues for the 21st Century," in *Intellectual Property Strategies for the 21st Century Corporation*.

17. USPTO web site, www.uspto.gov/news/pr/2009/09_33.js.

18. Tim Keating, vice president of marketing at Skyline Solar, a California-based manufacturer of high-gain solar arrays and former chip maker with Intel Corporation, personal communication, April 14, 2010.

19. Tim Keating, personal communication.

20. Larry Goldenhersh, CEO of Enviance Inc., a California-based manufacturer of software for helping businesses determine their greenhouse gas emissions levels, and a former intellectual property lawyer with the law firm of Irell & Manella LLP in Los Angeles, personal communication, April 14, 2010.

21. Joseph Daniels, a lawyer with the New York City-based law firm of Hodgson Russ LLP, Personal communication, April 14, 2010.

22. Joseph Daniels, personal communication.

23. Joseph Daniels, personal communication.

24. Eric Raciti, partner at the law firm of Finnegan, Henderson, Farabow, Garrett & Dunner, LLP in Cambridge, Massachusetts, and former patent examiner in medical device arts at the USPTO, personal communication, April 14, 2010.

25. Alan Taub, head of General Motors' Global Research and Development, personal communication, April 14, 2010.

26. General Motors web site, www.gm.com/experience/technology/news/2009/coolheat_102709.jsp.

27. Y. Tanaka, Y. Himuro, R. Kainuma, Y. Sutou, T. Omori & K. Ishida, "Ferrous Polycrystalline Shape-Memory Alloy Showing Huge Superelasticity," *Science* 327, no. 5972 (2010): 1488–1490.

28. Alan Taub, head of General Motors' Global Research and Development, personal communication, April 14, 2010.

29. Alan Taub, head of General Motors' Global Research and Development, personal communication, April 14, 2010.

30. Robert Stoll, personal communication, April 15, 2010.

31. Manny Schecter, Chief Patent Council for IBM, personal communication, April 16, 2010.

32. Manny Schecter, personal communication.

33. Article I, Section 8, Clause 8 of the United States Constitution.

34. Robert Stoll, April 15, 2010.

35. Robert Stoll, April 15, 2010.

CHAPTER 16

Accounting and Tax Policies as They Relate to Intellectual Property

Howard Fine and Andrew P. Ross
Gettry Marcus Stern & Lehrer, CPA, P.C.

Intellectual property often can be one of a company's most valuable assets.[1] It also could be one of the most difficult in terms of accounting treatment. Due to the intangible nature of these assets it is often hard to place values on them; determine whether any impairment has occurred or whether the asset has any future value and should be capitalized or expensed. There could be differing accounting treatment depending on whether the asset is internally developed or is acquired in an external transaction. In addition, the tax treatment of these types of assets can differ significantly from their accounting treatment. For example, for tax purposes certain costs associated with acquiring or creating intangible assets must be capitalized rather than be treated as deductible expenses. Generally Accepted Accounting Principles (GAAP) in the United States require that intangible assets possess three essential characteristics: (1) an entity embodies a future economic benefit by contributing directly or indirectly to future net cash flows, (2) a particular entity can obtain the benefit and restrict others access to it, and (3) a particular transaction or event giving rise to the benefit or control has already occurred. [2]

This chapter discusses the relevant issues one should be aware of in accounting for these types of assets under current U.S. accounting standards, along with possible changes under international standards. It will also address the related tax treatment of these assets.

Types of Intellectual Property

Intellectual property or intangible assets can be categorized into two basic categories: (1) intangible assets subject to amortization and (2) intangible assets not subject to amortization.

Intangible assets subject to amortization are those with a finite useful life, even if the length of life is not definite. In these cases, a best estimate would be utilized. If, subsequently, an intangible asset that is being amortized is determined to now have an indefinite useful life, this asset would then, at this point, no longer be amortized and would be accounted for as an intangible asset not subject to amortization. These assets are determined to have an indefinite useful life and are not amortized. Instead they should be tested for any impairment for each reporting period to determine whether a loss has occurred. If an impairment has occurred then a loss must be recognized on the company's income statement.

Examples of both types of assets are as follows:

Subject to amortization

- Patents
- Trademarks and trade names
- Copyrights

Not subject to amortization

- Goodwill
- Costs in research and development activities until the completion or abandonment of the project

Intangible assets are sometimes categorized into intellectual property or legal intangibles and competitive intangibles. Intellectual property consists of copyrights, patents, trademarks, and trade names and goodwill. These types of assets create property rights for exclusive usage and allow the owner to benefit from them. Competitive intangibles consist mainly of know-how or knowledge developed assets such as trade secrets, customer lists, and other internally developed items. Other types of intangible assets could be start-up costs (organization costs), covenants not to compete, and domain names.

Accounting for Intangible Assets

Recently there have been significant debates over the generally accepted accounting principle of utilizing the traditional historic cost approach in accounting for intangible assets. One argument against this approach is that intangibles drive businesses in the twenty-first century and that these knowledge-based assets are often not reflected on a company's financial statements. These assets under current standards generally are recognized as assets only if externally acquired rather than internally developed. By not reflecting such assets, arguments are made that a company's true net worth is not being stated properly.

However, these arguments have not been adopted yet and intangible assets are still recognized under the guidance established by the Financial Accounting Standards Board (FASB) under its Accounting Standards Codification. This is the single source of authoritative literature of U.S. generally accepted accounting principles.

There is specific guidance issued by the FASB in accounting for different types of intangible assets consisting of the following not all-inclusive list:

- FASB ASC730 Research and Development
- FASB ASC350 Goodwill Asset and Other Intangible Costs
- FASB ASC360 Accounting for Impairment of Long-Lived Assets
- FASB ASC805 Business Combinations
- FASB ASC820 Fair Value Measurements
- FASB ASC350–40 Accounting for Costs of Computer Software
- FASB ASC720 Accounting for Start-up costs

FASB ASC730 gives guidance on accounting for research and development activities exclusive of intangible assets acquired in a business combination. It states that these costs should be reflected as an expense when incurred.

FASB ASC350 gives guidance on intangible assets and states that they should be initially recognized and recorded based on their fair value. Intangible assets with finite useful lives should be amortized over their respective lives while those with indefinite useful lives should not be amortized. It also states that the costs of developing, maintaining, or restoring intangible assets that are not specifically identifiable, that have indeterminate lives, or that are inherent in the activities of a continuing business should be expensed when incurred.

This section of the codification also gives guidance on accounting for goodwill acquired in a business combination. Specifically it states that goodwill should not be amortized, but should be tested for any impairment at least annually. This also applies for other intangible assets not subject to amortization. The effective date of this treatment was June 30, 2009, so any goodwill acquired prior to that date would still be amortized over its useful life.

FASB ASC720 states that start-up costs, including organization costs, should be expensed as incurred.

FASB ASC820 establishes a framework to measure fair value when applying it to record specific assets and liabilities and also expands the disclosure requirements.

Recently there was a movement in the accounting industry for U.S. accounting standards to conform with international accounting standards due to the globalization of business activities. This would create one standard set of reporting requirements worldwide.

International Financial Reporting Standards

International Financial Reporting Standards (IFRS) are the rules and guidelines created by the International Accounting Standards Committee (IASC) and its successor, the International Accounting Standards Board (IASB).

Many of the IFRS were promulgated by the IASC and are known by its older name, International Accounting Standards (IAS). When the IASB assumed its responsibilities from the IASC on April 1, 2001, it immediately adopted the existing IAS standards as it continues to develop new standards titled IFRS.

In October 2002, the FASB and the IASB announced the issuance of a memorandum known as the Norwalk Agreement. The Norwalk Agreement reflects both organizations' commitment toward converging U.S. and international accounting standards.

In February 2010, the U.S. Securities and Exchange Commission (SEC) reaffirmed its commitment for the convergence of U.S. and international accounting standards. The SEC believes that domestic reporting entities should expect to make the transition, and a convergence with IFRS could be completed by 2015 or 2016.

International Financial Reporting Standards for Small- and Medium-Sized Entities

The IASB issued International Financial Reporting Standards for Small- and Medium-sized Entities (IFRS for SMEs). This simplified version of the IFRS standards is codified in a small fraction of the text that represents the full version of IFRS. The IFRS for SMEs "are aimed at meeting the needs of private company financial reporting users and easing the financial reporting burden on private companies through a cost-benefit approach."[3] The IASB understood "the full IFRSs were designed to meet the needs of equity investors in companies in public capital markets, they cover a wide range of issues, contain a sizeable amount of implementation guidance and include disclosures appropriate for public companies."[4] The IASB estimates that these SMEs represent more than 95 percent of all companies.

IFRS for SMEs apply to companies that issue financial statements for external users who do not have public accountability. The IASB defines a publicly accountable entity as an entity that "files, or is in the process of filing, its financial statements with a securities commission or other regulatory organization for the purpose of issuing any class of instruments in a public market; or it holds assets in a fiduciary capacity for a group of outsiders." The definition is irrespective of the size of the reporting entity and allows for many private United States companies to utilize IFRS for SMEs. Full IFRS and IFRS for SMEs are considered generally accepted accounting principles for financial statement reporting purposes.

International Accounting Standard 38—Intangible Assets

IAS 38 Intangible Assets was issued by the IASC in September of 1998. The standard replaced IAS 9 *Research and Development Costs*. Two subsequent revisions to IAS 38 resulted in the revised IAS 38, effective July 1, 2009. The objective of IAS 38 is to address the accounting treatment for intangible assets not discussed elsewhere in another standard.

Paragraph 9 of IAS 38 describes the applicability of the Standard. "Entities frequently expend resources, or incur liabilities, on the acquisition, development, maintenance or enhancement of intangible resources such as scientific or technical knowledge, design and implementation of new processes or systems, licenses, intellectual property, marketing knowledge and trademarks (including brand names and publishing titles)." Paragraph 9 further gives examples as "computer software, patents, copyrights, motion picture films, customer lists, mortgage servicing rights, fishing licenses, import quotas, franchises, customer or supplier relationships, customer loyalty, market share and marketing rights."

IAS 38 emphasizes that all the items described in paragraph 9 may not meet the definition of an intangible asset. In order to be classified as such, the item must reflect the characteristics of identifiability, control over a resource, and the existence of a future economic benefit. If an internally generated or acquired expenditure does not meet these criteria, then the item must be expensed when incurred.

Tax Treatment for Intangible Assets

Several Internal Revenue Code sections address the treatment of amortizable expenditures. Examples of these sections are:

- Section 197—Amortization of goodwill and certain other intangibles
- Section 195—Start-up expenditures
- Section 248—Organizational expenditures
- Section 174—Research and experimental expenditures
- Section 173—Circulation expenditures
- Section 167—Depreciation (including purchased software)

This classification will have a bearing on whether the cost should be expensed as incurred, amortized over a specified time period, or be considered an asset until disposal. Goodwill and other intangibles are examples of expenditures that require amortization. Start-up expenditures and organizational costs are generally amortized over a 15-year period. However, the taxpayer may elect to immediately expense amounts up to certain limitations. Circulation expenditures are generally expensed when incurred unless an election is made to amortize these costs.

Overview of Section 197—Amortization of Goodwill and Certain Other Intangibles

The Internal Revenue Service has issued its final regulations regarding when an intangible asset should be capitalized rather than immediately deducted. Under Reg. 1.263(a)4(b) capitalization is mandatory for amounts paid or incurred to:

- Acquire or create intangibles
- Facilitate the acquisition or creating of intangibles
- Facilitate the acquisition of assets constituting a trade or business, or an ownership interest in the taxpayer

Capitalization rules govern intangible assets acquired from another party as well as costs incurred for intangibles created by the taxpayer. An example of an intangible created by the taxpayer would be the costs paid for copyright or trademark rights.

In 1993, Congress added Section 197 to the Internal Revenue Code. Section 197 was part of the Omnibus Budget Reconciliation Act of 1993 allowing for the first time that goodwill and going-concern value acquired as part of an acquisition transaction be amortized over a prescribed 15-year period. Also addressed in Section 197 is the treatment of other intangible assets, such as covenants not to compete and customer lists that are traditionally allocated as part of an acquisition of assets of a trade or business.

The Section 197 legislation came about after years of conflicts between taxpayers and the Internal Revenue Service on the proper handling of these intangibles. Prior to its enactment, the Internal Revenue Service's position was that intangibles such as covenants not to compete and customer lists were indistinguishable from goodwill and going-concern value.

Conversely, taxpayers asserted that these non-goodwill intangibles have a limited identifiable useful life and thus should be amortized accordingly. Section 197(d) (1) served to curtail this heavily litigated area of the tax law by mandating a standard 15-year amortization period for the assets identified as "Section 197 Intangible" assets as follows:

(A) Goodwill
(B) Going-concern value
(C) Any of the following intangible items:
    (i) Workforce in place including its composition and terms and conditions (contractual or otherwise) of its employment
    (ii) Business books and record, operating systems, or any other information base (including lists or other information with respect to current or prospective customers)
    (iii) Any patent, copyright, formula, process design, pattern, know-how, format, or other similar item
    (iv) Any customer-based intangible
    (v) Any supplier-based intangible
    (vi) Any other similar item

The above listing of Section 197 assets generally consist of assets acquired by the taxpayer in a business transaction; however, Section 197 identifies certain "self-created" intangibles such as trademarks that are also amortized over the Section 197 15-year period.

Section 197 anti-churning provisions disallow the use of 15-year amortization where the buyer and seller are related parties. Congress was aware of the opportunity for certain family members to enter into transactions specifically for the purpose of converting previously unamortizable intangible assets, such as goodwill (prior to the enactment of Section 197) into amortizable assets.

Prior to the enactment of Section 197, amounts allocable to goodwill or going-concern value were capitalized and could not be amortized. This unfavorable tax treatment caused taxpayers to allocate as little as possible toward these types of assets.

The mechanics of allocating Section 197 intangible assets is straightforward. The parties to the transaction should identify and allocate the value of all assets associated with the acquisition of a trade or business. If the acquisition purchase price exceeds the value of these allocated assets, the excess should be applied toward goodwill and amortized over 15 years. The original allocation of assets can contain both tangible assets and intangible assets such as patents, trademarks, customer lists, and covenants not to compete. The allocated intangibles included in the original allocation are also amortized over the 15-year period as defined in Section 197.

Covenant Not to Compete

An example of the rigidity of the Code is the treatment of covenants not to compete in the context of a business acquisition transaction. This asset class is defined as a Section 197 asset and therefore amortized over a 15-year period. This seems counterintuitive since covenant not to compete agreements are usually for a period of two or three years. Courts are reluctant to validate covenants that exceed five years. The mandatory 15-year amortization period effectively serves to encourage taxpayers to allocate a minimal amount to the covenant causing potential conflict with the Internal Revenue Service.

Prior to the enactment of the Omnibus Budget Reconciliation Act of 1993, taxpayers had incentive to allocate a large portion of the purchase price to the covenant not to compete because the allocated amount would be amortized over the actual term of the covenant.

Taxpayers are prohibited from writing off the covenant not to compete agreement when it becomes worthless (i.e., after the term of the covenant has passed). Section 197 provides that the asset cannot be written off as worthless until there has been an entire disposition of the business unit. This is an even stricter provision than the rules contained in Section 197 relating to the write-off of other intangible assets.

Copyrights and Patents

Copyrights and patents are specifically excluded from Section 197 treatment if they are *not* acquired as part of an asset purchase or sale. Therefore, if an entity purchases the rights to a copyright or patent individually, the assets must be depreciated under methods governed under Section 167 Depreciation.

Computer Software

Computer software, defined in Section 197(e)(3)(B) as "any program designed to cause a computer to perform a desired function," is carved out of Section 197 classification. In these cases software will be depreciated under Section 167 over 36 months using the straight-line method. In cases where computer software is bundled with hardware, the asset will be considered 5-year MACRS property. Section 197(e)(3)(A) defines excluded software as follows:

(i) computer software which is readily available for purchase by the general public, is subject to a nonexclusive license, and has not been substantially modified, and
(ii) other computer software which is not acquired in a transaction (or series of related transactions) involving the acquisition of assets constituting a trade or business or substantial portion thereof.

Section 197(e)(3)(A)(i) uses the term *readily available* to describe software that is excluded from intangible asset recognition, and therefore, 15-year amortization.

This terminology is akin to "off the shelf software." Therefore, "custom" software would be classified as a Section 197 intangible asset if it were purchased along with other assets as part of a trade or business acquisition. In order for software to be considered custom software there must be evidence of substantial modification. Substantial modification is defined under Reg. 1.197-2(c)(4)(i) as software whose costs to modify exceeds the greater of $2,000 or 25 percent of the price at which the unmodified version is available to the general public.

Acquisition of Section 197 Intangibles—IRS Form 8594

IRS Form 8594, Asset Acquisition Statement Under Section 1060, is the reporting form that allocates assets in the purchase or sale of a trade or business. The instructions to Form 8594 state that "both the seller and purchaser of a group of assets that makes up a trade or business must use Form 8594 to report such a sale if goodwill or going concern value attaches, or could attach, to such assets and if the purchaser's basis in the assets is determined only by the amount paid for the assets." Both the purchaser and seller must file this form as an attachment to their respective income tax filing.

The form requires assets to be categorized into seven assets groups. Class VI assets are defined as "all Section 197 intangibles (as defined in Section 197) except goodwill and going-concern value." Goodwill and going-concern value are reported as a Class VII asset.

The Form 8594 is filed separately by the buyer and seller on their respective income tax filings. The parties must allocate the purchase/sales price to the first six categories. Any residual amounts are then carried forward into Class VII, thereby creating goodwill.

For the seller, the allocation will dictate which asset classes the sale will be reported under on the taxpayer's income tax filing. Assets generally fall under three categories:

1. Capital assets—for C–corporations capital gains are taxed at the same rates as ordinary income. Net capital losses cannot be deducted and can be carried back three years or forward five years to be applied against capital gains in those years.
2. Section 1231 assets—consisting of certain intangible property amortized under Section 197 and real property held by the business for more than one year. Generally, net Section 1231 gains are treated as long-term capital gains while net 1231 losses are treated as ordinary losses.
3. Other ordinary assets such as accounts receivables are treated as ordinary income to the seller.

Intangible assets can be classified as capital assets, section 1231 assets, or other ordinary assets depending on the characteristic of the asset sold. For example, intangible assets that are neither amortizable under Section 197 nor depreciable under Section 167 are capital assets. An example of such is goodwill generated by the seller in the resultant transaction.

Disposition of Section 197 Intangibles

The tax treatment for disposal of a Section 197 Intangibles held in a trade or business is governed by the length of the holding period. For intangibles held for more than one year, the gain up to the amount of allowable amortization is treated as ordinary income. Any remaining gain (or loss) is then treated as a Section 1231 gain or loss.

Section 197 Intangibles disposed of within one year of acquisition are treated as ordinary gains or losses.

A taxpayer cannot deduct any loss on the disposition or worthlessness of a Section 197 intangible asset that was acquired as part of a purchase transaction that consisted of other Section 197 intangible assets. Instead, the basis of the surviving Section 197 assets must be increased proportionately, to include the disposed-of intangible asset.

Overview of Section 195—Start-Up Expenditures

Section 195 defines start-up costs as expenses paid or incurred in connection with "investigating the creation or acquisition of an active trade or business, or creating an active trade or business, or any activity engaged in for profit and for the production of income before the day on which the active trade or business begins". Section 195 specifically excludes any amounts that qualify under Section 163(a), 164, or 174.

If Section 195 is elected, the taxpayer will be allowed an amount equal to the lesser of the actual expenditure, or $5,000, reduced by the amount by which such start-up costs exceed $50,000. The remainder of these start-up expenditures shall be allowed as a deduction, ratably over a 15-year period.

Overview of Section 248—Organizational Expenditures

Organizational expenditures are defined in the Code as costs incurred that are "incident to the creation of the corporation and if expended incident to the creation of a corporation having a limited life, would be amortizable over such life."

The deductibility rules governing Section 248 expenditures follow Section 195— Start-Up Expenditures.

Overview of Section 174—Research and Experimental Expenditures

A taxpayer can elect to amortize research and experimental costs over 60 months, deduct them as current business expenses, or write them off over a 10-year period. The Internal Revenue Service defines research and experimental costs as "reasonable costs you incur in your trade or business for activities intended to provide information that would eliminate uncertainty about the development or improvement of a product. Uncertainty exists if the information available to you does not establish how to develop or improve a product or the appropriate design of a product."

The IRS specifically addresses whether the costs of obtaining a patent would qualify as a research and experimental expenditure. Such an expenditure would qualify as research and experimental if it was incurred in making and perfecting a patent application. Costs incurred to purchase another's patent would not qualify as a research and experimental expenditure.

The IRS describes the following examples as products:

- Formula
- Invention
- Patent
- Pilot model
- Process, technique, and property similar to the items listed above

Specifically excluded are:

- Advertising or promotions
- Consumer surveys
- Efficiency surveys
- Management studies
- Quality control testing
- Research in connection with literary, historical, or similar projects
- The acquisition of another's patent, model production, or process.

A credit for increased research expenditures is available for amounts paid or incurred through December 31, 2009 and is reported on tax form 6765—Credit for Increasing Research Activities.

The credit is subject to the tax liability limitation and carryover rules.

Overview of Section 173—Circulation Expenditures

All expenditures incurred to establish, maintain, or increase the circulation of a newspaper, magazine, or other periodical shall be allowed as an immediate income tax deduction unless the taxpayer elects to amortize these costs over a 36-month period beginning with the tax year the costs were paid or incurred. The election is simply a statement attached to the taxpayer's return for the first year the election applies.

The Code Section specifically excludes the purchase of land or depreciable property from Section 173 treatment. Also excluded are costs relating to the acquisition of circulation through the purchase of any part of the business of another publisher of a newspaper, magazine, or other periodical.

Overview of Section 167—Depreciation (Purchased Software)

As stated previously, Section 197(e)(3)(A)(i) uses the term *readily available* to describe computer software that is excluded from intangible asset recognition. This computer software is also referred to as off-the-shelf software and is amortized over a 36-month period pursuant to Section 167(f) of the Code.

Conclusion

The accounting and tax treatment of intangible assets represents a challenge to the individual responsible for maintaining the organization's financial books and records. Special attention must be paid to the emerging financial reporting and tax issues.

Notes

1. See also James E. Malackowski, "Intellectual Property: From Asset to Asset Class," in *Intellectual Property Strategies for the 21st Century Corporation*.

2. IASB Project Update, "Intangible Assets" (June 2007).

3. The American Institute of Certified Public Accountants, International Financial Reporting Standard for Small- and Medium-Sized Entities, 2010.

4. International Accounting Standards Board: IFRS for SMEs, 2010.

CHAPTER 17

Intellectual Property Valuation Techniques and Issues for the 21st Century

David Blackburn and Bryan Ray
NERA Economic Consulting

The sale, licensing, and use of intellectual property (IP) are often aided by a contemporaneous economic valuation. A valuation, for example, can provide the owner of an IP asset with a benchmark price or royalty to seek when selling or licensing the asset, or an estimate of the future benefit to exploiting the IP or the opportunity cost of not using it. Similarly, a valuation can provide a prospective buyer with insight into the most it should be willing to pay for an IP asset. Valuations of IP can also be used for other purposes, such as intercompany transfer pricing, financial reporting, or the calculation of economic damages caused by the infringement or misappropriation of IP.

Proper valuations of IP are guided by economic principles. These principles and the approaches that stem from them provide a stable set of frameworks for most valuations. While these economic principles are stable, changes in legal and regulatory frameworks and innovations in technology and business practices have raised important new valuation issues. Some of these issues may play a role in valuation practice for years to come, even if not germane to every exercise. In addition, some advanced quantitative techniques have become available and more practical to apply to valuation. These technical advances have further changed valuation practice by adding to the toolkit of the practitioner.

In this chapter we discuss some of the key economic principles that underlie a proper valuation and, generally, each of the traditional frameworks: income-based, market-based, and cost-based. We then provide a brief description of recent technical advances in valuation methods. We conclude with a discussion of some important business practices, market structures, and institutional changes that have and may continue to affect how IP can create value and how that value can be measured.

Economic Valuation of IP Assets

Value can be an imprecise concept when it is not tied to a specific context. For example, the value of IP can be thought of from the perspective of a single entity that is using that IP (often referred to as value-in-use), or, alternatively, as the market price at which the IP is sold or licensed. Why this context matters is intuitive. The specific circumstances of a particular entity will determine how that entity can deploy the IP to generate profit, which will determine the value-in-use of the IP to that entity. The market price for IP is determined by the interaction of the individual values assigned to the IP by all relevant market participants.

Although the context for which value is being measured matters to the ultimate approach and outcome of a valuation analysis, there are several overarching economic principles that both illustrate how IP creates value and provide a general framework by which value can be measured. Most fundamentally, the value of an IP asset is based on the future *incremental* profits that the IP asset is expected to generate. What does that mean? In the most general sense, the incremental effect of something can be isolated by observing the effects of introducing (or removing) that thing when all other things are held constant. With respect to the valuation of IP, we can think of the IP being used in connection with some product or service that is expected (either directly or indirectly) to generate a future cash flow. The incremental contribution of a particular IP asset to that expected future cash flow is the difference between the expected future cash flow from using the IP asset and the expected future cash flow after replacing the IP with its next-best available alternative (after fully accounting for the costs of implementing that alternative).[1] Although conceptually this approach to measure the value-in-use of an IP asset is well defined, in practice this analysis can be complex. We discuss some of the analytical methods that have been developed to isolate the incremental cash flows that are expected to be contributed by an IP asset.

We focus on expectations because value is a forward-looking concept—what gives IP value is its expected ability to generate incremental profit *in the future*. As a result, the measurement of the incremental profit contributed by the IP should account for the effects of time and uncertainty about the future. That is, there is an opportunity cost of forgoing a payment of a given amount today in exchange for the same payment in the future. This is true because of: (1) expected inflation that, all else being equal, depreciates the future value (or purchasing power) of a given amount of money and (2) the risk of not realizing an expected future cash flow. To account for these facts, the expected incremental future returns from the IP are discounted. In practice, the amount of that discount may be measured by the opportunity cost of the capital required to generate the expected future returns. The opportunity cost of capital is the expected rate of return required by rational investors in financial securities that have equivalent risk to the project that is generating the cash flow being discounted. This rate of return can be used to capture the effects of both inflation and uncertainty on the measurement of the present value of the future returns.

Finally, though the concepts of incremental profit and the time value of money are in themselves abstract, they cannot be evaluated in a vacuum. IP is embodied (or expected to be embodied) in products or services that are sold in markets. Accordingly, the conditions (e.g., the competitive, legal, and regulatory forces) of those markets should be assessed to best understand how and to what extent the IP may generate future incremental profits. Furthermore, because value is forward looking, a valuation should be focused on the projected future conditions in the market (or markets) where the IP is (or is expected to be) used.

Income-Based Approaches to Valuation

As we previously described, an asset's value-in-use is the discounted value of the expected returns attributable solely to that asset. In practice, this assessment is often made using what is conventionally called a discounted cash flow (often referred to as a DCF) analysis. This approach is considered an income-based approach to valuation because it calculates the value of an asset based on the future income that the asset is expected to generate, relative to its next-best alternative.

Accordingly, a DCF analysis requires that: (1) the asset's expected future incremental returns (i.e., the cash flows, including possible cost savings, contributed by the asset) be estimated over a reasonable forecast period; (2) an appropriate discount rate be determined that adequately reflects the underlying risk of those future returns; and (3) when appropriate, the asset's expected returns beyond the forecast period (i.e., the terminal value) be estimated. A DCF analysis will produce what is referred to as a present value. In short, the present value is the value of the expected future cash flows that the IP is incrementally expected to contribute where those cash flows have been discounted to reflect the time value of money, including the expected risk associated with the future cash flows.

Market-Based Approaches to Valuation

Market-based approaches to valuation are based on the concept that the value of an asset can be discerned from real-world marketplace transactions either involving the IP asset at issue or involving other, substantially similar assets. This approach relies on market prices to assess value and, accordingly, may not measure the specific value-in-use of the asset to any particular entity.

The usefulness of a market-based valuation analysis depends on the comparability of the benchmark transaction(s) to the asset being valued and the context of the valuation. To provide a reasonable basis for the value of an IP asset, candidate benchmark transactions should be carefully evaluated to determine whether they provide meaningful indicators of the value of the asset at issue. The valuation analysis should assess, among other things, the extent to which the transactions present comparable circumstances to those at issue (e.g., in terms of the assets themselves, the competitive relationships of the parties, the scope and terms of the transactions, and the timing of the transactions). The valuation analysis should also consider the extent to which the market, in which the benchmark IP was expected to be used, differs from the situation at hand. Failure to properly consider and account for all the relevant differences can yield unreliable results.

Cost-Based Approaches to Valuation

There are at least two ways to obtain an asset: produce it or acquire it. Unless prevented, a profit-maximizing firm will choose the least-cost option of obtaining an asset. As a general matter, a prospective buyer of an asset therefore will not pay more than: (1) the full economic cost to create an equivalent asset or (2) the incremental economic benefits of having that asset relative to its next-best alternative. Thus, there are several types of cost-based analyses that may be relevant to valuation. These may be based upon, for example: (1) the historical cost to the IP asset's owner of creating the asset; (2) the current cost to the IP asset's owner of turning to its next-best alternative; and (3) the current cost to a prospective buyer/licensee of turning to its next-best alternative.

Companies ordinarily would not make an investment in any asset, tangible or intangible, unless the expected return on the investment exceeds its cost. Thus, the economic costs associated with the creation of an IP asset may provide a proxy for the economic cost to a putative buyer of turning to its next-best alternative and, therefore, the most it would pay for that asset. In addition, the IP asset owner's historical investment in the property at a particular time, if properly analyzed, may provide a basis for a lower-bound estimate of the return from that investment it expected to obtain at that time.

As a general matter, the availability of economic substitutes is an important determinant of the value of any IP asset. For example, a prospective licensee of a patent may evaluate the ease with which it can invent around the licensor's patented technology to avoid infringement. In effect, this is the same as evaluating the extent to which there is an acceptable alternative to which the licensee can turn and the full economic cost of doing so. The less costly it is to turn to that alternative, the less the licensee will be willing to pay for a license, all else being equal.

Recent Advances in the Methods of Valuation

While the general principles involved in valuation are largely unchanging, valuation methods evolve in response to advances in economic theory and quantitative techniques and to the availability of resources (e.g., data and powerful computers) to implement these new methods. Two recent advances in valuation that are now used by practitioners are discussed here.

The first advance is based on viewing the demand for goods and services as separable across their attributes. For example, the demand for a computer can be expressed as the demand for memory, computing speed, connectivity, and so on. Thus, it is not hard to imagine how this approach may be useful for the valuation of IP, given that the contribution of specific IP to a product may be isolated to specific features or attributes of the product.

For purposes of these methods of valuation, each of the identifiable attributes of a good is considered to have its own price (sometimes referred to as a shadow price) indicating how the attribute contributes to the market price of the good—for example, how much a gigabyte of memory contributes on average to the total price of the computer. Statistical regression techniques, using data collected from both actual market transactions and surveys, can be used to measure the value of these attributes. We discuss two such methods: hedonic price regressions and discrete choice models.

The second advance is the application of real options theory to the valuation of tangible and intangible non-financial assets. Valuing assets as real options can be thought of as a form of discounted cash flow analysis, one that recognizes that the return from certain decisions or investments may depend on future decisions taken by management, including subsequent investment, and outcomes.

Statistical Methods of Valuation

In general, regressions are statistical models that can provide an estimate of the relationship between one variable, say rainfall, and another, say crop yield. These estimates are made holding other relevant factors specified in the regression model constant. For example, temperature might be one of these other factors that could also affect crop yield. Advances in computing in the closing years of the twentieth century have made computers more powerful and prevalent enabling regression analysis to be more accessible.

There are many types of regressions. Hedonic price regressions are a way of looking at products as composite goods comprised of a number of product characteristics. A characteristic might be the inclusion of a particular patented feature. A hedonic price regression can be used to apportion the market price for the product as a whole across the product's various characteristics. Econometric models of discrete consumer choice can also be used for the same purpose. In the former, product characteristics are included as explanatory variables in a regression model of observed prices.[2] In the latter, product characteristics are included as explanatory variables in a regression model of consumers' observed choices.[3]

HEDONIC PRICE REGRESSIONS   A hedonic price regression can be viewed as a means of apportioning the price (or value) of a product across its constituent features, all else being equal. For example, we might find that by including a GPS in a model of automobile, the manufacturer is able to raise the average price of an automobile by a certain amount or percentage. Or, that increases to the resolution of a screen display support a higher price. As such, these models allow us to measure the price premium (or discount) associated with a characteristic of a product. As we go on to explain, because hedonic price regressions can be used to estimate price premiums, they can be useful for an income-based approach to valuation.

The estimated coefficients in linear hedonic price regressions can be viewed as estimates of the implicit prices of product characteristics. For example, we might estimate a hedonic price regression for automobiles that includes a parameter indicating whether each automobile has a curtain airbag. We might find the estimated coefficient of that parameter has the value of $500. Accordingly, we may conclude that the "price" of the curtain airbag, or its contribution to the overall price of the automobile, was $500. To be sure, it can be a complex exercise to construct a model that appropriately controls for all the relevant factors and get data on those variables that have sufficient variation.[4]

As a general matter, the observed prices used in a hedonic price regression are the result of the interaction of supply and demand. Instead of estimating demand or supply elasticities or the willingness to pay of consumers, we are measuring the price premium associated with the product characteristic (i.e., the incremental revenue associated with the characteristic).

For purposes of valuation, we can use the estimated price premium for a product characteristic in conjunction with measures of the incremental costs of providing the characteristic. Because this method attempts to assess the incremental income associated with a product characteristic (and its underlying IP), it follows that this is an income-based approach to valuation. For example, to help determine a royalty for a patent license or to calculate the economic damages as a result of the infringement of a patent, we may be able to use a hedonic price regression to measure the price premium for the patented feature. The particular facts and context of the valuation will direct the specific approach, but, as a general matter, the value of the feature can be measured based on the estimated price premium for the feature, the total number of units embodying the feature expected to be sold, the expected timing of the sales, the costs of providing the feature in those units, and an appropriate discount rate to reflect the fact that the profits attributable to the feature are expected to be realized in the future.[5]

Indeed, hedonic price regressions have been used to parse the prices of characteristics for many products, including, for example, computers, automobiles, housing, and agricultural products (including wine, horses, wheat, rice, and cotton). In addition, they have been used in the study of such diverse products as pharmaceuticals, crude oil, kitchen garbage bags, group health insurance, newspapers, breakfast cereals, child care, sculptures, common carrier services, and coal rail prices.[6] Hedonic price regressions are also often the first step toward the calculation of a quality-adjusted price index. The U.S. Bureau of Labor Statistics uses hedonic models in the Consumer Price Index (CPI) to control for concomitant changes in product quality and price for a number of products.[7]

DISCRETE CHOICE MODELS   Discrete choice models approach valuation from a somewhat different angle. Generally, hedonic price analyses are measuring a market price, inclusive of the interaction of supply and demand. In contrast, discrete choice models are generally used to measure the willingness of consumers to pay for a particular product or product attribute. Accordingly, they only measure demand, in particular, the influence of, for example, product characteristics on the likelihood of a purchase.

If we can trace out the likelihood of the purchase of a product at a sufficient number of prices, holding constant all the characteristics of the product, and then multiply the likelihood by the number of prospective consumers, we would have an estimated demand curve for a product with product characteristics corresponding to the fixed values we chose. If we were to repeat the process and make only one change, this time excluding the product characteristic of interest, we would have an estimated demand curve for a product that was in every way identical to that for which the first demand curve was constructed except for the excluded product characteristic. Taking the difference between the first demand curve and the second yields the incremental demand for the product characteristic of interest.

An important difference in working with an estimate of the willingness to pay for a product characteristic rather than a market price premium for that characteristic is that the factors of supply have not yet been accounted for in the analysis. Therefore, we have only an estimate of the willingness of consumers to pay, and not what the marginal consumer is paying in equilibrium. If we are willing to assume that the supply of the product characteristic is perfectly inelastic (i.e., that the quantity supplied may be considered to be, for all intents and purposes, fixed), then we may be able to interpret the willingness to pay as the implicit price for the product and use that in the valuation.

Frequently, the data used in discrete choice models are the results of choice experiments presented to consumers as part of a survey; however, one may also be able to use sales data. In some cases, survey data and transactional data, along with engineering and other descriptive data, might be combined.

In a consumer choice survey, the respondents are typically presented a number of alternatives, each with a price and a description of the product (or service) characteristics. The alternatives could include a "no buy" option. The respondent is then asked to indicate which of the alternatives is preferred. Using a variety of price and product characteristics provides the variation needed to identify the marginal utility of each attribute. Here, the respondents reveal, through their choices, their willingness to pay for the product (or service) characteristics.

As with hedonic price regressions, which product characteristics should be included in a discrete choice model should be considered carefully in order to capture those characteristics that are likely to influence the choices of consumers. Using a survey to collect data can be useful. A survey can control the variation in the characteristics of the products from which the respondents are asked to choose. Moreover, with a survey, respondents can be shown the actual products (or suitable representations) that embody the relevant characteristics.

Real Options

As we have discussed, income-based approaches to IP valuation attempt to measure the present value of the future incremental cash flows that a particular IP asset (or group of assets) is projected to generate. A conventional approach to this exercise is DCF analysis. Because a traditional DCF analysis assumes a single series of discrete cash flows, typically discounted at a constant rate, it can oversimplify the modeling of the possible outcomes with respect to the use of the IP asset at issue. The same applies to investment decisions more generally.

The future cash flows may depend on choices made and outcomes realized at various points in the future, such that one can describe the DCF as more than just a single series of cash flows. That is, it may be more accurate to model the possible future outcomes as a series of distinct cash flows, each of which is individually discounted. The real options approach to valuation attempts to model the uncertainty of these future outcomes with *ex ante* assumptions about the probabilities of those different cash flows being realized in the future. Under this approach, it is the "option" to pursue a course of action to realize those future cash flows—for example, to commercialize certain IP—that is often being valued.

Although there are several methods employed to capture the probabilistic nature of these future cash flow streams, one of the more common methods is based on a decision tree. Here, the series of expected future cash flows branch from decision node to decision node. At each node, the different possible outcomes are each assumed to occur with a specified probability. To illustrate the intuition and basic mechanics of this approach, consider the example of a patent on voice recognition technology for purposes of converting speech into text on mobile phones. At present, assume this technology is not used in any devices. However, a major handset manufacturer is considering incorporating the patented technology into its line of phones. Furthermore, although there are no industry standards with respect to this technology or issues of interoperability of the technology across different devices, if that phone manufacturer does adopt this technology, other manufacturers may follow suit. Accordingly, a real options-based approach to valuation can be used to enable the valuation of the patented technology to best reflect these possible outcomes. With this example, there are two decision nodes: (1) whether that major phone manufacturer adopts the technology and (2) whether other manufacturers follow the lead of that manufacturer. The probability of these events occurring and the trajectory of cash flows from each are the critical inputs to the valuation. In essence, the valuation weights the future cash flows based on their *ex ante* probability.[8]

Contemporary Business Practices and Market Structures and IP Value

To better understand the forces that may, in the coming years, change how IP creates value and how we will measure that value, it is useful to consider some business practices and market structures that are helping to motivate those changes. The securitization of and the development of secondary markets for IP assets have provided potentially useful market-based mechanisms to monetize IP. Furthermore, the technology in which IP is embodied and the markets for that technology present dynamic features that can significantly affect the value of IP. For example, the spillover and network effects often associated with IP and the importance of the standardization of particular technologies in a wide array of products are all factors that can strongly influence the value of IP and thus how we approach its valuation.

IP Securitization and Secondary Markets[9]

Securitization is a means to trade and monetize IP assets. In this context, the cash flows associated with an IP asset are packaged into a security and sold. In its most basic form, securitization enables the exchange of a claim on future (and thus uncertain) payments generated by an IP asset for a fixed payment now.

An early example of this type of securitization is the Bowie Bond, whereby in the late 1990s musical artist David Bowie in essence sold royalty streams associated with his music catalog for a lump-sum payment of $55 million.[10] Since then other musical artists have followed suit with this sort of securitization of the royalties on the copyrights on their music.[11]

Music copyrights are not the only IP assets to be used to create these asset-backed securities. For example, royalties on pharmaceutical patents have been securitized. In an early case, Yale University reportedly securitized and sold future royalty payments for a patent used in connection with the anti-HIV drug Zerit®.[12] More recently, Northwestern University sold a portion of its future patent royalties in connection with the drug Lyrica®.[13]

These transactions can serve as an effective means to manage risk by transferring the risk associated with future payments (e.g., a royalty stream) to a willing buyer of that risk (presumably in exchange for an expected return commensurate with the perceived risk). However, several factors complicate these transactions and may limit their prevalence and the formation of markets for these transactions. For example, agreements may be difficult to reach because of a high degree of unpredictability of future cash flows. Information asymmetries between buyers and sellers may also militate against transactions. Furthermore, the transactions themselves may create moral hazard, as the seller may still have an important role to play in generating the future cash flows but, after the sale, may have less incentive to play that role.

In addition to the securitization of cash flows related to IP assets, IP assets themselves are also increasingly trading in secondary markets, in part driven by a flow of assets from bankruptcy proceedings.[14] The presence of these transactions underscores the value of IP and the transferability of that value. All else being equal, this trend may also lead to markets for IP with greater liquidity. Although the high degree of differentiation of IP and the particular circumstances one may find in these secondary markets limit their ability to provide benchmarks for the value of any particular IP asset, going forward, these sorts of transactions may become useful indicators of more general trends in the market value of different types of IP and innovative ways of utilizing existing IP.

Spillovers, Network Effects, and Standards

We live in a world where technology is rapidly changing, both in terms of incremental improvements and significant new inventions. The interconnections between various technologies, some of which may have initially been thought to be unrelated, have seemed to become, more and more frequently, important elements of value. Following these trends, spillovers, network effects, and standards are gaining increasing importance in technology and other markets.

Innovations can often have spillover effects. Advances in satellites and computing brought us GPS in our cars and on our phones. Improvements in battery technology helped make mobile phones and personal media players hugely popular. The development of new data storage formats (e.g., CDs, DVDs, Blu-Ray discs, and MP3s) has heralded dramatic changes in the distribution of recorded music, films, and other media. Indeed, the development of new applications for existing technology can be a fundamental driver of innovation.

Because the current value of an IP asset is dependent on its prospects for generating cash flow in the future, spillover effects have important implications in the future value and valuation of IP. Spillovers may be difficult to anticipate, but methods like a real options-based approach can help incorporate available information about them that may be relevant to a specific valuation.

Technological advances and follow-on product commercialization can also generate network effects. Network effects arise when the value of a product is, at least in part, dependent on the degree to which multiple consumers use the product. Consider telephones: to be valuable as a means of communication, you need at least two phones connected so you have someone to call. As more phones are added to the network, the value of having a phone increases, as there are more people with whom you can communicate. As with spillover effects, network effects have important implications for the ability of IP to create value. A valuation improves to the extent these network effects can be included.

Finally, the extent to which many IP assets are used commercially can be influenced by the extent to which they become industry standards. Industry standards (either informal or facilitated by standard setting organizations) can foster interoperability between and among a variety of devices produced by many different firms. For example, consumers' ability to use any number of alternative tires from a variety of manufacturers, any of which would fit the standard size wheels on a car, helps enhance the value of the car. Similar effects on value can exist, for example, based on the interoperability of computers and peripherals, among other technology. IP rights that are used in connection with industry standards may be licensed between competitors through various types of cross-licensing agreements.

Selected Contemporary Institutional Changes

The value of IP is principally derived from the uses to which it can be put, regardless of the method used to value it. Therefore, in determining value, one must be careful to properly account for elements of the legal or regulatory environment that might curtail or enhance the extent to which any particular IP can be exploited. As recent years have demonstrated, institutional changes, including recent court opinions, can affect the ways in which holders of IP rights can monetize them. Therefore, a proper IP valuation may have to account for certain legal and regulatory frameworks and any recent or expected changes to those frameworks.

Recent Judicial Opinions Put More Stringent Standards on Calculating Infringement Damages

In recent years, U.S. courts, including the Court of Appeals for the Federal Circuit (CAFC), have issued a number of opinions that focused, at least in part, on the appropriate standards for calculating damages—and, in particular, reasonable royalties—in patent infringement suits. The economic lessons of these rulings may, therefore, be an important consideration in determining the value of patents (particularly in a litigation context), as well as other IP. These recent rulings, by indicating a movement toward more stringent standards for determining damages for patent infringement, suggest that damages experts in litigation, and other valuation practitioners, may need to focus more squarely on the specific economic benefits derived from the use of the particular IP at issue and away from analyses that may focus on rules of thumb or the use of what are purported to be comparable transactions. Indeed, by raising the standards for proving patent infringement damages, these rulings may limit damage awards, and may, therefore, reduce the ability to monetize patent rights. Moreover, to the extent that the ability to monetize IP rights outside the courtroom is derived from the threat of a successful infringement suit, these higher standards may play an important role in the value of IP more broadly.

In *Cornell University v. Hewlett-Packard Co.* (*"Cornell-HP"*), Judge Rader, a CAFC judge sitting by designation in a district court, overturned a jury award for reasonable royalty damages of over $180 million, awarding instead about $53 million.[15]

According to Judge Rader, Cornell did not provide sufficient evidence to tie the value of the patented technology (related to the ability of a computer processor (CPU) to handle instructions out of order) to the value of the entire so-called CPU brick. As a result, Judge Rader reduced the royalty award based on an estimate of the value of the processors themselves, rather than the CPU bricks that contain processors. Although this decision is particularly focused on the application of the so-called entire market value rule for determining patent infringement damages, Judge Rader's opinion may provide guidance about the sort of scrutiny that courts can be anticipated to apply to the determination of patent infringement damages and IP valuation, more generally.[16]

For example, Judge Rader claimed Cornell lacked evidence to show the "origin of consumer demand" as being related to the patented technology.[17] Indeed, according to the court, Cornell had an obligation to undertake studies showing the extent of the demand for the patented feature of a product. While recognizing that Cornell had provided evidence that use of the features provided by the patented technology "would be a competitive requirement," the court ruled that "Cornell did not offer any customer surveys or other data to back these predictive claims" and that "[n]owhere does Cornell offer evidence that the claimed invention drove demand for Hewlett-Packard's CPU bricks."[18]

Similarly, in *Lucent Technologies et al. v. Gateway, Inc. et al.* ("*Lucent-Gateway*"), the CAFC overturned a $350 million reasonable royalty damages award relating to a patent covering a pop-up form to be filled out by the user of a computer program (i.e., a so-called "date-picker" technology).[19] In reviewing the damage award, the CAFC highlighted the need for economically sound analyses that support a damages calculation and held that "[b]ecause the damages calculation lacked sufficient evidentiary support, we vacate and remand" the damages portion of the case.[20]

In *Lucent-Gateway*, the CAFC focused largely on the use of so-called comparable, or benchmark, licenses into which Microsoft had entered. The CAFC found that the purportedly comparable benchmarks cited by Lucent were not properly comparable. In the words of the court, "some of the license agreements are radically different from the hypothetical agreement under consideration" for the patented technology and "we are simply unable to ascertain from the evidence presented the subject matter of the agreements," which makes it impossible for a jury to determine "the probative value of those agreements."[21] The CAFC referred to the available information about some of these licenses as "superficial" and found that the "substantial" differences among the purported comparables and the hypothetical negotiation at issue rendered them not "sufficiently comparable" to support the original award.[22] Thus, to the extent that one relies on so-called benchmark market-based valuation methods, *Lucent-Gateway* suggests that the benchmarks should be carefully chosen to ensure that they are comparable to the context of the damages analysis.

The CAFC also found in *Lucent-Gateway* that, beyond the inappropriate use of purported comparable agreements, there was insufficient evidence to conclude that the patented feature generated much value to users. Indeed, while Lucent introduced "evidence, such as marketing material, product documentation, and expert testimony, that the accused features were important to the success of Microsoft's products and were promoted by Microsoft,"[23] the court found that "[t]he only reasonable conclusion that can be drawn from the evidence is that the infringing use of . . . [the]

date-picker feature is a minor aspect of a much larger software program."[24] Consistent with the *Cornell-HP* ruling, the CAFC in *Lucent-Gateway* apparently required data and/or analyses that more directly identify the sources of demand for infringing product(s), such as studies showing demand for the patented feature(s).

Following on *Cornell-HP* and *Lucent-Gateway*, the CAFC has continued its march to impose appropriate standards for calculating patent infringement damages. On January 4, 2011, in *Uniloc USA, Inc. et al. v. Microsoft Corporation*, the CAFC rejected the use of the so-called 25 percent rule of thumb in the calculation of reasonable royalty damages.[25] As a general matter, application of this rule of thumb would arbitrarily set a reasonable royalty at 25 percent of the profits earned from the product embodying the patented invention at issue. In its opinion, the court recognized that this rule of thumb "does not say anything about a particular hypothetical negotiation or reasonable royalty involving a particular technology, industry, or party" and, as such, is not appropriate for a damages analysis.[26]

Although the CAFC has not drawn the explicit connection, it appears to be demanding that damages calculations be thoroughly grounded in the basic economic principles and valuation frameworks that we discussed previously. As a general matter, IP owners should consider these demands in valuing their own IP rights whether they are pursuing litigation or not. Said differently, when valuing IP, practitioners should focus squarely on quantifying the incremental economic benefits derived from the rights afforded by the IP (e.g., to exclusively practice a particular invention). This focus will help ensure a sound and defensible valuation.

The Patent Settlement Debate in Pharmaceuticals

A much talked about issue in IP is that of patent settlements (or "reverse" payments or "pay-for-delay") in pharmaceuticals. Generally, settlement agreements to which objections are made involve a patent infringement suit between a branded pharmaceutical firm and a generic pharmaceutical firm threatening entry. The objection would be typically over terms to the agreement that allegedly provide for a division of the remaining patent life and a payment to the alleged infringer to delay its entry until the division date.

The U.S. Federal Trade Commission (FTC) has sought to ban settlements of patent infringement cases between a branded pharmaceutical patent holder and an alleged generic infringer when the terms include what might be viewed as a reverse payment to the alleged infringer from the patent holder. For example, the FTC supported a bill introduced in the U.S. House of Representatives that would prohibit such settlements.[27] While the FTC does seem to have won some support from President Obama, it has perhaps not been as successful as it would have liked in convincing courts to prohibit such agreements, proclaiming that "it has become increasingly difficult to bring antitrust cases to stop pay-for-delay tactics, and such agreements have become a common industry strategy."[28] In one decision, the Court of Appeals for the 11th Circuit stated that "the proper analysis of antitrust liability requires an examination of: (1) the scope of the exclusionary potential of the patent; (2) the extent to which the agreements exceeded that scope; and (3) the resulting anticompetitive effects."[29] The 11th Circuit then went on to find "the terms of the settlement to be within the patent's exclusionary power."[30] All in all, the court said, "we fear and reject a rule of law that would automatically invalidate any agreement where a patent-holding pharmaceutical manufacturer settles an infringement case by negotiating the generic's entry date, and, in an ancillary transaction, pays for other products licensed by the generic."[31]

Whether a per se rule is pursued by Congress or not, the prospect can create a valuation issue for pharmaceutical patent valuations. A per se rule would, all else equal, tend to weaken the "exclusionary power" of the patent holder described by the 11th Circuit, and, in so doing, would tend to make the patents less valuable.[32]

The Impact of the Supreme Court's Decision in *eBay v. Mercexchange* on Licensing Negotiations[33]

The Supreme Court, in its decision in *eBay Inc. et al. v. Mercexchange, L.L.C.* (*eBay-Mercexchange*), clarified the legal standard for granting injunctive relief to a plaintiff in a patent infringement lawsuit.[34] Rather than granting an automatic injunction in the event the patent in dispute is found to be valid and infringed, as was the past practice, courts must now apply the traditional four-factor test to determine whether an injunction is appropriate.[35] While this decision should directly affect parties' expectations of injunctive relief in a patent matter, it could also potentially affect the calculation of royalties, both outside the context of a damages analysis for litigation and in a reasonable royalty analysis of patent infringement damages.

The practical impact of *eBay-Mercexchange* is that certain patent holders would seem to be less likely than previously to be granted injunctions, even after the patent is upheld and infringement is found. Justice Kennedy, in his concurring opinion, noted that an injunction may not be appropriate "when the patented invention is but a small component of the product the companies seek to produce and the threat of an injunction is employed simply for undue leverage in negotiations."[36] He singles out a particular type of patent owner that may use the threat of injunction as a bargaining tool to increase the royalty income that it obtains from its patent(s), namely "firms [that] use patents not as a basis for producing and selling goods but, instead, primarily for obtaining licensing fees."[37] Court rulings following *eBay-Mercexchange* indicate that this characterization is consistent with the types of plaintiffs who are now being denied injunctive relief, despite their patents being upheld and found to have been infringed.[38]

A patent owner is now faced with at least the possibility that it will not be able to prevent the infringer from using its patented invention, even if it prevails in every other aspect of the litigation. Therefore, the patent owner's bargaining power—derived, in part, from a threat not to license—may be diminished.[39] Moreover, because the threat of a lawsuit (and the resulting damages and injunction) may be a primary negotiation tool for the patent owner, the impact of *eBay-Mercexchange* on patent infringement damages is an important consideration in licensing negotiations, as well. Because *eBay-Mercexchange* may diminish the threat of litigation by taking away the possibility of injunctive relief, it may change the relative bargaining positions of the parties to a patent licensing negotiation. Any such change could also manifest in the hypothetical negotiation for purposes of calculating a reasonable royalty in the context of litigation.[40]

This shift in the relative bargaining positions of the parties to a licensing negotiation could—other things being equal—result in lower royalties for a patent holder who, by virtue of *eBay-Mercexchange*, is now faced with an increased probability of not being able to enjoin an infringer, even if its patent were upheld and infringement found. Thus, the evaluation of a patent's value should now also consider the likelihood that a patent owner will be able to obtain an injunction against an infringer. A patent owner that is more likely to obtain a permanent injunction against an infringer owns a patent that, all other things equal, is more valuable to both the patent owner and any licensees because that patent can exclude others from using the patented technology and, thus, may limit the ability of others to compete. On the other hand, a patent owner who is similarly situated to those noted in Justice Kennedy's opinion may be less likely to obtain a permanent injunction, thus reducing the value of its patent(s).

The Importance of Accounting for Uncertain Enforceability of IP Rights

Because the value of any IP rights derives from their ability to deliver incremental profits going forward, it is important to consider how possible future changes to the enforceability of patent rights may affect the future ability to profitably exploit those rights (either positively or negatively). Some recent rulings regarding patent approvals demonstrate how these sorts of changes can affect the value of IP.

In its 1998 ruling in *State Street Bank & Trust Co. v. Signature Financial Group, Inc.*, the CAFC allowed for "business methods" to be patented, so long as the claimed invention met the standard of producing a "useful, concrete and tangible result."[41] This decision arguably led to an influx of business method patents (e.g., Amazon's "one-click" buying patent) being applied for and issued by the U.S. Patent and Trademark Office (USPTO).[42] However, in its recent *In re Bilski* decision, the CAFC has imposed more stringent limits on the patentability of such inventions, rejecting the "useful, concrete, and tangible result" test in favor of a test focused on whether or not the invention "is tied to a particular machine or apparatus, or . . . transforms a particular article into a different state or thing."[43] In doing so, and subject to the Supreme Court's June 2010 ruling in this case, the CAFC may have had a significant negative effect on the value of many business method patents.

Indeed, in *Cybersource Corp. v. Retail Decisions, Inc.*, the District Court for the Northern District of California struck down a patent covering "a method and system for detecting fraud in a credit card transaction between a consumer and a merchant over the internet" in light of the *In re Bilski* decision. In the ruling, Judge Patel noted that "[a]lthough the majority declined (*sic*) say so explicitly, Bilski's holding suggests a perilous future for most business method patents. . . . The closing bell may be ringing for business method patents, and their patentees may find they have become bagholders."[44]

That future was not fully resolved by the Supreme Court's opinion on this case that was issued in June 2010. While the Court upheld the ruling that the particular patents at issue in the *In re Bilski* case are not patentable, the Court went on to state that the "machine-or-transformation test is not the sole test" for patentability but rather that the focus should also be whether or not the method goes to an abstract idea.[45] Indeed, the USPTO's memorandum on *In re Bilski* states that it will use the "machine-or-transformation" as a first screen in determining patentability, but regardless of whether the test is passed, the patent office will then focus on whether the "method is directed to an abstract idea."[46] Arguably, then, the Court has made it less clear whether any particular "business method" patent is patentable or not by declaring that the "machine-or-transformation" test is not the sole test for patentability. This outcome highlights the risk inherent in evolving legal environments and the importance of considering the impact potential changes in the law may have on the value of IP. Moreover, this case shows how the value of IP generally, and patents, in particular, is crucially tied to the legal environment in which the IP is owned

Another area that has been the focus of an evolving legal environment and a concomitant effect on the value of IP is the biotech community and, in particular, gene patents. In 2009, the American Civil Liberties Union filed suit against the patent office and Myriad Genetics ("Myriad") seeking to invalidate a number of gene patents related to breast cancer tests using BRCA genes, on the grounds that "human genes are products of nature, laws of nature, and/or natural phenomena and abstract ideas, or basic human knowledge or thought" and are therefore not patentable under the U.S. Constitution.[47] Following this suit, the National Institute of Health's Secretary's Advisory Committee on Genetics, Health, and Society issued a draft report on "Gene Patents and Licensing Practices and Their Impact on Patient Access to Genetic Tests" recommending an "exemption from liability for infringement of patent claims on genes for anyone making, using, ordering, offering for sale, or selling a test developed under the patent for patient care purposes."[48]

In March 2010, Judge Sweet in the U.S. District Court for the Southern District of New York issued his ruling in the BRCA case, which stated that: "the patents at issue [are] directed to 'isolated DNA' containing sequences found in nature" and are therefore not patentable.[49] This ruling may result in reduced enforceability of similar gene patents, materially reducing their value and discouraging this type of innovation. However, Myriad may well appeal, therefore the status of its patents (and gene patents more generally) remain somewhat uncertain. If the ruling is upheld through an appeal, then gene patent holders could be left holding the bag. However, should the patentability of the gene patents be reestablished on appeal, the value of many of these patents could well be substantial.[50]

Conclusion

In this chapter, we have discussed economic principles and frameworks that underlie proper valuation of IP across the various different contexts and purposes for valuation. These core principles and frameworks provide a useful foundation as new techniques, business practices, and institutional structures continue to add texture to the valuation of IP in the twenty-first century. Of course, changes will persist. We expect there will be continued advances in valuation practice as, for example, there are new transactional structures developed for IP, courts converge on and enforce best practices, and other institutional changes affect how IP can be exploited in the marketplace.

Notes

1. As a general matter, we note that when multiple pieces of IP are "stacked" in a product, such that the values of different pieces of IP may be interdependent, isolating the incremental impact of any one piece of IP may be more difficult. This difficulty is analogous to determining the value of a lock and the key to that lock. Without the other, neither the lock nor the key provides any value (at least for their intended purpose), but when used together they can provide an important function.

2. We might represent the starting point as $p(z) = p(z_1, z_2, \ldots, z_m)$, where p is price and z is a vector of m product characteristics. This might then lead to an estimation based on the following specification, $p_i = \alpha + \sum_j \beta_j z_{ij} + \varepsilon_i$, where i indexes over n transactions, j indexes over the m product characteristics, β_j is the implicit price of the jth characteristic, the ε_i are unobserved random factors, and $m < n$.

3. We might represent the starting point with a basic relationship, different from the one posited in note 2, i.e., $P(z) = P(z_1, z_2, \ldots, z_m)$, where P is the probability of choice and z is a vector of m product characteristics. However, because we are now attempting to explain a probability rather than a price, and probabilities are bounded by zero and one, we would employ a discrete choice model (e.g., logit). For more details, see Kenneth Train, *Discrete Choice Methods with Simulation* (New York: Cambridge University Press, 2003).

4. For example, a hedonic price analysis of housing value may include characteristics relating to the structure and the lot, as well as to the location of the house and the associated schools and community amenities. Similarly, a study of wine or cigars may include not only characteristics about the vintages or tobaccos used, but also how these products have been rated by perceived authorities.

5. The particular specifications of hedonic price regressions, including determining which explanatory variables to include and the details of the estimation procedures—for example, the number of stages in the estimation procedure or use of instrumental variables—are driven by the market at issue in the study and the precise research question(s) and go beyond the purpose of this paper. For more detailed discussions of these issues see Sherwin Rosen, "Hedonic Prices and Implicit Markets: Product Differentiation in Pure Competition," *The Journal of Political Economy* 82, no. 1 (1974): 34–55; also see Zvi Griliches, (ed.), *Price Indexes and Quality Change* (Cambridge: Harvard University Press, 1971). As in any econometric analysis, one wants the observables to conform to the underlying assumptions of the model being used.

6. See Kandalpa Thanasuta et al., "Brand and Country of Origin Valuations of Automobiles," *Asia Pacific Journal of Marketing and Logistics* 21, no. 3 (2009): 355–375; also see Brad R. Humphreys and Michael Mondello, "Determinants of Franchise Values in North American Professional Sports Leagues: Evidence from a Hedonic Price Model," *International Journal of Sport Finance* 3, no. 2 (2008): 98–105.

7. See Bureau of Labor Statistics, U.S. Department of Labor, "Using a Hedonic Model to Adjust Television Prices in the Consumer Price Index for Changes in Quality," June 16, 2003, www.bls.gov/cpi/cpihe01.htm. See also Nicole Shelper, "Developing a Hedonic Regression Model for Camcorders in the U.S. CPI," October 16, 2001, www.bls.gov/cpi/cpicamco.htm and Brendan Williams, "A Hedonic Model for Internet Access Service in the Consumer Price Index," *Monthly Labor Review*, July 2008: 33-48.

8. For further discussion of these methods, see Avinash K. Dixit and Robert S. Pindyck, *Investment Under Uncertainty* (Princeton: Princeton University Press, 1994). Recent methods of real options analysis have also been developed to value portfolios of investment opportunities. See Gintaras V. Reklatis and Juan C. Zapata, "Valuation of Project Portfolios: An Endogenously Discounted Method," *European Journal of Operational Research* 206, no. 3 (2010): 653–666.

9. See also Scott Lebson, "Creating, Perfecting, and Enforcing Security Interest in Intellectual Property," in *Intellectual Property Operations and Implementation for the 21st Century Corporation*, (forthcoming).

10. For a more detailed discussion of how the financial transaction was structured see, Nicole Chu, "Bowie Bonds: A Key to Unlocking the Wealth of Intellectual Property," *Hastings Communications and Entertainment Law Journal* 21, no. 2 (1999): 469–499; Ronel Elul, "The Economics of Asset Securitization," *Business Review*, Third Quarter 2005, 16–25; Yal Bizouati, "Donuts to Dollars," *Investment Dealers Digest*, March 19, 2007; Vipal Monga, "Beyond Bowie," *IP Law and Business*, May 20, 2005.

11. See Yal Bizouati, "Donuts to Dollars," *Investment Dealers Digest*, March 19, 2007.

12. See Michael Gregory, "Baby Steps in IP: Sale/License-Back," *Asset Securitization Report*, April 8, 2002.

13. See "Royalty Pharma Acquires a Portion of Northwestern University's Royalty Interest in Lyrica® for $700 Million," *Pharma Business Week*, December 31, 2007.

14. See Gabe Fried, "IP: A Reason to Exist; Creatively Utilizing Collateral, Divestitures and Licensing to Get Deals Done," *Mergers & Acquisitions*, June 1, 2010; Shane Kite, "Intellectual Property May Soon Be Traded as its Own 'Asset Class,'" *Securities Industry News*, August 3, 2009.

15. *Cornell University v. Hewlett-Packard Co.*, 609 F. Supp. 2d 279 (N.D.N.Y. 2009).

16. The application of the entire market value rule and, more generally, the difficulties in treating a royalty rate separately from the royalty base to which it is applied, are beyond the scope of this chapter.

17. *Cornell University v. Hewlett-Packard Co.*, 609 F. Supp. 2d 279, 288 (N.D.N.Y. 2009).

18. Ibid. at 289.

19. *Lucent Technologies, Inc. et al. v. Gateway, Inc. et al.*, 580 F.3d 1301 (Fed. Cir. 2009). Microsoft intervened for the defendants in this case.

20. Ibid. at 1308.

21. Ibid. at 1327.

22. Ibid. at 1329.

23. *Lucent Technologies, Inc. et al. v. Gateway, Inc. et al.*, 580 F.Supp.2d 1016, 1043 (S.D. Cal. 2008).

24. *Lucent Technologies, Inc. et al. v. Gateway, Inc. et al.*, 580 F.3d 1301, 1333 (Fed. Cir. 2009).

25. *Uniloc USA, Inc. et al. v. Microsoft Corporation*, WL 9738, 19 (Fed. Cir. 2011).

26. Ibid. at 21.

27. See, e.g., "FTC Testifies in Support of Bill Banning 'Pay-for-Delay' Settlements Between Brand and Generic Drug Companies," FTC press release, March 31, 2009, www.ftc.gov/opa/2009/03/payfordelay.shtm). See also "FTC Testimony: Stopping 'Pay-for-Delay' Drug Settlement Agreements is a Top Competition Priority," FTC press release, July 27, 2010, www.ftc.gov/opa/2010/07/antitrust.shtm).

28. "FTC Testifies in Support of Bill Banning 'Pay-for-Delay' Settlements Between Brand and Generic Drug Companies," FTC press release, March 31, 2009, www.ftc.gov/opa/2009/03/payfordelay.shtm.

29. *Schering-Plough Corp. et al. v. Federal Trade Commission*, 402 F.3d 1056, 1065 (11th Cir. 2005). Other Circuits have taken different positions on these patent settlements. For example, the Second Circuit has held that there is "no sound basis for categorically condemning reverse

payments employed to lift the uncertainty surrounding the validity and scope of the holder's patent" and that "so long as the patent litigation is neither a sham nor otherwise baseless, the patent holder is seeking to arrive at a settlement in order to protect that to which it is presumably entitled: a lawful monopoly over the manufacture and distribution of the patented product," while the Sixth Circuit has held that the agreements are per se illegal. See *In re Tamoxifen Citrate Antitrust Litig.*, 466 F.3d 187, 207, 209 (2d Cir. 2006) and *In re Cardizem CD Antitrust Litig.*, 332 F.3d 896 (6th Cir. 2003). There is currently a petition for writ of certiorari pending for a case on which the Second Circuit ruled on the legality of these patent settlements. See Petition for a Writ of Certiorari: *Louisiana Wholesale Drug Co. et al. v. Bayer AG et al.*, No. 10-762, December 6, 2010.

30. *Schering-Plough Corp. et al. v. Federal Trade Commission*, 402 F.3d 1056, 1071 (11th Cir. 2005).

31. Ibid. at 1076.

32. That said, the effect of such a rule on consumer welfare in any given case may be harder to predict because of the tradeoffs between its potential short- and long-term effects.

33. See also James Markarian, "Strategic and Legal View of Licensing Patents," in *Intellectual Property Operations and Implementation for the 21st Century Corporation*, (forthcoming).

34. *eBay Inc. et al., v. Mercexchange, L.L.C.*, 547 U.S. 388, 126 S.Ct. 1837 (2006).

35. As stated by the Court, the plaintiff must demonstrate: "(1) that it has suffered an irreparable injury; (2) that remedies available at law are inadequate to compensate for that injury; (3) that considering the balance of hardships between the plaintiff and defendant, a remedy in equity is warranted; and (4) that the public interest would not be disserved by a permanent injunction."

36. *eBay Inc. et al., v. Mercexchange, L.L.C.*, 547 U.S. 388, 126 S.Ct. 1837, 1842 (2006). From an economic perspective, "small component" must mean that the economic contribution of that component, relative to its next-best non-infringing alternative, is minor in comparison with the total value of the product incorporating the patented technology. A patented component could be a small part of a product or one of a large number of components but still be the key economic contributor to the profits generated by the product.

37. Ibid.

38. See, e.g., *z4 Technologies, Inc., v. Microsoft Corporation and Autodesk, Inc.*, 434 F.Supp.2d 437 (E.D. Texas 2006); *Paice L.L.C., v. Toyota Motor Corp. et al.*, 504 F.3d 1293 (Fed. Cir. 2007); *Jan K. Voda, M.D. v. Cordis Corporation*, 536 F.3d 1311 (Fed. Cir. 2008); and *Sundance, Inc. et al. v. DeMonte Fabricating Ltd. and Quick Draw Tarpaulin Systems, Inc.*, 2007 WL 37742 (E.D. Mich.). In the z4 and Sundance rulings, the courts declined to grant injunctive relief in part due to a finding that the patented invention was a "small component" of the product. In the z4, Paice, and Jan Voda cases, the plaintiff's primary use of the patents was for licensing purposes. However, in *Commonwealth Scientific and Industrial Research Organization, v. Buffalo Tech., Inc.*, 492 F.Supp.2d 600 (E.D. Texas 2007) the court granted CSIRO, Australia's national science agency, a permanent injunction, despite the fact that CSIRO did not actively practice the patent at issue.

39. Depending on the facts of the case, the threat not to license may not result in substantial bargaining power at all, such as in the case of an infringer who has a readily available non-infringing alternative whose cost, market price, and market acceptance is little different from those of the accused technology.

40. This may imply that, even in trials occurring post-*eBay*, if the hypothetical negotiation is assumed to take place prior to the issuance of the *eBay* ruling, the parties would not have considered the *eBay* ruling and its implications.

41. *State Street Bank & Trust Co. v. Signature Financial Group, Inc.*, 149 F.3d 1368 (Fed. Cir. 1998).

42. See, e.g., Electronic Frontier Foundation, "Federal Circuit Reins in Business Method Patents," October 31, 2008, www.eff.org/deeplinks/2008/10/federal-circuit-limits-busi ness-method-patents; George H. Pike, "Business Method Patents in Jeopardy," *Information Today,* January 2009; "Patently Obvious," *Los Angeles Times,* October 30, 2006.

43. *In re Bernard L. Bilski and Rand A. Warsaw,* 545 F.3d 943 (Fed. Cir. 2008).

44. *CyberSource Corp. v. Retail Decisions, Inc.*, 620 F. Supp. 2d 1068, 1081 (N.D. Cal. 2009).

45. *Bilski v. Warsaw,* 561 U.S.____, Slip Op. 08-964, (2010).

46. USPTO Memorandum, "Supreme Court Decision in Bilski v. Kappos," June 28, 2010.

47. *Association for Molecular Pathology et al. v. United States Patent and Trademark Office et al.*, United States District Court for the Southern District of New York, Complaint, May 12, 2009.

48. "Revised Draft Report on Gene Patents and Licensing Practices and Their Impact on Patient Access to Genetic Tests," approved by SACGHS February 5, 2010, oba.od.nih.gov/oba/SACGHS/SACGHS%20Patents%20Report%20Approved%202-5-20010.pdf.

49. *Association for Molecular Pathology et al. v. United States Patent and Trademark Office et al.*, 2010 WL 1233416, 1 (S.D.N.Y.).

50. Further highlighting the uncertainty resulting from an ever-changing legal environment, Judge Sweet did not rule on the First Amendment challenge to Myriad's patents because he found the patents to be invalid as a result of being "directed to a law of nature." Thus, even if the district court ruling is overturned on appeal, the gene patents may yet be found invalid as a result of the constitutional challenge.

About the Editors

Lanning G. Bryer

Lanning G. Bryer is a partner in the New York office of Ladas & Parry and is Director of the firm's Mergers, Acquisitions and Licensing Group. Mr. Bryer is an active committee member of several intellectual property organizations, including the Trademark Licensing Committee of Licensing Executives Society (United States and Canada) and the Editorial Board of *The Trademark Reporter*. He recently served on the International Editorial Board of the International Trademark Association (formerly The United States Trademark Association) and currently serves as Editor-in-Chief of INTA's *The Trademark Reporter*. Mr. Bryer has written and lectured extensively on foreign trademark practice and IP commercial transactions and routinely counsels a diverse variety of clients on the acquisition, financing, and licensing of intellectual property. Mr. Bryer is co-author and co-editor of other books published by John Wiley & Sons, entitled *Intellectual Property Assets in Mergers and Acquisitions; Intellectual Property in the Global Marketplace;* and *The New Role of Intellectual Property in Commercial Transactions*. Mr. Bryer also co-authored and co-edited *Worldwide Trademark Transfers*. He is a graduate of Johns Hopkins University and Hofstra University School of Law. Mr. Bryer can be reached at (212) 708-1870 or via e-mail at lbryer@ladas.com.

Scott J. Lebson

Scott Lebson is a partner in the Mergers, Acquisitions and Licensing Group of Ladas & Parry LLP. Mr. Lebson's practice focuses primarily on counseling clients with respect to the acquisition, sale, licensing, and securitization of intellectual property rights and related technology. He is recognized as one of the leading authorities in the evolving field of securitization of intellectual property rights. Mr. Lebson also counsels clients with respect to the filing and recordation of documentation relating to the transfer of patents and trademarks in jurisdictions throughout the world. He is an accomplished speaker and has lectured and written extensively on a wide range of intellectual property matters and is a committee member of several intellectual property organizations, including the Licensing Executives Society, the International Trademark Association, and the New York State Bar Association Intellectual Property Section. He is a graduate of Villanova University and Hofstra University School of Law. Mr. Lebson can be reached at (212) 708-3460 or via e-mail at slebson@ladas.com.

Matthew D. Asbell

Matthew D. Asbell is an associate in the New York office of Ladas & Parry LLP. He considers himself an IP generalist, though he primarily practices trademark law domestically and internationally. With a diverse background in the entertainment industry, information technology, and medicine, proficiency in several languages, and a certification as a Social Media Strategist, he handles complex intellectual property matters, including those arising in the Web 2.0 space, for a wide variety of clients. Mr. Asbell is an active member of the American Bar Association, in which he serves as a Young Lawyer Fellow of the Section of Intellectual Property Law, and as current Chair of the Internet and Intellectual Property Law Committee of the Young Lawyers Division. He has chaired the Young Lawyers Committee of the New York State Bar Association Intellectual Property Section, and is an active member of several other bar association committees related to intellectual property. Mr. Asbell has authored and co-authored several publications and given presentations on the topics of trademark, licensing, copyright, patent, broadcasting, and Internet and privacy law. He is a graduate of the Benjamin N. Cardozo School of Law, Carnegie Mellon University, and The Episcopal Academy. Mr. Asbell can be reached at (212) 708-3463 or via e-mail at masbell@ladas.com.

About the Contributors

Marc Adler is the President of Marc Adler LLC, an intellectual property strategy consulting firm outside Philadelphia. Marc is the former chief IP counsel of Rohm and Haas Company, and past president of the Intellectual Property Owners Association and Association of Corporate Patent Counsel. He is a member of the bar of the State of New York and a registered U.S. patent attorney with undergraduate and graduate degrees in chemical engineering. He assists corporations and new technology ventures in devising and implementing patent strategies and the management of patent portfolios.

Marc Adler can be reached at (267) 265-4488, marcadler@mac.com, or at www.adlerip.com.

David Blackburn is a senior consultant at NERA Economic Consulting based in White Plains, New York. He earned a BSc in applied mathematics and economics from Brown University and a PhD in economics from Harvard University. Dr. Blackburn has extensive experience in the valuation of intellectual property in a variety of contexts, including litigation and the negotiation of licenses and settlement agreements.

David Blackburn can be reached at david.blackburn@nera.com.

Kimberly Klein Cauthorn is a director in the Houston office of Duff & Phelps and part of the Dispute Consulting and Legal Management service line. She has more than 21 years of experience in law firm, academic, consulting, and insurance environments. Kim has developed intellectual property (IP) risk management solutions, including insurance, and assisted clients with managing the costs of intellectual property litigation. In addition, she has conducted intellectual property audits and risk assessments, as well as prepared IP licensing and monetization analyses, and damages expert reports. Kimberly Klein Cauthorn can be reached at (713) 582-1676 or kimberly.cauthorn@duffandphelps.com.

Raymond DiPerna is an associate in the New York office of Ladas & Parry LLP where he specializes in the preparation and prosecution of patent applications, both domestically and internationally. Mr. DiPerna's practice focuses on the electrical, computer, and mechanical arts, with particular experience in technologies including Internet-related hardware and software, e-commerce, and business methods. In addition, Mr. DiPerna has experience in patent litigation, and prepares appeal briefs and opinion letters regarding patent infringement, validity, and enforceability. Mr. DiPerna is a graduate of Lehigh University with a BS in Electrical Engineering, and earned his JD from the University of Pittsburgh School of Law. Mr. DiPerna is admitted in New York and is registered with the United States Patent and Trademark Office. Raymond DiPerna can be reached at rdiperna@ladas.com.

Leib Dodell is co-founder and CEO of ThinkRisk Underwriting Agency, a specialty professional liability underwriting facility formed in 2009, where he founded and managed the company's media liability program and was the architect of the Multimedia Liability, NewsMedia Liability, and Safety'Net Internet liability products. Prior to entering the insurance industry, Leib was an attorney specializing in First Amendment and intellectual property litigation. Leib practiced at the Washington, DC law firm of Williams & Connolly, where he represented many of the firm's media clients, including the *Washington Post* and the *National Enquirer*. He has also served as an assistant attorney general for the Commonwealth of Massachusetts, as an attorney in Harvard University's Office of Legal Counsel, and as a law clerk in the U.S. District Court for the District of Columbia and the U.S. Court of Appeals for the First Circuit. Leib earned his JD summa cum laude from the George Washington University National Law Center and his BA cum laude from the University of Maryland at College Park. Leib is an active member of the Professional Liability Underwriting Society (PLUS), and is a frequent speaker on media liability, cyberliability, intellectual property risk management, and other professional liability topics. Leib Dodell can be reached at (816) 994-6401, www.thinkrisk.com.

Michael Downey is a St. Louis litigation attorney and partner in the national lawyer ethics and risk management practice at Hinshaw & Culbertson LLP. He teaches legal ethics and law firm practice at Washington University School of Law and is author of *Introduction to Law Firm Practice* (2010). Michael Downey can be reached at (314) 425-2104, mdowney@hinshawlaw.com, or through www.DowneyonLawPractice.com.

David Drews is founder and president of IPmetrics LLC, an intellectual property consulting firm. He has a great deal of experience with intellectual property, including valuation, negotiation and the calculation of infringement damages. David Drews can be reached at (858) 538-1533 x202, ddrews@ipmetrics.net, or www.ipmetrics.net.

Howard H. Fine is a partner at Gettry Marcus Stern & Lehrer, CPA, P.C. and provides accounting, auditing, and tax services to middle market closely held businesses. Mr. Fine has extensive experience in providing these services to diversified industries. He also specializes in conducting internal control reviews and is a member of the firm's Business Valuation and Litigation Support Group as well as the chairman of the Quality Control Committee. In addition to his CPA designation, Mr. Fine is a Certified Valuation Analyst with a Financial Forensics certification. Mr. Fine can be reached at (516) 364-3390 x212, or at www.gmslny.com.

Larry Greenemeier is the associate technology editor at ScientificAmerican.com and a frequent contributor to *Scientific American* magazine. Prior to joining *Scientific American* in 2007, he spent eight years as a technology journalist at *InformationWeek* magazine. Larry Greenemeier can be reached via e-mail at lggreenemeier@yahoo.com.

Jack L. Hobaugh Jr. is an associate with the firm of Blank Rome LLP, in Washington, DC. He concentrates his practice in the areas of intellectual property and intellectual property litigation. The views expressed are those of the author and not necessarily those of Blank Rome LLP. Jack L. Hobaugh Jr. can be reached at (202) 772-5954, Hobaugh@BlankRome.com, http://www.blankrome.com/index.cfm?contentID=10 &bioID=3127.

Robert Lamb is an adjunct Professor of Management at NYU Stern School. He has served as an advisor to the United States Federal Reserve, the Treasury, and the Securities and Exchange Commission, as well as many corporations, such as Goldman Sachs, J.P. Morgan, and Lehman Brothers. Professor Lamb frequently serves as an expert witness on the duties and industry practices of investment bank underwriters, sales, trading, market making, structuring of M&A corporations, joint ventures, strategic alliances, financial advisors, municipal bonds, corporate securities and derivatives markets. He has contributed to Professor Hugh Hansen's textbook, "International Intellectual Property Law and Policy" and has written over a dozen books and numerous articles on Corporate Strategy, Business Strategic Management and Investing in Government, Municipal and Corporate Securities Markets. Professor Lamb earned a PhD from the London School of Economics and an MBA from Columbia. Professor Lamb can be reached at rlamb@stern.nyu.edu.

Alicia Lloreda is partner and head of intellectual property at Jose Lloreda Camacho & Co., one of the leading full service law firms in Colombia with one of the largest IP practices in the country. Her primary practice areas are trademarks, copyrights, unfair competition, ADR, and IP litigation. Alicia Lloreda can be reached at 57-1-606-97-00 x1005 or alloreda@lloredacamacho.com and/or www.lloredacamacho.com.

James E. Malackowski is the chairman and chief executive officer of Ocean Tomo, LLC, an integrated Intellectual Capital Merchant Banc™ firm. Mr. Malackowski has advised clients and counsel on business valuation issues as well as all phases of the technology transfer process. His expertise extends to intangible asset portfolios as well as business segments and complete entities. On more than 30 occasions, Mr. Malackowski has served as an expert in federal court or for the International Trade Commission on questions relating to intellectual property economics, including the subject of business valuation and the impact of advertising programs. James Malackowski can be reached at (312) 327-4400 or jmalackowski@oceantomo.com.

Diane R. Meyers is corporate counsel for PPG Industries, Inc., where she manages global intellectual property matters for the company's coatings business units.

Steve Mortinger is a vice president, associate general counsel and Trust & Compliance Officer for IBM's Growth Markets based in Shanghai, China. He previously had responsibility for IBM's virtual worlds policies, cloud computing legal matters, acquisitions and divestitures for his division, and for IBM's open source policy, among other things. Steve was co-founder of and is past co-chair of the ABA IP section's Committee on Computer Games and Virtual Worlds and headed up the IBM team that created IBM's well-regarded Virtual Worlds Guidelines for employees. Steve has spoken extensively at legal conferences on legal issues in virtual worlds including as keynote speaker at the first Virtual Worlds Legal Conference. Steve has been quoted in numerous articles on legal issues in virtual worlds and authored an article entitled "An Avatar's Bill of Rights" published in the September 2009 issue of *IP Law & Business Magazine*. Steve is co-editor of a book entitled *Computer Games and Virtual Worlds: A New Frontier in Intellectual Property Law* released in April 2010. Steve was the first IBM lawyer supporting the Engineering & Technology Services group in IBM where he negotiated the chip design agreements for the Nintendo Wii and Xbox360 gaming consoles. Steve Mortinger can be reached at mortinger@cn.ibm.com and (011) (86-21) 6100 8067.

Olga Nedeltscheff is a graduate of Barnard College, Columbia University, cum laude, and earned her JD from Fordham School of Law in New York City. At present, she is employed by Limited Brands, Inc. as Director-Intellectual Property. Ms. Nedeltscheff has extensive and varied experience both as an attorney at law firms, and as in-house counsel, focusing on trademark, copyright, and design matters throughout the world. She is admitted to the bars of the State of New York and the Commonwealth of Massachusetts.

Toshiya Oka is a general manager of Canon Inc. in Tokyo, Japan. He has extensive experience in intellectual property licensing and contracts. He can be reached at oka1048@aol.com.

Marilyn O. Primiano is Vice President, Legal Services at Pangea3, LLC and is based, full-time, in Europe. Prior to this, Marilyn resided for over four years in Mumbai, India, where she oversaw large litigation and IP litigation document reviews, research projects, and contract abstraction work, and developed hands-on expertise in offshore project management and quality assurance. In her current capacity, Marilyn uses her expertise in offshore project management and Pangea3's operations to support the integration of IP, litigation, and corporate projects on behalf of U.S. and E.U. clients. She is a member of the Pennsylvania and New Jersey bars and regularly lectures as a teaching associate at the University of Malta School of Law. Ms. Primiano can be reached at (215) 301-6683, marilyn@pangea3.com, or through www.pangea3.com.

Bryan Ray is a vice president at NERA Economic Consulting based in White Plains, New York. He has extensive experience in the valuation of intellectual property in a variety of contexts, including litigation, regulatory compliance, and transactions. Bryan Ray can be reached at bryan.ray@nera.com.

Randie Beth Rosen is an intellectual property practioner in New York. She has an LLM in intellectual property from Yeshiva University (Benjamin N. Cardozo School of Law), and an MBA from New York University's Stern School of Business.

Andrew P. Ross is a partner at Getty Marcus Stern & Lehrer, CPA, P.C. In addition to his CPA designation, he is a certified valuation analyst with a professional financial specialist certification. Mr. Ross provides audit, tax, and litigation services to his clients, many of whom are in the service, manufacturing, and wholesale industries. He is also a mamber of the firm's business valuation and litigation support group and quality control committee. He can be reached at (516) 364-3390 ext. 246, (516) 426-3239, or through www.gmslny.com.

Deepica Capoor Warikoo is an intellectual property attorney in New York with a focus on trademark and copyright prosecution, litigation, and transactional matters. She received her Masters in Law (LLM) in intellectual property law from Benjamin N. Cardozo School of Law. She is also the founder and President of The Intellectual Property Committee (South Asian Bar Association of New York). She can be reached at deepica@warikoo.org and at http://deepica.blogspot.com/.

Index